W9-DET-585

THE
GREAT BOOK
OF
BIRDS

THE
GREAT BOOK
OF
BIRDS

The Comprehensive Illustrated Guide to 600 Species and Their Environments

AN IMPRINT OF RUNNING PRESS
PHILADELPHIA • LONDON

This 1997 edition published in the United States by Courage Books, an imprint of Running Press
Book Publishers

© 1990 Kodansha Ltd.-Arnoldo Mondadori Editore
Drawings and text © 1980, 1981, 1982 by Kodansha Ltd - Arnoldo Mondadori Editore

English translation © 1990 by Arnoldo Mondadori Editore S.p.A., Milan

All rights reserved under the Pan American and International Copyright
Conventions

This book may be not reproduced in whole or in part, in any form or by any means electronic or
mechanical, including photocopying, recording, or by any information storage and retrieval system
now known or hereafter invented, whihout written permission from the publisher.

9 8 7 6 5 4 3 2 1
Digit on the right indicates the number of this printing

ISBN 0-7624-0136-2

Library of Congress Cataloging-in-Publication Number. 96-72225

This book may be ordered by mail from the publisher. *But try your bookstore first!*

Published by Courage Books, an imprint of
Running Press Book Publishers
125 South Twenty-second Street
Philadelphia, Pensylvania 19103-4399

Printed and bound in Spáin by Artes Gráficas Toledo, S.A.
D.L.: TO 1390-1996

CONTENTS

PREFACE

Often only the sharp eye of the birdwatcher can spot a bird perched on a rocky crag, or hidden amidst the dense foliage of a tree. Even if the bird is quite close, the outline of the tiny creature can be lost to the inexperienced eye in the tangle of shapes and confusing outlines. Indeed, nature has created a world of intricate, deceptive patterns, far removed from the symmetry of man, providing perfect cover for her wildlife.

Learning how to see is a skill in itself, and the best way is by going out and watching, learning to recognize different shapes and movements. But it is no use learning if we do not know what we are looking for. Practice is by far the best way, but who can boast that they have seen every one of the species in this book? Who has seen the sudden acceleration of the roadrunner, or the courting ritual of a bowerbird in front of its bower, or the stark white of a flock of seagulls or gannets set against the gray rugged cliffs of the northern seas? Or who, in their lifetime, has had the opportunity of witnessing the oilbirds of the Venezuelan caves, or pheasant-tailed jacanas skimming the water, or the mounds of decaying plant matter beneath which the mallee fowl deposits its eggs, letting the fermentation provide the necessary warmth to hatch the chicks? Given the fact we will not see all these birds in the flesh, an admirable substitute can be found in printed form: not photographs, which inevitably reproduce the same problems as in the wild – the difficulty of clearly distinguishing the birds from their natural surroundings – but drawings; and only drawings of the highest quality which, combined with accurate factual text, direct the observer's attention to important details.

We have created *The Great Book of Birds* for this reason around a rich collection of color pictures, following in the prestigious tradition inspired by such unsurpassable works as *The Birds of America* by John James Audubon. These works have become masterpieces, not only in the field of natural history, but also in the history of figurative art.

INTRODUCTION

THE BODY STRUCTURE OF BIRDS

Birds are warm-blooded vertebrates adapted to flying; as a result of this, their forelimbs have been transformed into wings, and when moving about on land they make use only of their hind legs. A bird's body has a covering of feathers and the bones are lightweight and partly pneumatic, containing air sacs. Like reptiles, they are oviparous, laying eggs from which the young are hatched; and like mammals, they are homeotherms, capable of avoiding loss of heat and of maintaining a constant body temperature. They form a well-defined, homogeneous class, Aves; and, together with reptiles, they belong to the subclass Sauropoda.

The plumage

Structure of feather. All vertebrates possess special structures produced by the epidermis, such as scales, hairs, and feathers. Feathers, in fact, are simply extremely specialized products of the bird's epidermis, consisting mainly of keratin. Unlike the epidermic structures of cold-blooded vertebrates or mammals, the feathers vary considerably not only in function but also in shape, color, and arrangement. They are exclusive to birds, forming the similar plumage that immediately distinguishes them from all other animals. The origin and evolution of the plumage were veiled in mystery for centuries, and little light was shed on the subject until the comparatively recent discoveries of fossil remains of the first known bird *Archaeopteryx*. They revealed an animal that was already completely covered with feathers,

those of the forelimbs having been so transformed as to permit limited flight. Because of the very gradual processes of evolution, it was not easy for many scientists to accept the idea of an animal which exhibited completely new structural features, especially as it had clearly been derived, as its bone structure showed, from reptiles. We now know, thanks to recent finds of fossil beds in South Africa, that certain dinosaurs, totally incapable of flying and without the slightest trace of wings, were covered in feathers. The original function of these feathers was certainly to insulate creatures which were on the way to achieving a notable degree of independence in relation to their surroundings. They developed the ability, however limited, of regulating their own body temperature, becoming warm-blooded (homeothermic) animals.

A typical feather consists of a long, tapering central axis which has, on either side, a series of branches known as barbs, angled towards the tip. The composition of barbs on each side forms vanes. The axial rod is divided into two main parts. The cylindrical basal section is called the calamus, and it is continued in the solid distal part known as the rachis. Almost at the base, towards the end of the calamus, are two small pits, the inferior umbilicus and the superior umbilicus. Stemming from each barb, and similarly arranged, are even smaller structures, the barbules. The barbules on either side of the barb are of different types. The distal barbules, facing towards the tip of the feather, are flat, with a series of tiny projections (barbicels) which have hooks (hamuli) in the middle of the lower surface. The

proximal barbules are also flat at the base but do not have hooks. The overlapping and interlocking of barbules form a series of structures that in conjunction make up a solid, extremely flexible, compact and coherent feather. The initial development of the feather is very similar to that of a reptile's scale, so that it would not be incorrect to describe feathers as extremely modified scales.

Types of feather. Although there are many different kinds of feather that constitute a bird's plumage, they are generally grouped for convenience into the so-called contour feathers and flight feathers.

The contour feathers are those which help to distinguish the contour or outline of the bird's body. They have large vanes, a calamus, and, a small rachis which tends to be "downy" at the base. Some contour feathers, notably those covering the wing and forming the tail, are highly specialized for the function of flying; those on the wing are called remiges and those on the tail, rectrices. The contour feathers grow out of the skin only in particular areas of tracts, the pterylae. The spaces in the epidermis left bare between the places where the feathers are inserted are known as the apteria. The semiplumes are special types of contour feathers with loose vanes, small rachis, and barbules without hamuli. These semiplumes are found especially on the edges of the pterylae and usually form a layer covered by the mass of contour feathers. There are, however, innumerable transitional forms between true feathers and semiplumes. Other markedly specialized kinds, similarly grouped among the

contour feathers, are the filoplumes; and these, too, are varied in type, with different functions. Superficially like the filoplumes, but distinguished from them in structure, are the wire-like feathers found in certain species such as the hair-crested drongo (*Discrurus hottentottus*) and the bristle-thighed curlew (*Numenius tahitiensis*). Vibrissae are generally present at the base of the bill, close to the nostrils, and around the eyes of many species. They are stiff and wire-like, simply being highly modified feathers almost or wholly lacking vanes.

Another special type of plumage, formed from the down or plumules, is, in adult birds, generally hidden under contour feathers. The plumules are not restricted to the pterylae but may be scattered widely all over the body. Apparently they serve mainly as insulation. Various other modifications of plumage include the so-called powder down, made up of special plumules that grow in particular parts of the body and which flake off to produce a kind of dust, similar to powder, used by those birds possessing it for cleaning the rest of the plumage.

The primitive feather of a bird seems to have consisted of two rachises, one external and the other internal (the hyporachis). In some extant species there are clear traces of these structures. The emu and the cassowary, for example, possess a rachis and hyporachis of equal size, but in most other birds the hyporachis is very small or totally absent.

We come now to the flight feathers. The remiges attached to what is, anatomically, the hand of a bird are called the primary remiges; and there is a fixed number of these in the various bird groups. Flying birds have 9, 10, 11 or 12 primary remiges in each wing. Only a few birds that have lost their capacity for flight, such as the ostrich and the rhea, have a large number of primary remiges. But their function is wholly ornamental.

The secondary remiges are attached to the part of the body equivalent to the arm. In the more primitive bird groups, so-called carpal remiges and their coverts may be found between the primary and secondary remiges, but in the course of evolution these have gradually disappeared. It is not uncommon for some of the secondary remiges to be missing, the further in they grow. Many quite ancient species often have a space without a remige but with the corresponding wing covert after the fourth secondary. In the course of evolution this has tended to change and the gap filled by a true and proper flight feather. The former condition is known as diastataxy (literally "separated arrangement") and the latter as eutaxy ("good arrangement").

A group of feathers, generally rather small but quite strong, is inserted into the thumb of a bird's hand, and this is called the alula or false wing. In some birds, such as the hummingbirds, there are only 2 such feathers, but certain cuckoos, peacocks and other species have 5 or 6. The general rule for passerines is 3 or 4, while the lyrebird has 5. The comparative lengths of the alula feathers are important criteria for bird classification. In all passerines and in the majority of other orders the extreme distal feather is the longest, but among the cuckoos of the genus *Tapera* the two towards the distal end are both very long, so much so that the birds are sometimes called four-winged cuckoos. The alula has a strictly functional importance, for it is this part of the wing that acts as a brake for many species when they come in to land. In cases where the last secondary remiges are especially large, some authors refer to tertiary remiges, as occurs among some ducks, but this term is best avoided since it tends to be confusing.

An interesting phenomenon, probably associated with the increased structural efficiency of the remiges, is that in the course of evolution these feathers have shown an obvious tendency to become fewer in number. The greatest number of remiges among flying birds is exhibited by relatively primitive species with very long wings, such as certain albatrosses: the wandering albatross (*Diomedea exulans*) has about

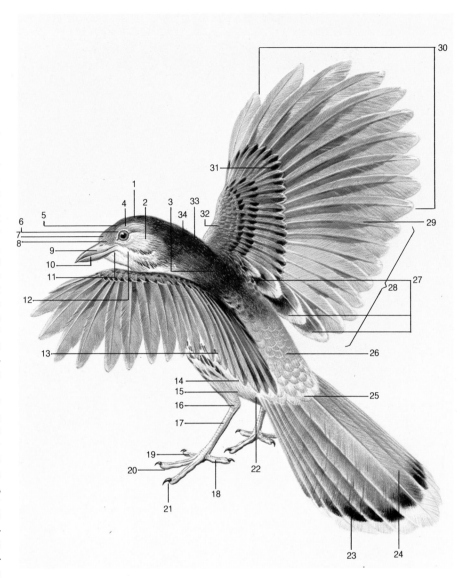

10 primaries and more than 32 secondaries. The Andean condor (*Vultur gryphus*) possesses 11 primaries and 25 secondaries. The minimum number of primaries for a flying bird is 9, as in several families of passerines that are particularly highly evolved and of recent origin, such as the buntings and the icterids. Naturally, nonflying birds such as the ratites and various flightless rails have less than 9 primary remiges, but this is clearly a degenerative phenomenon.

Each remige is covered, at the base of the wing's upper surface, by at least one primary covert feather; and as we look forward from the primary coverts to the front edge of the wing we find successive series of ever smaller feathers. These are the median and lesser coverts, etc., as well as the marginal covert feathers. On the lower side of the wing there is a similar arrangement of covert feathers but they are not as well developed and some rows are often incomplete. All

the remiges overlap one another sideways in a uniform fashion, the inner vane of each feather being covered, when viewed from above, by the next nearest feather. This arrangement is clearly a most effective way of providing the whole wing with coherence,

This page: different parts of a bird's body: 1) vertex; 2) ear region; 3) nape; 4) orbital fissure; 5) forehead; 6) eye; 7) cere; 8) lore; 9) upper mandible of bill; 10) lower mandible of bill; 11) chin; 12) cheek; 13) breast; 14) hip; 15) tibia; 16) heel; 17) tarsus; 18) first toe (hind); 19) second toe (inner); 20) third toe (middle); 21) fourth toe (outer); 22) under tail coverts; 23) rectrices; 24) tail feathers; 25) upper tail coverts; 26) rump; 27) tertiary remiges; 28) secondary remiges; 29) greater coverts; 30) primary remiges; 31) primary coverts; 32) lesser coverts; 33) scapulars; 34) back.

Facing page: changes in the plumage of the ptarmigan from winter to summer.

solidity, and elasticity.

The tail feathers are called rectrices and are usually even in number. They are normally counted from the central pair outwards. Many birds have 12 rectrices, or 6 pairs, but a few have 10. Among the latter are the Apodiformes, including hummingbirds and swifts, almost all the cuckoos, the motmots, the toucans, etc. Some rails and certain grebes have only 8 rectrices, and, as far as is known, there are three species of very small birds which have only 6 rectrices. The species with the most rectrices appears to be the ostrich, which has at least 50 or 60, but here the structural arrangement of the feathers is chiefly ornamental. The rectrices, too, possess upper and lower coverts, designed to protect the bases of the feathers, as is the case with the remiges.

Because the feathers covering the body of birds were primarily designed, as we have noted, for insulation, long before they evolved for purposes of flying, it is not surprising that the number of contour feathers in the various species should vary according to the environment, the period of the year, and also the size of the bird itself. Clearly the numerical variation mainly affects the contour feathers that are part of the organs for flying, and precise calculations in respect of different species are few and far between. The lowest total of feathers has been reported in the ruby-throated hummingbird (*Archilochus colubris*), which has only 940, whereas the record is apparently held by the whistling swan (*Cygnus columbianus*), credited with 25,216. On average the passerines possess from 1,500 to 3,000 contour feathers. There is not a great difference, proportionately, between species living in tropical surroundings and those frequenting areas subject to fluctuations of temperature and particularly cold climates. This is evidently due to the fact that it is not so much the number of feathers that count in achieving a greater or lesser measure of insulation so much as the ability to ruffle them and, even more importantly, the chance of acquiring an insulating cover of down, scattered, thinly or densely, over the whole body. The distribution of the feather-covered tracts, or pterylae, varies according to the overall shape of the body and, at least to some extent, the functions that the plumage has to fulfill.

Study of the pterylae is of considerable value for taxonomic purposes; and as a rule they are identified by the position they occupy. Thus ornithologists distinguish the head tract, the spinal tract which extends almost all the way along the dorsal region of the spine, the humeral tract, the femoral tract, the crural tract, the wing and tail tracts, the ventral tract , etc.

Molting

Because of the typical structure of the feathers, the continual use to which they are subjected and the need to keep them in the most efficient condition, birds go through a series of plumage changes or molts, beginning with a first covering of feathers as soon as they are born or shortly after they hatch, and continuing until they are fully adult. After that all the feathers are changed at least once a year, and among certain species twice or even three times every twelve months. Two kinds of molt, therefore, must be distinguished, one associated with growth, the other with replacement. Almost all species go through one annual postnuptial molt and some have a second prenuptial molt, which is complete only in a few cases and generally partial. Willow grouse (family Tetraonidae) go through three and in some instances four molts a year. The majority of migratory birds need to have their plumage in perfect condition before flying off in fall to their wintering zones and thus complete their postnuptial molt prior to departure. It is vital, however, for some birds not to be partially immobilized and to have their flight power diminished before the migration journey, a period during which they need to accumulate a sufficient quantity of fat to travel long distances without feeding. In such cases it is more convenient to postpone the exchange of feathers until the birds reach their winter quarters. Birds most affected are those that feed while flying, and in this category of species with a delayed postnuptial molt are groups that differ greatly from one another phylogenetically, such as swallows, the migratory American flycatchers, bee-eaters, and shearwaters (genus *Puffinus*). The dangers associated with molting are synchronized, above all, with the breeding cycle and of course with seasonal variations of climate. There have been innumerable studies and experiments designed to establish the factors that control the mechanism of the molt; apparently the principal factors are the increasing and decreasing amounts

of daylight which, by stimulating the hypophyses, condition the activities of the other endocrine glands and especially the thyroid, mainly responsible for the growth of certain tissues and particularly the production of melanin and other pigments that give color to the plumage.

The period when the different species reach the age of acquiring adult plumage varies considerably from group to group. Certain larks and pipits assume complete adult plumage with their first postjuvenile molt at the end of the summer or beginning of the fall in their year of birth, a mere three months or so after hatching. Many passerines acquire adult plumage with a more or less complete prenuptial molt around late winter or early spring of their first year, at about the age of eight months. A number of other passerines take on adult plumage some fourteen months after birth, when the first postnuptial molt is completed. Among those species that take some time to acquire adult plumage, going through several intermediate phases, are various medium-sized and large gulls, including the herring gull (*Larus argentatus*), which assumes its handsome pearl-gray and white adult plumage in its fourth winter, at the end of the postnuptial molt which lasts from August to mid January. The longer the entire process takes, the more individual variations are likely to occur. Some herring gulls may delay the acquisition of adult plumage until they are almost four years old. Yet many large birds of prey do not assume adult garb until much later, between five and ten years of age. It has to be pointed out, however, that many observations relating to birds of prey apply to individuals in captivity, where conditions for obtaining food, use of plumage, and illumination are probably very different from those pertaining to life in the wild.

Some species possess an extremely complex plumage with varied forms of adornment that play an important role in nuptial displays, territorial defense and all the behavioral postures and attitudes that facilitate communication among birds of the same species. There are also comparatively small birds whose metabolism and life cycle are fairly accelerated. Both types of bird need several years to obtain their adult plumage. This seems to be the case, according to certain authors, with the twelve-wired bird of paradise (*Seleucides melanoleucus*), the males of which species take on their splendid

nuptial plumage for the first time when they are seven years old.

The extent and form of molt tends to differ considerably, such variations apparently being connected with adaptation and affecting even subspecies of the same species. A classic example is the short-toed lark (*Calandrella cinerea*), which normally does not have a spring (prenuptial) molt, except for the Asiatic subspecies *C. c. dukhunensis*, which has a complete change of plumage every spring. There is a very good explanation for this difference. The Asiatic subspecies of the short-toed lark lives in deserts where constant and very strong winds cause serious and rapid abrasion to the feathers. It is equally noticeable that if individuals of the same species display different habits, the form of the molt may vary. The populations of phainopeplas (silky flycatchers) living in the Colorado Desert in California go through a more complete molt than those

inhabiting the cooler coastal strip, the latter birds starting to breed later and therefore having less time to complete their molt before the autumnal migration.

The molting process is usually extremely regular, affecting different tracts in sequence, except in the case of penguins where the change of feathers seems to happen in patches. The complete molt begins, as a rule, with the loss of the innermost primary remiges on both wings and then proceeds in regular succession to the changing of the other primaries as the original ones are replaced. This ensures that at any given moment the least number of feathers are missing, so that flying capacity is minimally affected. When the molt of the primary remiges is half finished, the secondaries normally start to fall out, commencing with the outer feathers and working inward. After the flight feathers begin to be molted, it is time for the other body feathers to be changed. The rectrices are also normally molted in series and in pairs, again so as to keep the tail functioning as well as possible. As a rule the central pair are exchanged first and the process continues in a centrifugal direction; but in some toucans, mousebirds and, above all, woodpeckers, the molt is in reverse (centripetal). It is extremely important that a woodpecker should not go for too long without its central tail feathers, which are very rigid and provide support for the bird when climbing a treetrunk.

There are, of course, exceptions to this molting procedure, and although at first glance they may appear to have little adaptive significance, these do, in fact, take on tremendous importance. Many aquatic birds, belonging to various orders, molt all their flight feathers almost simultaneously. Among such birds that lose their flight feathers and also some of their body feathers at the same time are virtually all ducks, geese and swans, certain auks and puffins, coots and moorhens, cranes, and some rails. The inability to fly puts such birds in a state of risk with respect to their surrounding conditions, particularly predators; so it is obvious that this method of molting applies in the main to those species that can find refuge in lakes, rivers, and ponds that are inaccessible to most of their predators, where they can feel comparatively safe even during the period when they are out of action. Many of these birds display particular kinds of behavior in relation to molting. Geese, for example, may assemble in relatively inaccessible areas, traveling some distance if need be, coming together, as it were, for the purpose of molting. Undoubtedly, one of the most comprehensive adaptations associated with a simultaneous molt of all the wing and tail feathers, as well as many of the body feathers, occurs in various species of hornbill (family Bucerotidae). The females spend almost the entire incubation period "walled up" inside their tree-hollow nest, undergoing a virtually complete molt in total seclusion. When the chicks hatch and the females are able to emerge from their prison, they appear in totally new garb. In this context it is worth mentioning that the different patterns of behavior exhibited by males and females are often enough, on their own, to determine varied forms of molt.

We can now sum up the types of plumage that may succeed one another from the hatching of the egg to the attainment of adult status. First comes the so-called natal plumage, absent in some species, particularly those that nest in tree hollows, and in certain quite primitive groups such as the pelicans. In other groups, instead of a single covering of down at birth, there are two, as in penguins, certain nocturnal birds of prey, and a few primitive passerines. From the viewpoint of adaptation it is evident that the majority of birds furnished with an efficient covering of down belong to those groups that give birth to "precocious" nestlings, while the opposite is true of nestlings that are more or less helpless.

After the disappearance of the down, and at a rate that varies enormously from one species to another, birds acquire a proper covering of feathers, the juvenile plumage, which is usually worn for a fairly short period. There are instances of very rapid successions of plumage, as in some passerines, among them the house sparrow, which already possesses a subadult or fully adult plumage even before the feathers of the juvenile plumage have had time to develop completely. The next form of garb, usually known as the winter plumage, is the first type to bear a close resemblance to that of the adult. In some cases this plumage is incomplete and there are still clear signs of the juvenile plumage. This happens frequently with many wading birds and gulls, helping to determine the age of the individual concerned. In quite a

number of species there is then the first nuptial plumage, which is generally acquired not by molting but by the abrasion of the edges of the feathers comprising the preceding plumage. Thus the very vivid colors typical of this garb tend to appear initially on the borders of the feathers. Nevertheless, it is not strictly correct to talk about nuptial plumage, since in many cases sexual maturity is not yet complete. Eventually there is the second winter plumage, which in the huge majority of birds differs very slightly, and only in the comparative intensity of some tones, from the winter garb of the adults.

It is important to remember that as the individual bird matures, all the mechanisms associated with the functioning of the plumage are perfected, whereas the maturing of other elements of behavior does not necessarily keep pace with the various phases of the plumage itself. Recent research has shown that in certain species of colonial birds, where the plumage may be spectacular but generally with no sexual distinction, some individuals are already mature enough to couple, build a nest, lay eggs and incubate them, etc., while still bearing juvenile plumage. The adaptive significance of this condition is very interesting. In fact, the plumage of the adult normally indicates to a partner that the individual is physiologically capable of breeding, whereas juvenile plumage denotes both immaturity and inexperience. In times of need, however, it is essential for a species to recruit individuals that may be relatively inexpert from the viewpoint of behavior but are certainly fit to breed thanks to the full maturation of the gonads.

A special kind of plumage that is particularly widespread among the males of duck species in the northern hemisphere is the so-called eclipse plumage. When they have finished breeding, the males often assemble in groups, leaving the care of eggs and chicks to the females. Around midsummer they begin to molt their flight feathers simultaneously. The vivid colors that pinpoint the males of many duck species when their normal capacity for moving around is temporarily diminished would be a grave disadvantage for individuals that could be quickly located by predators and not be able to get away in time. To overcome this handicap the males of such species go through a genuine molt that entails an extraordinary change in appearance; for the plumage they

adopt is in almost every way like that of the females and thus extremely mimetic. The only differences are the wing speculum and a few other small details enabling the various species to be identified.

The skeleton

The skeleton of birds shows special adaptations both for flying and walking. Indeed, the forelimbs (wings) have undergone such drastic changes that they have become quite different, anatomically, from the hind limbs. The body is typically short and stocky, the skull compact and relatively small, and the neck (in many species) long and flexible. As a rule, too, the bones contain air sacs.

Birds' skeletons are very similar to those of reptiles, particularly of the Archosauria, comprising the extinct pterosaurs and dinosaurs as well as crocodilians.

Vertebrae. The number of vertebrae ranges from 40 (in small passerines) to a maximum of 60 (in swans).

The cervical vertebrae vary, according to the different groups, from 8 to a maximum of 25 in long-necked species. Each vertebra is hinged to the next by means of a saddle-shaped articulation which allows the individual vertebral parts to move quite freely. The thoracic vertebrae, on the other hand, are not very mobile. They range in number from 5 to a maximum of 10; and in many birds, such as the Galliformes and Falconiformes, the front ones are fused. The lumbar and sacral vertebrae are likewise fused and form the synsacrum. The 4 to 9 caudal or tail vertebrae, also fused, form the pygostyle.

Ribs. Each rib comprises two parts, one dorsal and vertebral, the other ventral and sternal, the latter making contact with the sternum (breastbone). As in the case with certain reptiles (the tuatara, for example), most birds have hooked processes over the greater part of the rib surface. The ribs overlap to form a fairly inflexible cage.

Scapular girdle. The scapular girdle linking the forelimbs with the skeleton is made up of the scapula (shoulderblade), the clavicle (collarbone), and the coracoid. This last bone is joined to the sternum. The scapula is a flat, sickle-shaped bone in close contact with the rib cage. The lower surface of

the clavicle is often fused to form a furcula (wishbone); and in certain parrots and owls the clavicles are linked by cartilage. The sternum, with its articulated sternal ribs, varies in form from species to species; but in all birds apart from ratites it is keeled. The pectoral muscles are attached to the surface of the sternum, which is particularly large in species poorly adapted for flying, such as the owl parrot (kakapo).

Forelimbs (wings). The wings of a bird are formed mainly by the bones of the arm and the forearm, unlike those of other flying vertebrates such as bats, whose wings are formed principally by the bones of the hand.

The arm is constituted of a large bone, the humerus, the proximal part of which is flattened and characterized by two crests, the radial (on the back) and the ulnar (on the front). The length of this bone varies according to the bird's propensity for flight. In powerful, speedy fliers such as swifts and hummingbirds, the forearm and hand are longer than the humerus; but the reverse is true of gliding birds such as the albatross. The forearm comprises the ulna and radius. The former is the larger and has projections on the surface to which the secondary remiges (flight feathers) are connected.

In the adult bird the first and second fingers have disappeared, although vestiges are present in the embryo. Among the majority of living birds the fingers of the forelimbs have lost their claws, but in ratites and certain species of keeled birds, such as the turkey vulture (*Cathartes aura*), there are claws on one or two fingers. Chicks of the hoatzin possess claws on their first two fingers, using these when making short journeys in the vicinity of the nest. In the adult the claws have vanished.

Pelvic girdle. The pelvic girdle (hip) is made up of three bones: the ilium, the ischium, and the pubis. These are fused and closely linked to the synsacrum, so that there appears to be only a single bone. In most birds neither the ilium nor the ischium are joined at the front and thus the pelvic cavity is not completely surrounded by bone. This feature is clearly associated with the relatively large size of the eggs. Exceptions to this rule are ostriches and rheas. The three bones in conjunction form the acetabular cavity, into which the head of the femur is fixed.

Hind legs. These have been modified to facilitate bipedal locomotion.

The bones of the hind leg are the femur (thighbone), the tibiotarsus (shinbone), and the fibula. The femur is large, usually short and facing forward. The tibiotarsus is formed by the distal fusion of the tibia and the tarsal bones; and the fibula is fairly small, thin, and roughly two thirds of the length of the tibiotarsus. The fibula and the tibiotarsus form an articulation with the femur in the knee.

The feet of a bird, important for purposes of classification, are highly specialized and the tarsal bones are fused. Most species have 4 toes (first, second, third, and fourth). The big toe is short and directed to the rear. The second, third, and fourth toes have 3, 4, and 5 phalanges respectively, while the big toe has no more than 2.

The first and fourth toes of parrots and woodpeckers are turned backward. Those of pelicans and swifts, however, all face forward. Ratites lack a big toe and ostriches have only 2 toes (probably the second and fourth).

The skull. A bird's skull displays a number of reptilian features, such as a single occipital condyle and a mobile quadrate bone which articulates with the mandible. The cranial cavity is made up of parietals and a large frontal bone which covers the orbits and is hinged to the nasals. In an adult bird the various bones that form the skull are fused in such a way that the different components cannot be distinguished. At the front of the cranium are two large cavities separated by a perforated septum. The orbital cavities accommodating the eyes are particularly large.

In the case of the palate, there is an incomplete separation of the nasal and buccal cavities, whereas in mammals the opposite is true, the two cavities being wholly separated. The palate is very interesting from the viewpoint of classification. There are at least two principal types, the paleognathic and the neognathic.

The circulatory system

Birds are warm-blooded animals with a complete double circulatory system. Indeed, although they are derived from reptiles, their blood circulation functions more efficiently than that of mammals. The heart is relatively larger and the rate of heartbeat is higher than that of a mammal, so that a greater quantity of blood is pumped through within any given period. This undoubtedly has much to do with the vast amount of energy needed by a bird when flying.

As a rule, smaller species have bigger hearts. A famous example is the hummingbird, the weight of whose heart is roughly 2 per cent of its whole body.

The heart is situated in the central part of the thoracic cavity below the lungs; and is separated by an oblique septum from the visceral cavity. The heart is additionally surrounded by a pericardial sac.

Blood flows back from the body through the anterior and posterior venae cavae into the right atrium. In the lower vertebrates the two venae cavae come together in a venous sinus, but in birds this is part and parcel of the right atrium. In the ostrich the venous sinus is still present, whereas in wild and domestic fowl only the vestiges can be seen. The blood entering the right atrium flows through the atrio-ventricular opening into the right ventricle, and from there it courses through the lungs. The lungs are furnished with three semi-lunar valves which prevent the blood flowing back, and two pulmonary arteries carry the blood which supplies oxygen to the lungs. The oxygenated blood then passes from the lungs into the left atrium and from there through the bicuspid valve into the left ventricle. From here the blood travels to the aortic arch.

The blood contains corpuscular features that evidently have affinities with the blood of reptiles; the red corpuscles, in fact, are oval in shape and possess a nucleus.

The digestive system

The principal characteristics of a bird's digestive system are a horny mouth opening (the bill), the absence of true teeth, the division of the stomach into at least two sections, and (in some species) the presence of a crop, formed by the enlargement of the esophagus (gullet). The bill of a bird is extremely variable in form, depending on the nature of the food that is normally taken. The tongue shows similar variation. In woodpeckers, for example, the tongue is very long, in hummingbirds it is tubular or subtubular (adapted for sipping nectar from flowers), in penguins the rear part is provided with hooks for capturing food, and so on. The tongue is covered by a horny epithelium which is especially thick at the front; and, except in parrots, it does not possess any internal muscles.

Esophagus. The esophagus is a long tube extending from the mouth and connecting this with the stomach. As a rule it is expandable and contains a large amount of food; and sometimes the lower part enlarges into a special pouch (the crop) which, apart from being used for storage, may have other functions as well. In doves and pigeons, for example, it is a glandular organ; and in many seed-eating species it is likewise glandular, with a predigestive function. The dimensions of the esophagus vary according to the type of food eaten. When operating as a storage chamber it may take on various forms: thus in cormorants it is oblong, in vultures it is lopsided, and in pigeons and fowl it comprises a double pouch.

Gastric cavity. There are two regions of the stomach, one glandular, the other muscular.

Food travels gradually from the esophagus to the glandular part of the stomach and there is an isthmus between the latter and the muscular part or gizzard.

The gizzard performs a variety of functions although it is basically considered an organ designed for grinding food. In seed-eating birds, for example, it is used for storage, food particles remaining inside until broken down by the gastric enzymes. It is here that the preliminary proteolytic (breaking down of protein) stages of digestion occur but, as we have seen, it also plays an important role in the mechanical breaking up of food. In many species the grinding action is improved by the presence of tiny pebbles swallowed by the bird. The gizzard serves, too, to filter indigestible parts of a prey, such as feathers, hairs, bones, scales, and fish skins.

The shape of the muscular gizzard is adapted to every particular type of diet. Thus in species that digest food which is easily assailable by enzymes and gastric acids, the stomach is in the form of an elongated pouch, typical of geese, diurnal birds of prey, pelicans, etc. In fruit- and nectar-eating species such as parrots, flowerpeckers, tanagers, etc., the gizzard is very small and it is the glandular part which has the job of storing food. An extreme instance of adaptation to diet is found in the flowerpeckers of the genus *Dicaeum*, fruit-eating birds which possess a diverticulum between the stomach and intestine. These species feed both on berries and arthropods. The berries travel directly from the glandular stomach to the intestine, while the arthropods pass into the muscular stomach in the course of breakdown and peptic digestion.

The typical muscular stomach, as found in seed-eating species, is furnished with strong muscles. With their powerful tongue, these birds can get rid of the outer covering of seeds, swallowing only the soft pulp so that they do not have to grind up their food.

Intestine. Chemical digestion and the absorption of nutritious substances take place in the intestine. As in the human body, there is the small intestine and the large intestine. The former begins with the duodenum, although only relative position distinguishes it from the next section, the ileum. The duodenum is like a rather narrow handle at the point where it connects with the pancreas. The intestine's form is clearly adapted to different diets, being comparatively long in herbivorous species and relatively short in carnivorous, insectivorous, and frugivorous species.

The mucus of the small intestine is constituted by a layer of cube-shaped epithelial cells with round or oval nuclei. The mucus possesses folds or villi designed to increase the internal surface of the intestine. These folds vary in shape from one species to another and constitute a useful criterion for classification, although they do not seem to be associated with diet.

The large intestine extends from the caecum to the cloaca. It is not as long as the small intestine, accounting for 3 to 10 per cent of the total length. This part of the intestine is shorter in seed-eating birds than in fruit-eating species. Although little is known about the function of the large intestine, its main purpose is certainly to absorb the water recovered from the food.

The pairs of blind sacs or caeca situated at the junction of the small and large intestines assume different forms according to the taxonomic groups concerned. Some species, such as the parrots, do not have these; and others, like the kingfishers, only exhibit them as adults. They are either absent or rudimentary in the hummingbirds, the falcon family, the woodpeckers, the hoopoes and, generally, in insect-eating species. Nor are they very well developed in seed-eating species. On the other hand, the caeca are pronounced in herbivores and frugivores as they are in birds that feed on mollusks, such as waders and gulls.

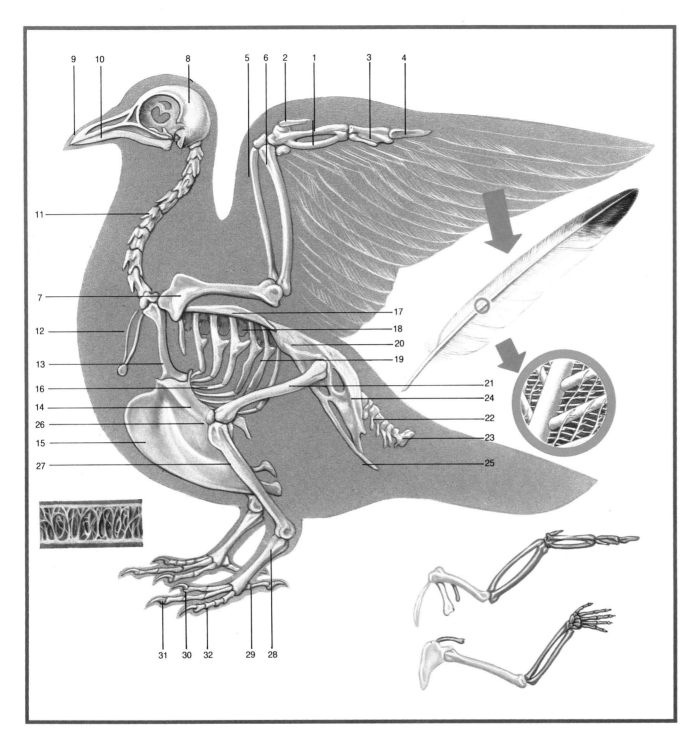

Skeleton of a bird; 1) metacarpal bone; 2) first toe of hind legs; 3) second toe; 4) third toe; 5) radius; 6) ulna; 7) humerus; 8) neurocranium; 9) splanchnocranium; 10) mandible; 11) cervical vertebrae; 12) furcula; 13) coracoid; 14) sternum; 15) keel; 16) sternocostal bones; 17) scapula; 18) thoracic vertebrae; 19) ribs; 20) ilium; 21) femur; 22) caudal vertebrae; 23) pygostyle; 24) metatarsal bones; 29) first finger of forelimbs; 30) second finger; 31) third finger; 32) fourth finger.

Below right: skeleton of bird's wing compared with that of human arm; equivalent bones are shown in same colors. Left: section of pneumaticized bone. Right: a feather with enlargement of the rachis; note the parallel series of barbs stemming from it and the parallel series of barbules, joined by hooks.

Liver. In birds the liver is a large, bilobate organ, the right lobe being the larger. Its chief digestive function is to produce bile. The most important of the non-digestive functions is to accumulate fats and glycogen, others being intermediary metabolism, the synthesis of protein and glycogen and the production of uric acid. During the development of the embryo and the immediately succeeding stage, the liver has a blood-forming function. It is largest in insect- and fish-eating species, smaller in others. Anatomically, the inner surface protected

inside the abdominal cavity is somewhat irregular and convex in shape.

The two lobes are separated by a deep cleft. The top part of the liver extends as far as the lungs. The surrounding organs adapt to it and appear in relief on its surface. Thus the heart is visible in the top part of the parietal surface, while the outline of the glandular and muscular stomachs appear on the visceral surface of the left lobe, and those of the top part of the duodenum and of the pancreas can be seen on the right lobe. The spleen is connected to the central section of the

liver's visceral surface. Blood circulates to the liver through the vena cava which crosses the top of the right lobe.

The hepatic veins and the vena cava have their respective entrances and exits at the same point. The two parietal hepatic veins and the two arteries enter by way of the transverse fossa in the center of the visceral surface; and the two bile ducts stem from the same fossa. These ducts, one for either lobe, lead to the duodenum. The left duct communicates directly with the intestine but the right duct may deviate to flow into the gall bladder or become enlarged so as to form such an organ. In some groups of birds the gall bladder is absent. Its function is to concentrate the bile liquids which serve to neutralize the acid of the chyme and to emulsify the fats.

Pancreas. The pancreas is a gland with a double function, namely endocrine and exocrine. In the former capacity it produces two hormones, insulin and glucagon, and in the latter capacity pancreatic juice. The dimensions of the pancreas vary according to the bird's diet: in insectivores it is fairly large, whereas in carnivores it is comparatively small. Pancreatic juice plays an important part in neutralizing chyme; and thanks to the presence of digestive enzymes it assists the process of molecular breakdown in the small intestine.

The excretory apparatus

Kidneys. The kidneys, situated in the pelvic region, represent approximately 1 per cent of the body weight. They are are made up of three lobes (cranial, median, and caudal).

The ureter, located on the lower surface, receives the principal ducts from each lobe. Venous blood flows into the kidneys from the feet, the tail and the mesentery by way of the portal system. Arterial blood is carried to the kidneys by the renal artery. The kidneys rest against the sacrum and the ilium, fitting their outlines. Flat in shape, they have ureters which lead directly to the cloaca. In contrast to mammals, the nephron, which is the functional unit of the kidney, has a very short Henle's loop, this being associated with the fact that the kidneys of birds absorb more water.

Salt glands. These glands are situated in the head, more specifically in the region of the nose. Present mainly in marine birds, the glands produce a secretion that contains a high concentration of sodium chloride. Although they may be different in shape and arrangement, the salt glands all have features in common. In the embryonic stage they stem from the infolding of the nasal epithelium and may have a double series of ducts on either side which come together in a common duct penetrating the nasal cavity. The glands are formed of tubular lobes surrounded by a thick layer of connective tissue. Each lobe possesses a central canal which leads into the duct of the gland. The secretion is produced in tubules arranged radially around the central canal. These glands mainly produce sodium as well as modest quantities of salts.

The respiratory system

Birds possess a fairly complicated respiratory system which is very different to that of other vertebrates, especially mammals. From both the anatomical and physiological aspects, there are still gaps in our understanding of this system, despite all the research that has been done. The apparatus consists of two relatively small lungs and voluminous air sacs poor in blood vessels. The air sacs may actually penetrate the bones. The whole respiratory system occupies from 5 to 20 per cent of the body volume. The upper section of the system comprises a pair of nostrils leading into the nasal chambers, which are themselves divided into three parts (turbinals).

Air passes from the nasal chambers through the internal nostrils into the mouth cavity. From the mouth air travels into the trachea (windpipe) via the glottis, which is closed by the laryngeal cartilages. The larynx (unlike that of mammals) does not constitute the vocal organ. Air continues to pass through the trachea, which is circular in cross-section because it is formed of complete cartilaginous rings, and then into the bronchi. At the dividing point of the trachea is the syrinx, which is the true vocal organ of birds. This is formed by a tracheal-bronchial expansion and furnished with one or two membranes capable of vibrating when disturbed by air. The muscles causing the membranes to vibrate are of two kinds: the extrinsic muscles stem from the sternum and are inserted in the trachea, and the intrinsic muscles have their origin or the bronchi. These muscles vary in number and position from one

species to another and are consequently regarded as a valuable criterion for classification.

The bronchi, provided with a cartilaginous framework, are joined to the two lungs.

Lungs. The lungs, small and not expandable, are situated in the rear part of the thorax and are protected by the ribs. Equal in size, birds' lungs may contain a lesser volume of air than the lungs of mammals. The bronchi do not branch out as in mammals; indeed, the main bronchus, having entered the lung, continues as a mesobronchium for the entire length of the lung itself, having its outlet in the abdominal air sac. Stemming from the mesobronchium are the secondary bronchi, interlinked by small ducts known as parabronchia; and leading from each parabronchium are air-carrying capillaries joining up with the parabronchium.

Air sacs. These vary in number (12 in waders and gulls, as well as in herons

Anatomy of a bird, with indications of the various internal organs: 1) esophagus; 2) cervical muscles; 3) trachea; 4) crop; 5) hand muslces; 6) tensor, extensor and flexor muscles; 7) pectoral muscles; 8) biceps; 9) lungs; 10) triceps; 11) liver; 12) thoracic and abdominal air sacs; 13) small intestine; 14) sterno-tracheal muscle; 15) heart; 16) gizzard; 17) duodenum; 18) pancreas; 19) cloaca.

Below left: plan of the female genital system of a bird: 1) follicle of left ovary; 2) tube; 3) left oviduct; 4) uterus; 5) vagina; 6) cloaca; 7) right oviduct (atrophied in all birds).

Below right: plan of the heart and principal blood vessels of a bird (the venous blood is shown in darker color): 1) carotid; 2) pulmonary artery; 3) pulmonary vein; 4) aorta. Birds lack a second left aortic arch, and this is shown, therefore, in a neutral color.

and their allies, 6 – 7 in passerines), and make up about 80 per cent of the volume of the lungs. There are various kinds of air sacs, according to position and size. Thus there are two small cervical air sacs, located between the tenth vertebra and the front edge of the lungs; a single interclavicular sac between the trachea, esophagus and cervical sac, the front of which borders the heart; two anterior thoracic air sacs extending from the base of the lungs to the edge of the sternum; two asymmetrical posterior thoracic sacs (the left one being larger than the right), connected to the rear section of the lungs; and finally two large abdominal sacs, of which the left-hand one is the larger. These sacs occupy the spaces between the viscera.

The air sacs are usually connected to the primary and secondary bronchi and also possess other indirect links (recurrent bronchi) with the secondary and tertiary bronchi. The sacs also have diverticula which go inside the bones. As a rule the bones of larger

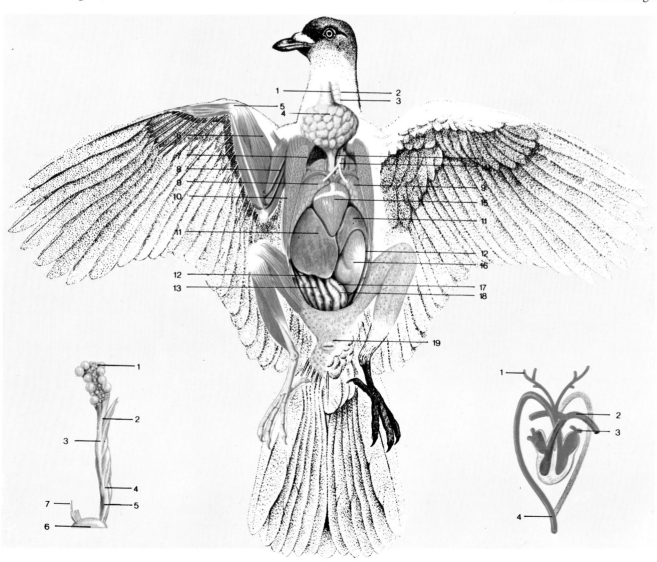

species and powerful fliers tend to be more pneumatic. This is an adaptation that clearly has a connection with flying, even though certain details concerning the true function of this phenomenon remain doubtful. It is interesting to note, for example, that this structural adaptation occurs, too, in some land animals, including the dinosaurs.

The muscular system

Because they are adapted for flying, birds possess a muscular system that is highly developed, particularly at the front of the body, so as to enable them to move their wings powerfully and rapidly. The rigidity of the thoracic and lumbar regions helps them to accomplish such movements. A bird's body contains about 175 different muscles, which are ranged into distinct groups according to their anatomical position. Thus there are muscles in the head, the mandible, the eyes, the trachea, the syrinx, etc.

The muscles responsible for moving the wings are inserted in the sternum or its keel, the principal kinds being the following: 1) the large pectoral muscle which fits into the keel, the sternum and the humeral crests, used for lowering the wings and therefore the most important muscle for flying; 2) the small pectoral muscle, assisting the large one, inserted in the coracoid and the humerus; 3) the antagonistic muscle which raises the wings, known as the supracoracoid muscle, inserted into the front of the sternum, with a distal tendon that goes through the articulation of the scapula, the coracoid, and the clavicle, and which is inserted into the rear part of the humerus.

The muscles of the hind legs are equally specialized, for in addition to helping the bird to walk, sometimes very rapidly, they provide the impetus for the initial leap that every flying bird has to make when taking off. These muscles also permit the bird to land after flight without sustaining any damage to the body. The various leg muscles together form a triangular pattern, the base being in the pelvic region and the apex terminating in the knee (where the femur articulates with the tibiotarsus).

Taxonomists recognize four groups of muscles for purposes of classification, namely the tracheal muscles, the mandibular muscles, and the muscles of the front and hind limbs.

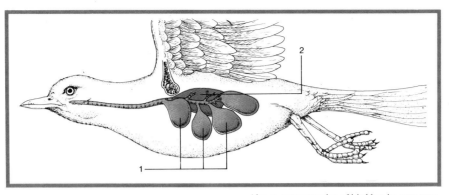
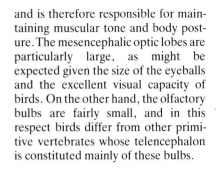

The brain

The brain of a bird is characterized by voluminous cerebral hemispheres and a fairly large rhombencephalon. This brain is considerably larger than that of a reptile, and very different; it is protected by a thin brain box and, because of the large size of the eyeballs, it has shifted upward and backward.

Unlike mammals, birds possess well-developed corpora striata; but the cortex is not large and lacks the circumvolutions found among mammals. This undoubtedly has much to do with the fact that bird behavior is far more stereotyped. The cortex, for example, makes no direct contact with the spinal medulla, as is the case among mammals by virtue of the pyramidal fascicles.

Consequently the rhombencephalon is well developed. This controls the reflex activity of the skeletal muscles

Above: every species of bird has its own type of flight and what generally distinguishes one from the other is the amount that the wings beat. Common to all species, on the other hand, are the anatomical features which ensure the lightness of the body, such as the air sacs (1) in association with the lungs (2). Below: examples of visual adaptation in birds, which for the most part involves binocular vision, characterized by a particular area where the two visual fields are superimposed. A) Sight in the sparrow. This little bird, which feeds on worms and insects, needs to have forward binocular vision but also a wide lateral field in order to escape from predators. This is made possible by the position of the eyes far back in the head. B) Sight in the woodcock. The bird's forward binocular vision is fairly weak as it finds food by searching in the mud with its flexible beak; the position of the eyes, on the other hand, is far back in the head to allow good all-round vision with visual fields superimposing both front and back. C) Sight in the hawk. This bird of prey has two foveae in the retina. When the focus of the two central spots overlap, it can measure distance exactly which is vital for homing in on prey. The lateral spots give accurate vision of other distinct areas. D) The owl has a wider field of vision than any other bird. However, because it has no central foveae, it judges distances through an acute sense of hearing. It is also able to turn its head 270° to look sideways or over the shoulder.

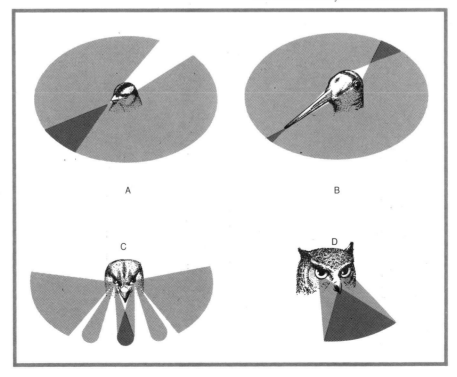
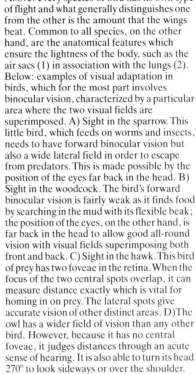

and is therefore responsible for maintaining muscular tone and body posture. The mesencephalic optic lobes are particularly large, as might be expected given the size of the eyeballs and the excellent visual capacity of birds. On the other hand, the olfactory bulbs are fairly small, and in this respect birds differ from other primitive vertebrates whose telencephalon is constituted mainly of these bulbs.

The sense organs

Apart from the overall sensibility of receptors dispersed through the entire body, the organs governing the senses proper are related to smell, sight, hearing, and taste.

Smell. The organ governing scent or smell is situated in the nasal cavities and is innervated by the cranial nerve. It is not very large in birds and its real significance is still not known. Research has shown that it is actively employed for finding food by certain species such as the turkey vulture, the kiwi and the petrels, albatrosses, and shearwaters, but in the majority of birds it is no more than a rudimentary organ.

Sight. In contrast to smell, a bird's sense of sight is fairly good, which is hardly surprising when one realizes that the two eyeballs may be heavier than the whole brain. Birds' eyes are not very mobile and for this reason they have to rely on a highly flexible neck. The eye is usually bell-shaped, which reduces the volume of the eye without affecting its visual capacity.

The position of the eyes differs greatly from one group to another. Broadly speaking, there is one eye on each side of the head in an arrangement that makes it possible to cover a broad field of vision even if there is a fairly reduced measure of binocular vision. Some groups, including the nocturnal birds of prey, have their eyes at the front of the head and this improves binocular vision, so essential for pinpointing prey.

An extreme example of how the eyes may be adapted to the surroundings and especially for finding food is found in the woodcock. The eyes of this bird are placed far back so that when it hunts for food, probing into the soil with its long bill, it can literally look back over its shoulders.

The retina of the eyes contains a very large number of rods and cones, and in general possesses more nerve cells than the human eye. Certain parts of the retina, known as areae, have a very large number of such nerve cells, which causes the retina to thicken. Other zones, the foveae, are thinner and only possess cones. The foveae are the areas of the eye with the keenest vision. In hunting species, such as the diurnal birds of prey, there are two foveae in either eye. In addition, a bird's eye is characterized by a pecten, a structure containing numerous blood vessels. The function of the pecten seems to be the nourishment of the retina, but it may accomplish other things as well, such as increasing the eye's sensibility or compensating for changes in pressure brought about by the bird's adjusting movements.

The eyes are innervated by the second cranial nerve which, emerging from the eyeball, leads to the optic chiasma where the optic tracts commence.

Hearing and balance. The hearing mechanism of birds conforms to the standard anatomical structure of the higher vertebrates. There are, in fact, three sections: the outer ear, the middle ear, and the inner ear. The outer ear lacks a true auriclè, but the arrangement of feathers around the ear opening provides a good substitute, carrying sounds, into the interior. The outer ear terminates in the tympanic membrane. The middle ear, where this membrane begins, possesses a special bone called the columella and it communicates with the pharynx by means of the Eustachian tube. The columella transforms acoustic vibrations into mechanical energy, which then transmits to the cochlea of the inner ear. The cochlea is the organ that transforms the mechanical vibrations into nerve impulses, but in contrast to the corresponding cochlea of mammals, it does not contain spiral folds.

Three canals of membranes are present in the inner ear. These semicircular canals are responsible for balance. The inner ear is innervated by the eighth (acoustic) cranial nerve, which performs functions connected both with hearing and balance.

Taste. It does not appear that this sense is highly developed and it is still not known what role it plays in the selection of food; clearly it is not as important as in mammals. The taste receptors are situated at the rear of the tongue and are scattered over the mouth region. They comprise taste buds which are not linked to form papillae, unlike those of mammals, and they are innervated by the seventh, ninth, and tenth cranial nerves.

REPRODUCTION

The Darwinian theory, maintaining that natural selection works in favor of the best adapted and strongest individual in the so-called "struggle for existence," has been partially revised in recent years. Nowadays, experts tend to agree that within a species the favored individual is not necessarily the strongest but the one that succeeds in procreating the greatest number of descendants, thus disseminating his genetic inheritance more prolifically than others of his species. The moment of reproduction is therefore the focal point in the life of any organism. Among the higher vertebrates, birds have undoubtedly been more closely studied in this respect than other groups, and their reproductive behavior exhibits many extremely interesting features.

Among birds, the arousal of the breeding instinct is partly environmental and partly physiological. As far as surroundings are concerned, at least in temperate regions, the most important factor is without doubt the increasingly long period of daylight as winter progresses to spring, this being recognized by birds as a reliable signal that the breeding season is approaching. By virtue of a complex interplay of physiological and hormonal factors, the response to this biological "clock" is evident in the pronounced enlargement of the gonads in both the males and females, which increase in volume some 2,000 times in relation to the period of winter inactivity, and in the development of authentic patterns of reproductive behavior. Other important causative factors are the abundance of food and of materials used for nest building. In the case of species living in equatorial zones, other elements, of course, control breeding behavior, regulating the levels of the various sexual hormones in the blood and provoking a sufficient hormonal increase to stimulate the reproductive instincts. In temperate zones the breeding season is more or less clearly defined; and in the course of this period some birds have a single brood whereas others, especially small and medium-sized species, often have two or even three successive broods. Among the many factors helping to determine the number of broods are the amount of food available in the vicinity, the pressure of predators, life expectancy, competition among members of the same species, etc. In tropical areas, as a result of certain constant physical

parameters, many birds do not observe a definite breeding season, so that nesting and reproductive activities occur right through the year. As a rule, therefore, every single species tends to follow its own annual rhythm. There are, nevertheless, some exceptions, as in the case of the sooty tern (*Sterna fuscata*), whose annual cycle really comprises ten lunar months, and sometimes this species breeds twice a year.

The age at which various birds start breeding differs enormously. Among the majority of passerines, ducks, geese and swans, doves and pigeons, and some owls, the first brood occurs at about the age of one year, while many African waxbills are capable of breeding only four months after birth. Other species, particularly among the birds of prey, do not attain sexual maturity for 4 – 5 years; and the royal albatross (*Diomedea epomophora*) is only ready to breed in the eighth year. These slow breeding cycles mean that such species become extremely vulnerable and have to be given ample protection, since the death of only a few individuals may have very serious repercussions on the various local bird populations.

Territory

One of the most characteristic features of the reproductive behavior of birds is the defense of territory, either by the male alone or by both partners. The term "territory" applies to any area that is defended, no matter how large or small. It may consist of the zone where the pair builds the nest, feeds and performs all the activities associated with breeding; or it may comprise a relatively large area which contains the nest alone, the birds flying off to other areas to feed and not displaying marked aggressive tendencies while so occupied. Among colonial species the breeding pair only defends the nest and a restricted area around it, while all members of the colony forage for food together. Finally there is the defense of territory known as the lek, namely an arena where the males display in ritualized parades that are sometimes extremely complex.

The territorial instinct may also be manifested as a simple defense of eggs, newly hatched young or even a mate, as happens, for example, with the black rosy finch where the male only defends the female, following her about whenever she leaves the nest to look for food. Territoriality among

birds is so commonplace as to indicate that there is clearly an evolutionary advantage associated with such behavior. Indeed, it guarantees the breeding pair isolation, permitting them to reproduce without interference, chiefly from others of their species; and it avoids too many birds collecting in zones which could not then support the whole population, likewise making it easier for the young to find food by removing the competitive pressure of other individuals with the same needs and habits.

Courtship

A period varying from a few hours to several months will elapse prior to the formation of pairs, and this is devoted to courtship. This term applies to all the procedures of behavior designed to link the pair and keep them united until the culminating act of copulation. It is a field of bird activity which has led to a vast amount of controversy, so that it is difficult to devise neat schemes of classification; but it seems clear that courtship, particularly when prolonged, serves to stimulate in the opposite sex internal physiological processes connected with reproduction, as well as to suppress the aggressive tendencies that invariably come to the fore at this time, especially among males of those species with strong territorial instincts. The various attitudes adopted during courtship are typical of, and exclusive to, each bird species; and the entire ritual is of the utmost importance in isolating a pair prior to copulation, enabling every bird to verify that its potential mate belongs to its own species. This considerably reduces the risk of crossbreeding between different species, so that each can preserve and transmit its characteristic, unaltered genetic material. Many species show marked sexual dimorphism, in that the color of the male is far more vivid than that of the female, whose coloration is generally drab. Furthermore, in many instances, the male plumage, apart from color, is notable for its extremely well-developed feathers, as in the African widowbirds (family Ploceidae) and the famous birds of paradise from New Guinea. In all these birds the colored parts, or at any rate the visible parts, of the plumage, are displayed in various ways by the males, assuming a role of fundamental importance during courtship. Even though such gaudy colors increase the likelihood of the males being spotted and perhaps attacked by predators, the selective process ensures that such birds will mate and produce young.

Among species where both sexes look alike, courtship is based on audible signals, often accompanied by characteristic postures, as in most of the passerine songbirds, and also, as occurs among birds of prey, by display rituals. The latter are performed either by the male or by both birds, frequently entailing spectacular dives or other exhibitions of dexterity in the air. Parades involving both partners are particularly typical of many gannets and grebes. An integral part of the courtship ritual is frequently the offering of miscellaneous objects and items of food by the male to his mate. In some heron species, for example, the offering may be a branch, a stick, tufts of algae or simply a prey. This ritual can occur at various stages of the reproductive cycle, during actual courtship, while the female is incubating or even when the newly born young are in the nest. In all cases the attitude of the female when receiving the gift imitates that of the chicks when demanding to be fed. The male may quite simply place the food directly in the female's beak; alternatively he will regurgitate it into her mouth or onto the ground in front of her. Many birds of prey perform spectacular aerial acrobatics, in the course of which the male drops the prey and the female snatches it in midair. The significance of such behavior would seem to be that the male has the opportunity of proving to his mate his ability to obtain food, which in itself satisfies her that when the young are born they will be adequately cared for. Objects other than real food may therefore be regarded as symbols for actual items of prey. When the young are already being reared, this form of courtship is basically intended to reinforce the bonds that already exist between the adult pair. Such bonds, formed after the initial courtship phase, differ enormously both in nature and duration. Among certain pheasants, for example, male and female come together only to mate, often in huge arenas where a number of males display simultaneously; in such cases the female alone attends to the egg-laying activities and parental cares. Naturally there is a wide spectrum of intermediate patterns of behavior. Some couples stay together only while a single brood is raised, others for an entire breeding season. In some cases

the bonds formed by a pair of birds are, as far as can be ascertained, permanent, as among swans, geese, many members of the crow family, but also some of the smaller bird species: such links will apparently be broken only by the death of one of the partners. There are numerous examples of polygyny, as among the hummingbirds and some buntings, where a single male fertilizes several females. Polyandry is also known, one female mating with more than one male, as happens, for instance, among the phalaropes.

The common oystercatcher (*Haematopus ostralegus*), on the other hand, seems to behave quite promiscuously at the start of the breeding season,

ground, in water, in a tree or even, as among some swifts, in midair. As a rule this sexual behavior, which commences while the nest is being constructed, ceases as soon as the eggs are laid. Nevertheless, it is quite usual to observe species whose mating activities begin about two months before egg laying or continue during the period of parental care; in such cases these activities also have the important function of reinforcing the bonds of the breeding pair.

The nest

Once a pair is formed, the most important job for one or both birds is to look for a suitable place for laying the eggs and then to begin building the nest. The architectural solutions to this problem are infinitely varied and offer ornithologists opportunities for studying one of the most interesting and absorbing aspects of bird behavior, with particular emphasis on ethology and evolution. According to the environment, nests are likely to be found in many different places – in trees, bushes and caves, in buildings, on the ground and among rocks, floating on water or hanging from a branch, in the hollow of a trunk or cactus, in a termite mound or postbox, and so forth. Equally fascinating is the ingenuity displayed by birds in making use of diverse materials for their nest-building activities, depending on what is locally available. Large branches or stones, lichens and spiders' webs, snake skins or leaves, feathers plucked from the female's own breast or even her saliva – all these and more may go towards the construction of a suitable nest where the eggs can be laid and the young given refuge. The dimensions of the nest are just as variable, ranging from a couple of inches in diameter in the case of certain hummingbirds to some 9 ft (3 m) for the bald eagle (*Haliaëtus leucocephalus*). Yet there are many species that do not build a true nest at all, simply depositing their eggs in hollows on the ground or on outcrops of rock, as happens with some raptors and many members of the puffin family. The fairy tern (*Gygis alba*), a tropical bird, lays its single egg, precariously balanced, on a horizontal branch.

The actual nest-building process occupies the two sexes to a varying extent. In many species the female does all the construction work while the male collects the materials; in others both birds share the labor

Eggs of various species of bird. This selection illustrates the enormous variety of size, colors, and shape that nature achieves in this area.

inasmuch as mating will occur in a wholly casual manner.

All courtship rituals culminate in actual copulation, which in the majority of birds is achieved by simple contact of the respective cloacal orifices.

The male balances on the female's back often flapping his wings; and in certain cases, such as many of the Anseriformes and Galliformes, there is also a characteristic copulatory organ. Mating may take place on the

equally. Among some of the African weaver birds, however, the male alone is responsible both for the assembling of materials and the building of the nest. The majority of passerines complete their nest in less than a week, but larger and more complex structures, such as the nests of the ovenbirds or of the hammerhead (*Scopus umbretta*), may involve several months of uninterrupted work. As a general rule, northern species tend to get their nests constructed more quickly than tropical birds, adapting to the relative shortness of the breeding season; and for the same reason many of the former species tend to make use of the same nest for several years, repairing and renewing it from time to time. Those birds that use larger quantities of saliva in the construction of their nest may be occupied for a variable length of time, simply because there is a limit to the functional capacity of their salivary glands. Thus it has been verified that some of the tropical cave swiftlets (genus *Collocalia*) take 30 – 40 days to complete their nest.

Egg laying

The female generally lays her eggs immediately after the nest is finished. Once detached from the ovary, the mature egg receives nourishment in the form of albumen while traveling through the oviduct. In the uterine tract of the oviduct the egg doubles its volume by absorbing water, and while lodged in the uterus it is furnished with its calcareous shell. The egg takes 24 hours to travel through the entire oviduct.

A bird's egg varies considerably in shape, size, and color. Depending upon the comparative size of the pelvis, the eggs of various species may be elongated, pear-shaped or oval, as in many owls. Dimensions differ enormously in relation to body weight, although smaller birds lay proportionately larger eggs. The pigments, which are deposited in the final tract of the oviduct, may be distributed uniformly or in small spots when the egg is stationary in the tract, or in stripes and streaks when the egg resumes its movement. Species that lay in a hollow or enclosed nest usually have white eggs, while the others often produce eggs with drab or pale colors, although this is by no means an invariable rule. Many storm petrels, penguins, puffins, and other species lay a single egg, while large birds of prey frequently lay two. In the case of the bigger

Falconiformes, only the first of the two chicks born may frequently survive, since the younger is liable to die of hunger or be killed by the elder at various stages of growth. This apparently ridiculous waste of energy on the part of the parents is actually an efficient method of controlling the population. In fact, it generally happens that among birds of prey the firstborn gets more food mainly because, being bigger, it can tussle for it more energetically; and if there is insufficient food locally to provide for both chicks, one of them will be eliminated before it can fly, thus assuring the fullest possible development of at least one youngster and avoiding bitter competition which would eventually harm the prospects of both contenders. Many species of ducks and pheasants are, however, far more prolific, in some cases laying up to 20 eggs. Whereas in many of the less prolific species the number of eggs in a brood tends to remain constant, fluctuations often occur as a result both of environmental and physiological factors. The number of eggs laid may, indeed, vary according to the amount of food available in the vicinity (as happens among some birds of prey) or even the latitude, for as a rule the more northerly populations of a species tend to lay a larger number of eggs than the

Below left: cross-section of an egg: 1) albumen; 2) vitelline membrane; 3) shell; 4) yolk; 5) air chamber; 6) shell membrane. Below right: egg with a six-day old embryo. As the embryo develops, the yolk is slowly consumed as nourishment until it disappears totally.

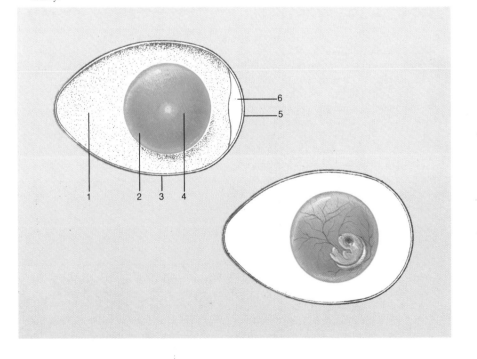

equivalent southerly populations. Eggs are laid at regular intervals ranging from 24 hours among many passerines to 10 – 12 days in the case of some megapodes.

Incubation

Incubating eggs means providing them with warmth. To this end the females (and sometimes the males) of all species, with the exception of ratites and pelicans, develop bare epithelial zones in the abdominal region, known as incubation patches. These areas are characterized by a thickening of the network of surface capillaries and a temporary loss of feathers, making it possible for body heat to be transmitted more effectively to the surface of the eggs. Furthermore, the adult's body temperature increases markedly in the course of incubation. The duration of this phase varies considerably from one family to another. In many small birds the eggs hatch after 11 – 13 days, whereas in the case of the royal albatross about 80 days elapse before the first chick is born. Parasitic species such as the European cuckoo manage to avoid wasting a lot of energy by placing their own eggs in the nests of other species. The coloration of the cuckoo's eggs is virtually indistinguishable from that of the eggs of the host bird. Another strategy for getting eggs to hatch without directly incubating them is that adopted by the Australian megapodes. These species deposit their eggs at the base of mounds of vegetation. The heat generated by the gradual rotting of the vegetable matter serves to

incubate the eggs; and after a couple of weeks they hatch tiny chicks that are perfectly capable of finding their own food. During incubation the male controls the temperature in the mound, ensuring that it does not fluctuate too much or get too hot by adding or removing bits of vegetation. This is the only form of parental care discernible in these species, for in many cases youngsters and adults never come into contact with one another.

In the course of incubation the eggs will be tended for periods of varying length, interspersed with intervals when the brood is left uncovered. Although this may result in fairly pronounced fluctuations of temperature in relation to the eggs and their surroundings, such changes do not constitute any real risk to the development of the embryos. Among small passerines the adult incubates, as a rule, for 20 – 30 minutes at a time, then abandoning the nest for 6 – 8 minutes. In species where both sexes share incubation, the nest is likely to be left untended for much shorter periods. Adult birds of prey and other large species remain in the nest for a much longer time. The royal albatross, a bird whose breeding behavior has been extensively studied, may incubate uninterruptedly for 10 – 14 days. In some species the male will return to the nest frequently with food for his mate; but this does not happen with penguins, so that it is not uncommon, as in the case of the emperor penguin (*Aptenodytes forsteri*), for the male to stay absolutely motionless and to go without food for more than 60 days, incubating the single egg in a special abdominal pouch, while the female is off feeding in the open sea. An extreme example of the female remaining permanently in her nest is provided by the hornbills. Once the eggs are laid, the male narrows the entrance of the nest, situated in a tree hollow, with mud and other materials. The female is thus unable to leave the nest, staying inside until incubation is completed or even longer, being fed regularly by her mate.

The nestlings

The cracking of the shell at the moment the eggs hatch is made easier by the presence, at the tip of the nestling's upper bill, of a horny projection known as the egg tooth, which soon disappears. The newborn chicks are generally divided by ornithologists into nidifugous and nidicolous species.

The former are covered in down and within only a few hours are ready to abandon the nest, moving about and feeding by themselves, although assisted by the adults. The young of nidicolous species, however, are helpless, often with eyes closed; they may possess a thin covering of down but generally have none. They spend a variable period in the nest, during which time the adults provide them with food and shelter them from extremes of temperature. Body growth tends to be particularly rapid in small insectivorous species, and the babies may be fed up to 45 times an hour, leaving the nest around the tenth or twelfth day. At the opposite extreme is the young royal albatross, who stays in the nest for approximately eight months.

There are many elements of risk that may intervene at any stage of the reproductive cycle, thus preventing the brood from hatching. Among numerous predators are birds, mammals, reptiles and sometimes spiders, who feed either on the eggs or the chicks and may even kill one of the adults. In this last eventuality the surviving member of the pair may succeed in rearing the young until they can fly. Environmental factors may also affect the brood, such as adverse weather conditions, as well as human interference, all too common among certain species. Species that construct open nests are likely to sustain a mortality rate among the young of up to 60 per cent which enables the population to remain fairly constant. Birds that lay eggs in closed nests have a success rate of between 60 and 90 per cent. Parental care may continue even after the young learn to fly, and during this period the latter exhibit a wide range of behavior patterns and strategies associated with feeding that will enable them to attain sexual maturity and eventually help propagate the species.

BEHAVIOR

The science of ethology (meaning the comparative study of animal behavior) stems mainly from the work of ornithologists. Certain aspects of bird behavior can be applied as valid criteria for other animals, but matters are, of course, not that simple. The literature on the subject embraces such a wealth of observations, experiments, and theories that there must inevitably be ample scope for discussion and controversy in many areas of animal behavior.

In simple terms, behavior, by definition, is the manner in which we act, such action being conditioned by everything that surrounds us and concerns us. A slightly more precise way of defining behavior is to envisage it as the expression of coordinated vital processes, including all the actions that enable an animal to look after itself in relation to its surroundings (Hemlen, 1955).

In order to have a full understanding of how birds (and, for that matter, other animals) behave, it is essential to know something about their organs of sense. Birds certainly have better eyesight than all other orders of animals. Their eyes are so large as to take up a considerable part of the skull structure, ofter surpassing and in any event equaling the weight of the brain. The eyes of the many birds have

Various types of nest: A) nest of weaverbird hanging from a branch; B) a duck's nest; C) nest of a bird of prey; D) the characteristic nest of the flamingo made of mud; E) a swallow's nest.

limited mobility, exceptions being penguins, cormorants, pelicans, gulls, and hornbills, who can move their eyes to some extent. At the opposite extreme are nocturnal birds of prey, such as owls, whose eye is practically immobile within its socket. The retina possesses more visual cells, proportionately to surface, than that of almost any other vertebrate, and this explains why a bird's vision is so sharp. Because the eyes are more or less fixed, the neck tends to be exceptionally mobile. It is clear that the extra-

ordinary visual capacity of birds is also related to their food habits, a rather obvious example being the ability of a diurnal bird of prey to spot its potential victim at a great distance. Birds possess binocular vision, in varying measure depending on species, this being more marked in birds with predatory habits.

The next best sense, after vision, is undoubtedly hearing; and consequently the organs involved are highly developed, notably the middle and inner ear. The sense of balance, closely linked, anatomically, with the hearing organs, is equally remarkable, and indispensable to birds, which have to maintain their equilibrium in a rarified element such as the air. The hearing ability of birds is by far superior to that of many mammals and of humans. The ear of a bird can pick up more sound frequencies than a human ear, especially in the high frequency range, so that a bird is able to detect what we call ultrasounds.

In other words, birds live in a world of sounds, shapes, and colors. There is an analogy between the development of their senses and our own, which explains why it is easier for us to understand the behavior of birds than that of many other animals.

The sense of smell is one of the least developed, although it is not necessarily correct to say, as so often is affirmed, that birds cannot detect odors. There is great variability in the size of the brain's olfactory bulbs, and certain species, such as the kiwi and some of the tube-nosed swimming birds, certainly have a good sense of smell.

The sense of taste, like that of smell, in some measure entails the perception of the chemical characteristics of particular substances. Birds possess a very small number of nerve fibers associated with taste, and the species with the largest quantity of taste buds, about 400, appear to be the parrots. The taste buds of mammals are concentrated in the tongue, but among birds they are found mainly in the palate, the pharynx, and the lower surface of the epiglottis. The tongue, by contrast, has practically no taste receptors.

Touch is a fairly well-developed sense. Birds are furnished with diverse tactile corpuscles, and aquatic birds in particular seem to possess all types in their bill. Tactile buds are found not only on the bill but also in the mouth cavity, the cloaca, the forearm, and the skin, especially in the pterylae or feathered zones. In addition, there are other sensory nerve endings that allow the bird to respond to the complex conditions of its environment, whether internal or external. These include neuromuscular and neurotendinous sensory endings, as well as sensitive fibers that react to pain and temperature. They are not the only attributes, although the other mysterious senses attributed to birds are probably, in the main, the fruit of human fantasy; an exception may be certain special magnetic receptors that enable birds to possess a perfect sense of orientation.

In everyday life a bird has to resort to a range of fixed habits in order to perform its various activities. These sequences of actions relate to activities connected both with survival and reproduction; and they cannot be learned because there simply is not enough time available to achieve the desired result, particularly if it is a matter of life and death. Fixed patterns of action are therefore adopted by birds as a means of communicating with other individuals of the same species; and in this context there may be postures and attitudes of aggression, defense, submission, sexual invitation, courtship, and so forth. For such purposes birds often make use of special features such as the coloration and form of plumage, which serve as signals and are recognized as such by individuals observing them. For this to happen there must always be a local stimulus, even if only constituted by the presence of another member of the species.

There are, naturally, other considerations. A large part of bird behavior stems from relatively simple situations and stimuli. David Lack, in his study of the territorial behavior of the robin, has observed that when stuffed adult robins are introduced to the territory of a live robin, the latter will adopt threatening postures; yet if the stuffed birds exhibit juvenile plumage (lacking the red patch on breast and throat), the owner of the territory will ignore them. The mere sight of a tuft of red feathers provokes the threat reaction, and clearly the color is the stimulus signal that triggers off the response itself.

A similar explanation applies to the food-demanding response of young herring gulls, studied by Tinbergen and Perdek. The adults of this species have a red mark on the tip of the lower bill and various experiments show that this patch is enough to stimulate pecking and food-demanding behavior among the young. The shape of the head and the coloration of other parts of the bird's body do not have the same signaling function. A similar type of response can be obtained by other sensory means. Thus the song of the white-throated sparrow (*Zonotrichia albicollis*), a small American passerine, consists of a series of well-defined notes in precise order. If the type and sequence of notes are altered artificially, different reactions or no response at all will be obtained from the other males defending their territory in the breeding season. The conclusion is that in order to provoke an appropriate reaction such a song must contain pure notes without harmonics and that notes and intervals have to be of determined length. These are just a few examples of features producing an automatic response, clearly implying a capacity of selection on the part of the individual reacting to such stimuli.

It is by virtue of these mechanisms that each individual species has evolved structural features associated with shape, song or attitude. Stimulus signals, in other words, consitute an unmistakable means of identification within the species. Nevertheless, a particular stimulus does not invariably evoke the identical response. If the outside situation remains constant, the altered reaction can only be attributed to changes in the animal itself. For convenience, temporary and reversible changes in the internal condition of the animal are described as motivational, although as a rule, as noted by Hinde, changes that last more than a second or those which occur in the sensory organs or effectors should not be included in this category. The factors influencing such responses are various. The stimuli have already been mentioned. The influence of hormones on a bird's behavior is extremely important. Then there are activities that show a clearly defined daily rhythm, which are governed by internal factors. Thus an extremely interesting example is the "mobbing" response exhibited by finches when faced by a predator.

It is evident, too, that there are almost always environmental factors that are likely to provoke more than one pattern of behavior. Take, for example, the contrasting urges to look for food and to fly off with the rest of the flock. Alternatively (and this is especially characteristic during the breeding season) an individual may be called on to respond to the stimuli of a partner, be it aggression, flight or sexual invitation. Because it is often impossible to adopt more than one behavior pattern at the same time, birds sometimes find themselves facing a situation of conflict, which may have various outcomes. It may be that all responses are inhibited, except for one: thus the appearance of a winged predator will spur many passerines to seek refuge under cover, blocking virtually every other pattern of behavior. There are many examples, too, of alternating forms of behavior, as when a bird engaged in a fight with a rival, impelled to attack and flee simultaneously, repeatedly exhibits both attitudes in turn. A conflict situation may result in what are defined as intentional movements. Thus a bird may carry out a series of incomplete movements which express one or the other intention, or perhaps both the opposing urges. In other cases there will be a response that appears to be the result of combining the two incompatible tendencies, this being known as compromise behavior. When a hungry bird is unable to get near its food because it is frightened in some way by a disturbing presence, it flicks its tail, a movement that simultaneously expresses hunger and the wish to fly towards the food, and fear, with the desire to fly away. In either contingency the act of flying involves moving the tail. Sometimes a bird will adopt a position which clearly expresses the two urges simultaneously; this is called an ambivalent posture. Many of the threat and courtship postures are of this type.

One particular form of behavioral activity is known to ethologists as redirected activity. In such situations the movement triggered off by one of the conflicting urges is directed towards an object different to the one arousing it. The male black-headed gull (*Larus ridibundus*), for example, whose territory is invaded by a female, will often turn his aggressive instincts against other individuals, even though it is she who initially aroused such feelings.

Conflict situations also provoke various responses of an automatic kind, such as defecation, ruffling of feathers, etc. Sometimes a bird, driven by two or more conflicting urges, will behave in an apparently senseless manner. A great tit, while fighting, will suddenly break off the attack to peck at a trunk or shoot. A male duck, during courtship, may unexpectedly start smoothing his wing feathers. Such actions are defined as substitution activities, designed, as it were, to release the tension built up inside the animal, which for some reason it cannot express in the proper way. (A human analogy immediately comes to mind here. A person may annoy us for some trivial reason, but instead of taking direct action we resort to a completely irrelevant act such as thumping a fist on the table, scratching our face or nervously squeezing an object between our hands.)

Similar irrelevant actions may be carried out in situations that do not seem to pose any conflict, and the explanation for this kind of behavior is unclear. The only conlusion, based on close research, is that in some circumstances substitution activity of this nature may release a certain amount of pent-up energy.

All kinds of behavior displayed by the different species can also be classified as functional, such as nest building, sexual activity, feeding habits, and so forth. In general, a behavioral reaction to particular stimuli allows the animal to then cope with a succession of other stimuli, and it is by responding to these in the correct sequence that it expresses its intentions in complex patterns of behavior. There is no doubt, however, that birds, like all other animals, are capable of modifying their behavior in the light of acquired experience. In other words, birds are able to learn; and this learning capacity is a feature of behavior which, by definition, is contrasted to instinct. Learning may be described as the process which manifests itself in changes of individual behavior as a result of adapting to experience. In this context even the simplest activities of an animal can be said to be learned; and such learning finds expression in different ways. Habituation is the term applied to an activity of the central nervous system whereby innate responses to relatively simple stimuli, especially those of great potential value such as danger warnings, become weaker if such stimuli continue for some time without any unpleasant consequences. In other words, the animal learns not to respond to stimuli which are insignificant in that they do not lead to a threatening outcome. This, according to Thorpe, is the simplest and most elementary form of learning. Naturally, excessive habituation would be disastrous for a species. A nestling that has been reared artificially or in the wild by its own parents must learn, for example, that a butterfly is not a source of peril. A typical instance of habituation is seen among certain birds which are no longer frightened by the sounds of shooting once these have proved to have no adverse effect on them.

Another kind of learning is conditioning, which is simply the introduction of an additional or substitute stimulus to a preexisting association of stimulus and response. Conditioned reflexes are extremely useful for the experimental study of behavior, but we do not know what role they play in nature. Learning by trial and error is really a procedure whereby one response is chosen out of a series of possible responses in a complex situation. There are typical examples of this in feeding activities. The young of many birds have to learn what kind of food can be eaten and what kind cannot be eaten; and this must be learned quickly so as to avoid them dying from hunger.

The most complicated form of learning is that in which an appropriate response is chosen for a problematical situation, which has to be effected, unlike a trial and error procedure, in an extremely short time, without alternative attempts. According to Thorpe, the perception of temporal and spatial relationships is an innate faculty of all animals. On this basis it can be said that intuition is merely the perception of such relationships and the correct use of them. Naturally the interpretation of intuitive behavior and of reasoning, even in its simplest form, is

Konrad Lorenz (left) and Niko Tinbergen (right) who carried out extensive research into animal behavior and, along with Karl von Frisch, were awarded the Nobel prize in 1973. Lorenz, in particular, is often cited as the "father of ethology." His work, which provoked much discussion both inside and outside the world of science, confronted the difference between innate and learnt behavior in a new light. He is mainly to be remembered for the introduction of the concept of imprinting which recognized a process of learning experienced by an animal in a brief receptive period, typically just after birth or hatching, that produces a series of long-lasting behavioral responses. The concept of imprinting abandons the traditional division of innate and learnt behavior. Tinbergen contributed above all to the beginnings of research into the ethology of the countryside.

an extremely delicate problem, but it is quite obvious that in some situations many species of birds, admittedly on an elementary level, show a capacity for reasoning.

One special kind of learning, widespread among animals but first studied among birds, is so-called imprinting. This can be defined as the rapid formation of associations between stable stimuli and responses, which are made in the very first moments of an individual's life, during the so-called impressionable period. The classic example of imprinting is that mentioned by Lorenz in reference to geese born in an artificial incubator, who accept as "mother" the person who looks after them and is also the first moving object they come across. Numerous experiments have shown that this type of learning is absorbed in the first hours of life, that it is almost irreversible and that it conditions the later activities of the animal when adult. The geese raised by Lorenz, in fact, looked upon him as a member of their own species and directed many behavioral activities towards him, including sexual attentions. Nowadays the irreversibility of imprinting has been challenged, and it has certainly been demonstrated that birds which recognize the person who has reared them as being their true partner, having gradually been restored to normal situations, shed this unnatural attachment and become capable of conducting a straightforward relationship, turning their attention towards an individual of their own species.

The objective study of animal behavior is a comparatively new science. Modern theories, moreover, are constantly being modified as more precise information comes to hand and as more is understood about various aspects of the subject, especially concerning the physiology of the nervous system which conditions patterns of behavior. It is quite likely that the traditional clear-cut distinction between instinctive and learned behavior will be discarded, because it is now evident, for example, that in certain cases the absence of a motor response within an expected period may simply be due to the complex relationship between nerves, muscles and body structures, not necessarily to lack of experience. There is, admittedly, a marked distinction in the world of birds between nidifugous and nidicolous nestlings, whose respective states of development at birth are very different. There is no doubt, however, that

many sophisticated patterns of behavior, such as those resulting in the building of complex nests or particularly elaborate forms of song, stem from a combination of instinctive reactions and habits that have been acquired through experience.

MIGRATION

The mass activity known as migration, common to many groups of animals all over the world, is a fascinating subject for zoologists and clearly of great importance. The migration journeys of birds are, in addition, highly spectacular.

Migration can be regarded as a means whereby certain species of animals manage to adapt to environmental conditions. But before examining the phenomenon more closely we must attempt a reasonably precise definition of the term (especially important in its application to birds) which will distinguish it from other occurrences that resemble it in some respects. Migration, in the true sense, implies a regular movement of animals, at different times of the year, away from and back to the zones where they usually live. In the case of birds, one of these areas is where they breed and the other is the place most suitable for their normal living requirements during the season when they are not occupied with reproduction. The latter is known as the wintering zone, even though, from the viewpoint of the yearly calendar, the stay here may extend beyond the winter proper.

Modern research in this field, which is by no means complete, is based on the information derived from several principal sources: 1) data concerning the distribution of certain species, and in many cases subspecies, at different times of the year, given the dates of their arrival, departure, and movements within particular areas; 2) direct observation of what is termed "visible migration" of birds which tend to appear in unusual numbers in places such as promontories, ocean peninsulas

or small islands; 3) night-time observations of flying birds attracted by the beams of offshore lighthouses or lightships, which can either be heard calling in flight, seen through a telescope as they cross in the light of the moon, or tracked on the radar screen; 4) the ringing method, whereby birds are invariably marked so that they can

be recognized, once captured, and their points of departure verified; 5) experiments under strictly controlled conditions, especially those designed to clarify phenomena such as the restlessness displayed by birds prior to migration and their capacity for orientation and navigation.

Ornithologists recognize that very many bird species, representing virtually every order and family, are to some extent migratory. Although migration is commonest among birds that breed in the higher latitudes, it is not all that unusual in tropical species as well. But whenever it occurs, the pattern of migration varies enormously, not only in scope but above all in degree of precision and regularity. In numerous instances there are marked variations among populations of the same species or even among individuals and age groups within a single population. It may be helpful if we try to list the principal kinds of migration.

1) Local movements. Here the migrations may range from short journeys to flights of considerable distance. Sometimes the birds may simply move from a breeding zone in the hinterland to a winter feeding area along the coast. Alternatively, the birds will fly off in a definite direction but only travel a few hundred miles, such a journey perhaps not compelling them to cross any stretch of sea. Whatever the length of the journey or distance involved, such movements are strictly local, without further qualification.

2) Vertical movements. This is an example of local migration in which the birds seek higher altitudes. There are many birds that nest up in the mountains and come down to the valleys below in the winter. The opposite occurs in the area of the Dead Sea, where certain species breed in the depression, almost 900 ft below sea level, and return in winter to the surrounding hills where the climate is not so unbearable.

3) Long-distance migrations. Here the differences are of degree rather than kind, but all are genuine migrations in the sense that they entail journeys of several hundred or sometimes thousands of miles. Thus numerous bird species, for example, leave their breeding zones in northern Europe to spend the winter season along the African coasts of the Mediterranean or even south of the Sahara. Equally long journeys are made without a significant change of latitude, as in the case of species that migrate from the interior of continental Europe towards

Migrating birds usually travel in large groups. While flocks of smaller species often seem disordered and somewhat chaotic, larger birds fly in more regular and characteristic formations. We can identify above, from left to right, a skein of geese, the line formation of mallards and the V-formation of lapwings. The arrival of a flock of migrating birds can suddenly change the scenery, as the photograph of flamingos below illustrates.

the Atlantic coasts. An instance of this is provided by the populations of rooks (*Corvus frugilegus*) which travel from the Russian plains to winter along the Atlantic shores of France.

4) Transequatorial migrations. These involve birds not only in journeys across the same continent (from one zone at higher latitude to another where the winter is milder) but also in flights over the equator to reach temperate areas in the other hemispheres where "wintering" really occurs during the local summer season, when native species are actually breeding. There are species that breed in Europe and winter in South Africa, others that journey from North America to South America and still others that travel from northern Asia to Australasia. These are all migrations of many thousands of miles, and surely one of the most famous and spectacular examples is that of the sea swallow or Arctic tern (*Sterna arctica*), which is found nesting in the Arctic as far as latitude 82°N and outside the breeding season flies south to the Antarctic, where it has been observed at or even beyond latitude 74°S. The journey there and back, reckoned by the most direct route, is certainly not less than 9,000 miles (14,000 km).

Although there are species from the southern hemisphere which migrate northward as far as the tropics, no case is recorded of ground birds with a southern distribution migrating to northern temperate zones. The main explanation of this is probably that the continental masses are differently distributed. In the southern hemisphere there is no large land mass, apart from Antarctica, found at latitudes equivalent to those from which the long-distance migrators of the northern hemisphere originate. Only in the case of some sea birds, especially the Procellariiformes (petrels, albatrosses, and shearwaters), are there species from the southern hemisphere which "winter" in the northern hemisphere during the local summer season. These are migratory birds that not only make a transequatorial journey but also a transoceanic one. The Manx shearwater (*Puffinus puffinus*) flies from its breeding grounds in the British Isles to the shores of South America. Another extraordinary example is that of the bristle-thighed curlew which after nesting in the Alaskan tundra flies over the vast expanses of the Pacific, crossing the equator, to winter in Tahiti and some other islands.

In order to prevent confusion and to understand how the phenomenon of migration has evolved under various forms of pressure, let us now look briefly at other examples of movements among bird populations.

5) Dispersion. Certain types of annual journeys cannot truly be defined as migrations. These involve individual birds moving away from the center of the distribution area of the species, the number of such birds dwindling with distance from the center. These movements are not all in one direction. Certain species, particularly among marine birds, scatter, outside the breeding season, over vast areas and although such dispersion is not entirely a matter of chance, there does not appear to be any fixed rule to it. Often these tend to be seasonal journeys related especially to the availability of food as affected by the direction and strength of ocean currents.

6) Some birds may be described as partial migrators. The lapwing (*Vanellus vanellus*) from the British Isles, the robin (*Erithacus rubecula*) from various parts of central Europe, and the song thrush (*Turdus philomelos*) are just a few examples. In these and other species, always within one area, there are some birds that do migrate and others that do not. It is not known for certain whether it is the young, in particular, that tend to migrate, although in the cases of the gannet (*Sula bassana*) and the Australian gannet (*Sula serrator*) it is undoubtedly the young who undertake fairly regularly these journeys that take them a considerable distance from the breeding zones.

7) Premigratory movements. Among certain migratory species the young born in the same year often show a tendency to disperse or even lead a nomadic life during the interval between the end of breeding and the beginning of migration proper. They may move about in various directions, although quite often the direction preferred by the majority is the very opposite of that adopted later when the real migration gets under way. These wanderings are therefore unconnected with true migrations and probably occur for a completely different reason.

8) Some species, particularly those of northerly temperate zones, move about in periods of prolonged bad weather. These journeys have nothing to do with migrations since they do not occur at regular times of year nor do they start or finish at any fixed period. Another type of activity, linked to weather conditions, is described as "reverse migration." During their spring return northward, some species may interrupt the migration journey or even reverse their route if held up by bad weather. Then, too, there are so-called "irruptions," that is decidedly irregular flock movements which are only observed occasionally, since the flight will remain undisturbed under normal conditions.

Migration periods and routes

As regards the period chosen for migration, it is obvious that mass population movements will be avoided during the seasons when weather conditions are at their worst. In temperate zones, therefore, fall sees the large-scale exodus of species that have nested in high latitudes and spring sees their return. In tropical zones, migrations appear to coincide with the seasonal contrasts of drought and rains. As a rule, and especially in the case of long-distance migratory birds, the period of departure and actual travel tends to be fairly constant from year to year. Thus the duration of the entire journey, given the regularity of departure and arrival dates, does not fluctuate very much.

Because migration is clearly associated with climate and therefore definable as behavior designed to adapt to the seasonal variations of the environment, it is true to say that weather conditions exert a direct influence. This is of two kinds, one conditioning the start of the exodus, the other affecting the migrating birds in the course of the journey. Low pressure systems result in a general lowering of temperature in fall, and such conditions determine and favor the birds' departure. In spring, however, precisely the opposite occurs. During the journey it is evident that adverse conditions such as storms, gales, and prolonged periods of rain will impede migration and often have a disastrous effect on the migratory bird populations.

Migrations, especially those that take place on a vast scale, usually involve a change of latitude and the general direction is likely to be from north to south or vice versa. Nevertheless, climatic conditions and geographical locations are extremely influential factors that often bring about deviations from the standard pattern. The Po Valley in the north of Italy, for example, is regularly crossed by massed flocks from east to west or vice versa. Taking all these facts into account, it is clearly permissible, without laying down rigid rules, to talk of migration routes. Such routes may be narrow corridors through which masses of migratory birds fly or, in some cases, broader land belts. Everything suggests that migrating birds have an inborn capacity to keep flying in a particular direction without the aid of a compass. Some topographical features are undoubtedly used by birds as points of reference, landmarks, guidelines, etc. The shape of a coast is also a factor that determines the flight direction of all species that prefer to stick to the land rather than venture out over the open sea. Strong head winds, rain, snow, and the like often force flocks of migrating birds to swerve far off their set course. This so-called migratory drifting is thought to be one of the most important reasons for some species colonizing new territories.

Although adverse weather such as gale-force winds may cause many birds to lose their way, it is interesting to note that as a rule the migratory flocks are able to correct such an error, at least during the daytime. At night, when landmarks are scarcely visible, it is less easy for them to get back on course. Their normal ability to follow a fixed route with unerring precision is also undermined by the powerful sideways thrust of the winds. Similar diversions may occur by day as well if cloud, mist, and fog obscure familiar landmarks below.

Migration routes may vary with the season, many species following one fixed course in the fall and taking a completely different path in the spring. Classic examples are those of the garganey teal (*Anas querquedula*) and the subalpine warbler (*Sylvia cantillans*). During the winter journey the warbler is often observed in the Nile Valley on its way to winter quarters in Ethiopia, Kenya, and neighboring areas. In spring the species is very seldom seen over the Nile and it has been confirmed that it returns by a route much farther to the east.

The term abmigration has been given by Landsborough Thompson to a phenomenon that occurs in certain species and which is particularly frequent in the Anatidae. A few birds, having remained in the zone where they were born during the winter, fly off in spring to breed in other areas, probably because they mate with other migrating birds (pair-forming among the Anatidae takes place prior to migration).

Migration patterns

Some species migrate during the day,

some by night and others elect to travel either in light or darkness as circumstances dictate. The daytime migrators may be medium sized or large (some of the Corvidae), or small, like the swallows. The majority of small passerines usually migrate and make shorter journeys at night, probably to avoid the risk of predators en route but also so that they can build up energy with food during the day. Many migrating birds tend to assemble in flocks, sometimes comprising vast numbers, for their journeys, and this marked tendency applies, too, to species that are not normally gregarious by habit. Nevertheless, there are also species that retain their solitary habits when migrating.

It is interesting to note that there is often a clear distinction among different age groups. The juveniles may travel apart from the adults, sometimes leaving first, sometimes departing later. This is a phenomenon that has given rise to much speculation, indicating as it does that newborn individuals have the innate capacity of flying off to their winter quarters without any previous experience.

At what height do birds fly when they migrate? The information on this point is much more accurate now that radar can be used to track and record the journeys of many species. Normally migrating birds fly at moderate heights (about six hundred feet) but various small passerines have been sighted and tracked at heights of over 10,000 ft (3,000 m). One of the best known examples of high-flying is that of the bar-headed goose (*Anser indicus*); migrating birds have been observed over the Himalayas at an altitude of more than 32,800 ft (10,000 m).

The speed of flight during migration varies considerably from one species to another, ranging from 20 – 25 mph (35 – 40 kmh) to 55 – 60 mph (90 – 100 kmh) in the case of some geese. Of course not every migration journey is nonstop, although many birds undoubtedly cross the Mediterranean, the Sahara, the Gulf of Mexico, and probably the Himalayan mountain chain in a single stage, given that they cannot survive in the sea or any area where weather and climatic conditions are wholly intolerable.

Because birds have to expend an enormous amount of energy during a migration flight (despite their ability to store such energy for the journey in the form of accumulated fat beneath the skin) many of them interrupt their travels at regular intervals during the daytime. Migrating birds generally fly for 6 to 8 hours by day, spending the remainder of the time resting and feeding. The autumn migration journey seems to be less hurried than the spring return, because species living in northern temperate zones tend to leave the breeding grounds before weather and climatic conditions become really bad. So the flight towards the south takes place when the weather is fairly favorable, and the birds, in a sense, are in no great rush to get to their winter destinations. During the return journey, however, there is a feeling of urgency to reach the breeding grounds as soon as possible, and the routes are likely to be more direct and regularly timed.

Apart from the speed of flight and the total duration of the journey, ornithologists will take note of the rate at which a species advances across the "seasonal" zones occupied at various times. During the spring migration, for example, areas of plain where climatic conditions are already good will be visited first, and only later will the birds fly on to higher altitudes where spring's arrival is delayed.

From the physiological point of view it is interesting to see how the beginning of migration is preceded, in the case of many species, by a period of intense psychomotor restlessness, known in German as *zugunruhe*, which, even among captive birds, indicates the urge to migrate. A classic example in nature is that of the swallow (*Hirundo rustica*). Large flocks, sometimes containing thousands of individuals, come together in the fall to perform group acrobatics, as if they had decided to compete against one another. This restlessness is an extremely significant feature of migration because it can be measured quantitatively and has revealed that, to some extent at least, it is influenced by hormonal action.

The significance of migration

Migration is clearly a highly important feature of many animals' lives. Although complex in detail, the striking thing about it is that it occurs so regularly from year to year. The biological implications of such a phenomenon are bound to be of extreme interest. Apart from anything else, behavior of this nature, entailing so much expenditure of energy and so many risks to the lives of individual animals, must surely have some general value which far outweighs the various disadvantages. Granted that

Opposite: the prairie chicken (*Tympanuchus cupido*). This species, with several subspecies, inhabits the prairies of North America. The type subspecies *T. c. cupido* became extinct in 1932; the remaining ones are also in danger of extinction and are protected.

The great auk (*Pinguinus impennis*). These birds lived in the North Atlantic up to 1844, the official year of their extinction. They were discovered in 1534 by the French explorer Jacques Cartier, and it was then that they began to be indiscriminately massacred throughout their vast range. The birds were killed for their flesh and plumage, and even their fat was sometimes used as fuel.

this is so, it has to be seen as a positive contribution to survival. But it is not enough just to say that migration is useful. Explanations have to be sought to explain why it exists, and the concern of zoologists is both to investigate its likely causes and the different ways in which it is accomplished.

Taking first the question of adaptive value and utility, it is obvious that migration enables birds to exploit opportunities offered by the environment that would otherwise be denied them. The breeding grounds provide the best conditions for reproduction with plenty of places for nesting and abundant food both for the parents and the newborn babies; and the farther north, the better the conditions for in spring and early summer the days are that much longer. In other seasons, however, these same zones cannot provide the same opportunities for a large number of individuals and species. The effect of climate is, in a sense, indirect, adverse conditions preventing birds from finding enough food. (Incidentally, the fact that birds nest at a definite time of year is in itself proof of adaptation to seasonal opportunities for procuring the largest quantities of food; and the phenomenon of migration is clearly linked to this.) It is possible, therefore, to envisage the annual life cycle of a bird as an alternation of reproductive and nonreproductive phases coinciding with the seasonal fluctuations of food resources, and to see migration as a secondary adaptation which has to take into account a period in which birds can restore the feathers, their instruments of flight, by means of molting.

As to the causes of migration, it is obvious that animals do not all consciously decide to go off together at the same time. Birds often take their departure even before the climatic conditions in the breeding zones deteriorate, and the long-distance migrators follow such regular patterns of activity that it is hard to believe they can make departures and arrivals depend on weather factors which are far from regular. There appears to be little doubt, therefore, that the migratory instinct is inborn, so that scientists have to look both for the general causes of their behaving in this manner and for the immediate causes, the actual stimuli, that come into operation year after year. The origin of the migratory instinct is undoubtedly associated with the evolution of each species, to the history of its distribution and the long-term modifications of geographical and climatic conditions to which it has been subjected. This is not the place to discuss in detail the many theories that have been put forward. Suffice it to say that the migratory phenomenon must have originated quite independently on many occasions among different species. Not only that, but the process is still continuing, so that in some cases there is evidence of a weakening of the migratory urge when the immediate motives that trigger off the instinct are absent. This is true of certain birds which remain sedentary in their breeding grounds because modifications brought about by human activity have made it possible for them to obtain as much food in winter as during the actual breeding season. Yet other species continue to undertake traditional, ancestral journeys which apparently make no sense except that they reflect habits that had meaning before the species acquired its present-day geographical distribution. A classic example is the Greenland wheatear (*Oenanthe leucorrhoa*) which flies from the American Arctic via Iceland, the British Isles, and the western shores of Europe to winter in Africa south of the Sahara. Then there is a subspecies of the Arctic warbler which nests in Alaska and in the fall, instead of flying towards South America like most of the birds breeding in the region, crosses the Bering Strait and spends the winter in southern Asia, giving away the fact that its distribution was originally Asiatic. With regard to the immediate stimuli triggering off migration twice a year, there would appear to be two distinct components of such behavior: first internal or endogenous factors that prepare the birds for the journey and, secondly, external or exogenous factors which interfere with such mechanisms.

BIRDS AND NATURE CONSERVATION

Today it is possible to say, quite calmly and objectively, that there is hardly an existing natural habitat that has not, either directly or indirectly, been affected by man. There are many ways in which man has gradually destroyed his natural heritage. He has progressively impoverished the soil and the vegetation (of fundamental importance for storing oxygen and transforming solar energy, indispensable to life on earth), indiscriminately polluted the atmosphere, the water, the soil and the subsoil, and directly exterminated certain species, notably through hunting.

The ecologist Duncan Poore (IUCN, 1978) listed the following as the main evolutionary effects of human activity on living species: 1) the direct extinction of species and genotypes; 2) direct predation; 3) competition with other species for food and living space; 4) the selective breeding of new varieties of plants and animals, either deliberately or incidentally (by the crossbreeding of indigenous species and introduced species); 5) the creation of selective pressures that have favored the development of new types; 6) the destruction or modification of many habitats and the creation of new ones; 7) interference with the patterns of species dispersion, due to the creation or removal, either intentionally or accidentally, of barriers, and by the deliberate introduction of species from a particular area.

As far as birds are concerned, many species have been sadly affected by man's damaging and destructive activities. The ornithologist Paul Geroudet (WWF, 1969) listed the following seven criteria for measuring the condition of those species most in danger of extinction: 1) the extension of breeding grounds and the relative changes that have occurred in recent decades; 2) the numbers of a popula-

tion and its tendency to evolve; 3) ecological and ethological sensitivity (especially dependence on a particular biological environment or type of food, the need for company and security, the faculty of adaptation); 4) viability (especially the natural birth and mortality rates); 5) direct dangers (hunting and other activities, use of pesticides, etc.); 6) indirect dangers (changes to or destruction of biological environment and food resources); 7) the possibility of introducing effective protection and thereby improving the situation.

The International Union for the Conservation of Nature and Natural Resources (IUCN) is the largest organization in the world for protecting the environment and has for years published the Red Data Books, giving detailed lists, constantly updated, of species all over the world that are threatened with extinction.

The species and subspecies mentioned in the Red Data Books are placed in five categories according to their situation: 1) endangered species – threatened with extinction, whose survival is at risk if the factors currently endangering them continue unabated in the future; 2) vulnerable species – could easily fall into the

category of endangered species should the present negative factors continue to operate in the immediate future; 3) rare species – with small or limited world populations, not at present endangered but running the risk of so becoming; 4) unendangered species – belonging to one or other of the preceding categories in the past but now considered relatively safe as a result of protective measures or the removal of factors that once threatened their survival; 5) species of indeterminate situation – likely to belong to one of the first three categories but for which current information is insufficient for determining status.

Many bird species have disappeared for ever. The elephant bird (*Aepyornis maximus*), belonging to the order Aepyornithiformes (now extinct), is probably the largest bird that has ever lived on earth. It looked like an ostrich, stood about 10 ft (3.5 m) high, may have weighed 1,102 lb (500 kg), and had a long neck and small, atrophied wings. Its eggs were 12 in (30 cm) in length. The remains of this bird have been found only in Madagascar and a complete skeleton exists in the Paris Museum. The species probably became extinct during the latter half of the seventeenth century. The giant moa (*Dinornis maximus*), largest representative of the order Dinornithiformes (also now extinct) was up to 10 ft (3 m) high and probably weighed about 550 lb (250 kg); remains of this bird have been discovered only in New Zealand. A poor flier, it, too, resembled an ostrich. Ruthless hunting led to its extinction.

The great auk (*Pinguinus impennis*), family Alcidae, became extinct in 1884, the last two specimens being killed on Eldley Island off the southwest coast of Iceland. It measured up to 2 ft (80 cm) long and lived on the islands and continental coasts of the North Atlantic. The impact of humans was lethal for this species, as it proved, too, for the dodo (*Raphus cucullatus*), a member of the pigeon family (Columbiformes), standing 30 in (75 cm) high, and inhabiting the island of Mauritius in the Indian Ocean. Hunting, the introduction of domestic animals to the island, and the deterioration of the environment caused by humans were fatal to the dodo, which became extinct in 1681. Today there is not even a stuffed specimen left (Oxford University had one until 1775), so this is a species of which literally no trace remains.

FOSSIL BIRDS

About 150 million years ago, during the Jurassic period of the Mesozoic era, many parts of Bavaria were covered by extensive swamps surrounded by forests. The trees were of various types but still fairly primitive. Through the branches of these Jurassic forests scampered different kinds of reptiles, many of them very similar to lizards. They were agile climbers and runners, darting along the branches to catch their prey, consisting of other small reptiles or, more probably, insects. Among these scaly creatures there was one animal that moved about with particular dexterity and speed. This animal already possessed wings with perfectly formed feathers, in every way resembling those of modern birds. The body, too, was covered with feathers and the hind legs were so structured as to permit the animal to grasp branches firmly and to perch like present-day birds. The only major outward difference was the long lizard-like tail covered with feathers and with vertebrae extending into it. Another was the head, fairly naked and with a long forward portion that was not shaped like a beak and contained powerful teeth. This strange feathered creature was roughly the size of a modern magpie, and although its pectoral muscles were not particularly developed, it could "fly" from branch to branch and from tree to tree, in this manner crossing fairly broad stretches of treeless swamp. The name given to the species was Archaeopteryx lithographica. Fossil remains of this first bird were initially found in a cave of lithographic limestone near Solnhofen, Bavaria; and they are now to be seen at the British Museum of Natural History in London. What is left of the skeletal portions of this animal shows a clear structural affinity with reptiles, especially with certain thecodonts such as Euparkeria, known to be a divergent branch of that vast assemblage of Mesozoic reptiles that were ancestors of the dinosaurs. Actually, had fossil impressions of feathers not been noted on this specimen of Archaeopteryx, no anatomist or student of evolution would have dared classify the animal among the birds. But the presence of feathers and wings for flying are essential attributes of the class Aves, and it is evident that

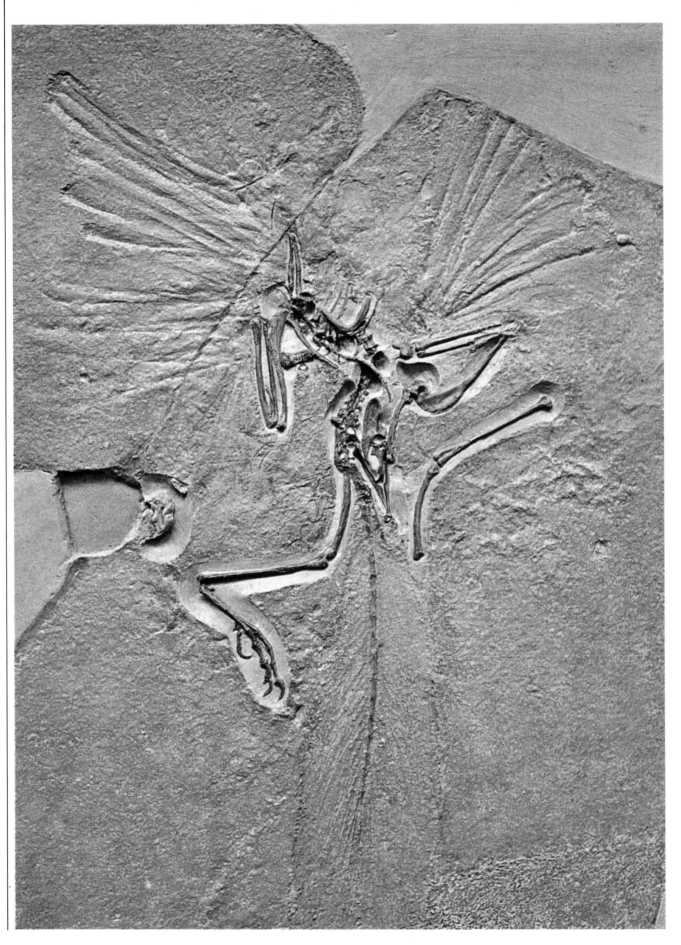

Archaeopteryx has a perfect right to be classified as a bird.

The fundamental problem raised by the discovery of this fossil (and two more were found in 1877 and 1956) is determining exactly how birds came to be descended from reptiles and pinpointing the transitional stages. In fact, despite the long tail with its many vertebrae, the still typically reptilian head, the presence of teeth, the absence of a keeled breastbone, etc., in many other ways, as well as for the possession of feathers and wings, *Archaeopteryx* must be regarded as a bird that was already quite highly evolved. Scientists were eager to discover something of a more primitive nature that would have justified the evolution of feathers and, more particularly, wings. Until a few years ago, the hypothetical ancestor of birds, the link between these and reptiles, was more a matter of fantasy on the part of researchers than solid fact. Several authors even went so far to satisfy their whims as to propose reconstructions of an imaginary creature called *Proavis* as the ancestral form. Only about ten years ago did the discovery of fossil deposits in South Africa's Karroo region help ornithologists to understand how feathers evolved. It was in this area that paleontologists unearthed the perfectly preserved remains of a fairly small dinosaur measuring about 13 ft (4 m) long, tail included, with a body wholly covered in feathers but without the slightest trace of wings. This dinosaur was given the name *Syntarsus*. Feathers, therefore, must already have been present before certain reptiles developed the particular aptitude for flight with feathered wings. This means to say that plumage evolved, as had long been suspected, essentially as a protective, insulating adaptation for animals which had by now become homeothermic (warm-blooded), capable of regulating their own body temperature independently of the surrounding conditions.

The missing link between reptiles and birds had been found. It has now been established that birds are directly descended from certain types of dinosaur, and for that reason, even though the largest forms became extinct under the influence of other selective pressures, we can confidently assert that the dinosaurs have not vanished. Their direct descendants are the present-day birds.

The oldest known fossilized bird is *Archaeopteryx lithographica*, whose partial remains and outlines were found for the first time embedded in limestone at Solnhofen, Bavaria, in 1861 (photograph opposite). This unusual feathered creature, with long, lizard-like tail and mouth equipped with strong teeth, was already capable of flying, although only for short distances. Three sharply clawed fingers on either wing enabled it to grip surfaces firmly. *Archaeopteryx* lived in dense forests about 150 million years ago. In Bavaria, such forests were, at that time, surrounded by wide tracts of swamp. The bird probably spent much of its life perched or hanging from branches, moving about in search of food or when forced to flee from a predator.

It has now been established that birds are directly descended from certain types of dinosaur, as is evident from the remains of a small dinosaur, body wholly covered in feathers, which was found in South Africa. Such dinosaurs must already have possessed feathers before developing flight capacity.

RATITES AND TINAMIFORMES

The name ratite is commonly applied to those birds possessing a flat sternum or breastbone, without a keel, in contrast to those that do exhibit this feature and are consequently referred to as keeled birds. The keel is essential to such birds for, among other things, it provides the basis of attachment for the large pectoral muscles which make it possible for them to fly efficiently. The ratites are, therefore, by definition, birds that are unable to fly. But it must be pointed out that a structure comparable to the sternum is sometimes present in other flightless birds that belong to different orders and which are not normally regarded as ratites.

The interesting problem, still much discussed, is to determine how the different orders are related to one another. It has often been suggested that the ratites have a common evolutionary origin. Some authors claim, basically because of the primitive characteristics of the palate, that the ratites constitute a primitive group of birds descended from ancestral forms that were never able to fly, and that in this respect the ratites should be considered more primitive than other birds. Yet there are a number of reasons to show that this theory does not really hold water, for there is no denying the solid evidence for believing that the ratites are descended from birds that were quite capable of flying and which only later, by adapting to their environment and conditions of life, turned into birds that were runners rather than fliers.

Zoogeographical considerations have also persuaded ornithologists to reach the same conclusions regarding the ratites' secondary loss of flight capacity. When *Archaeopteryx* lived in Europe, during the Jurassic, there was no land link with New Zealand from that time on, so that the ancestors of moas and kiwis could only have reached its shores by flying. The same reasoning would seem to apply to the elephant birds of Madagascar. Comparison of the different ratites shows that it is possible to regard them merely as a succession of degenerate forms. In fact, the wings of the ostrich,

One of the most distinctive characteristics of the flightless ratites is the presence of a flattened sternum or breastbone, in contrast to the keeled sternum of other birds. In the drawing below, which compares the skeleton of an ostrich (above) with that of a pigeon, this important anatomical feature is shown in red.

The crested tinamou (*Eudromia elegans*) is notable for the absence of a rear toe. All members of the order Tinamiformes are ill adapted for flying. It seems, in fact, that some species are so reluctant to take wing that, if compelled to do so, they show very little aptitude and frequently end up by colliding with obstacles.

Kiwi
(*Apteryx australis*)

Rhea
(*Rhea americana*)

Cassowary
(*Casuarius casuarius*)

Emu
(*Dromaius novaehollandiae*)

Some present-day ratites: the rhea (order Rheiformes), the cassowary and the emu (order Casuariiformes), and the kiwi (order Apterygiformes).

The only surviving species of ostrich (order Struthioniformes) appeared during the Pleistocene and was widely distributed through much of Africa as well as Asia Minor and Palestine. Because man has wiped out entire populations, either for commercial reasons or simply for sport, the range of the species is nowadays restricted to areas of West and East Africa and certain zones in the south of the continent. 1) Ostrich (*Struthio camelus*).

the rheas, the emu and the casso-waries, although fairly small, are still recognizable as such and may some-times come in useful as a kind of sail when the birds are running with the wind. The wings of the kiwi are extremely small and quite useless, while the extinct moas and the elephant bird probably had no wings at all.

South America, the so-called neo-tropical region, harbors a group of birds which look very much like cer-tain Galliformes. They are found in various surroundings but especially in the open zones of pampas, llanos and other types of prairie. The interest they have for zoologists derives chiefly from those features that give them a resemblance to the ratites, even though, as already mentioned, they are perfectly keeled and thus possess strong pectoral muscles which undoubtedly enable them to fly, at any rate for short distances. The different species of tinamou, all belonging to the family Tinamidae, vary in size from that of a quail to that of a hen. There is no difference between the sexes as far as plumage color is concerned but females are generally a little bigger than males. The bill differs somewhat from that of wild and domestic fowl in being rather slender and curved, the head is fairly small, and the neck decidedly thin when fully erect. The body, on the other hand, is compact and rounded, all the more so because of the virtual lack of a tail which comprises only a few short, fluffy feathers. The feet, too, differ from those of Galliformes. The struc-ture of the foot clearly shows it to be associated with running and, indeed, all the tinamous are fast runners who prefer to get away on foot and hide among the vegetation rather than to take wing.

Most of the tinamous have fairly drab, mimetic plumage, whereas the eggs, by contrast, are extremely bril-liant, almost lacquered and vividly col-ored. They are incubated by the male, virtually alone, who takes over all parental duties. Although mostly soli-tary by habit, some species may live in family groups except during the breed-ing season. The diet is basically vegetar-ian, although the chicks, in particular, will not refuse food of animal origin. The nest is a simple depression in the ground covered with scraps of plants, and in this respect, too, the tinamous show some affinity with the true ratites.

Reconstructions of the outward appearance and skeleton of some of the many extinct birds. Furnished with a paleognathic palate, *Dinornis* and *Aepyornis* were gigantic birds, 11 ft (3.30 m) and 10 ft (3 m) tall respectively, and they disappeared, as a result of human action, less than three centuries ago. Standing more than 6 ft 7 in (2 m) high, *Diatryma* was an archaic bird with a neognathic palate; it lived in Europe and North America during the Eocene.

Giant moa
(*Dinornis maximus*)

Elephant bird
(*Aepyornis maximus*)

Diatryma

OSTRICH

Struthio camelus

Order Struthioniformes
Family Struthionidae
Size Height 8¼ ft (2.5 m); length 6 ft (1.8 m)
Weight 300 lb (136 kg)
Distribution Central, east and southern Africa
Eggs 10 – 25
Chicks Nidifugous

A glance at the body structure of the ostrich (*Struthio camelus*) reveals how exceptionally well adapted this animal is to life in open surroundings where many predators roam. The head is small and practically hairless, with large, prominent eyes which are protected against dust and sandstorms by long lashes. It has a very long neck which functions as a periscope for surveying the surrounding terrain from on high, often rearing up above the low acacia bushes. The wings, despite not being used for flying, still retain long flight feathers. These have no real function except perhaps ornamentation and are more an ancestral residue. The plumage of the male is fairly striking: black over about a third of the neck and the rest of the body, with white flight and tail feathers which grow in large tufts. The coloring in the female is less noticeable and in fact she is far more camouflaged: all the plumage is a uniform brown and the flight feathers do not grow outwards like they do in the male.

The ostrich's diet is very varied despite being mostly composed of leaves and shoots. When feeding, they graze in scattered flocks of variable size. The total intake also includes quite a high percentage of animal food. This is mainly made up of insects, for example larvae or the adults of numerous species of ornithopter, though they will also often catch small mammals and saurians by rooting them out of the bushes.

The fact that ostriches have practically no natural enemy other than man is due to their amazing running ability. They are endowed with an incredible degree of physical resistance which allows them to maintain high running speeds for many miles, while other mammals can only keep up for a brief spell. At maximum speed an adult can touch 43 mph (70 kmh), with long

The evolutionary history of the ostrich began on the steppes of Asia, perhaps during the Eocene, when groups of small running birds broke off from the original branch of flying birds. These flightless birds soon adapted to their new ecological niche, successfully exploiting this environment. Indeed, during the Pliocene giant forms already existed, having extended their range as far as Mongolia in the north and the tip of Africa in the south.

The ostrich (*Struthio camelus*) is today the only bird to have mastered the conditions of the African savanna, where sheer speed is the basic key to survival both for predator and prey, the hunter and the hunted. The ostrich has developed to perfection the capacity for spotting, in good time, the danger posed by large predators such as lions and cheetahs, and of escaping on foot as rapidly as possible.

strides that can carry it along up to 10 ft (3 m) at a time. The wings play an important part when the bird is running as they serve to keep its balance. As it increases its speed, the bird holds the wings further out, moving them together with the neck, especially when swerving suddenly during flight.

The ostrich normally leads a communal life, spending most of the year in flocks of varying size and composition. It is generally polygamous, each male coupling with two, three or even more females. It is the male that makes the first move, pursuing one of the females of his group and separating her from the others. He spreads his large wings and beats them rapidly, and the couple take off in search of an isolated clearing in the undergrowth.

In due course the male courts and copulates with all the females in his harem, and by this time he is looking around for a suitable place to build the nest. This is usually found in an area of sandy terrain because it is easier to dig the round hole where the eggs will be laid in soft ground. Only the male will make the choice for the site of the nest and, once he has roughly shaped the hole, he will line it with various soft materials. When the nest has been constructed, several females approach and lay their eggs. After all the eggs have been laid, the dominant female sometimes chases all the others away from the nesting site, remaining alone with the male and assisting him with the duties of incubation.

After 39 – 42 days of incubation, the eggs hatch at varying and often fairly long intervals. Generally, hatching is completed by the end of two days. This occurs because the female is able to slowly distance the eggs one by one from the heat of her body and place them in little holes that she digs round the nest; in this way the development of the embryos slows down at this late stage, and to varying degrees according to the order in which the eggs are laid.

The chicks can take more than a day to break the shell and when they emerge they have a rough, stiff plumage. After 2 – 3 days, they leave the nest, pursuing the parents and learning how to search for food and to recognize their enemies. At the slightest warning of danger, the chicks lie immobile on the ground. The parents' vigilance helps keep chick mortality low, but it is still quite considerable.

The legs are long and sturdy, covered with horny plates; and there are only two toes on the foot, both strong and clawed.

When the breeding season approaches, males form harems composed of two, three or more females.

The male pays court to the female by means of a complex ritual, spreading his wings and so displaying the white tufts of wing feathers.

When incubating the eggs, the female blends so cleverly with the surroundings that she may easily be mistaken for a mound of sand. Should an intruder approach the nest, she ruffles and spreads her feathers in a characteristic threat attitude.

The chicks are born, after 40 days of incubation, with hard, stiff plumage. It may take them more than a day to break the shell of the egg.

The frightened chicks find refuge beneath their mother's wings. A few months after birth they are left to their own devices, forming large groups of young individuals who find safety in numbers from the many predators which pose a threat to their survival.

RHEA

Rhea americana

Order Rheiformes
Family Rheidae
Size Height 5½ ft (1.7 m); length 4¼ ft (1.3 m)
Weight 55 lb (25 kg)
Distribution South America
Eggs 15 – 20
Chicks Nidifugous

Not so powerful as the ostrich, the rhea has a relatively compact body, which, except for the almost naked legs, is uniformly brown. The wings are larger than in all other ratites, being used by the rhea to balance itself when running at speed. Frequently, while running, the rhea will suddenly stop and throw itself to the ground, somewhat like an ostrich, stretching its neck along the surface. The legs, very strong as in all running birds, are covered by a series of horny plates.

In the dry, flat expanses of the pampas the rhea feeds on the fruits of various species of crowberry (*Empetrum*) as well as cultivated fruits. An important part of the diet is additionally made up of the shoots and leaves of many leguminous and graminaceous plants, insects and lizards.

Rheas normally live in stable flocks outside the breeding season, but older males, which are markedly larger than the females, usually live on their own. With the approach of spring, when the days become longer and the temperature rises, the males turn decidely territorial and engage in combat, often very violently, with rivals, dealing out powerful kicks and blows of the beak. Having won a portion of territory, each individual male starts courting females. One male may, within a short time, assemble a harem of 15 – 20 females inside his territory. Then, having chosen a patch of sandy ground well concealed by trees, he will dig a hole and proceed to line it with leaves and grass. He mates with the various females and they begin laying their eggs either in the principal nest or in any of the other holes dug by the male. As soon as the nest is full of eggs, he starts incubating them. After 35 days' incubation, the eggs start to hatch and the male stays on the nest for another 48 hours. The chicks grow very fast and within a couple of months are one-third the weight of the adults.

▲ Although not so impressive in appearance, the rhea is very similar to the ostrich and plays the same role in South America as its counterpart does on the African savanna. This affinity suggests that they may have had a common ancestor, the progenitor of a group of birds which later became diversified when natural barriers appeared, isolating one from the other.

▼ Incubation of eggs is the task of the male, who drives away the female when the nest is full. After the eggs hatch he remains on the nest for a further 48 hours. The chicks grow quickly and soon become independent.

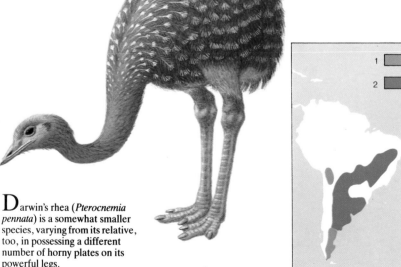

◄ Darwin's rhea (*Pterocnemia pennata*) is a somewhat smaller species, varying from its relative, too, in possessing a different number of horny plates on its powerful legs.

◄ Distribution of the two South American rheas: 1) Darwin's rhea (*Pterocnemia pennata*); 2) Rhea (*Rhea americana*).

EMU

Dromaius novaehollandiae

Order Casuariiformes
Family Dromaiidae
Dimensions Height almost 6 ft 7 in (2 m); length 6 ft 3 in (198 cm)
Weight 120 lb (55 kg)
Distribution Australia
Eggs 7 – 16
Chicks Nidifugous

The emu, next to the African ostrich, is the largest of living ratites. Up to 6 ft 7 in (2 m) high, with most of its neck covered in feathers, the emu, like other flightless birds, has strong, muscular legs for running; but each foot, unlike that of the ostrich, has three instead of two toes. The very thick plumage is uniformly brown. A part of the head and the uppermost section of the neck are almost naked and a vivid blue color. Other predominant features are the large reddish eyes and a bill that is very broad at the base.

The emu's diet is very varied. Essentially a vegetarian, the bird feeds mainly on flowers, fruits and seeds of many different plants but is also partial to caterpillars and orthopterans. In the central and eastern parts of the continent large flocks of emus undertake regular journeys of 250 – 300 miles (400 – 500 km) at the onset of the cold, dry weather. At that season they leave the hinterland to travel southward to regions where there is frequent rainfall and consequently more food. In summer, when the rains return to the central plains, the birds retrace their tracks to the northeast. The regularity of such migrations is therefore solely due to the cycle of rains.

In contrast to the ostrich, a typically polygamous species, the emu forms monogamous pairs. Male and female join forces from November onwards, feeding and moving around together; and thanks to their remarkably sharp vision, they can keep in touch with each other even when grazing a mile or so apart. Mating occurs from April onwards, after a short and very simple courtship.

In this species it is the female who builds the nest, a simple hole dug in the ground and lined with soft material. Between April and May the female lays 5 – 10 large, dark green eggs. With rare exceptions, incubation is carried out by the male.

As colonization has spread, emus, during their occasional travels in quest of food, have tended to interfere more and more with human activities, consuming cereal crops and invading zones reserved for cattle grazing. Farmers, therefore, virtually declared war against these birds, proceeding to exterminate them with any weapons at their disposal, including heavy artillery. Today, fortunately, such tactics have been abandoned, and the emu population appears to be relatively stable.

◀ Standing some 6 ft 7 in (2 m) high, the emu (*Dromaius novaehollandiae*) is second only to the ostrich as the largest living ratite. Adapted to life on the arid Australian plains, where it feeds and breeds, it is a nomad, moving about periodically in large flocks, in rhythm with the alternating cycle of rains of the continent.

▼ The emu is a monogamous species. The female lays her dark green eggs in a simple hollow on the ground, while the subsequent stage of incubation is the exclusive responsibility of the male.

▼ After about two months the chicks are born, covered in striped down, and capable of fending for themselves in a very short time.

▼ Shining objects, in particular, arouse the curiosity of the emu.

CASSOWARY

Casuarius casuarius

Order Casuariiformes
Family Casuariidae
Size Height 3¼ ft (1 m); length 5¼ ft (1.6 m)
Weight 187 lb (85 kg)
Distribution Northeast Australia, New Guinea
Eggs 3 – 6
Chicks Nidifugous

The cassowary is a large running bird adapted to the dense forest that still covers much of New Guinea. There are three distinct species, two of which are found exclusively in New Guinea and on the island of New Britain; the third, the common or Australian cassowary (*Casuarius casuarius*), is also an inhabitant of the Queensland peninsula in northeast Australia.

Although they stand up to 3¼ ft (1 m) high at the back, cassowaries give the impression of being extraordinarily stocky. The body, like that of the emu, is noticeably elongated and is supported by fairly short, though heavy, legs. The feet, broad and powerful, are those of an accomplished runner; they have three toes, the innermost one being short but furnished with a strong claw which constitutes a terrible weapon. The extremely thick plumage is glossy black with vivid blue reflections.

As is the case with the ostrich, a cassowary, as it runs through the forest, will extend its stumps of wings, not so much in order to maintain balance as to open gaps in the dense vegetation. The abundant, compact plumage is, furthermore, useful for lessening any pain or damage that the bird might sustain by colliding with branches or trunks as it runs through the trees.

It would seem that cassowaries are monogamous birds. Outside the breeding season it is usual to encounter only solitary individuals. Pairs form before August. The female lays 3 – 5 dark green eggs in a small hole on the ground, the nest being wadded with vegetation. Incubation is the responsibility of the male. At birth the chicks are covered with striped plumage and are nidifugous.

▼ The cassowary has an exceptionally robust build, its sturdy legs being covered by horny plates and the broad, heavy feet indicating that the bird is a powerful runner.

▲ The most spectacular feature of the cassowary (*Casuarius casuarius*) is the huge, horny growth jutting out, like a helmet, from the head. The shape and size of this casque vary from one species to another, and it has a very precise function; as the bird runs through the undergrowth at speeds of up to 31 mph (50 kmh) it stretches out its neck and head parallel to the ground, using the casque to prise open gaps in the vegetation without risk of injury.

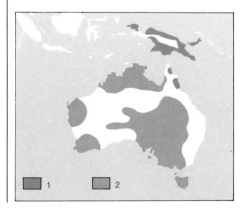

1) The cassowary lives in dense forests which cover a large part of New Guinea. The single-wattled cassowary (*Casuarius unappendiculatus*) and Bennett's cassowary (*C. bennetti*) are found only in New Guinea and on the island of New Britain, whereas the common or Australian cassowary (*C. casuarius*) is also an inhabitant of northeastern Australia, in the York Peninsula. The cassowary has no enemies apart from man; the natives hunt it for its flesh but this has never put its survival at risk. There is a greater potential threat in the progessive destruction of its forest habitats. 2) The emu has colonized the dry plains of the Australian continent. It, too, has been adversely affected by the indiscriminate hunting to which it was subjected until quite recently. Tens of thousands of birds were slaughtered every year, the incentive being a money reward offered by the governments to anyone bringing in an emu's beak.

KIWI

Apteryx australis

Order Apterygiformes
Family Apterygidae
Size Length 22 – 27 in (55 – 68 cm)
Weight Male about 4½ lb (2 kg);
female about 7 lb (3 kg)
Distribution New Zealand
Eggs 1 – 3
Chicks Nidicolous for about 3 – 4 days

The dense, luxuriant forests which still cover large areas of New Zealand harbor the kiwi, a strange bird quite unable to fly, its wings being reduced to two stumps into which the 13 remiges are inserted. Its plumage has an unusual consistency, rather like coarse hair. The tail has completely vanished, while the legs are very strong yet short, dark brown in color and partially covered by horny plates. Very remarkable is the bill, long and slightly curved downward, the upper jaw jutting out a little above the lower and the nostrils opening at the tip.

After spending the hours of daylight hidden in dark ravines or dense bush, the kiwi becomes very active as soon as night falls. Darting about, head lowered, it scratches at the ground in search of food, which consists in the main of insects and other invertebrates. The long beak probes into the moist forest soil for worms, myriapods, and larvae, digging them out so that they can be swiftly swallowed. It is likely that the kiwi makes use of its highly acute hearing to find this type of prey, for its ear openings are very large. Moving through the bracken and around the rotting trunks, it also catches spiders, snails, and many orthopterans. But when the climate is at its driest the bird turns largely vegetarian.

The kiwi seems to be monogamous; once the pair is formed, the male builds a rudimentary nest on the ground. The shiny white egg is remarkably large in relation to the female's body size – up to 14 per cent of her weight. Incubation is almost the exclusive responsibility of the male, who sits on the nest for about 84 days, except when he leaves it at night to look for food. At birth, the chicks are covered in soft brown down which is exactly like that of the adults.

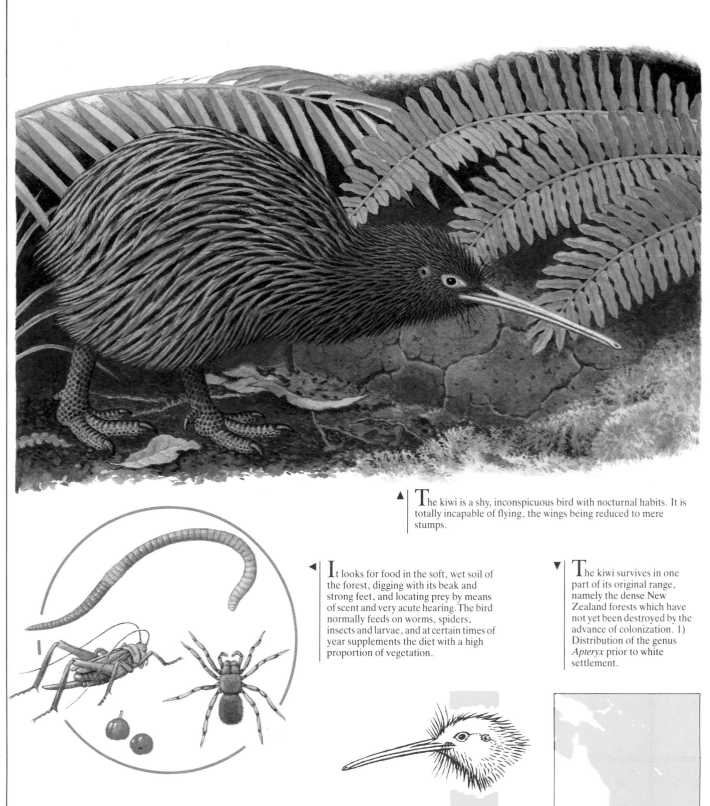

The kiwi is a shy, inconspicuous bird with nocturnal habits. It is totally incapable of flying, the wings being reduced to mere stumps.

It looks for food in the soft, wet soil of the forest, digging with its beak and strong feet, and locating prey by means of scent and very acute hearing. The bird normally feeds on worms, spiders, insects and larvae, and at certain times of year supplements the diet with a high proportion of vegetation.

The kiwi survives in one part of its original range, namely the dense New Zealand forests which have not yet been destroyed by the advance of colonization. 1) Distribution of the genus *Apteryx* prior to white settlement.

A characteristic feature of the kiwi is its bill, long, slightly curved downward and with nostrils that open at the tip. This last detail distinguishes the kiwi from the majority of other birds, whose nostrils are situated on the bottom of the beak, and it emphasizes the importance of scent in the search for food.

KING PENGUIN

Aptenodytes patagonica

Order Sphenisciformes
Family Spheniscidae
Length About 38 in (95 cm)
Weight 33 lb (15 kg)
Distribution Antarctic and subantarctic zones
Eggs 1
Chicks Nidicolous

Virtually everyone knows what a penguin looks like, its body being perfectly adapted, in the long course of evolution, to life in water, particularly the sea. Broadly speaking, penguins are marine birds, incapable of flying, that are typical of the southern hemisphere and better suited to an aquatic existence than any other family of birds.

By means of their flipper-like wings penguins can travel astonishingly fast through the water, steering themselves with feet and tail. Almost all penguins swim more or less like dolphins, traveling underwater for considerable distances and occasionally leaping clear of the surface. This can take them along at speeds of up to 2½ mph (4 kmh) and the leaps out of the water may reach a height of about 39 in (1 m), sufficient to propel them straight out of the sea on to dry land, a rock or an ice floe. When crossing ice or firmly packed snow, penguins can not only waddle in an upright position but also get along by flopping belly down and sliding over the surface, using flippers and feet for steering. The height of present-day penguins ranges from 1 ft to 4 ft (30 to 120 cm) or more. All penguins feed on fish, mollusks, and crustaceans.

Penguins are demonstrably gregarious and their calls are loud and sharp, including a wide range of grunts, rumbles, brays, and similar sounds which help to identify the species. Breeding colonies often contain an enormous number of birds, sometimes exceeding half a million pairs.

As far as distribution is concerned, the penguin family is typical of the southern hemisphere, performing more or less the same ecological role as do the auks in the northern hemisphere. The penguins probably originated in the antarctic or subantarctic regions, for it is here that fossils dating from the Tertiary have been found.

▲
◄ A group of king penguins (*Aptenodytes patagonica*) with chicks. Each pair tends a single egg which is incubated beneath an abdominal fold of skin and balanced on the feet so as to protect it from the ground below. When exchanging the egg, the parents perform the maneuver with such dexterity that it never comes into contact with soil or snow. Nevertheless, not all the chicks manage to survive the rigors of the southern winter and the inevitable scarcity of food in the nesting colonies.

◄ The waters of the Arctic Ocean are rich in food, especially in spring and summer, when the adult penguins find plenty for themselves and their young.

Not all species, however, are restricted to these zones. The breeding distribution of the family virtually follows the course of the cold sea currents northward as far as New Zealand, the coasts of Australia and South Africa, and the western shores of South America. In one case it extends to the equator, with a species actually breeding in the Galapagos Islands. Outside the breeding season the different species spend considerable time in the open sea, covering long distances.

As far as the king penguin (*Aptenodytes patagonica*) is concerned, one interesting feature is that this large species, like the emperor penguin, can have difficulty in raising the relatively sizeable chicks given that the environment in which it lives is very harsh and food is scarce for eight to nine months of the year. It lays the eggs in spring and summer and keeps the chicks in the colony until the next spring.

The adult king penguins sit on the eggs for 54 days and both parents are involved in the hatching and raising of the offspring. Growth is very quick and, by the end of the autumn, chicks born early in the season, hatching in November, are already almost as big as the parents. Those born later, towards the beginning of the winter, will only be three quarters fully grown and will remain this size until the next spring. During the months of April and May the penguins begin to feel the effects of the harsh climate and worse weather conditions, especially as far as the search for food is concerned. In fact, during these months egg laying and hatching cease and for the rest of the winter the chicks are only fed every two to three weeks.

They lose weight rapidly and the smallest chicks may even die. Only the healthiest ones with sufficient fat reserves will survive during these months of famine. By October and November, the largest chicks have already lost half their autumn weight. Finally, in spring, the abundance of plankton means there are good food provisions for the penguins and they are able to catch fish and cephalopods in the surface waters and feed the young generously.

Macaroni penguin
(*Eudyptes chrysolophus*)

King penguin
(*Aptenodytes patagonica*)

Emperor penguin
(*Aptenodytes forsteri*)

Magellan penguin
(*Spheniscus magellanicus*)

Jackass penguin
(*Spheniscus demersus*)

Gentoo penguin
(*Pygoscelis papua*)

Galapagos penguin
(*Spheniscus mendiculus*)

Little penguin
(*Eudyptula minor*)

Peruvian penguin
(*Spheniscus humboldti*)

Chinstrap penguin
(*Pygoscelis antarctica*)

The order Sphenisciformes is made up of the single family Spheniscidae, which in turn comprises six genera. All species of penguins are widely distributed over the southern hemisphere, particularly in the polar and subpolar latitudues around 50°S. Of the 18 recognized modern species, only five inhabit tropical and subtropical zones (as, for example, the Galapagos Islands), the remainder being native to colder areas. In these latter surroundings they choose breeding sites along the Antarctic coasts, farther inland and on the innumerable archipelagos fringing the Antarctic Ocean, ranging as far as New Zealand and Tristan da Cunha.

— Jackass penguin (*Spheniscus demersus*)
— Peruvian penguin (*Spheniscus humboldti*)
— King penguin (*Aptenodytes patagonica*)
— Magellan penguin (*Spheniscus magellanicus*)
— Adélie penguin (*Pygoscelis adeliae*)
— Little penguin (*Eudyptula minor*)
● Emperor penguin (*Aptenodytes forsteri*)
● Gentoo penguin (*Pygoscelis papua*)
○ Galapagos penguin (*Spheniscus mendiculus*)
● Macaroni penguin (*Eudyptes chrysolophus*)
● Chinstrap penguin (*Pygoscelis antarctica*)

ADÉLIE PENGUIN

Pygoscelis adeliae

Order Sphenisciformes
Family Spheniscidae
Length About 28 in (70 cm)
Weight 11 lb (5 kg)
Distribution Extreme southern coasts of Antarctica and neighboring islands
Eggs Generally 2, greenish-white
Chicks Nidicolous

One of the best known of the many species of penguins is the Adélie penguin (*Pygoscelis adeliae*), with a widespread distribution along the southeastern shores of the Antarctic and some of the surrounding islands. This is an average-sized penguin, about 28 in (70 cm) in total length, with white plumage on throat and abdomen, black on the head and the back down to the tail, without any special distinguishing marks.

Colonies of Adélie penguins tend to be confined to rocky zones, often extending for some distance, either on the flat or on gentle slopes close to the sea. The penguins start arriving and assembling in these areas at the beginning of the southern spring, at the end of October. They emerge from the sea in small, scattered groups and are seldom seen in large numbers; and in most cases the latest arrivals remain on the fringes of the zone that is subsequently filled by the whole colony. Within a few days some thousands of birds will have appeared, seeking sites for building their rudimentary nests. Pairs of penguins return punctually every year to the same spot in the colony. It is usually the male who comes back to take possession of his territory and begins building the nest even before his mate emerges from the sea.

Once they have commenced building the nest, the males summon the females, taking up a characteristic position with beak held high and wings flapping slowly against the sides, and giving out a succession of guttural sounds, followed by a loud cry. Mating normally begins soon after the female reaches the colony, when the construction of the nest is still in its early stages. The sexual act clearly fulfills a social function in cementing links between the breeding pair.

The first egg is laid a few days after

Adélie penguins live in large numbers along the southeastern shores of the Antarctic and on some of the surrounding islands. They form crowded colonies near the sea in flat, rocky zones, building nests and breeding every year.

There are various theories concerning the relationship of penguins to other orders of birds, and the picture is far from clear. Probably these species have affinities with the Procellariiformes (albatrosses, storm petrels, shearwaters, etc.) but there are also indications that they may have derived from a specific group of Charadriiformes, as has definitely been verified in the case of the auks.

Albatross

Penguins

?

Shearwaters

mating, and as a rule a second egg appears three to four days later. The first is usually larger than the second; and in exceptionally difficult years the female will lay only one egg. By the time egg laying is completed more than three weeks will have elapsed since the birds returned to the colony and as yet not a single penguin has ventured down to the sea in order to feed. At this point the females, weakened by their breeding activities, leave the nests en masse and head for the sea to feed on krill, planktonic crustaceans whose teeming populations are also the principal source of food for the enormous baleen whales. The Adélie penguins waddle off in long lines, sometimes sliding swiftly over the ice, belly downwards, and eventually reach the fringes of the pack ice. Having survived a long period without food and overcome the most critical phases of reproduction, they can now plunge into the waters that teem with nutritious krill, but may still have to brave certain dangers. One potential peril is the presence of that fearsome predator, the leopard seal (*Hydrurga leptonyx*). This seal is a selective hunter, concentrating on the Adélie penguin. Observations show that just ten leopard seals are capable of hunting and killing some 15,000 penguins in a single season. The penguins try to escape the seals by swimming about in large groups and trying to avoid being caught by surprise on their own.

When the females return to the colony after ten days or so in the sea, it is the turn of the males to quit the nests and go off to find food, having fasted for more than a month.

The eggs are incubated for 34 – 36 days and when almost ready to hatch are tended by both parents, alternating at frequent intervals, so as to be ready to feed the babies the moment they are born. The hatching process takes 24 – 48 hours and it may happen that the chicks have to go without food for two or three days. During their first few days the penguin chicks are covered uniformly by down of a variable color. Although there is no sexual dimorphism as such, there are hues ranging from silver to dark brown, even in chicks born in the same nest. After about ten days the initial covering is replaced by a thicker layer of down, and within three weeks or so this second covering begins to give way to real plumage consisting of feathers.

▲ They swim long distances, sometimes leaping like dolphins.

▲ Penguins will travel for dozens of miles in pursuit of food, shoals of krill, or cephalopods and crustaceans.

Principal stages of the breeding cycle.
1) Towards the end of October penguins emerge from the sea in small groups; 2) tobogganing, belly down, over the soft snow, they reach the sites where the colony assembles regularly year after year; 3) the nest is often rebuilt in the same place, intruders being driven away; 4) having started to make the nest, the males call and pay court to the females; 5) as a rule the male collects the stones from which the nest is constructed; 6) the male takes first turn in incubation; 7) the parents feed the chicks by regurgitating half-digested food; 8) after an initial period of attentive parental care, the chicks are left to the their own devices and live together in small groups.

EMPEROR PENGUIN

Aptenodytes forsteri

Order Sphenisciformes
Family Spheniscidae
Size Length about 45 in (115 cm)
Weight About 65 lb (30 kg)
Distribution Antarctic continent
Eggs 1
Chicks Nidicolous

The coasts of the vast continent fringing the Antarctic Ocean are the home of the emperor penguin (*Aptenodytes forsteri*), the largest species of its order, which breeds here in enormous colonies. The large dimensions of the body are a vital part of this species' adaptation to the harsh climate of the Antarctic: if the body is large, a proportionately smaller surface is exposed than is the case with a smaller creature and, given that heat is lost across the body surface, a larger animal will have more success in keeping in body warmth.

Linked again with the heat regulation of the fatty tissue is the form the plumage takes. In the emperor penguin, like other members of the family, the entire body is covered by dense plumage. Immediately over the skin is a layer of down which maintains the body temperature very efficiently. The feathers grow out of this down, numbering as many as 22 – 24 per square inch (2.5 cm). The wings are very short in relation to the body, and the legs, completely feathered, terminate in comparatively small feet. The color of the plumage follows the general pattern found in most penguins; back, wings and head down to the throat are shiny black while the abdomen is white with visible yellow tints. The emperor penguin chicks are covered in a thick layer of light-colored down.

The emperor penguin feeds on many kinds of marine animals, particularly the shoals of squid that often inhabit these relatively deep waters. The penguins skim through the water after their prey and when close to the surface leap right out, rather like dolphins, to replenish their supply of air.

The breeding cycle of the emperor penguin is determined by the amount of food available in the vicinity and the ease or difficulty in obtaining it at

▲ The emperor penguin, largest of living Sphenisciformes, is particularly adapted for withstanding the terrible southern winter. It, too, forms huge colonies: the one on Coulman Island brings together more than 300,000 birds.

The egg is incubated beneath a fold of abdominal skin, supported on the feet of the adult, thus ensuring that it does not come into contact with the ice.

◄ The burden of incubation falls entirely on the male. Motionless in the freezing cold winter, he carries out the task which, when complete, will have forced him to go more than three months without food.

different times of the year. Natural selection over the centuries has, in fact, ensured that the breeding season commences when climatic conditions are deteriorating and comes to an end at the very time when food is once again more abundant and easily obtained by the newly born penguins, who leave the colony while still inexperienced in fishing techniques.

The penguins begin to arrive at their breeding sites in small groups, the numbers steadily increasing the closer they get to the zone where the colony regularly assembles. The journey from the coast, which is already covered by pack ice, entails a considerable expenditure of energy, because the areas selected for reproduction may be a long distance from the sea. Apparently the emperor penguin, like the Adélie penguin, returns to the same site year after year. The largest colonies, such as the celebrated Coulman Island colony, number over 300,000 birds.

The species does not build a nest. Indeed, one of the most fascinating adaptations to the harsh, hostile surroundings is the development of a fold of skin between the feet, where the egg is incubated. Resting on the top of the feet and covered by this warm layer of tissue, the egg is protected from the cold of the icy surface and receives enough heat for the embryo to develop. Within 6 – 12 hours of laying the egg, the female passes it over to her mate, who places it beneath his pouch.

The burden of incubation now falls exclusively on the male who is compelled to prolong his own fast. After the departure of the female, the male penguins are faced with the none too easy task of caring for the eggs in conditions that steadily continue to worsen, with searing winds and temperatures several dozen degrees below zero. At this difficult stage of the reproductive cycle the males instinctively come closer together, forming large groups in which each individual is in contact with another; this helps to build a protective wall against the violence of the wind and at the same time takes full advantage of individual body warmth to create as favorable a microclimate as possible within the colony.

The females arrive back at about the time when the eggs are almost ready to hatch, so that the newborn chicks can receive fresh food from their mothers.

Among emperor penguins the end of the breeding cycle coincides with the period when food is most plentiful and thus easily obtained for the as yet nexperienced young: 1) the young penguins enter the sea; 2 – 3) the colony disperses; 4 – 5) the colony assembles, followed by mating and egg laying; 6 – 7) the male incubates the egg, the female feeds at sea; 8) the egg hatches and the females return; 9 – 12) the female cares for the chick, the male feeds at sea.

▲ Soon after laying her egg, the female passes it to the male for incubation and leaves the colony, making her way to the sea to find food.

If the chick is born before the female returns with the necessary supply of fresh food, the male is capable of feeding the baby with a special liquid consisting of partially digested food.

▲ The chick is fed by both parents on regurgitated fish.

◄ Baby emperor penguins are covered with a thick layer of light gray down, not shiny like the plumage of the adults but opaque and woolly. This covering ensures that they absorb as much heat as possible, vital at this early stage when they are not yet capable of regulating their body temperature. After a little more than a month they leave the adult's incubating fold and go to live together, waiting for the arrival of summer when, having acquired their complete plumage, they can abandon the safety of the colony and venture out on their own in the open sea.

▲ Emperor penguins can dive to a depth of up to 195ft (60m) and stay under water for as much as 15 minutes, chasing schools of cephalopods which they often capture in comparatively shallow water.

RED-THROATED DIVER

Gavia stellata

Order Gaviiformes
Family Gaviidae
Length 22 – 26 in (56 – 65 cm)
Wingspan 39 – 43 in (99 – 110 cm)
Weight (3 – 5 lb) 1,300 – 2,000 g
Distribution Europe, Asia and North America, Greenland
Eggs Usually 2, greenish-brown or olive-green, speckled with brown
Chicks Nidifugous

The order Gaviiformes is made up of a small group of aquatic birds which bears no relationship whatsoever to any other group of modern birds. The most recent genus, *Gavia*, comprises four present-day and five fossil species. The four living species are the great northern diver (*Gavia immer*), the white-billed diver (*G. adamsii*), the black-throated diver (*G. arctica*), and the red-throated diver (*G. stellata*).

The great northern diver is an inhabitant of North America, Iceland, Bear Island, Jan Mayen Island and Greenland. The white-billed diver is found on the American continent from Alaska to the Boothia peninsula, the northern Kola peninsula, the Kolguyev Islands, Novaya Zemlya and the Siberian arctic from Vaygach Island to the Chukchi Sea. The black-throated diver has three geographical races: *Gavia arctica arctica* from Europe and northern Asia east of the Lena river basin, *G.a. viridigularis* from northeast Asia, and *G.a. pacifica* from North America and the zones closest to the northeast Siberian Sea from the basins of the Indigirka and Kolyma to that of the Anadyr. It is mainly migratory, wintering along the coasts of the Arctic Ocean and the North Pacific as well as the large bodies of inland water (Lake Baikal, the Black Sea and the Caspian Sea). The fourth species, the red-throated diver, is found in the same areas as the black-throated diver but extends its range to Greenland.

The red-throated diver is especially easy to identify during the breeding season because of the conspicuous reddish-brown patch on the throat and the almost total absence of vivid black tones or, indeed, black anywhere on the body. The upper part of the head is glossy ash gray and, to all appearances,

A diver hunting a stickleback. Divers, mainly aquatic, are expert swimmers.

The food of divers consists chiefly of fish such as gobies, sand-eels, young salmon, lampreys, etc.

The webbed feet ensure that divers are swift, accomplished swimmers.

Black-throated diver resting on land and on the surface of the water.

striped. The remaining upper parts are dark brown with heavy white speckling. The sides of the head, neck, chin and throat are dark gray, offset by the distinctive reddish brown mark on the center of the neck. The nape, the back of the neck and the lower flanks are dark with white borders which appear striped. The upper parts of the back and wings are gray-black, delicately speckled with white. The speckling is clearly visible in the early stages of the molt and then tends to fade. The underparts of the body are whitish. In winter the coloration changes and the upper parts of the body and wings become gray-brown, while two white marks usually appear on each feather.

The red-throated diver is an example of perfect adaptation to an aquatic environment; indeed it spends the greater part of its life in water. No other bird, with the exception of the penguin, can rival it for swimming and, more especially, diving. As a rule the bird dives to depths of 19 – 32 ft (6–10 m) but often exceeding 100 ft (30m). One individual was found enmeshed in a fishing net 229 ft (70 m) down.

The diver's absolute mastery of its watery environment is due not only to its perfect hydrodynamic outline but also to its ability to vary its weight to match that of the water by expelling air. Furthermore, the bird's muscle tissues and blood have a greater resistance to the toxic effects of carbon dioxide, basically because it is better able to retain reserves of oxygen in the blood. A diver can therefore swim 1,650 – 2,620 ft (500 – 800 m) under water without any difficulty, propelling itself with the feet and using its wings to maintain balance and to turn.

With the approach of spring the divers fly back to their breeding grounds, and at this time of year the banks of lakes and ponds are crowded with birds. The nest is built on the banks of deep, still northern lakes or on ponds with plenty of grass all around. Each pair of birds patrols a territory surrounding the nest and chases away intruders.

The eggs, generally two in number, are incubated in turn by both parents for 24 – 29 days. The chicks leave the nest almost as soon as they are born and are warded off by their parents.

The food of adult divers is composed of fish and, to a lesser extent, mollusks, crustaceans, amphibians, and aquatic insects.

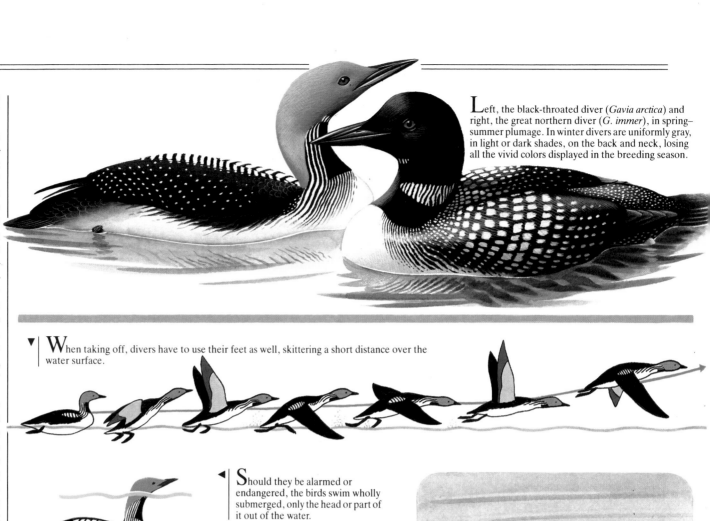

Left, the black-throated diver (*Gavia arctica*) and right, the great northern diver (*G. immer*), in spring–summer plumage. In winter divers are uniformly gray, in light or dark shades, on the back and neck, losing all the vivid colors displayed in the breeding season.

When taking off, divers have to use their feet as well, skittering a short distance over the water surface.

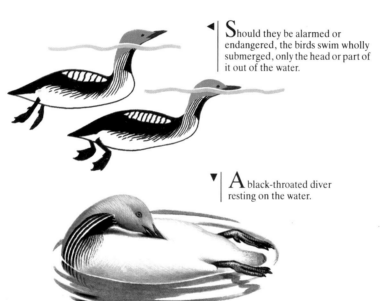

Should they be alarmed or endangered, the birds swim wholly submerged, only the head or part of it out of the water.

A black-throated diver resting on the water.

The nest is usually situated on small islands or embankments near the water.

During the first few days of life the chicks are often carried about on the back of one of the parents.

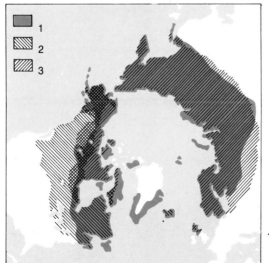

Nesting areas of divers: 1) Great northern diver (*Gavia immer*); 2) Red-throated diver (*G. stellata*); 3) Black-throated diver (*G. arctica*).

GREAT CRESTED GREBE

Podiceps cristatus

Order Podicipediformes
Family Podicipedidae
Length 15 – 21 in (40 – 54 cm)
Wingspan 5 ft 11 in – 6ft 6 in
(180 – 198 cm)
Weight 1½ – 2½ lb (700 – 1,200 g)
Distribution Europe, Asia, Africa,
Australia, Tasmania, and New
Zealand
Habits Gregarious, from a few pairs to
breeding or wintering colonies
Eggs 3 – 4, sometimes 5 – 6, elongated
in shape
Chicks Nidifugous

The order Podicipediformes comprises a group of aquatic birds, primitive in structure, distributed all over the world. The order is unrelated to any other order of present-day birds and probably not even to other extinct orders. At present there are more than 20 recognized species belonging to four genera, *Aechmophorus*, *Centropelma*, *Podiceps*, and *Podilymbus*. The genera *Aechmophorus* and *Centropelma* are monospecific, containing only one species each, namely the western grebe (*Aechmophorus occidentalis*), found in the western parts of North America, and the short-winged grebe (*Centropelma micropterum*), a flightless bird native to Lake Titicaca in Bolivia. The genus *Podilymbus* is exclusively American, comprising two species, the pied-billed grebe (*Podilymbus podiceps*) and the giant pied-billed grebe (*P. gigas*). The former is found throughout America from Argentina to British Columbia, and the latter is endemic to Lake Atitlan in Guatemala. The genus *Podiceps* has a cosmopolitan distribution. Among the group of little grebes are the least grebe (*Podiceps dominicus*) from tropical America; the little grebe (*P. ruficollis*), an inhabitant of the Old World; the black-throated little grebe (*P. novaehollandiae*) from Australasia; two species from Madagascar, Delacour's little grebe (*P. rufolaratus*) and the Madagascar little grebe (*P. pelzelnii*); the hoary-headed grebe (*P. poliocephalus*), native to Australia, and the New Zealand dabchick (*P. rufupectus*).

The grebes proper are represented by five South American species: the

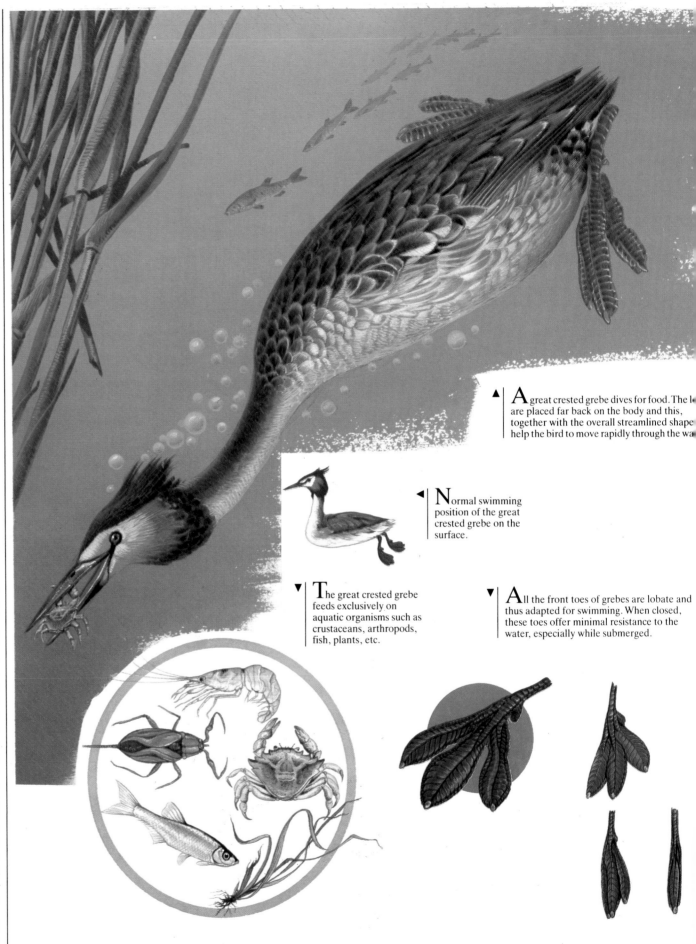

A great crested grebe dives for food. The l[e]
are placed far back on the body and this,
together with the overall streamlined shape
help the bird to move rapidly through the wa[ter]

Normal swimming
position of the great
crested grebe on the
surface.

The great crested grebe
feeds exclusively on
aquatic organisms such as
crustaceans, arthropods,
fish, plants, etc.

All the front toes of grebes are lobate and
thus adapted for swimming. When closed,
these toes offer minimal resistance to the
water, especially while submerged.

lesser golden grebe (*P. chilensis*), the great grebe (*P. major*), the silvery grebe (*P. occipitalis*), the white-tufted grebe (*P. rolland*) and the Puna grebe (*P. tachzanowskii*); three species from North America and Eurasia: the horned grebe (*P. auritus*), the red-necked grebe (*P. grisegena*) and the black-necked grebe (*P. nigricollis*); one species confined to the Lakes of the Colombian Andes, the Colombian eared grebe (*P. andinus*); and the great crested grebe (*P. cristatus*).

The great crested grebe is the largest of the Old World Podicipedidae. It is easy to recognize this bird in the wild during summer because of its size, its black ear tufts (only in the adults), its long bill and its slender neck. The bird's upper parts are blackish, the feathers edged with dark brown. The head is black, with a white line over the eyes, the lores, chin and front of the face are white, and the cheeks are reddish with thin, elongated feathers that form a kind of collar, brown to black at the tips. The female is very similar to the male, except that she is smaller. The species and its various races are distributed throughout Europe, Asia, Africa, Australia, Tasmania, and New Zealand.

The great crested grebe, essentially a water bird, only ventures on to dry land if absolutely necessary, whether to shift from one body of water to another, to build a nest, to incubate its eggs, or simply to rest and dry off. It can swim and dive with consummate ease; but it is also a strong flier once it has taken off by running some distance over the water surface. In flight it holds the neck outstretched, the head slightly below the line of the body, the legs extended backwards. It swims with body half-submerged and neck held high. The bird's diving technique is remarkable, the body so perfectly streamlined as to carry it down to a depth of about 65 ft (20 m), although in the stagnant waters where it is most often seen, the grebe seldom dives deeper than 22 ft (7 m).

The grebe builds its nest on the water, generally choosing a pond or lake where conditions are calm, with reeds and plants on the fringes. The nest is usually hidden among the reed, rush, and sedge vegetation. The female normally lays 3 – 4 eggs, more rarely 5 – 6. Coupling is preceded by a preliminary series of complex ceremonies designed to reinforce the links between the mating birds.

▲ Both sexes collaborate in building the nest out of heaped water plants; the nest forms a tiny floating island or may sometimes be anchored to swamp vegetation.

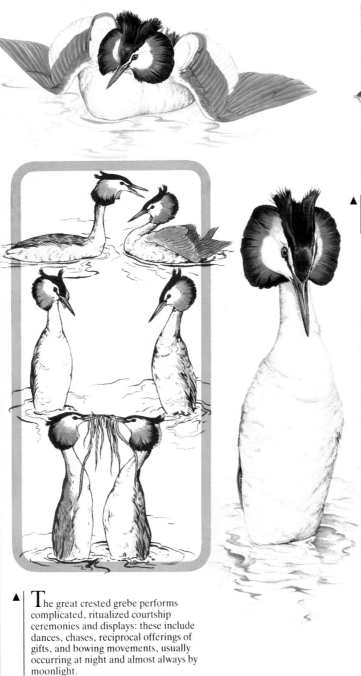

▲ The great crested grebe performs complicated, ritualized courtship ceremonies and displays: these include dances, chases, reciprocal offerings of gifts, and bowing movements, usually occurring at night and almost always by moonlight.

▲ From top to bottom: pied-billed grebe (*Podilymbus podiceps*), little grebe (*Podiceps ruficollis*), and red-necked grebe (*Podiceps grisegena*).

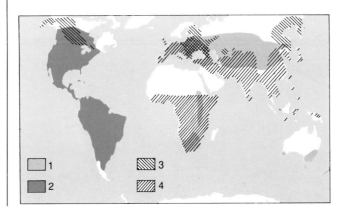

◄ Nesting areas of the four species illustrated on these pages: 1) Great crested grebe (*Podiceps cristatus*); 2) Pied-billed grebe (*Podilymbus podiceps*); 3) Red-necked grebe (*Podiceps grisegena*); 4) Little grebe (*Podiceps ruficollis*).

1
2
3
4

PROCEL-LARIIFORMES

The Procellariiformes are an order of marine birds with one special and distinctive characteristic. The bill terminates in a hook and is made up of juxtaposed horny sections, the sutures being clearly defined; and the tube-like nostrils, separated from the upper mandible, explain why the group used to be called Tubinares ("tube-noses"). The nasal or salt glands are well developed, secreting a solution with a high saline content, which, in effect, eliminates excess salt from the blood. The tubes of the nostrils possibly serve to conduct this saline solution away from the eyes, also preventing sea spray getting into the nostrils themselves. The tubes terminate in large nasal fossae or olfactory cavities, the significance of which remains obscure; but their function may be to detect the slightest differences in direction of the light winds that play over the surface of the sea.

The order Procellariiformes is nowadays divided into four families: Pelecanoididae, Hydrobatidae, Diomedeidae and Procellariidae. The Procellariiformes are found in all the world's oceans, especially those of the southern hemisphere. Present-day distribution, extremely restricted in the case of certain species, undoubtedly depends upon the availability of food and suitable breeding sites. Clearly, the quantity of plankton and fish in the sea is influenced by many factors, such as water temperature, currents, salinity, etc.

Faithful to their breeding sites, the Procellariiformes are highly gregarious, especially in the actual breeding season. The females lay a single, very large egg which, in the larger species, weighs from 6 to 10 per cent of her body weight and, in the smaller species, from 10 to 25 per cent. Nests may be built on the ground, in clefts, against rock walls, in underground tunnels excavated by the birds themselves or abandoned by mammals, or even in the crater of an island volcano.

Without any doubt, they are the world's best flying birds as well as the most formidable transoceanic migrants. Many investigations have shown that a large number of species follow

Black-footed albatross
(*Diomedea nigripes*)

Steller's albatross
(*Diomedea albatrus*)

The diving petrels are the most untypical of the Procellariiformes. In fact, they are not good fliers but use their short wings as paddles when submerged. Their body is very similar to that of the ancient auks.

Leach's petrel
(*Oceanodroma leucorhoa*)

Fulmar
(*Fulmarus glacialis*)

Cape pigeon
(*Daption capensis*)

1
2
3

▲ From left: black-footed albatross, widely distributed in the North Pacific; Steller's albatross, feared to be in danger of extinction, with only about 60 nesting pairs now left on the Japanese islands of Torishima and Isa; fulmar, with two distinct races in either hemisphere; Cape pigeon, very common in the southern hemisphere, migrating long distances outside the breeding season; Leach's petrel, one of the most abundant species, with millions of individuals in North America alone.

◄ Distribution areas of some Procellariiformes: 1) Fulmar (*Fulmarus glacialis*); 2) Steller's albatross (*Diomedea albatrus*); 3) Diving petrel (*Pelecanoides urinatrix*).

precise and well-defined flight paths. Wilson's petrel covers 7,450 miles (12,000 km) twice a year, but this is modest compared with the distances traveled by the albatrosses, whose flights have for centuries been described in legendary terms. Assisted by the trade winds of the southern hemisphere, these birds can actually circumnavigate the globe twice in the interval between two breeding cycles. Two wandering albatrosses (*Diomedea exulans*) have, for example, been recovered from 6,000 – 8,000 miles (10,000 – 13,000 km) away from the place where they were ringed.

These birds also have exceptional powers of orientation. One of 700 Manx shearwaters (*Puffinus puffinus*) ringed on their nests in Wales was taken by air to Boston, Mass., and released there. It made the return journey in 12 days, covering at least 3,100 miles (5,000 km). Another Manx shearwater, released in Venice, took 14 days to find its way back, probably because it flew across the whole Mediterranean. Nevertheless, it still managed to fly, on average, 280 miles (450 km) a day.

The Pelecanoididae, the diving petrels, are considered the most atypical and primitive of the Procellariiformes. They are excellent divers, with short wide wings which serve little pupose in the air but act as efficient paddles in the water. They are similar in appearance to auks with a very long sternum, an upright position and a small beak with the characteristic tube-like nostrils on the upper end, short and turned upwards, separated by a septum. There are four species, all small in size, distributed around the Antarctic Ocean.

The Hydrobatidae or storm petrels are the smallest of all the Procellariiformes. The flight pattern is very characteristic. Undaunted by the fiercest storms, they flutter securely below the crest of the waves; but if they venture too high above the surface they are often at the mercy of the wind, the flimsy body too light in weight to resist its buffeting. The petrels can also hover in midair by rapidly flapping their wings. Each species, however, possesses a distinctive flight technique. Thus Leach's storm petrel (*Oceanodroma leucorhoa*) has a zigzag flying pattern, frequently changing speed and direction, while the common storm petrel (*Hydrobates pelagicus*) flits about like a bat.

Storm petrel
(*Hydrobates pelagicus*)

Wilson's petrel
(*Oceanites oceanicus*)

◄ The storm petrels are smaller than the shearwaters, but also possess tube-like nostrils. There are two principal forms in either hemisphere, identifiable, too, by the ways in which they capture food. Their habits are similar to those of shearwaters. The birds fly close to the surface of the sea, following ships, feeding on various types of animal plankton.

▲ The chick, like that of the shearwaters, puts on large quantities of fat until it may be one and a half times the size of the adult.

▲ The storm petrel uses its feet both for checking its flight and catching small fish. The dangling legs sometimes give the bird the appearance of walking on the water surface and this is the reason why it was once known as St Peter's bird, petrel being a diminutive form of this name.

◄ The common storm petrel lives in the Atlantic and the western Mediterranean (1) while Wilson's petrel (2) populates the oceans in its millions, especially in the southern hemisphere.

WANDERING ALBATROSS

Diomedea exulans

Order Procellariiformes
Family Diomedeidae
Size Length 28 – 48 in (71 – 122 cm)
Weight 13 – 18 lb (6 – 8 kg)
Distribution Southern hemisphere,
North Pacific
Habits Gregarious; pelagic,
transoceanic migrants
Nesting On ground
Reproductive period Autumn – winter
or spring – summer
Eggs 1
Chicks Semi-inept
Sexual maturity 6 – 10 years
Maximum age About 40 years

The albatrosses, members of the family Diomedeidae, are the largest known flying birds. A simple distinguishing feature is the huge bill made up of numerous horny plates. The nostrils, in the form of short tubes, are situated on either side of the central slab of the upper mandible. On both the upper and lower surfaces of the long, narrow wings there is a distinctive color pattern, but this is not a reliable means of identifying young or immature individuals.

Albatrosses are to be found in almost all of the world's oceans: nine species live in the southern hemisphere, three in the North Pacific and one in the tropics. They are exceptional fliers and their migrations embrace the entire globe. One species noted for traveling immense distances is the Laysan albatross, which nests in Hawaii and migrates regularly across the Pacific, sometimes reaching Kamchatka and New Zealand. The wandering albatross, distributed throughout Oceania, spends approximately 12 – 13 months, the period between two successive breeding cycles, flying the world's oceans, sometimes reaching northern Europe and the Mediterranean. The ocean is, of course, the natural habitat of these huge birds, but during the breeding season they venture on to dry land, nesting mainly on small islands and isolated parts of the continents. Their ability to find their way across the oceans and back to their original sites is astonishing.

No other bird can rival the albatross in remaining for hours on end

The albatrosses are the largest representatives of the order Procellariiformes. The wandering albatross (the drawing shows an adult and, on the right, an immature individual) is the largest of all marine birds. There are three species of albatross in the northern hemisphere and ten in the southern hemisphere. They are carried along by the strong sea winds, seldom flapping their wings; in flight they hold the bill downward, repeatedly skimming the waves.

The bill of the albatross, composed of horny plates, is very stout, the nostrils being situated on either side of the central plate of the upper mandible.

suspended in the air, hardly ever moving its wings. It takes advantage of all the air currents playing over the water surface, gaining altitude by flying upwind (into the wind) when wind velocity diminishes because of friction with the waves, soaring upward when the wind is stronger and gliding downwind (with the wind) so as to obtain the thrust and acceleration needed to gain altitude once more when it encounters the immobile layers of air below. This zigzag pattern of flight, with minor variants, may last for hours. If the wind is very high, the albatross hurls itself down towards the sea with half-closed wings; and if there is no wind at all, it prefers to settle on the waves, often holding the wings slightly open on the back.

All the albatrosses feed chiefly on cephalopod mollusks (especially squid), caught on the surface either in flight, or when at rest. Other important elements of diet are crustaceans (notably shrimp), fish, and tunicates.

The birds normally nest in colonies. The nests are situated in small holes scooped out with the beak or simply on the ground, and consist of soil and mud. Ornithologists have made careful studies of the courtship rituals of these birds. The wandering albatross starts paying suit to his mate by beating his wings while she takes on a submissive posture, both birds pecking each other gently. Once his overtures are accepted, both partners spread their wings, stretch the neck and give out loud, penetrating cries. This courtship ceremony, studied thoroughly by Tickell, is regarded as a competitive encounter between two birds that have not yet mated; both the vocal and visual signals probably help to calm the female.

The birds are normally very regular in returning to the same nesting sites. The female lays one large egg, white or delicately streaked red at the bigger end, which is incubated for a period ranging from 60 to 80 days. Both parents take part in incubation.

Man is the only real enemy of the albatross. This was especially true during the eighteenth century when shipwrecked sailors were stranded for long periods on small islands where the birds nested, feeding on their eggs and chicks and almost wiping out entire populations in some areas. Today it appears albatross species are no longer endangered in view of the fact that they nest only in isolated places.

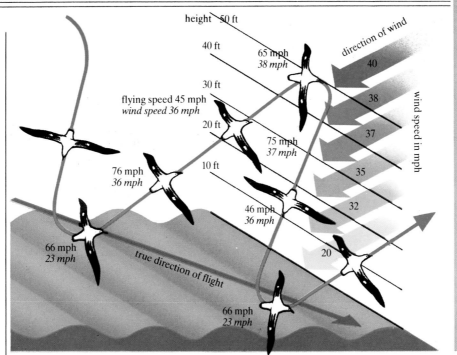

height 50 ft
40 ft
65 mph 38 mph
30 ft
flying speed 45 mph *wind speed 36 mph*
20 ft
75 mph *37 mph*
76 mph *36 mph*
10 ft
46 mph *36 mph*
66 mph *23 mph*
true direction of flight
66 mph *23 mph*
direction of wind
wind speed in mph
40
38
37
35
32
20

▲ The albatross exploits the air currents at the sea surface in the following manner: initially the bird swoops downward, picking up speed until it is almost skimming the surface; then it ricochets off the lowest, unmoving layers of air and soars up on the original air current. The strong trade winds of the southern hemisphere are invaluable for flying and migrating. The wings are used as rudders to change direction.

▼ During the courtship display the male wandering albatross snaps his beak and opens his wings; then both partners spread their wings and let out loud cries.

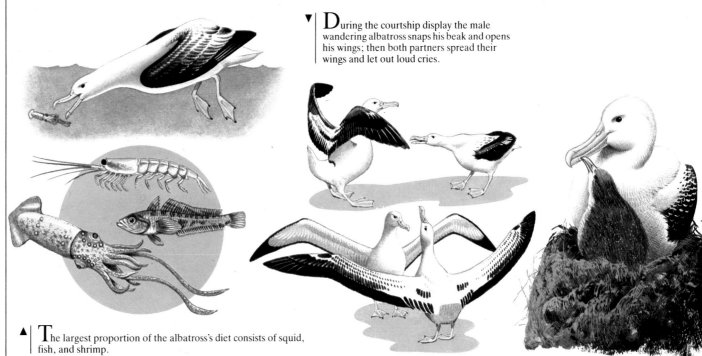

▲ The largest proportion of the albatross's diet consists of squid, fish, and shrimp.

▲ The chicks demand food by repeatedly tapping the parent's beak.

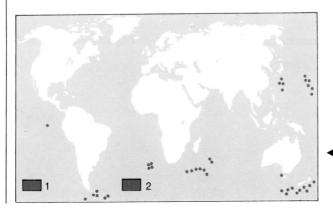

1
2

◀ Albatrosses are exceptional fliers and cover the world's oceans in the course of their migrations. They range over the southern hemisphere and the North Pacific, one species being tropical. 1) Distribution of family Diomedeidae; 2) Distribution of wandering albatross (*Diomedea exulans*).

PROCEL-LARIIDAE

The most distinctive characteristic of the family Procellariidae is the bill, slightly curved and with the nostrils opening at the end of a double tube in the upper mandible. The length of the body varies from 10 to 35 in (25 to 90 cm), depending on species, and the weight from 3.5 oz to 8.8 lb (100 g to 4 kg).

Differences in specialization and diet help to divide the 59 species of shearwaters into four subfamilies: Fulmarinae, Pachyptilinae, Pterodrominae and Procellariinae. The Fulmarinae range in size from 14 to 36 in (35 to 90 cm) and possess a tall beak, large head, strongly muscled lower mandible, and short tail. The Pachyptilinae are smaller (between 10 and 11 in [25 and 28 cm]) and ash gray in color with a black W-shaped line on the wings and back, similar to that of young kittiwakes (*Rissa tridactyla*); the bill is particularly broad, with filtrating pads. The Pterodrominae comprise 27 species in two genera, measuring from 10 to 18 in (25 to 45 cm) and identifiable by their short, powerful, sharp-edged beak. The Procellariinae are also of average size (11 – 22 in [28 – 55 cm]) and the nostrils of the slender bill open obliquely upwards.

The Procellariidae are distributed all over the world. The Fulmarinae are birds of the southern hemisphere, with the exception of the fulmar (*Fulmarus glacialis*), present in the Atlantic, the North Pacific and the adjacent arctic seas. This species is notable for its characteristically active, darting form of flight, with sudden changes of direction in which the feet seem to be employed as rudders. Very common in northern Europe, the fulmar has a light and dark color phase. The latter, for reasons that are still being studied, is predominant only on Spitzbergen (about 95 per cent), but is rare elsewhere, as in Ireland where it represents only 1 per cent of the population.

The giant fulmars of the genus *Macronectes* have a wingspan of around 6½ ft (2 m); they are antarctic and sub-antarctic birds, nesting in New Zealand and other smaller islands. Of the two species, *M. halli* and *M. giganteus*, the former is the more northerly, but both

Manx shearwater
(*Puffinus puffinus*)

▲ The Procellariidae are medium-sized birds li sea. They return to land only in the breeding and are seldom observed. They fly on the oce currents, occasionally flapping their wings to little altitude.

▼ The shearwater's bill is furnished with tubu nostrils like those of all Procellariiformes; the exude the salt filtered from the sea water dru the bird. The shearwater's sense of smell is so that it can find its mate and nest in pitch dark

live alongside each other on Macquarie Island. Here they do not compete, for the first lays eggs in August and the second in October. Furthermore, the southern species tends to be more colonial than its relative. The plumage of the two species varies only in shading, but the coloration of the bill is a sure guide to identification.

The Procellariidae, except during the breeding season, spend their life at sea, braving the most violent storms, skimming continuously over the waves and flying in broad circles, taking advantage of the slightest rising air currents and breaths of wind to go into its glides. Evidently these birds can spend considerable periods without sleep. Their food is comprised of crustaceans, cephalopod mollusks (mainly squid), fish, and plankton which are sometimes caught beneath the surface. They swoop on any type of organic waste matter that happens to be available and for this reason follow in the wake of fishing vessels for hours on end.

These birds are easily recognized by their characteristic skimming flight low over the waves. Apart from a few species that nest directly on the ground, most make use of holes or rock cavities to lay their egg. The single egg is white and very large in proportion to the adult bird's size. Incubation lasts 40–60 days, according to species, and both partners take turns to guard the egg for periods of between 2 and 12 days. The young, covered in two successive layers of brownish or grayish down, are fed on the regurgitated oily pulp of fish and other marine animals, inserting their bill sideways into that of the parent. When threatened by an enemy (and on some islands shearwater chicks are hunted by rats), they bring up their stomach oil, which in certain cases can be spat out to a distance of 3 ft (1 m).

The Procellariidae are the most remarkable of all migrating birds, winging their way across the boundless oceans and always returning to their birthplace. Ancient writers such as Pliny, Virgil, Ovid, and others coined the name *Avis diomedea* for a bird from the Tremiti Islands in the Adriatic, which during the night let out sounds similar to those of a crying baby. The name *Avis diomedea* arose from an ancient superstition, for the birds were taken to be the reincarnated souls of the companions of Diomedes, condemned to wander the seas for ever.

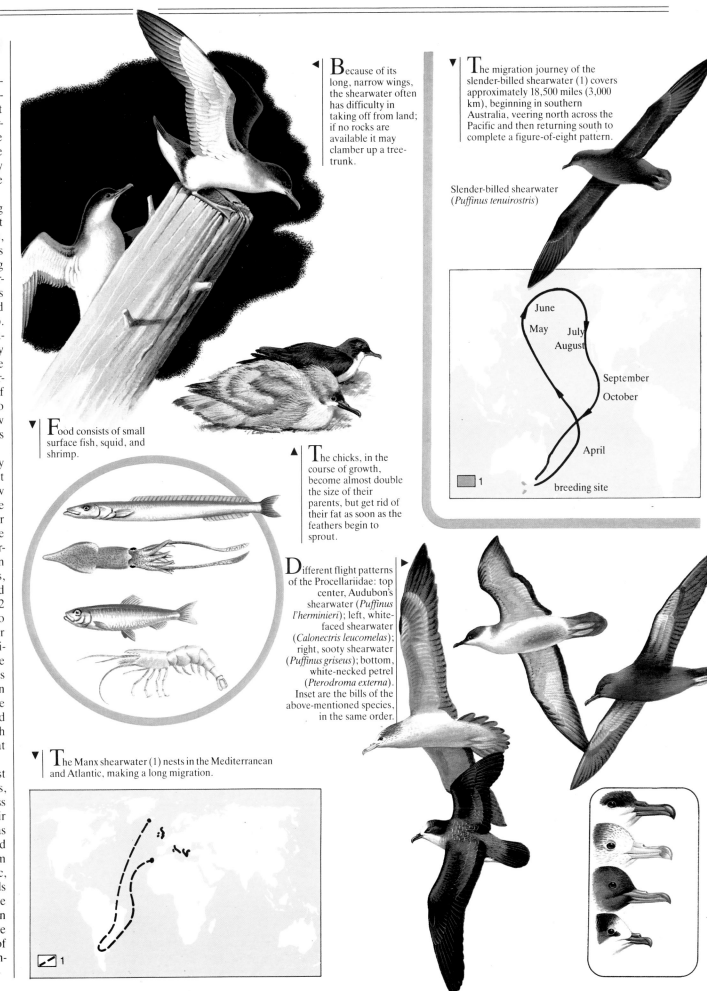

◀ **B**ecause of its long, narrow wings, the shearwater often has difficulty in taking off from land; if no rocks are available it may clamber up a tree-trunk.

▼ **F**ood consists of small surface fish, squid, and shrimp.

▲ **T**he chicks, in the course of growth, become almost double the size of their parents, but get rid of their fat as soon as the feathers begin to sprout.

▼ **T**he migration journey of the slender-billed shearwater (1) covers approximately 18,500 miles (3,000 km), beginning in southern Australia, veering north across the Pacific and then returning south to complete a figure-of-eight pattern.

Slender-billed shearwater (*Puffinus tenuirostris*)

June
May   July
August
September
October
April
breeding site
☐ 1

Different flight patterns of the Procellariidae: top center, Audubon's shearwater (*Puffinus l'herminieri*); left, white-faced shearwater (*Calonectris leucomelas*); right, sooty shearwater (*Puffinus griseus*); bottom, white-necked petrel (*Pterodroma externa*). Inset are the bills of the above-mentioned species, in the same order.

▼ **T**he Manx shearwater (1) nests in the Mediterranean and Atlantic, making a long migration.

⬚ 1

PELE-CANIFORMES

The order Pelecaniformes groups together birds whose four fingers are joined by a complete web. They are furnished with large air sacs, sometimes dilatable, as is the case with frigate-birds. The skin hangs loosely on the body, the bill is long and sturdy, and the upper mandible is composed of visibly sutured horny plates. As a rule, the nostrils are closed and the tongue atrophied. At the base of the lower mandible is an elastic gular pouch. The wings are very long and, in certain species, very wide as well. The eggs are somewhat elliptical, colored uniformly white or greenish, with a chalky shell.

The order is subdivided into 6 families: Anhingidae (2 species), Sulidae (9 species), Fregatidae (5 species), Phaëthontidae (3 species), Pelecanidae (8 species) and Phalacrocoracidae (29 species).

The Anhingidae, also known as darters or snakebirds because of their long, snake-like neck which is made up of 20 vertebrae, are distinguished by the structure of the joints and muscles attached to the eighth and ninth cervical vertebrae. This enables them to flex the neck with lightning speed so as to harpoon fish under water by means of their long, narrow, pointed and slightly saw-edged bill. The back of the skull is equipped with a small, bony stylet. The body is fairly slender and about 3 ft (1 m) in length. These birds frequent fresh and brackish water in tropical and subtropical zones as far as the Mediterranean region, Florida, New Zealand, and Argentina.

The Sulidae (gannets and boobies) are large birds, measuring from 30 to 40 in (70 to 100 cm) in length and weighing between 3¼ and 7½ lb (1.5 and 3.5 kg). The pointed wings facilitate sustained flight and the wedge-shaped tail comprises 12 – 18 rectrices. The nostrils are closed, so that the beak is often kept partially open for breathing. The naked skin of the head and the toes is generally brightly colored. The air sacs are linked with the lungs and can also be inflated at will. The plumage is white or dark brown.

Gannets and boobies are capable of diving to a depth of 30 – 50 ft (10 – 15 m)

Cormorants swim by moving their legs sideways to the body whereas other aquatic birds, as for example the divers, move them under the body.

Pelicans are found in many tropical and temperate regions. They live on inland bodies of water, fresh and brackish, apart from the brown pelican, which has typical marine habits. 1) Brown pelican (*Pelecanus occidentalis*); 2) White pelican (*P. onocrotalus*); 3) Australian pelican (*P. conspicillatus*); 4) American white pelican (*P. erythrorhynchos*).

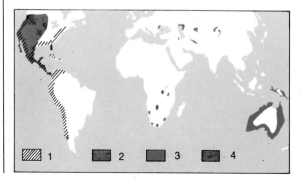

The order Pelecaniformes comprises totipalmate birds, with fully webbed feet, including the rear toe, in contrast to other aquatic birds. They capture prey by diving from a moderate height or by swimming and pursuing the victim under water. Apparently the order evolved from *Elopteryx*, a bird that lived in the Cretaceous, between 135 and 70 million years ago. In addition to the Pelecanidae (pelicans) there are five other families in the order, namely Phalacrocoracidae (cormorants), Anhingidae (anhingas), Fregatidae (frigate-birds), Phaëthontidae (tropic-birds) and Sulidae (gannets and boobies). The drawings below depict representative species of these five families.

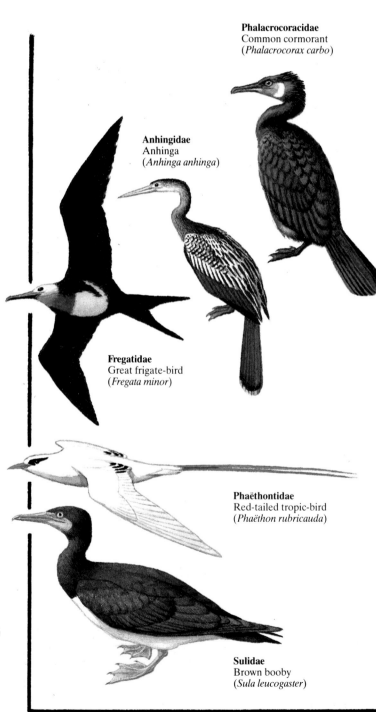

Phalacrocoracidae
Common cormorant
(*Phalacrocorax carbo*)

Anhingidae
Anhinga
(*Anhinga anhinga*)

Fregatidae
Great frigate-bird
(*Fregata minor*)

Phaëthontidae
Red-tailed tropic-bird
(*Phaëthon rubricauda*)

Sulidae
Brown booby
(*Sula leucogaster*)

to catch fish, descending at the rate of about three feet (a meter) per second. Tropical species do not dive from a very great height and enter the water at a more oblique angle. Food consists of fish and cephalopods. They are colonial birds, nesting very close to one another. Females lay 1 – 2 eggs, pale blue with a chalky white shell, and these are incubated by both parents.

The frigate-birds of the family Fregatidae, also known as man-o'-war birds, are the most accomplished fliers of all the Pelecaniformes. The nostrils are small and the long, powerful beak is concave in shape with a strongly hooked tip. They are large birds, measuring 29 – 44 in (75 – 112 cm) in length and weighing 3¼ lb (1.5 kg), with very large pectoral muscles that constitute about one half of the body weight. A large patch of skin under the throat is naked, the head is elongated, the wings are very long (spanning more than 6 ft [2 m]), and the tail, too, is long and forked, with 12 rectrices. The tarsi, however, are short and there is only a partial web between the toes, reduced at the base; the toes are furnished with long, curved claws. The plumage is black or partially white. Males are smaller than females. All species are excellent fliers, inhabiting the warm waters of inter-tropical seas, with a temperature of at least 77°F (25°C).

Of the five known species, the largest is the magnificent frigate-bird (*Fregata magnificens*), with a wingspan of up to 7 ft 11 in (240 cm). Frigate-birds mainly inhabit ocean zones where there are plenty of flying fish, their favorite prey, caught on the surface usually in the early hours of the morning. They are also capable of attacking other large birds, such as gannets and boobies, and snatching their prey; and they often feed on the nidifugous chicks of terns and sometimes of other sea birds. Their distribution appears to be limited by the distances from the coasts that can be covered in a single day.

The tropic-birds, also nicknamed bosun birds, are so called because of their habit of never straying beyond tropical seas; and they have a merited reputation of being tireless, exceptional fliers. They dive from on high into the water, closing their wings to catch flying fish, cephalopods and crustaceans, which are swallowed while the birds bob about on the surface. They often hunt in pairs.

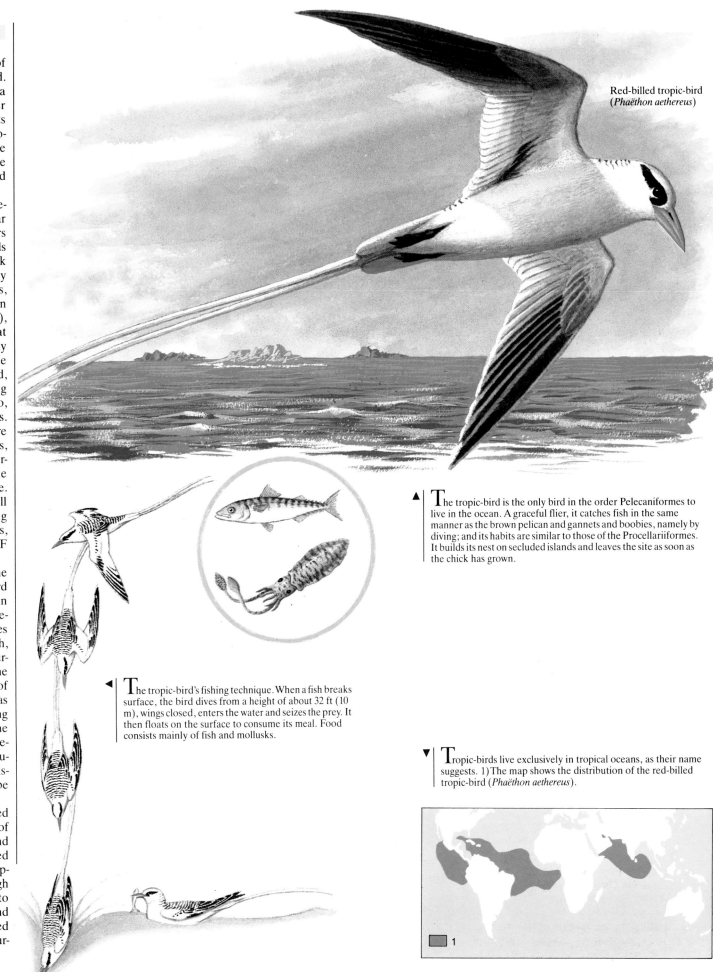

Red-billed tropic-bird
(*Phaëthon aethereus*)

▲ The tropic-bird is the only bird in the order Pelecaniformes to live in the ocean. A graceful flier, it catches fish in the same manner as the brown pelican and gannets and boobies, namely by diving; and its habits are similar to those of the Procellariiformes. It builds its nest on secluded islands and leaves the site as soon as the chick has grown.

◄ The tropic-bird's fishing technique. When a fish breaks surface, the bird dives from a height of about 32 ft (10 m), wings closed, enters the water and seizes the prey. It then floats on the surface to consume its meal. Food consists mainly of fish and mollusks.

▼ Tropic-birds live exclusively in tropical oceans, as their name suggests. 1) The map shows the distribution of the red-billed tropic-bird (*Phaëthon aethereus*).

1

WHITE PELICAN

Pelecanus onocrotalus

Order Pelecaniformes
Family Pelicanidae
Size Length 43 – 70 in (110 – 178 cm)
Weight 15 – 31 lbs (7 – 14 kg)
Distribution Europe, Asia, Africa, America, and Australia
Habits Gregarious and migratory
Nesting In trees or on ground
Reproductive period Spring and summer
Incubation 30 – 42 days
Eggs 2 – 3
Chicks Inept
Sexual maturity 3 – 4 years

Pelicans are large birds, commonly associated wtih tracts of water, either fresh or brackish. Their large, broad wings, spanning almost 10 ft (3 m), facilitate the characteristic gliding flight. The bill is very large and the upper mandible terminates in a small hook. From the lower mandible hangs a voluminous, dilatable pouch, with a capacity of 2 gallons (13 liters) and this gives the bird its characteristic and easily recognizable appearance. The pouch not only stores fish but is used as a net to catch them. The plumage is white or dark gray in the adults of the various species but immature individuals tend to be darker in color.

Pelicans live in tropical and temperate regions, where they are fairly numerous. There are five species in the Old World and three in America. All normally live on tracts of inland waters, both fresh and brackish, except for brown pelicans which are marine birds. Pollution of wetlands and coastal areas has played a significant part in reducing the numbers of these birds.

Although pelicans occasionally feed on crustaceans, worms, and organic refuse, they are, first and foremost, fishing birds. Their technique for catching fish varies according to species and provides an additional clue for distinguishing the two main types of pelican. White pelicans indulge in communal fishing while the brown ones catch their prey by diving. The former technique is the more widespread. Several birds form a semicircle in the water and beat their wings against the surface, driving all the fish in the vicinity towards a single

White pelican (*Pelecanus onocrotalus*)

▲ Pelicans, among the largest of all aquatic birds, are famous for the pouch of skin hanging from the lower mandible, which is used for netting fish. Their feet are webbed and this extends to the rear toe as well. There are white and brown pelicans, each with a different method of catching fish, their principal prey.

Foot of a pelican: all four toes are joined by a single web. ▶

place where the water is generally quite shallow. Once trapped, all the pelicans in the group can easily scoop up the victims in their elastic pouch. The second type of fishing technique, diving, is employed exclusively by the brown pelicans (*P. occidentalis* and *P. thagus*). These birds reconnoiter above the sea, usually in small groups, each individual some distance from the others; as soon as they detect a zone full of fish, particularly anchovies (*Eugralis ringens*), they start performing a series of extraordinary dives, rather like those of the closely related gannets and boobies, sometimes from a height of 66 ft (20 m).

With their large, broad wings, pelicans glide with extreme elegance, resembling birds of prey and storks. Pelicans are not nearly so graceful, indeed quite ungainly, when walking on land or taking off from the water; in the latter case, they have to push repeatedly with the feet in order to gain the necessary upward thrust. Thanks to the air sacs under the skin which help to buoy up their heavy body in water, pelicans are good swimmers. These birds are also famous for their migrations and ornithologists have frequently observed immense concentrations of adults and immature individuals outside the normal breeding areas, mainly in the autumn and early spring but occasionally in the summer as well.

During the courtship period pelicans build a nest with reeds, twigs, and scraps of vegetation. The female lays 2 – 3 bluish or yellowish eggs with a dirty white calcareous shell. She takes up her position in the nest some days before laying the eggs, but the duration of incubating is not exactly known, ranging from 30 to 42 days. The naked, completely inept chicks remain in the nest for a period that varies from 85 to 105 days.

The parent birds swallow the prey and reduce it to a consistent pulp inside the crop; then it is regurgitated into the expansible pouch beneath the lower mandible so that the chicks can thrust in the whole head at right angles for feeding. During the first few days of life this is a tricky operation for the baby.

The pelican has had a long relationship with man. Easily recognized by its distinctive anatomy, the bird may have inspired the earliest human fishing techniques.

▼ In Europe the pelican is known as a bird of the spring and summer, migrating enormous distances by virtue of its capacity for gliding flight.

▲ When hunting fish, pelicans take up a semicircular position in calm water, flapping their wings vigorously so as to drive their victims towards one place where they can easily be caught. They are often assisted by other birds, including cormorants and gulls.

◄ During the breeding season the pelican's head is tinged pale pink and the rostrum of the bill turns reddish. The nest consists of a heap of sticks and twigs and is placed either in a tree or on the ground, hidden in a reed-bed.

▼ Method of feeding the young.

▲ Silhouette in flight.

▲ Fishing technique of the brown pelican (*Pelecanus occidentalis*). When it sights prey in the water, it dives with closed wings, extending its entire neck like a dart.

▼ Left, the Dalmatian pelican, identifiable by the tuft on the nape; center, the American white pelican; right, the Australian pelican during the breeding season.

COMMON CORMORANT

Phalacrocorax carbo

Order Pelecaniformes
Family Phalacrocracidae
Size Length 18 – 36 in (48 – 92 cm)
Weight 1½ – 7½ lb (0.7 – 3.5 kg)
Distribution Worldwide, excluding polar regions
Habits Colonial; some species migratory
Nesting In trees and rocks
Reproductive period Spring – summer or winter – spring
Incubation 27 – 30 days
Eggs 2 – 4
Chicks Inept
Sexual maturity 3 years

One distinctive feature of cormorants is the skull, characterized by a supplementary bony stylet behind the occiput. Into this is inserted a band of sphincter muscles which constrict the head and neck and which make it possible to keep a hold on prey. The neck is long, the wings are fairly small and rounded. The bill is cylindrical at the base but terminates in a large hook. The bones are not very pneumatic and the body weight is relatively high so that the birds swim mainly submerged. The plumage is relatively permeable, lacking any secretion from the uropygial gland, which is absent; for that reason cormorants bathe in the water and spend several hours a day perched, often with wings open, drying themselves.

There are 29 known species of cormorants. Size varies a great deal, from 18 to 36 in (48 to 92 cm) in length, as does the weight, from 1½ to 7½ lb (0.7 to 3.5 kg). The plumage is generally dark, but species from the southern hemisphere also have white underparts.

Cormorants are found almost everywhere, except for the polar regions: Of present-day species, eight live only in America, eleven in Europe, Asia and Africa, six in Australia and the remaining four virtually all over the globe. Cormorants are also remarkable migrants. Thanks to ringing, it has been possible to follow their mass movements quite thoroughly; and because the birds are frequently hunting victims, a high proportion of ringed individuals are recovered in this way.

Common cormorant
(*Phalacrocorax carbo*)

▲ Cormorants, belonging to the order Pelecaniformes, are expert at fishing. They catch their prey by swimming underwater to a depth of about 33 ft (10 m) or even, exceptionally, to 100 ft (30 m). The rather stiff tail helps them to maintain standing position. The body weight is quite high and this makes underwater swimming easier. In western Europe there are two species of cormorant, shown on the left, the common cormorant and the shag.

▼ Common cormorant (left) and shag in flight.

Shag (*Phalacrocorax aristotelis*)

Cormorants acquire their adult livery in the second year of life but are only capable of reproducing in their third year. The nesting site is chosen by the male who tries to attract the female with a special form of nuptial display, raising and lowering his wings repeatedly and folding the primary remiges behind the secondary and tertiary feathers. Nest-building materials are assembled by the male but the female partner helps in the construction as soon as the eggs are laid. From that moment the nest is not left empty, even for the shortest period. Both birds take it in turns to incubate. Incubation of the 2 – 4 eggs lasts 27 – 30 days. The chicks remain naked for about seven days, demanding food by chirping and opening the beak wide. As they grow, they cease to chirp but simply point their bill at the parent's throat, flapping their wings; this action stimulates the adult to regurgitate semi-digested fish from the esophagus so that the chicks can get to it.

All species feed chiefly on fish but the diet may also include cephalopod mollusks, crustaceans, and amphibians. Because their plumage is not impermeable they can slip silently into the water, like the darters, but they, too, have to expose their feathers to the air so as to dry off. They also spend many hours every day cleaning themselves, two birds often tending to each other's needs. They observe more or less fixed hours during the day for fishing and for the rest of the time perch in groups or individually on rocks or trees, normally in full view. They have a distinctive method of swimming, using the feet only and moving them in turn on either side of the body, the tail serving only as a rudder. After fishing they pause to digest their food; and should they be disturbed in the process, they are forced to bring up the entire meal in order to take wing.

In some parts of the world cormorants are still hunted because of the alleged harm they do in catching their daily ration of fish. The truth is, however, that the birds feed on comparatively small fish and also on the less healthy individuals which are easier to capture, thus operating an effective system of natural selection. In Africa and Asia (particularly in Japan) cormorants are still caught and kept in captivity as an aid to fishing in rivers and seas. The birds are trained to fly home and then let loose with a hemp or leather ring around their neck to prevent them swallowing any fish they catch.

▲ Cormorants swim with almost the whole body submerged because of their weight, keeping the legs on either side.

▲ They capture fish at a depth of about 10 ft (3 m) and can stay under water for up to a minute.

▲ The reason cormorants perch with wings open may be both behavioral and practical. It is a way of keeping distance between one another and at the same time enables them to dry their feathers in the sun.

▲ The parents regurgitate half-digested food for their young.

▲ The meal is eaten in the water.

Red-legged cormorant (*Phalacrocorax gaimardi*)

▲ Cormorants form vast colonies and large quantities of their droppings are exported from Peru as guano, a high-quality fertilizer.

Flightless cormorant (*Nannopterum harrisi*)

Temminck's cormorant (*Phalacrocorax capillatus*)

▲ Abundance of food has rendered the wings of the flightless cormorant of the Galapagos completely useless; they are, in fact, atrophied.

◄ Cormorants are distributed almost throughout the world, with the exception of the polar regions. 1) Shag (*Phalacrocorax aristotelis*); 2) Flightless cormorant (*Nannopterum harrisi*); 3) Red-legged cormorant (*P. gaimardi*); 4) Common cormorant (*P. carbo*), the species with the widest distribution, found almost all over the world; 5) Temminck's cormorant (*P. capillatus*).

ANHINGA

Anhinga anhinga

Order Pelecaniformes
Family Anhingidae
Size Length 36 in (90 cm)
Distribution Tropical America
Habits Aquatic; gregarious in breeding season
Nesting In trees, sometimes on ground
Eggs 2 – 5
Chicks Nidicolous

There are two species of anhingas, water birds inhabiting tropical and subtropical regions all over the world: the anhinga (*Anhinga anhinga*) from America and the African darter (*A. rufa*).

Anhingas, also known as darters or snakebirds (because of their long, flexible neck) have an elongated body, a hooked bill and a very long, slender neck composed of 20 vertebrae; the eighth and ninth vertebrae possess a bony outgrowth, into which are inserted powerful muscles that allow the neck to fold into an S-shape and to be released like a spring. The feet are wholly webbed for easy movement through the water.

The American anhinga is widely distributed in the southern parts of the United States, extending its range to Central America and northern Argentina. It lives in lakes and freshwater swamps as well as river estuaries thickly planted with mangroves. The bird feeds on fish and other aquatic creatures (crustaceans, mollusks, and insects).

During the courtship display both birds face each other, tail raised, head resting on neck, beak down and holding a twig. The male then assembles branches and twigs for the nest and the female arranges them in the form of a platform.

The pale blue-green eggs have the same calcareous covering as those of cormorants and are incubated by both parents for 25 – 28 days. The chicks are fed by the parents with partially digested regurgitated pulp.

Anhingas or darters are able to expel all air from their plumage, enabling them to submerge completely and silently. Prey consist of fish, crustaceans, frogs, salamanders, aquatic insects, and larvae.

The birds spend many hours a day on a perch protrud from the water in order to dry their plumage, the open-winged posture being typical, too, of cormorants.

The drawing shows the perfect fishing technique of th anhinga. The S-shaped neck is thrust out and the bill impales the fish which is then tossed in the air to be swallowed, head first.

Anhingas inhabit the tropical, equatorial and subtropical regions of the world. According to some authors there are only two species: 1) Anhinga (*Anhinga anhinga*) from the New World; 2) African darter (*Anhinga rufa*) from the Old World.

1
2

BROWN BOOBY

Sula leucogaster

Order Pelecaniformes
Family Sulidae
Length 25 – 29 in (64 – 74 cm)
Distribution Atlantic, Pacific and Indian Oceans
Habits Marine, gregarious
Eggs 1 or 2, sometimes 3
Nesting On ground
Chicks Nidicolous

Gannets and boobies are large sea birds which visit land only for breeding purposes. Their body is streamlined, the wings are long and narrow, and the strong, conical bill has sharply notched edges towards the front.

The birds have a powerful, gliding flight, the grace of which is enhanced by the presence of large air sacs beneath the skin. They feed on fish and other sea animals which are caught under the surface after a spectacular dive from quite some height.

The colors of the brown booby's plumage are clear and distinct, the head and top of the body chocolate brown, the underparts white. The legs are yellow, the bill bluish and the naked facial skin yellow to purple. The young are uniformly brown. The adult wingspan is about 60 in (150 cm).

This is the most abundant species in tropical and subtropical areas of the Atlantic, Pacific, and Indian Oceans, never straying too far from rocky coasts or coral reefs where it breeds. Much of the day is spent flying over the sea, short periods of standard flight alternating with long glides above the surface. When it sights a school of fish the booby pauses for an instant in midair, closes its wings and nosedives into the sea. Propelling itself with wings and legs under water, it soon emerges with its prey, ready to take flight again. Sometimes it performs acrobatic movements in pursuit of flying fish.

The breeding cycle of the bird is not strictly annual but often eight monthly, directly linked with the greater or lesser availability of food in the neighborhood of the nesting sites. Nests are located on rocky shores, colonies being of fair size and each pair of breeding birds defending a small territory. The courtship ceremony is quite elaborate, similar in some ways to that of albatrosses.

Fishing technique employed by the northern gannet: the bird dives into the water and drives the fish up to the surface. Flying fish and pelagic cephalopods are among the most frequent victims in tropical zones.

The brown booby breeds on rocky islets. The large webbed feet, with their many blood vessels, cover and warm the eggs during incubation, this method replacing the standard one because the birds have no area of naked skin on the belly.

During the courtship ritual of the red-footed booby the two birds face each other, bill pointed high, tail spread, wings erect over the back, rocking on their feet. Special importance is attached, in the course of the ceremony, to displaying the brightly colored, naked parts of the body (beak, face, and legs).

The members of the family Sulidae live in warm and temperate seas and in the North Atlantic as far as the Polar Circle. The map shows the distribution of two species: 1) Brown booby (*Sula leucogaster*); 2) Red-footed booby (*S. sula*).

MAGNIFICENT FRIGATE-BIRD

Fregata magnificens

Order Pelecaniformes
Family Fregatidae
Size Length 40 – 44 in (103 – 112 cm), head to tail
Wingspan About 7½ ft (2.3 m)
Weight 3 – 3¼ lb (1.4 – 1.5 kg)
Distribution Galapagos, Antilles and Cape Verde Islands
Habits Gregarious
Nesting In trees or on shrubs, sometimes on rocks
Eggs 1
Chicks Nidicolous

The best fliers in the order Pelecaniformes are the frigate-birds of the family Fregatidae. Half the total weight consists of the pectoral muscles and feathers; so because of their fairly low wing load they are among the most accomplished of all gliding birds, with great powers of endurance. Their wings are very long and narrow with pointed tips. The male has iridescent black plumage with metallic-blue tints. Under his throat is a pouch of naked skin, rough in texture and colored dull orange, except during the breeding season when it swells up and turns crimson. The female is slightly larger than the male and her sooty-black plumage, with grayish overtones and no blue reflections, is less spectacular. She has a white patch on the breast and no red gular pouch.

The magnificent frigate-bird lives in tropical zones of the eastern Pacific and Atlantic Oceans. Naturalists, travelers, sailors, and all who have seen this bird cannot fail to be impressed by its elegant and most unusual silhouette in flight. In the air this bird is unrivaled for speed and grace, soaring and gliding for hours with occasional lazy flaps of its huge wings. The outline is unmistakable as it rides the winds tirelessly and with no hint of effort, vigilant for signs of life below. In addition to possessing enormous powers of endurance, the bird has an exceptionally keen sense of direction, this being absolutely essential in the ocean where there are virtually no guidelines apart from the sun and the stars.

The magnificent frigate-bird is noted for its parasitic habits, and

▲
◄ The magnificent frigate-bird, like other species belonging to the same family, is an excellent flier. The plumage of the males (shown here in flight) is shiny black with blue reflections; and the throat is adorned with a crimson pouch of naked skin. The female (shown perched) is duller in hue with a whitish patch on the breast. This species spends much of the time in the air, moving slowly and awkwardly on land: for this reason it usually perches or rests fairly high up, in trees or on rocks and cliffs, from which vantage points it can easily take wing.

▲ Because the species has such markedly aerial habits, the feet have adapted by losing most of the interdigital webbing that typifies other Pelecaniformes. The birds compensate for poor swimming and walking powers by the development of prehensile claws that are ideal for gripping branches and rocks.

▲ Food consists in the main of tiny marine creatures, especially flying fish, cuttlefish, small turtles, and jellyfish.

because of its flying powers it manages to obtain much of its food by pursuing other birds such as gulls, cormorants, pelicans, and, above all, boobies, harassing and tormenting them until they regurgitate the fish they have only recently swallowed. The frigate-bird swoops down on the morsel neatly catching it before it can hit the ground or water. Because the frigate-bird's plumage contains little oil, it is relatively porous and rapidly soaked. For this reason the bird never dives but fishes only at the surface, merely dipping its long beak in the water.

This species tends to nest at any time of year. Materials include sticks and dry branches, collected in the bill and for the most part taken on the wing either from the ground or from nests of other birds. The nest is situated on or near the shore, generally in trees or low bushes, but also on cliffs or hillside slopes, sites where it is as easy to land as to take off. Breeding colonies are close to those of other sea birds such as boobies, cormorants, pelicans, terns, gulls, etc., all of which are regularly parasitized by the frigate-bird.

Prior to mating, the birds indulge in courtship and nuptial displays. The males crouch on the nests while the females circle over the sites where the chicks are to be born and reared. When a male sights a possible mate, he opens his wings, trembles and lets out excited cries; at the same time he shakes his head rhythmically from left to right and vica versa, neck thrown back so as to give special prominence to the huge gular pouch of naked skin, now bright crimson and so taut and swollen with air that it seems about to burst. The pouch is a visual signal, serving both to attract the female and to mark out each individual portion of territory. After a courtship of varying duration the birds mate and the female subsequently lays a single white egg which weighs about 3½ oz (100 g). Incubation lasts appoximately 40 – 50 days and is undertaken by both parents, who also continue to collaborate in raising the young.

The magnificent frigate-bird, like many social animals, has a certain aptitude for learning. This fact, plus its keen directional sense, has been exploited by some local people who have managed to train the bird in the manner of a homing pigeon. In parts of the tropics, therefore, this species is used for transmitting information and messages from island to island.

▼ The magnificent frigate-bird often procures food by robbing other birds such as boobies, pursuing them until they regurgitate the prey they have barely swallowed. The frigate-bird then adroitly catches the fish before it hits the ground or water.

▼ The bird can also directly capture various small animals such as flying fish, grabbing them by the dorsal fins that protrude above the surface, or baby turtles, only just hatched, as the latter make their way down to the sea.

During the courtship period the male frigate-bird boasts a large pouch of naked red skin under the throat, which fills with air and inflates. This serves to attract the female to the chosen nesting site and also stakes out the individual male's territory. During rest and at times other than the breeding season, this pouch dwindles in size and turns dull orange.

▼ The nest is made of branches and twigs, collected from the ground or from the nests of other species.

◀ The family Fregatidae comprises five similar species, inhabiting the tropical belts of all the world's oceans. They are, however, restricted to particular islands or archipelagos. 1) Magnificent frigate-bird (*Fregata magnificens*), nesting in the eastern Pacific (Galapagos and neighboring islands) and the Atlantic (Antilles, Cape Verde Islands); 2) Ascension frigate-bird (*F. aquila*), an Atlantic species exclusive to Ascension Island, where there are 2,000-3,000 individuals; 3) Christmas Island frigate-bird (*F. andrewsi*) from the Indian Ocean (Christmas Island and neighboring islands); 4) Lesser frigate-bird (*F. ariel*), found on some islands in the Atlantic (Trinidad), the Indian Ocean (Aldabra), and the eastern and southern Pacific; 5) Great frigate-bird (*F. minor*), inhabiting various islands in the Atlantic (Trinidad), the Indian Ocean (Seychelles, Aldabra), and the Pacific (Galapagos, Hawaii, Laysan).

1
2
3
4
5

CICONIIFORMES

The most obvious characteristic of all the Ciconiiformes (storks, herons, ibises, etc.) are the long legs, designed for wading in shallow water, the equally long neck, necessary for reaching food at ground level in counterbalance to the legs, and the large, usually pointed bill, ideal for capturing live prey such as fish and aquatic insects. Body shape and size vary, of course, from one species to another, reflecting adaptations to different environments and individual modes of life; the beaks, in particular, sometimes assume very strange forms as in the shoebill stork or the spoonbill.

The color of the plumage is generally white, gray or black, often with metallic reflections; the naked parts, such as legs and neck, as well as the horny beak, may be red or bright yellow. The birds are medium-sized or large, the Indian marabou weighing 13 – 15 lb (6 – 7 kg). In flight, the true storks hold their long legs behind them, forming a straight line with the outstretched neck, so that the broad, voluminous wings create a cross-shaped silhouette; the herons, however, keep their neck folded and the head tucked between the shoulders.

The Ciconiiformes inhabit every continent, except for Arctic and Antarctic zones, most species being found in Africa and tropical Asia.

These birds mainly frequent zones of shallow water such as swamps and the edges of lakes and rivers, their distribution being determined by these surroundings; but some species, such as the white stork, are often found on steppes and cultivated grasslands, while the hermit ibis shows a preference for arid and desert habitats.

The species of Ciconiiformes that live in the higher latitudes are migratory, heading toward the equator in winter.

Ciconiiformes nest in groups or colonies of varying size, numbering up to several thousand pairs. The nests are situated in trees, among marsh vegetation or, more rarely, on rock ledges (hermit ibis). The most common type of nest is a huge pile of branches or interlaced reeds, slightly cup-shaped.

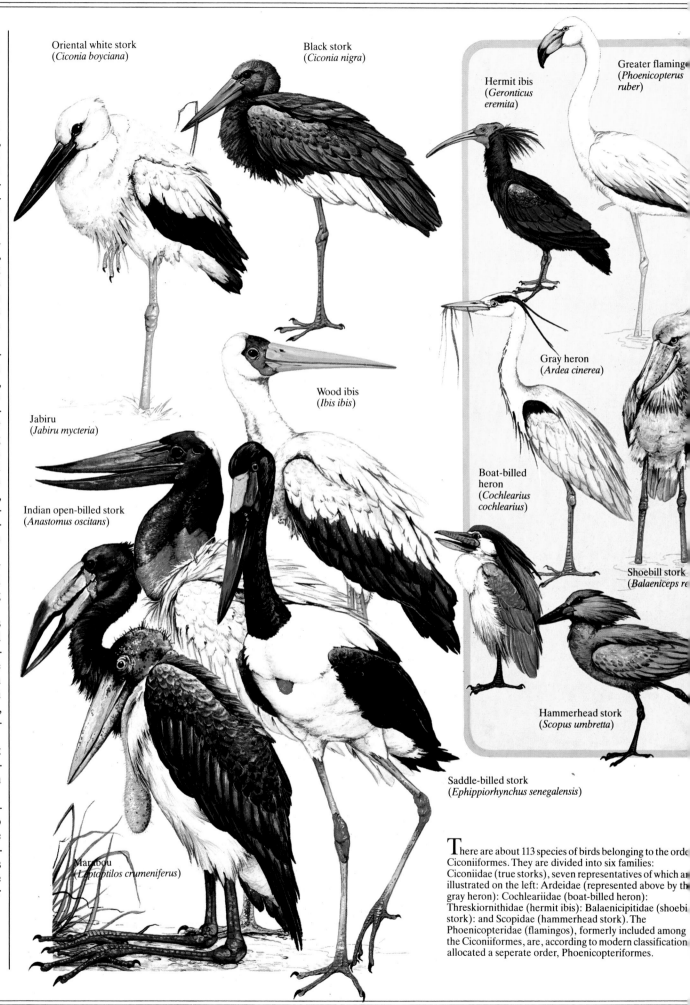

Oriental white stork
(*Ciconia boyciana*)

Black stork
(*Ciconia nigra*)

Hermit ibis
(*Geronticus eremita*)

Greater flamingo
(*Phoenicopterus ruber*)

Jabiru
(*Jabiru mycteria*)

Wood ibis
(*Ibis ibis*)

Gray heron
(*Ardea cinerea*)

Indian open-billed stork
(*Anastomus oscitans*)

Boat-billed heron
(*Cochlearius cochlearius*)

Shoebill stork
(*Balaeniceps re...*)

Hammerhead stork
(*Scopus umbretta*)

Saddle-billed stork
(*Ephippiorhynchus senegalensis*)

Marabou
(*Leptoptilos crumeniferus*)

There are about 113 species of birds belonging to the order Ciconiiformes. They are divided into six families: Ciconiidae (true storks), seven representatives of which ar illustrated on the left: Ardeidae (represented above by th gray heron): Cochleariidae (boat-billed heron): Threskiornithidae (hermit ibis): Balaenicipitidae (shoebi stork): and Scopidae (hammerhead stork). The Phoenicopteridae (flamingos), formerly included among the Ciconiiformes, are, according to modern classification allocated a seperate order, Phoenicopteriformes.

MARABOU STORK

Leptoptilos crumeniferus

Order Ciconiiformes
Family Ciconiidae
Length 47 in (120 cm)
Wingspan 7 ft 11 in (240 cm)
Weight 14 lb (6.5 kg)
Eggs 2 – 3

The marabou or adjutant stork (*Leptoptilos crumeniferus*) is a strange-looking bird, standing 47 in (120 cm) high, with a disproportionately large head, a conical, broad-based bill that measures almost 12 in (30 cm), a sturdy body and long, powerful legs. The neck, with its drooping gular pouch, is naked and red, as is the head with its tiny yellow eyes. The pouch hanging from the throat is not used for storing food because it has a cavity connecting with the breathing apparatus; in fact, the function of this pouch is not known. The plumage is bicolored, blackish above and whitish below; and the feathers on either side of the neck and on the under tail coverts are soft and snow white. The stork spends long periods at rest on the top of a tall tree or on the ground, head tucked between the shoulders, bill turned obliquely downward.

Normally the bird engages in slow, flapping flight, but it can soar gracefully and seemingly without effort to great heights, rising with wings wide open on warm air currents. Although the African species is a large bird, the Indian marabou is even bigger, 5 ft (150 cm) in height.

The marabou stork lives throughout Africa south of the Sahara. Its counterparts in southern Asia are the Indian marabou and another very similar species with almost identical habits. With its varied diet, the marabou is found in many habitats.

Nesting occurs according to the progress of the local rainy season. When the hungry babies are still growing in the nest, the parents are obliged to collect as many insects, amphibians, and other forms of prey as they can, these being easier to catch when the water level in pools and ponds is still quite low. Because of this fact, eggs tend to be laid late in the dry season, so that the chicks can grow at about the start of the rainy season.

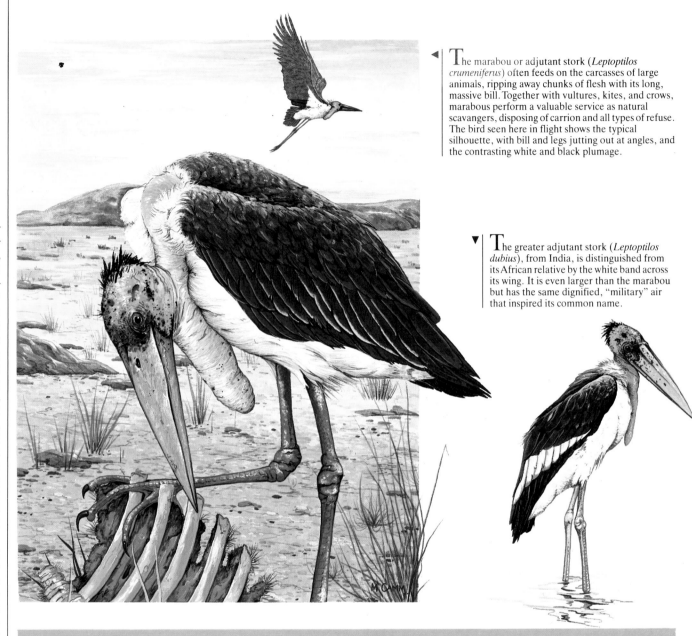

The marabou or adjutant stork (*Leptoptilos crumeniferus*) often feeds on the carcasses of large animals, ripping away chunks of flesh with its long, massive bill. Together with vultures, kites, and crows, marabous perform a valuable service as natural scavangers, disposing of carrion and all types of refuse. The bird seen here in flight shows the typical silhouette, with bill and legs jutting out at angles, and the contrasting white and black plumage.

The greater adjutant stork (*Leptoptilos dubius*), from India, is distinguished from its African relative by the white band across its wing. It is even larger than the marabou but has the same dignified, "military" air that inspired its common name.

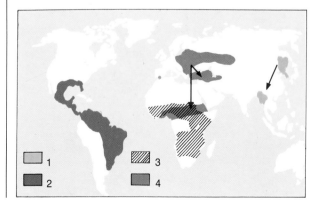

Distribution of some Ciconiiformes.
1) The Oriental white stork (*Ciconia boyciana*) nests in Asia, in the river basins of the Amur and the Ussuri, wintering farther south.
2) The jabiru (*Jabiru mycteria*) lives in America, from southern Mexico and Florida to the Buenos Aires region of Argentina.
3) The marabou (*Leptoptilos crumeniferus*) has a broad distribution in Africa south of the Sahara.
4) The black stork (*Ciconia nigra*) nests in eastern Europe and in certain parts of Spain, wintering in Asia Minor and Africa.

WHITE STORK

Ciconia ciconia

Order Ciconiiformes
Family Ciconiidae
Length 40 – 50 in (102 – 130 cm)
Wingspan 75 – 83 in (190 – 210 cm)
Weight 5½ – 9 lb (2.5 – 4 kg)
Distribution Europe, Asia, and northwest Africa
Habits Gregarious during migration to winter quarters; in pairs during breeding period
Nesting On trees, posts, and pylons with suitable platforms; buildings of all kinds; ruins
Eggs 3 – 5
Chicks Nidicolous

A comparatively large bird, the white stork (*Ciconia ciconia*) is easily distinguished from other European storks by the color of the adults, mainly white, except for the longer scapulars, the greater wing coverts, the primary coverts and the primary and secondary remiges, all of which are shiny black. The bill, the legs, and the feet are red, the naked parts around the beak are black, and the sides of the chin are red. The iris of the eye is gray. Both sexes are similar.

The white stork, with its measured, stately walk, is an elegant bird; and in the air, too, its slow, majestic flight is a marvel of harmony and grace, especially when the bird is gliding and soaring at a great height or when it spirals upward or downward to change altitude. When resting, the stork usually stands on one leg, often pulling back its neck on the shoulders and pointing the beak downward: in this position it looks extremely relaxed and dignified.

Storks fly at considerable heights, making full use of rising warm air currents, with slow, measured wingbeats. They can often be seen from aeroplanes, particularly over their breeding grounds or winter quarters, flying at altitudes of 13,000 – 14,800 ft (4,000 – 4,500 m).

The white stork is represented by two different subspecies. The nominal form nests in northwest Africa (Tunisia, Algeria, and Morocco), in Europe (Portugal, central and western Spain, eastern France, Holland, Germany, Denmark, southern Sweden, Poland, Czechoslovakia, Austria, Hungary, Romania, and the Balkan peninsula), and in Asia (Asia Minor,

▲ A pair of white storks on their nest. This species, in addition to nesting in trees, also settles on rooftops and specially prepared platforms. In central and eastern Europe there are villages with almost every roof accommodating a stork's nest. The particular choice of site is partly due to the fact that ever since the Middle Ages the bird has been considered a symbol of good fortune and treated with respect. As indicated by the illustrations on the opposite page, at bottom right, the stork also builds its nest in ancient ruins and on telegraph wires. The nest is a fairly bulky construction, more than 3 ft (1 m) high, of roughly interlaced branches and twigs; the interior is lined with feathers, moss, grass, and down.

western Iran, northern Israel, and Iraq).

This bird, using rising air currents for its long-distance flights, has been obliged to follow migration routes which take it across those zones where such meteorological conditions occur. Starting from the breeding zones, these migrations clearly branch off in two directions, one to the west and the other to the east; and there is a neat demarcation line between these two routes, extending more or less from Austria (River Lech) to Holland. This imaginary line divides the storks into two groups, one of which nests to the southwest of the line, the other to the northeast.

The white stork generally nests on rooftops, and in central and eastern Europe there are many country villages whose houses each accommodate a nesting pair. The choice of such sites and the relative abundance of such nests stem from the fact that ever since the early Middle Ages this species has been well treated and considered to bring good luck. It finds its food on wet, grassy plains subjected to flooding and in zones covered with pools, rice-paddies, and swamps, sometimes close to habitation.

The storks begin nesting from the end of March and continue all through April. They return from winter quarters individually (in contrast to the departures for the south, when they fly off separately or in large groups), and as a rule the males are first to arrive, usually settling on the nest constructed the previous year. This nest is indeed an impressively large structure, more than 3 ft (1 m) high, made of roughly interlaced sticks and twigs, the interior lined with feathers, moss, down, grass, etc. The materials for building and decorating the nest are usually collected and carried by the male, and arranged in place by the female.

Each family normally lays 3 – 4 white eggs and incubates them at night for a period of 25 – 30 days. The newborn chicks are fed by the parents, inside the nest, on regurgitated food; and as they grow, they are taught by the adults how to pick it up themselves. The young are fed for a period that varies from 53 to 55 days and in some cases for a few weeks after they embark on their first flight.

In Europe many countries have tried to bring in measures to protect the species.

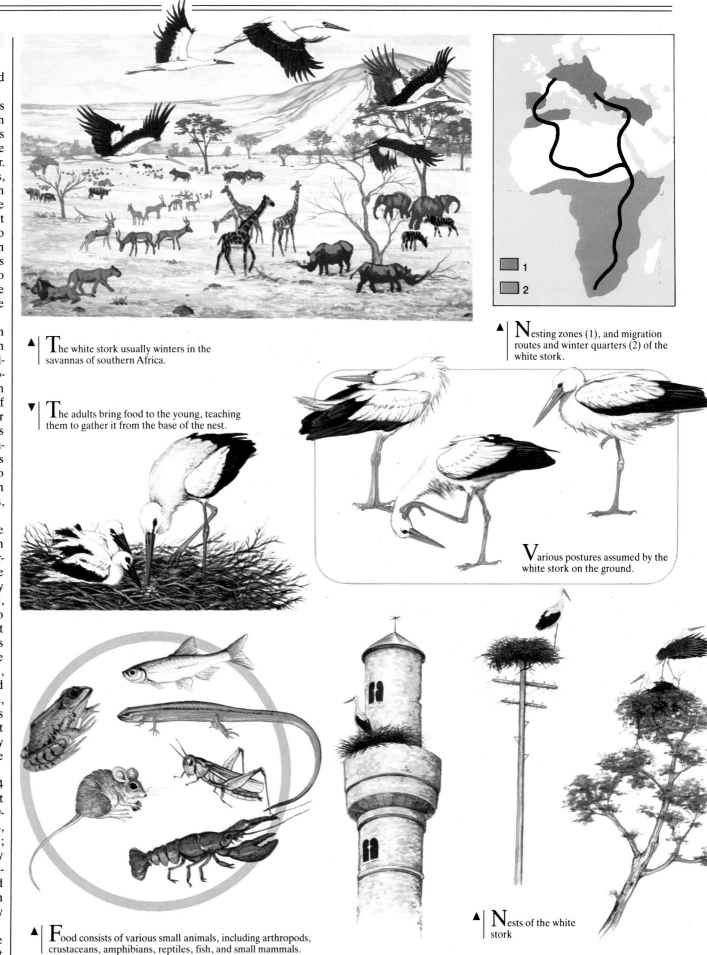

▲ The white stork usually winters in the savannas of southern Africa.

▲ Nesting zones (1), and migration routes and winter quarters (2) of the white stork.

▼ The adults bring food to the young, teaching them to gather it from the base of the nest.

V arious postures assumed by the white stork on the ground.

▲ Food consists of various small animals, including arthropods, crustaceans, amphibians, reptiles, fish, and small mammals.

▲ Nests of the white stork

SACRED IBIS

Threskiornis aethiopica

Order Ciconiiformes
Family Threskiornithidae
Length 26 in (65 – 67 cm)
Distribution Africa and Persian Gulf
Habits Aquatic; gregarious
Nesting On trees, sometimes on ground
Eggs 2 – 4
Chicks Nidicolous

The sacred ibis (*Threskiornis aethiopica*) has a wingspan of about 47 in (120 cm) and white plumage with contrasting black head and neck; the long, down-curved bill, the soft scapular feathers and the tips of the wings are likewise black. The species is found in the tropical and equatorial regions of Africa; and a small population breeds in Iraq. Long ago the bird nested along the banks of the Nile in Egypt, as is shown by hieroglyphics in which it is depicted as symbolizing the god Thoth. It lives in lakes and swamps and on the banks of slow-flowing rivers with mud-banks and thick clumps of reeds and papyrus.

Gregarious by habit, sacred ibises venture out together in quest of food, slowly making their way over mud-flats and sandbanks in wet zones but sometimes settling on cultivated land and dry plains. They feed on insects (especially locusts), crustaceans, and mollusks; and this diet is supplemented by frogs, reptiles, fish, and birds' eggs.

The nests are built in colonies on tall trees, especially acacias, but sometimes on the ground or among rocks and papyrus. The male supplies the materials and the female arranges them into a platform of dry branches, shells and aquatic grasses. The dates for laying eggs, which are white with red spots and blue streaks, vary according to place and climate. As soon as they arrive, the females choose a section of male territory and pairs are then formed. During the courtship ritual the partners face each other, raising and lowering the head, frequently interlocking necks and interrupting the ceremonial from time to time in order to preen the plumage.

Both birds change places, every 24 hours, to incubate the eggs, which hatch after 28 days. Once nesting is over, the birds depart on migrations,

▲ Sacred ibises, elegant birds with black-and-white plumage, feed on a large variety of small creatures that are speared with the long, curved beak. They move in ranks over plains, the sandy banks of rivers and savannas, capturing insects, worms, mollusks, crustaceans, small reptiles, and amphibians. Gregarious by habit, they often associate with other birds that have similar feeding requirements (marabous, storks, and herons) and also spend the night together with them.

◀ Japanese crested ibises are also typical birds of
▶ temperate and subtropical zones. Dramatically diminished in numbers during the nineteenth century as a result of alterations to the environment and intensive hunting, they are very handsome birds with pink-orange plumage. At the approach of the breeding season the roots of the feathers covering the head and the back exude a gray secretion so that these parts of the body turn pure gray. This phenomenon occurs only in this species and the white ibis.

these being more common in the northern parts of the breeding area and conditioned by the availability of food during the dry season.

The hermit ibis (*Geronticus eremita*) boasts splendid black plumage with purple and green reflections. It has the sad distinction, along with the Japanese crested ibis (*Nipponia nippon*), of being one of the rarest birds in the world. Until 1600 the species bred in certain parts of Austria and Switzerland, and possibly also in Italy and Germany: but because both adults and young were ruthlessly hunted, partly to furnish what was considered a rare delicacy at the dinner tables of princes and nobles, the European population was wiped out. Today only a few colonies remain on the Atlas Mountains of Morocco, with another small colony to be found in southern Turkey.

The scarlet ibis (*Eudocimus ruber*) and the white ibis (*E. albus*), substantially differing in the color of their plumage, were once regarded as the same species; the former is an inhabitant of South America (there are about 3,000 pairs in Venezuela) and the latter of Central America. These birds frequent broad stretches of marshland and nest in colonies on mangrove trees, willows, and cacti. Both species are fairly silent and each pair defends a small breeding territory around the nest.

The hadada ibis (*Hagedashia hagedash*) is an exclusively African species, chestnut in color with a white band on the cheeks. It breeds on the wettest savannas, in forest galleries and in woods crisscrossed by rivers, up to an altitude of 6,560 ft (2,000 m). The bird finds its food on cultivated land, in fields, and along rivers. Each pair lives on its own, constructing a nest of dry branches in a tree close to the water.

The glossy ibis (*Plegadis falcinellus*) is the most widely distributed species (although this distribution tends to be somewhat irregular and fragmented). It has a liking for freshwater zones, where it hunts aquatic insects and their larvae, small crustaceans and mollusks, fish, and leeches.

The habitat of the Japanese crested ibis (*Nipponia nippon*) consists of wooded hilly zones. It finds food in rice paddies, swamps, and streams. The nest is flat, made of interlaced twigs in the branches of a tree. It is a migratory bird, breeding in the north and wintering in warmer southern climes.

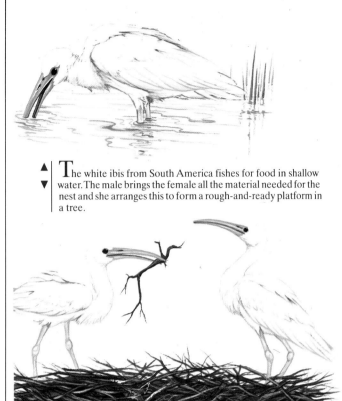

▲ ▼ The white ibis from South America fishes for food in shallow water. The male brings the female all the material needed for the nest and she arranges this to form a rough-and-ready platform in a tree.

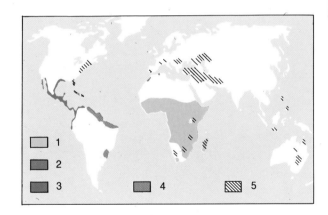

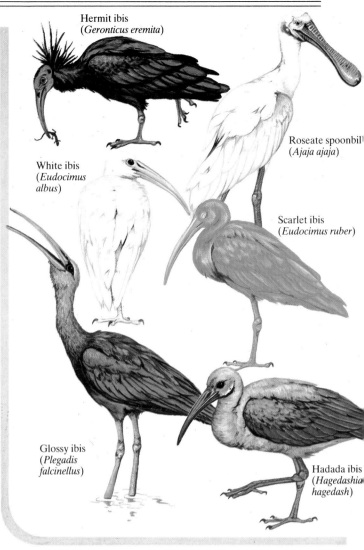

▲ The family Threskiornithidae displays a great variety of forms.

◀ Ibises are typical birds of tropical, subtropical, and warm temperate regions, being found mainly in wet zones. Many species are migratory and regularly cover long distances between breeding grounds and winter quarters. 1) Sacred ibis (*Threskiornis aethiopica*); 2) Hermit ibis (*Geronticus eremita*); 3) White ibis (*Eudocimus albus*); 4) Scarlet ibis (*Eudocimus ruber*); 5) Glossy ibis (*Plegadis falcinellus*).

Hermit ibis (*Geronticus eremita*)

Roseate spoonbill (*Ajaja ajaja*)

White ibis (*Eudocimus albus*)

Scarlet ibis (*Eudocimus ruber*)

Glossy ibis (*Plegadis falcinellus*)

Hadada ibis (*Hagedashia hagedash*)

Japanese crested ibis (*Nipponia nippon*)

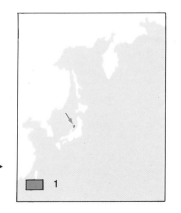

The last six specimens live on the Japanese island of Sado. 1) Japanese crested ibis (*Nipponia nippon*). ▶

1

ROSEATE SPOONBILL

Ajaja ajaja

Order Ciconiiformes
Family Threskiornithidae
Size Length 26 – 31 in (68 – 81 cm)
Distribution Central and South America
Habits Aquatic; gregarious
Nesting On trees
Eggs 1 – 4, usually 2 or 3
Chicks Nidicolous

In the roseate spoonbill, the plumage of the adult is pink with scarlet-tinted wings. The neck is white, the legs red and the tail feathers yellow to orange. The naked skin of the head and the broad, flat-tipped bill are gray-green. The young bird's plumage, however, is completely white, while the bill and the head, which is wholly covered with feathers, are yellowish.

This species, the only American spoonbill, inhabits a few zones in the southern states of the USA (Texas, Florida, and Louisiana) and in Central and South America. Formerly common, the roseate spoonbill population has been systematically destroyed because of the commercial demand for its handsome feathers. The bird is mostly found in remote areas of swampland surrounded by dense concentrations of aquatic plants, and in mangrove woods close to the coasts.

The nests are built in colonies, often in company with those of other aquatic birds such as ibises, herons, and egrets, and comprise heaps of branches and plant stems with a lining of leaves and softer grass. The female lays 1 – 4 eggs, usually 2 or 3, which are white with brown spots. Incubation lasts 23 – 24 days and is shared by both parents. The chicks are able to fly within 40 days.

A related species is the European or white spoonbill (*Platalea leucorodia*), which has white, ocher-tinted plumage on the breast, a tuft of feathers on the head and a black bill with a yellow tip. Slightly larger than the roseate spoonbill, the species lives in southern and eastern Europe, in Asia and in a few parts of Africa. Breeding colonies are located in dense reedbeds surrounded by stretches of deep water that guarantee them protection from predatory mammals.

Roseate spoonbill
(*Ajaja ajaja*)

▲ Roseate spoonbills live on marshy terrain, in ponds and lakes with plenty of aquatic vegetation and bushes jutting straight out of the water, especially in remote areas where they feel secure and to which have retreated because of the intensive hunting that has practically wiped them out. It was only thanks to the National Audubon Society of America that an end was put to the capturing of these birds for their plumage, with sanctuaries established for them and for other marshland birds.

White spoonbill
(*Platalea leucorodia*)

▲ Both species feed on a wide range of small water creatures, such as crustaceans, insects and larvae, mollusks, amphibians, and small fish. They supplement this animal diet with aquatic plants and seeds.

▶ The European or white spoonbill, slightly larger than the roseate spoonbill, looks more slender and graceful and is further embellished by the crest of feathers on its head. It is an inhabitant of the Old World, found in Europe, Asia, and Africa.

BOAT-BILLED HERON

Cochlearius cochlearius

Order Ciconiiformes
Family Cochleariidae
Length 18 – 20 in (45 – 51 cm)
Distribution Central and South America
Habits Aquatic; solitary
Nesting In trees
Eggs 2 – 4
Chicks Nidicolous

Stocky in build, with fairly short legs, the boat-billed heron has slate-gray plumage which is paler on the underparts and reddish on the flanks. The head is unusual not only for the long tuft of feathers which fall down the neck but also, and especially, for the broad, flat bill, about 3 in (7.5 cm) long and 2 in (5 cm) wide, ending in a hook. Because the beak is so broad, the membrane extending to the base of the two mandibles is very wide and elastic, and the skin of the throat stretches to form a deep, hanging gular pouch.

This bird is found in the tropical and equatorial regions of America from Mexico to northern Argentina. Its habitats are along courses of water with a slow current, in ponds surrounded by vegetation, in marshes and mangrove swamps. The boat-billed heron, like many other birds that are active at dusk and by night, have very large eyes. It is, in fact, around dusk that the bird goes fishing in shallow water for the small invertebrates on which it feeds, these being caught with great ease thanks to the huge beak. It appears the bill is also used for raking the muddy bottom, so providing a rich haul of worms, crustaceans, mollusks, insects, and larvae.

The nest is constructed from dry branches on bushes or small trees, especially mangroves, either fringing or protruding from the water. The nests are secluded and usually situated some distance from one another, although sometimes built closer together to form small colonies. Each female lays 2 – 4 white eggs, incubated by both members of the pair who also share the rearing of the nidicolous chicks.

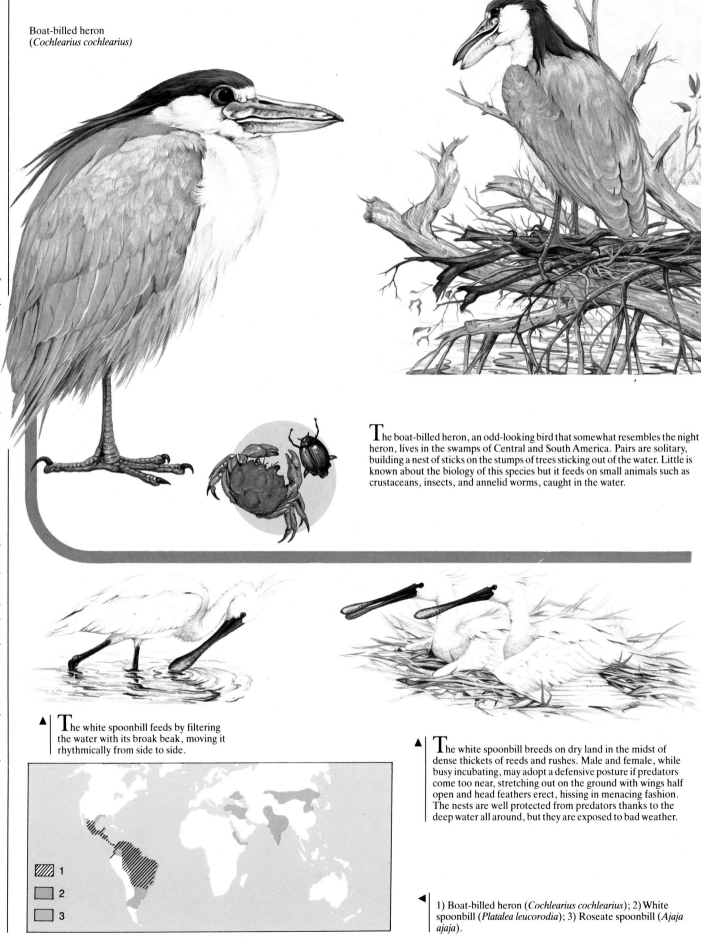

Boat-billed heron
(*Cochlearius cochlearius*)

The boat-billed heron, an odd-looking bird that somewhat resembles the night heron, lives in the swamps of Central and South America. Pairs are solitary, building a nest of sticks on the stumps of trees sticking out of the water. Little is known about the biology of this species but it feeds on small animals such as crustaceans, insects, and annelid worms, caught in the water.

▲ The white spoonbill feeds by filtering the water with its broad beak, moving it rhythmically from side to side.

▲ The white spoonbill breeds on dry land in the midst of dense thickets of reeds and rushes. Male and female, while busy incubating, may adopt a defensive posture if predators come too near, stretching out on the ground with wings half open and head feathers erect, hissing in menacing fashion. The nests are well protected from predators thanks to the deep water all around, but they are exposed to bad weather.

◀ 1) Boat-billed heron (*Cochlearius cochlearius*); 2) White spoonbill (*Platalea leucorodia*); 3) Roseate spoonbill (*Ajaja ajaja*).

1

2

3

ARDEIDAE

For the most part the 64 species belonging to the family Ardeidae are of average size, slender in build, with long legs, a flexible neck, and a pointed beak, but because there are so many types of watery environment, from marshes and swamps to lakes and rivers, a number of species, although retaining the basic body structure of all members of their family, vary to some extent in dimension, build, and behavior so that each can get the most from its chosen habitat. Most of the Ardeidae are active by day but some species, such as the night herons, hunt at night. The least bittern measures 12 in (30 cm) in length and weighs only 1.7 – 2.8 oz (50 – 80 g) whereas the giant or goliath heron is 60 in (150 cm) long and weighs almost 7 lb (3 kg).

The two sexes are very similar and can only be distinguished visually by their behavior while breeding. The young are usually similar to the adults but their coloration is less vivid and they have no ornamental feathers. Certain species are entirely white (a feature of very few of the world's birds) and some wholly black. Others have plumage of various shades but always in a mixture of the same white, gray, black, and reddish brown colors; and a few are brown flecked with white spots. A difference of color is the most striking feature distinguishing the two subfamilies of the Ardeidae: the herons (Ardeinae), including the egrets and night herons, are brightly colored, while the bitterns (Botaurinae) are brown or black to blend with their surroundings.

The Ardeidae walk with ease through the water, supported by their long toes on the slimy bottom. They are capable of swimming but only venture into really deep water on rare occasions. They fly slowly, powerfully and majestically, with long, broad wingbeats. In flight the neck is folded in an S-shape, the head is tucked between the shoulders and the legs are stretched out backward.

Closely dependent upon water, the number of herons present in a particular region will be in proportion to the extent and nature of the swamps, lakes, and rivers in that area. Some species are cosmopolitan (present in most parts of all the continents); they include the

Little egret
(*Egretta garzetta*)

Cattle egret
(*Ardeola ibis*)

Reddish egret
(*Dichromanassa rufes*)

Louisiana hero
(*Hydranassa tri*)

Purple heron
(*Ardea purpurea*)

Goliath heron
(*Ardea goliath*)

Great white heron
(*Casmerodius albus*)

Little bittern
(*Ixobrychus minutus*)

Least bittern
(*Ixobrychus exilis*)

Jap
nigh
(*Go
goisc*)

Bittern
(*Botaurus stellaris*)

Night heron
(*Nycticorax nycticorax*)

Black heron
(*Melanophoyx ardesiaca*)

night heron, the cattle egret, and the great white heron. The majority of species migrate during the cold season to equatorial regions but those already living in warm latitudes, such as the goliath heron of Africa, confine themselves to short journeys in zones where the water contains plenty of fish.

Food consists of aquatic creatures such as fish, frogs and tadpoles, adult insects and larvae, small mammals, worms, and crustaceans. Although the type of food is often the same, several heron species will manage to feed in the same pond or lake without competition, because each captures prey of different dimensions, in water of varying depth and at different times of day.

With the exception of bitterns, which are always solitary by habit, the other Ardeidae are more or less gregarious, coming together to roost at night and to breed in colonies (known as heronries) which may contain thousands of nests, belonging to various heron species as well as other water birds such as spoonbills, ibises, and storks. The nests, sometimes only a few yards from one another, are built on trees, bushes, or clumps of reeds in marshy zones. At the beginning of the breeding season the males perform displays that attract the females and lead to pair formation. They then take up characteristic postures, revealing their ornamental feathers, lifting the head, folding their legs and ruffling the feathers of the neck and back. Each species has its particular courtship rituals which constitute a form of sexual communication exclusive to itself. Because of this, even though thousands of males of different species may be around, the females will make no mistake, choosing to mate only with males of the same species, avoiding the formation of hybrid pairs that must prove in fertile. Pairs stay together only for one breeding season, and both sexes collaborate equally in the laborious task of incubating and raising the brood.

The chicks are born unfeathered and incapable of doing anything, becoming self-sufficient between the ages of 40 and 60 days, according to the size of the species. As they grow rapidly they demand a good deal of food, which the parents collect by making journeys that may take them dozens of miles from the colony in search of suitable fishing grounds.

▲ Cattle egrets owe their name to their habit of following herds of cattle and feeding on the insects that are put to flight as the huge animals advance.

▲ A special hunting technique used by certain herons, including the reddish egret, is to locate the prey and disturb it by casting a shadow on the water with outspread wings.

▲ The bittern lives in red thickets and in order to hide from predators takes up a stance in which the upturned beak and stripes of the neck blend with the swamp vegetation.

▲ The night heron hunts at night for frogs, tadpoles, fish, and insects, which are enticed by its beak vibrating against the water, or by the moving feet.

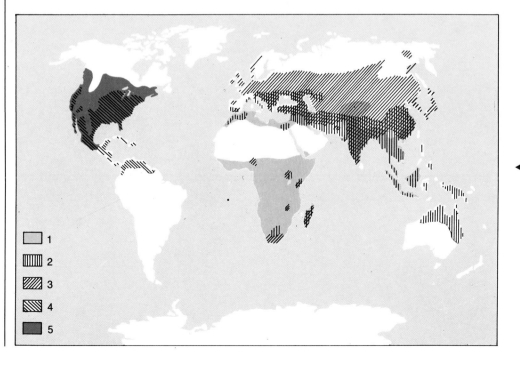

◄ The family Ardeidae comprises species of various sizes and colors, predominantly white, gray, black or reddish; but all have the same basic body structure, with very long legs and neck. These birds are found in every continent except Antarctica, their presence closely linked to wet habitats and the quantity of food to be had in such parts. 1) Cattle egret (*Ardeola ibis*) before its recent expansion into the Americas; 2) Little egret (*Egretta garzetta*); 3) Gray heron (*Ardea cinerea*); 4) Green heron (*Butorides virescens*); Great blue heron (*Ardea herodias*).

GRAY HERON

Ardea cinerea

Order Ciconiiformes
Family Ardeidae
Length 38 – 42 in (95 – 100 cm)
Wingspan 70 – 76 in (175 – 190 cm)
Weight 2½ – 4¼ lb (1,200 – 1,900 g)
Eggs 4 – 5
Maximum age in wild 25 years

The gray heron (*Ardea cinerea*) is one of the largest species of the family Ardeidae. It uses its long legs to strut through fairly deep water where it catches fish and other forms of prey by virtue of its long, flexible neck. The streamlined build and characteristic silhouette, reflected in the water of a swamp, confer an elegance which is heightened by the sober white, gray, and black plumage and the calm, dignified air of the bird.

The white neck merges with the gray of the back, contrasting with the two black bands on either side of the head and the black marks that run down the center of the neck. The wing feathers, which are concealed by covert feathers when the bird is at rest and visible only in flight, are blue-black. The plumage is at its most glittering and resplendent during the breeding season when long ornamental feathers develop on neck and back, and when the feathers at the rear of the head extend up to 8 in (20 cm). For a short period, when the males are displaying, legs and bill also assume an orange-pink hue. During the rest of the year they are yellowish, and the eye is bright yellow. The two sexes have a very similar appearance, while the first-year chicks are grayer in color. The gray heron's flight is slow (about 25 mph [40 kmh]) but direct and stately, the long wings beating deeply with a measured and continuous rhythm.

The gray heron nests over large parts of Europe, Asia and Africa (from latitude 60°N to the southern tip of that continent), and from Spain to Japan. Favorite nesting places are swampy regions or dry spots surrounded by water, safe from human interference and the curiosity of animal predators. If not disturbed, it will also build a nest near castles or in a city center, as in London's Regent's Park. As a rule the nest is situated in reeds, bushes or trees between 3 and 165 ft (1 and 50 m) from ground or water level;

▼ The gray heron (*Ardea cinerea*) lives in wet zones of either fresh or brackish water. It frequents inland and coastal swamps, slow-flowing streams and rivers, river deltas, lakes, and rice paddies.

tall trees are preferred to any others because the gray heron is one of the most arboreal members of its family.

The gray heron is a partial migrant, so that while many birds fly from their breeding zones on genuine migrations to warmer latitudes between September and February, other individuals of the same species remain sedentary. Throughout the year, as is the case with many other representatives of the Ardeidae, these herons gather in groups to spend the night resting in fixed places, forming colonies that are known as heronries. During the day the birds disperse in all directions to find food. In the breeding season they tend to form even larger heronries which may comprise anything from a few pairs to many thousands.

The breeding season commences in February-March in the middle latitudes of the northern hemisphere, when males take over old nests or suitable forks of branches in the heronries, displaying the typical nuptial plumage with its ornamental feathers. Then they perform their characteristic displays, adopting stereotyped, instinctive movements which signal to the females that they are available to form breeding pairs. A pair is formed when a female approaches a displaying male and is accepted by him. In the course of a few days a nest is built or reconstructed; invariably it is the male who collects branches and brings them to his mate, who in turn interlaces them in a rough and ready fashion so as to make the large, cup-shaped nest. Every time one member of the couple arrives at the nest, he or she greets the partner by raising the neck and head feathers and emitting a special sequence of guttural cries.

The two adults share the duties of incubating and of supervising the young during the first few weeks of life. At birth, in fact, the chicks are almost naked and incapable of looking after themselves, so that the parents have to protect them from predators and shelter them from heavy rain or the strong rays of the sun. Fed by both adults in turn, one always staying behind to guard the nest, the youngsters grow rapidly and at three weeks are already capable of climbing the branches around the nest. Thereafter both parents devote themselves to obtaining food, venturing out a couple of times a day and traveling some dozens of miles from the colony.

Sequence of catching fish (lasting only half a second). If the fish is large, the heron will need several minutes to swallow it, with many twists and jerks of neck and head.

Breeding colonies, known as heronries, comprise many nests. At the start of the breeding season each male occupies a nest of the previous year as a base for his courtship displays.

Greeting ceremonies are performed by both members of the pair every time they meet.

Food consists of small animals living in the water and the immediate vicinity. Some are very mobile and have to be caught by means of a sudden thrust of the long neck and pointed bill.

Of the various heron species, those with the longest legs are able to fish in the deepest water. Techniques adopted also include movements of feet and wings to frighten small prey.

Parades by males involve lifting and lowering the neck and ruffling the ornamental breast feathers.

Green heron   Louisiana heron   Snowy egret   Reddish egret   Great blue heron

HAMMERHEAD

Scopus umbretta

Order Ciconiiformes
Family Scopidae
Length About 20 in (50 cm)
Wingspan About 40 in (100 cm)
Distribution Africa south of the Sahara, Madagascar, and southwestern part of Arabian peninsula
Habits Solitary or in pairs, or for short periods in family groups
Nesting On trees
Eggs 3 – 6
Chicks Nidicolous

The hammerhead (*Scopus umbretta*) is so called because of the shape of its head which, by reason of the feathers jutting from the nape and the chisel-like bill, resembles that of a hammer. Male and female look similar. The plumage color is uniformly nut brown with bronze or golden tints. It is found all over Africa south of the Sahara, in Madagascar and southwestern Arabia. It lives in swampy surroundings close to lakes, ponds and large rivers where the water is shallow and the vegetation (of reeds, rushes, etc.) thick, and in waterside woods with plenty of tall trees, necessary for nest building.

The hammerhead is a solitary bird, spending much of the day hidden in the dense vegetation that grows near swamps, lakes and rivers. It resumes activity towards dusk and during the night, foraging in shallow waters, through which it slowly struts, catching small fish, amphibians, crustaceans, larvae, mollusks, and worms. Like many Ciconiiformes, it spears prey with its beak.

As a rule it remains silent, but in the course of the breeding season it becomes quite noisy, emitting strange cries. Courting pairs perform special nuptial flights, consisting of aerial acrobatics and simulated flights. They display staunch loyalty to each other and remain together throughout life. Reproduction normally occurs twice a year, coinciding with the rainy season.

The female lays from 3 to 6 eggs which are initially white but later darken as a result of dirt. They are incubated in turn by the parents for about 30 days; both sexes also collaborate in raising the brood.

The hammerhead has black eyes, bill, and legs, the plumage being uniformly nut-brown with bronze tints. Like most Ciconiiformes, legs and beak are fairly long. The nape feathers form a curious tuft which extends backwards, giving the head its hammer shape and so explaining the bird's vernacular name.

Food is made up principally of fish, amphibians, and crustaceans, hunted in shallow water.

This species builds a characteristically bulky nest over 6½ ft (2 m) in diameter. It is placed in the forking trunk of a tall tree and is clearly visible, thus attracting human attention. It is in the shape of a hollow sphere, communicating with the exterior through a small side opening. The nest is made of straw, dry twigs, branches, and leaves, all stuck together with mud and thus very strong.

The eggs are laid and incubated in the inner chamber of the nest. The hammerhead enters the nest by performing a very strange maneuver, flying towards the entry hole without slackening speed and at the last moment folding the wings and shooting in like a bullet.

SHOEBILL STORK

Balaeniceps rex

Order Ciconiiformes
Family Balaenicipitidae
Dimensions Length 48 in (120 cm); wing 28 in (700 mm); tail 10 in (250 mm); legs 9½ in (245 mm); bill 7½ in (190 mm)
Distribution Central and East Africa
Nesting On ground
Eggs 1 – 3, usually 2
Chicks Nidicolous

The shoebill stork is a blue-gray bird with a small tuft at the back of the head. The enormous bill is pinkish-yellow, spotted and/or streaked blue-gray; the mandibles have cutting edges and the upper one is clearly keel-shaped, ending in a hook. The eye is blue-gray or amber, the legs lead gray. The female is similar to the male but as a rule slightly smaller.

The shoebill is a bird of broad fresh-water swamps, densely covered with grasses, reeds, and papyrus, seldom venturing onto dry land and roosting on floating vegetation, empty termite mounds or, occasionally, in trees. Thanks to its long toes, it can move nimbly over submerged and floating plants with slow steps, often sinking up to the tibio-tarsal joint or even deeper. Essentially diurnal and solitary by habit, the bird does not hunt at night except occasionally in the light of fires lit by fishermen. Preferred food consists of fish, particularly bichir, lungfish, and catfish, and it also catches amphibians, snakes, and other swampland reptiles.

The shoebill stork's nesting period, particularly in regions subject to seasonal flooding, is timed to coincide with the moment when the water level starts to recede. Pairs of shoebills will therefore nest in a zone especially rich in food, but always keeping a fair distance from one another so that in no sense is a colony formed. Both sexes cooperate in building the nest, placed on a floating platform in quite deep water or on top of a termite mound that is temporarily semi-submerged. The same site and nest will be used year after year. The female lays 1 – 3 (usually 2) opaque white eggs at intervals of 4 – 5 days. Both sexes incubate for about 30 days.

The drawing at lower right deliberately shows an attitude formerly attributed to the shoebill stork. Although it is true that this bird feeds to a large extent on lungfish (eel-shaped fish belonging to the subclass Dipnoi, which are able to withstand the temporary drying-up of pools where they live by rolling themselves up in the mud and breathing atmospheric air by using their swim bladder in the manner of lungs), there is no proof in the belief that the shoebill actually digs down into the mud for lungfish. As far as is known, these fish are only caught when fully active.

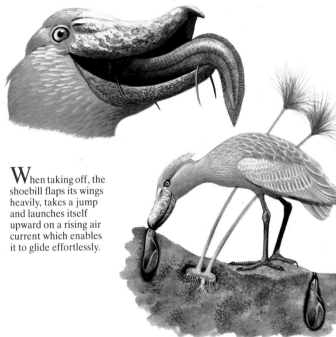

When taking off, the shoebill flaps its wings heavily, takes a jump and launches itself upward on a rising air current which enables it to glide effortlessly.

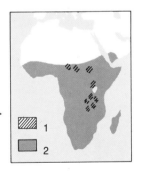

1) Distribution of shoebill stork (*Balaeniceps rex*).
2) Distribution of hammerhead (*Scopus umbretta*).

▨	1
▥	2

With a frequent local distribution and even common in some zones, the shoebill stork, by and large, is everywhere threatened by the progressive drainage of swamps, irrational farming activities, and excessive grazing by domestic livestock. The total world population is probably not more than 10,000 individuals, but this is an approximate estimate needing detailed verification, especially in peripheral northern areas. What cannot be denied, however, is that this species, depending on a very particular habitat, is no longer as abundant as are most other African Ciconiiformes.

FLAMINGOS

Order Phoenicopteriformes
Family Phoenicopteridae
Size Lesser and James' are the smallest
species, having a total length of 31 – 39 in
(95 – 100 cm) and a wingspan in the order
of 37 – 39 in (95 – 100 cm). Greater/
Caribbean is the largest and can reach
a total length of 78 in (200 cm) with a
wingspan of up to 70 in (187 cm)
Weight From about 3½ lb (1.6 kg) in
the Lesser to over 9½ lb (4.4 kg) in
large male Greaters
Incubation From 27 – 31 days
Eggs 1, exceptionally 2
Sexual maturity At least 2 – 3 years
Maximum age 27 years recorded in
wild (Camargue) and up to 50 years in
captivity (Basle Zoo).

Flamingos are among the most spectacular of birds, especially in flight,
their neck and legs outstretched,
wings flashing red and black, accompanied by goose-like honking calls.
There are six races of flamingo in the
world. Two species are to be found
throughout the Old World and four in
the New. All have a similar preference
for areas of shallow brackish or salt
water, varying in altitude throughout
the world from sea level to about
13,000 ft (4,000 m). The most typical
habitat, at least throughout the Old
World, is the temporary salt lagoon,
which is flooded during periods of
heavy rain, then dries out again when
drought conditions prevail.

The Caribbean flamingo (*Phoenicopterus ruber ruber*) has the darkest color
of the six races being reddish once
adult. The bill has a yellow base while
the grayish pink legs are darker at the
joints. It is widespread throughout the
Caribbean, as south as Venezuela and
Surinam and north to Mexico.

The Greater flamingo (*Phoenicopterus ruber roseus* or *Ph. antiquorum*) is a
race of the former species having an
entirely different distribution and
being much paler in color. Body plumage is almost white but with a pinkish
tinge, much more pronounced on the
head and neck. The legs and feet
are wholly pink and the black tipped
bill has a pink base. It occurs on three
continents of the Old World. In Europe
it is confined to the Mediterranean
region.

Greater flamingos on their
nests. The colony usually
comprises thousands of pairs,
generally on islands in
inaccessible areas where the
birds are safe from predatory
mammals and from man.

The Chilean flamingo (*Phoenicopterus chilensis* or *Ph. ruber chilensis*) is noticeably smaller than the former and has a body plumage almost intermediate in color between the Caribbean and Greater, being an orangy pink. It has slightly more black at the tip of the bill but differs most strikingly in having grayish legs with pink feet and "knee" joints. It ranges over much of temperate South America occurring along both coasts and on high-altitude lakes in the Andes where most of the breeding sites are located. The world population is estimated at about 250,000 individuals.

The Lesser flamingo (*Phoeniconaias minor*) is the smallest, pinkest, and most abundant of the tribe. The generally pink plumage is interrupted only by the red and black of the wings while the bill is a deep blood red, looking almost black at a distance. It is the second of the two Old World species, cohabiting with the Greater on many wetlands of Africa.

The Andean flamingo (*Phoenicoparrus andinus*) has a very pink body plumage, a yellow base to the bill and is the only species to have yellow legs. It is a bird of high-altitude salt lakes in Peru, Chile, Bolivia and Argentina where it often occurs with the Chilean and the James' flamingos.

The James' flamingo (*Phoenicoparrus jamesi*) is a little larger than the Lesser flamingo, and has a pale body plumage, orange-pink legs and a yellow base to the bill. It has the most restricted distribution of all and because of the remote areas it frequents, was thought to have become extinct until its rediscovery in the mid 1950s. It occurs on salt lakes above 11,483 ft (3,500 m) within the range of the former species.

All species of flamingo are gregarious and sometimes congregate in flocks numbering thousands or even hundreds of thousands. Prior to breeding, flamingos of all species form ritualized displays. These may be started sometimes months before the onset of egg laying and not necessarily close to the breeding grounds. They usually increase in intensity with the season and come to an end once nesting is under way. Flamingos usually build a conical-shaped nest, using their bill to scrape up the mud from around the spot chosen for breeding. The single egg is laid in a shallow depression on top and incubation, by both sexes, takes from 27 to 31 days.

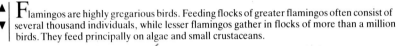

▲
▼ Flamingos are highly gregarious birds. Feeding flocks of greater flamingos often consist of several thousand individuals, while lesser flamingos gather in flocks of more than a million birds. They feed principally on algae and small crustaceans.

◄ Moving the tongue rapidly to and fro like a piston, the bird filters water and mud, retaining food particles in the beak.

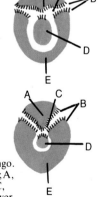

▲ Bill of the greater flamingo (above) and of the lesser flamingo. At right are the various sections; A, upper mandible; B, lamellae; C, soft lamellae; D, tongue; E, lower mandible.

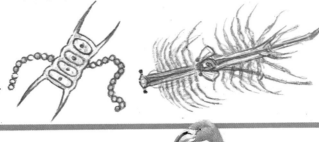

European greater flamingo (*Phoenicopterus ruber roseus*)

American greater flamingo (*Phoenicopterus ruber ruber*)

Andean flamingo (*Phoenicoparrus andinus*)

James' flamingo (*Phoenicoparrus jamesi*)

Chilean flamingo (*Phoenicopterus chilensis*)

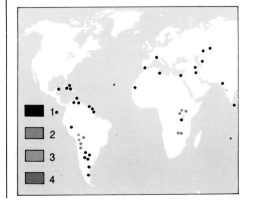

1
2
3
4

◄ Flamingos are among the most spectacular of all birds, especially when flying with neck and legs extended, wings striped red and black, and giving out cries similar to those of ducks. Their exotic appearance has long stimulated man's imagination from the Stone Age through the great periods of ancient Egyptian and Greek civilization. Artists have depicted them in many forms and the birds feature in many myths and legends. Even today flamingos are popular as decorative species in parks and zoos.
They are found in four of the five continents, the exception being Australasia, although fossil remains have been discovered in Australia.
1) Greater flamingo (*Phoenicopterus ruber*); 2) Lesser flamingo (*Phoeniconaias minor*); 3) James' flamingo (*Phoenicoparrus jamesi*); 4) Andean flamingo (*Phoenicoparrus andinus*).

ANSERIFORMES

This order comprises birds which are, to a lesser or greater extent, dependent on a watery environment. They vary considerably in size but most of them possess a fairly long neck which is held outstretched during flight. There are two families: Anhimidae and – much larger – Anatidae.

The Anhimidae comprise species with webbed feet, a bill without lamellae or plates but furnished instead with bony spurs, and with the "wrist" of the wing, namely the metacarpus, covered by a horny substance. The family Anatidae is in turn subdivided into three subfamilies: Anseranatinae, Anserinae and Anatinae. The first of these contains one species only, which can be seen as a transitional form between Anhimidae and Anatidae. The other two subfamilies contain the major number of species commonly known as swans, geese, and ducks.

With the exception of the magpie goose (*Anseranas semipalmata*) and the South American geese of the genus *Chloephaga*, feather molt coincides, in large measure, with the period when the young are being reared. Geese, swans, and ducks, for short periods that vary from 2 to 4 weeks, are wholly incapable of flying because the remiges fall out almost all at the same time. During this period it is vital for the birds to be in a place that is both safe and provided with sufficient food in the water or in the immediate vicinity.

Geese have a strong bill furnished with lamellae modified into a series of small teeth designed to cut and rip the plants on which they feed, unlike the lamellae of other Anatidae, which are genuinely used for filtration. The legs are comparatively long and sturdier than those of swans, which seldom engage in long journeys on land. Geese, on the other hand, are excellent walkers and will occasionally break into quite a fast run, though with a typical swaying gait. They are also very strong fliers and can cover hundreds of miles without resting and without any apparent difficulty. The broad, long, pointed wings enable them to fly quite rapidly and in a straight line, with flocks adopting the classic V-formation.

There are two principal groups of species: those of the genus *Anser* (the

White-fronted goose
(*Anser albifrons*)

Bean goose
(*Anser fabalis*)

Swan goose
(*Anser cygnoides*)

Lesser white-fronted goose
(*Anser erythropus*)

Brant goose
(*Branta bernicla*)

Some Anseriformes

Anhimidae
Horned screamer
(*Anhima cornuta*)

Anatidae
Whooper swan
(*Cygnus cygnus*)

Anatidae
Magpie goose
(*Anseranas semipalmata*)

Anatidae
Graylag goose
(*Anser anser*)

"gray" geese) and those of the genus *Branta* (the "black" geese). The geese belonging to the genus *Anser* exhibit a combination of colors ranging from gray or white to chestnut brown. In addition to the graylag goose (*Anser anser*), species that are quite common and widely distributed in the Palearctic region include the bean goose (*A. fabalis*) and the white-fronted goose (*A. albifrons*). The bean goose has a distinctive beak, base and tip being black and the middle part orange. The lesser white-fronted goose (*A. erythropus*) resembles the foregoing species but is much smaller; also it has a clear yellow circle around the eye and the white area of the head is broader. The swan goose (*A. cygnoides*), distinctive in the wild by virtue of its very long swan-like bill, is generally better known in its domestic form, with a shortened beak and large frontal knob.

The "black" geese of the genus *Branta* are recognizable by their plumage, containing, in parts, distinctive black and white patches which generally form a characteristic pattern. The function of these marks is probably to enable single individuals to identify conspecifics from a distance. Each species, in fact, has its particular feeding habits, which is obviously an advantage, among other things, when it comes to breeding, for it prevents birds mating with different species. The Canada goose (*Branta canadensis*), nowadays widely distributed, by introduction, in various regions of northern Europe, has a large number of subspecies, ranging from *B. c. maxima*, weighing about 17½ lb (8 kg) to *B. c. minima*, whose weight averages barely 3¼ lb (1,500 g). The Hawaiian goose (*B. sandvicensis*) is probably derived, by reason of isolation, from an ancestral form of Canada goose, but by now exhibits so many structural differences that it is always treated as a separate species. Quite rare (with perhaps under 20,000 individuals remaining) is the splendid red-breasted goose (*B. ruficollis*), which features in a singular instance of symbiosis with various species of raptor.

The South American Magellan goose (*Chloephaga picta*) is an interesting example of convergence with the various "gray" and "black" geese, for it shares their sturdy build, long legs, and bill structure.

Hawaiian goose
(*Branta sandvicensis*)

Emperor goose
(*Anser canagicus*)

Canada goose
(*Branta canadensis*)

Magellan goose
(*Chloephaga picta*)

Red-breasted goose
(*Branta ruficollis*)

Snow goose (dark phase)
(*Anser caerulescens*)

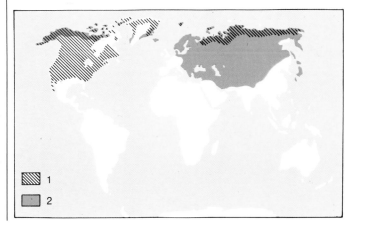

1
2

The order Anseriformes contains two families, Anhimidae and Anatidae. The Anatidae, in their turn, are subdivided into three subfamilies, Anseranatinae, Anserinae, and Anatinae. The drawings on the left illustrate some of the most representative species of the order, namely the horned screamer, the trumpeter swan, the magpie goose, and the graylag goose. Above, on both pages, are illustrations of the principal goose species, including the Magellan goose which actually belongs to the subfamily Anatinae and therefore, despite its name and appearance, should strictly be included among the ducks.
There are two principal groups of geese, the "black" geese of the genus *Branta* (distribution 1 on the map) and the "gray" geese of the genus *Anser* (distribution 2) which are generally gray, although also white and chestnut.

HORNED SCREAMER

Anhima cornuta

Order Anseriformes
Family Anhimidae
Length 32 – 36 in (80 – 90 cm)
Weight 4½ – 6½ lb (2 – 3 kg)
Distribution Colombia and Venezuela to eastern Bolivia (basin of Amazon)
Habits Gregarious
Nesting On ground
Eggs Usually 2
Chicks Nidifugous

The horned screamer (*Anhima cornuta*) has mainly dark, blackish plumage with green or violet tints. The wings are fairly broad but not very strong, and the tail is long and truncated. On the head is a short tuft of upward-turned feathers and a long whitish feather, measuring 4 – 6 in (10 – 15 cm), without barbs, sprouting forwards above the bill. The sexes, as in all species, are similar. Thanks to its long toes, the bird can tread delicately over floating vegetation, rather like rails and coots.

The black-necked screamer (*Chauna chavaria*) is a slightly smaller bird. Its head is adorned with a short tuft of backward-facing feathers which match those of the nape. The cheeks are white, the region round the eye is red and the neck is black. Other parts of the body are dark gray to blue, and the legs are fleshy orange. The crested screamer (*C. torquata*) is very like the black-necked screamer but has no white spaces on the cheeks and boasts a narrow white collar, bordered below by a black band.

Screamers are typical birds of the South American swamplands, and also frequent wooded zones, perching on trees thanks to the special shape of their feet and the great length of the rear toe. They are gregarious by habit, especially when feeding, mainly on vegetation, and often standing in shallow water among the swamp plants. During the breeding season males engage in fairly spectacular battles, exchanging pecks, kicks, and wing-butts. Screamers use large quantities of aquatic plants to build their bulky nests. The two parents share this work and also take turns in incubation and rearing. The horned screamer generally has 2 chicks and the other species 5 or 6.

Horned screamer
(*Anhima cornuta*)

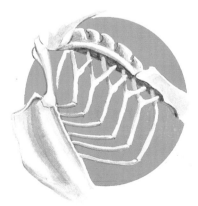

They do not possess the hooked or uncinate processes which strengthen the ribs of all other birds. The absence of this structure is found in the extinct *Archaeopteryx*, and for this reason, too, screamers are regarded as very primitive.

Black-necked screamer
(*Chauna chavaria*)

Crested screamer
(*Chauna torquata*)

The screamers are very strange birds for, although from the classification viewpoint they are closely related to the Anatidae, they do not have many characteristics in common with geese and ducks. They are easily distinguished by their feet with four large unwebbed toes, and the shape of the beak, which is rather short, curved, and somewhat similar, generally, to that of Galliformes.

These birds are typical inhabitants of swampy regions in South America, but also frequent tree-covered zones, being capable of perching on the branches. 1) Horned screamer (*Anhima cornuta*); 2) Black-necked screamer (*Chauna chavaria*); 3) Crested screamer (*Chauna torquata*).

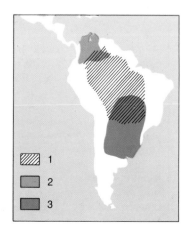

1

2

3

MAGPIE GOOSE

Anseranas semipalmata

Order Anseriformes
Family Anatidae; subfamily
Anseranatinae
Length About 32 in (80 cm)
Distribution Australia, Tasmania,
southern New Guinea
Habits Gregarious
Nesting On ground
Eggs 5 – 14
Chicks Nidifugous

The magpie goose (*Anseranas semipalmata*) is the sole representative of the subfamily Anseranatinae, since its ancestral characteristics are closely related neither to true geese nor to ducks. The long, sturdy bill is pinkish yellow with small lamellae. The hook at the tip of the beak is broad and curved, and pointed down. The plumage is black with large white patches on the rump and underparts. The female is slightly smaller than the male.

The magpie goose is a good walker although it moves about cautiously and usually quite slowly. It flies easily, preferring to glide rather than adopt flapping flight over long distances. It often perches in trees, choosing the thinnest branches situated as high as possible. The bird is not, however, a strong swimmer even though it spends a good deal of its time among marshes and lakes.

Mild in disposition, these birds usually live together in large colonies which break up with the approach of the breeding season. Nevertheless, as is the case with many other Australian species, reproduction does not occur at fixed times but may take place at various periods of the year.

Among other strange aspects of behavior, the magpie goose mates out of the water, which is completely at variance with the habits of swans, geese, and ducks in general. Evidently the reason is that these birds are less adapted to the watery environment. Male and female, indeed, change places during incubation and cooperate in raising the chicks. Such behavior is paralleled among other Anseriformes only by the screamers, certain tree ducks, and the black swan; for other species it is normally only the female who attends to parental duties.

The magpie goose, like the screamers, is almost a living fossil. It cannot be considered a real goose, nor a swan, nor a duck. Unlike geese and ducks, it does not molt its feathers regularly and therefore has only one form of plumage. It spends much of its time in lagoons and lake-covered zones, where it builds its nest.

This bird lives nowadays in the swampy regions of northern Australia, but at one time it was widely distributed in suitable places throughout the continent. It was then exterminated because of its excessive trust in humans and, above all, because of the damage done to rice paddies as a result of it sometimes feeding on growing plants and trampling on others. 1) Magpie goose (*Anseranas semipalmata*).

GRAYLAG GOOSE

Anser anser

Order Anseriformes
Family Anatidae; subfamily Anserinae
Size Length 30 – 36 in (75 – 90 cm)
Wingspan 58 – 72 (147 – 180 cm)
Weight 6¼ – 8¼ lb (2.9 – 3.7 kg)
Distribution Europe and Asia
Habits Gregarious, except during breeding season
Nesting On ground
Eggs 4 – 7, exceptionally up to 12
Chicks Nidifugous

The graylag goose is the best known, if not the most abundant, species of goose, one reason being that it is the ancestor of various domestic strains.

In the wild the bird is easy to identify because it is the only one of the "gray" geese to have a large, uniformly pink or orange bill (with a whitish hook). In flight the graylag goose displays the broad silvery zone on the upper wing which, from a distance, appears almost white. The upper parts of the body are gray-brown and the feather tips are whitish so that they form a series of thin white transverse stripes. These stripes are broader and clearer among birds of eastern populations, who thus have a lighter appearance overall. The underparts are more or less uniformly pale and the legs are flesh-colored. The short tail is blackish and makes a striking contrast with the white rump. Because the sexes are similar it is somewhat difficult to distinguish them in the wild; but sometimes this is possible by comparing the sizes (males are larger) and attitudes.

On the other hand, there is never any problem in recognizing the young of the year, for they are darker and more brownish than the adults, displaying fewer white stripes on the back.

This species at one time nested over a much wider area, both in Asia and in Europe. Nowadays there are large, well distributed populations in much of central Asia and European Russia, but the bird has practically disappeared as a nesting species from western and southern Europe.

The graylag goose has a preference for wet grasslands, often, but not invariably, near areas covered by swamps and lakes. Like many other

▲ The family Anatidae (swans, geese, and ducks) comprises many species of aquatic birds, furnished with short but robust legs and capable of swimming and flying long distances. The graylag goose, like other geese, possesses long legs which are particularly suited for walking on dry land. They are easily distinguished from other species by the almost uniform pink or orange color of the bill and the gray-brown body.

◄ Geese feed mainly on plants which they rip and chew with the tiny teeth or lamellae along both mandibles of the bill.

geese, it relies on water more for reasons of safety than for purposes of feeding. Indeed, without exception, when dusk approaches, flocks of geese that have been feeding in fields simultaneously take their departure for the places where they regularly spend the night; their "nocturnal quarters" are usually situated along low-lying shores, in muddy or sandy river estuaries or in lagoons, perhaps where a strip of land, surrounded by water, juts out.

The nest of the graylag goose is usually a somewhat rough-and-ready construction, formed mainly of scraps of vegetation heaped up on the ground into a cone which is then stuffed with feathers. During the breeding season the birds relinquish their gregarious habits and each pair defends its own small territory, not allowing any other members of the species to intrude. The young hatch after 25 days of incubation and are capable of embarking on their first flights after a couple of weeks. During this time they are attended and protected by both parents. In the second (or, more often, the third) year the geese mate, remaining loyal to their partner for the rest of their life.

The ethologist Konrad Lorenz, author of some of the first and most celebrated studies on the behavior of graylag geese, emphasizes that among geese monogamy is the rule, but that every rule has its exceptions. Of particular importance is the description of the phased learning process known as "imprinting," a phenomenon encountered among many animals, particularly those species with a measure of social organization. Lorenz has affirmed that a young goose, shortly after hatching, may learn to regard almost any animal or human, or even an object, as its parent, in the event of the latter moving close by and making occasional sounds that are similar, but not necessarily identical, to the "contact" call generally used by the species. In this way the young goose receives the imprint of its foster parent, which may be a hen, a turkey, a human being or even a self-propelled, sound-equipped cardboard box. The goose thus identifies with its adoptive parent, behaving in the latter's presence exactly as it would with one of its kind; having reached maturity, it may even attempt to mate with individuals or objects resembling its fosterparent, refusing other geese.

▼ When they fly long distances, the geese adopt the typical V-formation used by all large, gregarious birds when they migrate.

▼ Graylag geese usually feed in fields and grasslands, not necessarily in wet zones.

▶ Young graylag goose shortly after hatching.

▶ Position of graylag goose while asleep.

▼ A female (who incubates alone) recovering an egg that has rolled out of the nest.

▲ Graylag goslings may follow their mother around within a day of hatching.

▲ During the days after hatching, should the mother not be available, baby geese will accept as a foster parent virtually any object or animal that happens to move nearby, including humans.

WHOOPER SWAN

Cygnus cygnus

Order Anseriformes
Family Anatidae
Size Length 58 – 64 in (145 – 160 cm)
Distribution Europe and Asia
Nesting At water's edge
Eggs 5 – 6, exceptionally 4 – 8
Chicks Nidifugous

Swans are birds of considerable size, larger than the biggest geese (wild). They have a very long neck and their plumage is white (among species of the northern hemisphere) or black or black-and-white (in southern hemisphere).

The birds spend much of their time swimming and find most forms of food in the water, straining the surface layers or submerging head and neck, to reach the plants growing on the bottom.

These birds need broad tracts of water, especially while they are growing, for the considerable weight of the body might hamper the development of the legs if the latter had to support the bird too frequently on dry land.

As a rule the bill of a swan is high at the base but fairly long. The cygnets are grayish or brownish, and this plumage distinguishes them immediately from the adults when they mingle in large flocks.

The five existing swan species are all classified in the genus *Cygnus* and do not differ much from one another. Contrary to what might be supposed, given their size, swans are excellent and powerful fliers, capable of migrating many hundreds of miles.

The whooper swan (*Cygnus cygnus*) is easily distinguished by the absence of a frontal knob; its body has a square appearance and the neck is held straight and rigid rather than elegantly folded. Its voice is deep and musical, similar to the sound of a trumpet. For this reason the American subspecies *C. c. buccinator* bears the vernacular name of trumpeter swan. It is the largest of all the swans and may weigh more than 33 lb (15 kg).

The whooper swan nests in Iceland, Norway, Sweden, Finland, Russia, Siberia as far as Kamchatka, Sakhalin, the Commander Islands, and Japan, as well as some zones of central Asia. It winters in the British Isles, Europe, North Africa, Asia Minor, Iran, northern India, China, and Japan. The

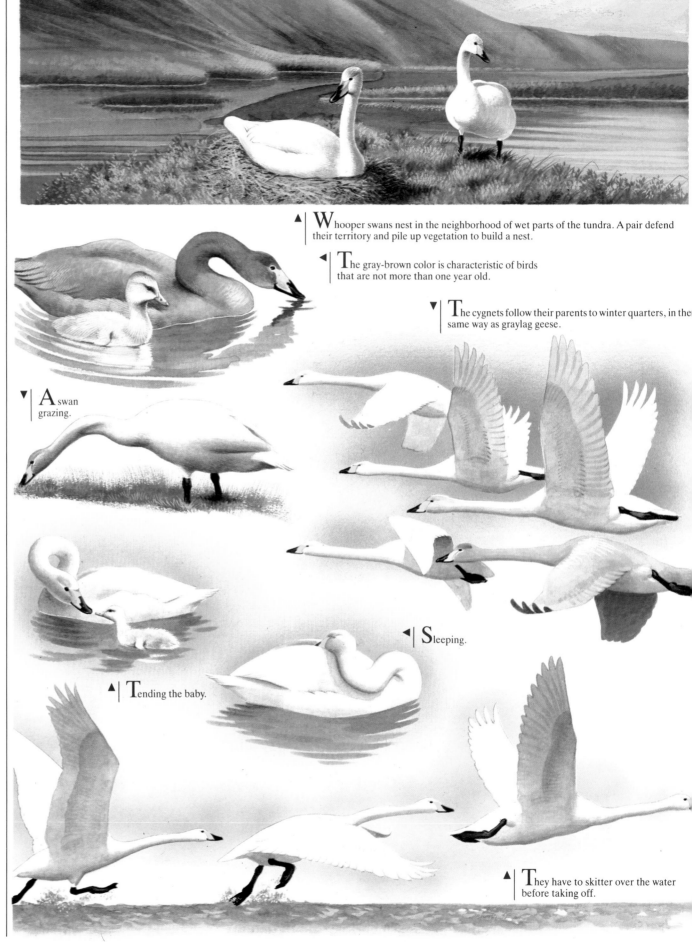

▲ Whooper swans nest in the neighborhood of wet parts of the tundra. A pair defend their territory and pile up vegetation to build a nest.

◀ The gray-brown color is characteristic of birds that are not more than one year old.

▼ The cygnets follow their parents to winter quarters, in the same way as graylag geese.

▼ A swan grazing.

◀ Sleeping.

▲ Tending the baby.

▲ They have to skitter over the water before taking off.

trumpeter swan once had a wide distribution in various parts of North America, but is nowadays restricted to a zone on the borders of Canada, the United States, and Alaska.

Whooper swans nest for preference close to lakes, in the tundra, on heathland or in swampy areas near the estuaries of arctic rivers. In winter they assemble in zones farther to the south because of ice and snow which, if extensive, prevent them obtaining food.

The mute swan (*C. olor*) may be distinguished from similar species by the color of its beak, which is almost wholly orange, with black edges and black knob on the base, connected to the forehead. The legs are also black (rarely fleshy or gray) and the pointed tail is fairly prominent.

The range of the mute swan includes Denmark, central and southern Sweden, northern Germany, Poland, Roumania, central Russia, Asia Minor, and central and eastern Asia to Mongolia and the Dagur province of northern Manchuria. In winter it migrates southward.

The nest of the mute swan is preferably situated on an islet in the water of a swamp, but semi-domesticated birds will build a nest anywhere close to water. Both birds help to build it and the male later stations himself nearby while his mate incubates. She lays 4–7 (exceptionally 12) eggs and incubates them for 36 days. The chicks are tended by the parents and are able to fly 120–150 days after hatching.

The whistling swan (*C. columbianus*) is in many respects similar to the whooper swan, with all the main characteristics of the latter except that it is a good deal smaller. The neck, in fact, is rather short and the body tends to be rounded rather than elongated; the voice is musical and resonant.

The best-known species from the southern hemisphere is undoubtedly the black swan (*C. atratus*), with elegant curly black plumage, and deep red bill barred with white at the tip.

The comparatively small black-necked swan (*C. melanocoryphus*) from South America, flies northward for winter migration. It has a white body, a deep, velvety black neck and a white stripe across the eye. The bill is gray, with a large, bilobate, flesh-pink frontal knob at the base.

The female has the odd habit of carrying her babies on her back when they go swimming.

Trumpeter swan
(*Cygnus cygnus buccinator*)

Black-necked swan
(*Cygnus melanocoryphus*)

Mute swan
(*Cygnus olor*)

Black swan
(*Cygnus atratus*)

1
2
3
4
5

▲ From left: the different bills of the mute swan, the whooper swan, and the whistling swan.

◄ Apart from the mute swan, which has a wide distribution almost everywhere, the other species require absolute and total protection because of their rarity and their exceptional ornamental value. 1) Whooper swan (*Cygnus cygnus*); 2) Mute swan (*Cygnus olor*); 3) Black swan (*Cygnus atratus*); 4) Whistling swan (*Cygnus columbianus*); 5) Black-necked swan (*Cygnus melanocoryphus*).

MALLARD

Anas platyrhynchos

Order Anseriformes
Family Anatidae; subfamily Anatinae
Length 20 – 26 in (50 – 65 cm)
Wingspan 33 – 39 in (81 – 98 cm)
Weight About 2 – 3 lb (900 – 1,400 g)
Distribution Widespread throughout Europe, Asia, and North America. A separate subspecies (*A. p. conboschas*) has been identified in Greenland, another 2 (3 according to some authors) in the southern parts of the United States and Mexico; and 2 subspecies are considered endemic to the Hawaiian Islands.
Habits Gregarious
Nesting Generally on the ground, but occasionally in all sorts of nest.
Eggs Normally 9-13, sometimes up to 18
Chicks Nidifugous

The mallard (*Anas platyrhynchos*) is the commonest and best known of all Anatidae. Like the graylag goose, the mallard was also domesticated by man thousands of years ago and is therefore the ancestor of innumerable domestic strains. In its original pure form, which is also often observable in the semi-domesticated state, the livery is unmistakable and very characteristic, at least in the case of the male in nuptial plumage. The head is bright green with metallic tints, the bill is greenish yellow, and the upper breast brick red, with a narrow white band separating it from the green head and neck. The rectangular patch (speculum) on the wing is metallic blue, edged with black and white. The tail is gray and white, and the upper and under tail coverts are black. There are a few curly black feathers on the rump.

The female is striped chestnut brown, with a paler abdomen, and with the same blue speculum on the wings. The male mallard in eclipse plumage looks almost like the female but may be distinguished from her by the grayer color of his head and, more particularly, by the color of his bill which remains yellow-green, while hers is black and orange. It is interesting to note that sexual dimorphism, so marked in individuals living in northern regions, is far less noticeable in the small populations from the southern parts of the U.S.A., Mexico, and Hawaii.

Mallard drakes (*Anas platyrhynchos*) take on showy colored plumage between fall and spring; during this period the difference in sexes is very striking among most duck species. The drawing shows both duck and drake, as well as a duckling with a "tooth" on the tip of its beak, used for breaking the shell of the egg while hatching.

Like all dabbling ducks, mallards are excellent fliers, capable of traveling hundreds of miles without a halt. Only the northern populations set off on true migrations, whereas the birds from the south can be regarded as sedentary. Populations of temperate climes are partial migrants, with only some individuals moving from the zones where they were born.

The sexual behavior of ducks has been the subject of precise research by many authors, including, once again, Konrad Lorenz. Pairs usually form in autumn, and this normally takes place in winter quarters. It may happen that a male will pair with a female wintering in the same locality but coming from a completely different region. When the two migrate again in spring, the male will follow the female.

The female mallards not yet paired give out, in their turn, a succession of cries gradually decreasing in intensity. When one or more drakes are gathered around a female, she swims with head held low and neck extended, this attitude evidently exciting the males who usually begin raising and lowering their head rhythmically with a pumping movement. After making her choice, she allows the drake to approach, and he swims round her, neck outstretched, until he succeeds in gripping her by the feathers of the nape, when he mounts on her back to mate. Courtship does not always proceed, however, in such a "romantic" fashion; indeed, the males often display aggressive and violent behavior, pursuing their intended mate even through the air in a rough, insistent manner. Nor is it rare for a group of squabbling males to maltreat a female who is not fast or strong enough to evade her pursuers. Once the pair is formed, however, the drake will defend his legitimate partner from the incursions of other males. Having selected a suitable site, the female of the pair concentrates on building the nest, carefully lining the interior with feathers (which immediately start to regrow) plucked from her own underparts. In the course of incubation (lasting 27 – 28 days) the male defends a section of beach close to the nest.

Being so abundant, and growing to such a good size, the mallard is inevitably of commercial interest. Since it is extremely easy to rear, provided there is plenty of water available, the species is a prime attraction both for hunters and breeders.

Dabbling ducks collect their food while floating on the surface; they swim under water only in exceptional cases and if in danger. They can raise themselves vertically to fly.

Diving ducks swim under water to find their food and take wing only after running a short way over the surface.

By day ducks generally rest in the water or among the vegetation. Sometimes they feed on land by night. They sleep with the bill and part of the head tucked between the wings.

Nuptial parade of the mallard. During courtship they assume strange attitudes, often accompanying such movements with particular calls or boldly displaying parts of their plumage.

Immediately after the mating season, from June to August, the male's plumage becomes mimetic, like that of the female. This is the so-called eclipse plumage.

Some mallards, like mandarin ducks (but also goldeneyes and certain mergansers), nest in hollow treetrunks.

DUCKS

Ducks that normally feed on the surface without completely submerging their bodies in water, leaving at least the rear portion exposed, are generally known as dabbling ducks. Among these species the secondary remiges form a rectangular zone on the wings which is clearly defined and brightly colored, with metallic and often variously reflected tints; this patch is called the speculum. The presence of this "wing mirror" is probably explained by the need of individual ducks to easily recognize others of their kind from a distance and while flying.

The so-called diving ducks mostly have black and white zones on their wings, or wings of uniform color. They are so named because they are in the habit of submerging their bodies entirely when looking for food, often diving to a depth of several feet. Diving ducks are more reliant on water. The dabbling ducks have smaller webs on their feet and fairly short toes, relative to body dimensions. The diving ducks, on the other hand, have feet that are broadly webbed so as to facilitate underwater swimming. The feet, furthermore, are positioned some way back on the body so that diving ducks tend to look more upright when on the surface. Dabbling ducks have bills suitable for filtering and chewing, namely, flat and fairly long. Diving ducks, particularly those spending the winter on the seacoasts, have beaks that are fairly high at the base, and a large head.

Ducks are classified into several tribes and genera. The whistling ducks of the Dendrocygnini tribe are found plentifully in the tropical and subtropical regions of the New World as well as Africa, Asia, and Australia, being represented by eight different species. One of the most representative species of the tribe of Tadornini is the shelduck (*Tadorna tadorna*), a bird closely associated with broad tracts of salt water and so generally found along the seacoasts, especially on low lying sands or muddy shores. A fairly common form of behavior exhibited by some members of this tribe, particularly the shelduck, is the manner in which the female "instigates" her mate, inciting him against intruders by facing him squarely but turning her

Shelduck
(*Tadorna tadorna*)

Lesser whistling duck
(*Dendrocygna javanica*)

Egyptian goose
(*Alopochen aegyptiacus*)

Shoveler
(*Anas clypeata*)

American wigeon
(*Anas americana*)

Falcated teal
(*Anas falcata*)

Wigeon
(*Anas penelope*)

Garganey teal
(*Anas querquedula*)

Gadwall
(*Anas strepera*)

head in the direction of the adversary. It has been noted that the degree of aggressiveness displayed by the drake depends on the presence of such an instigating female, especially as males without female companionship live most harmoniously together, even within a confined space.

The tribe of Anatini comprises the dabbling ducks. The shoveler (*Anas clypeata*) is easily recognizable from the shape and size of its bill, which is adapted mainly for filtering water so that the duck can collect the plankton which constitutes an important part of its diet. This species is widespread over the entire Holarctic region. The garganey teal (*A. querquedula*) is slightly smaller and is easily distinguished from the shoveler by its much smaller bill and the peculiar colors of the male in his nuptial livery. The falcated teal (*A. falcata*) is a handsome bird that ranges widely over northeast Asia and reaches China and Japan in the winter. Its name is derived from the sickle-shaped tertiary remiges, which are particularly long and curving in the males. Very similar in general body structure and behavior is the gadwall (*A. strepera*), whose area of distribution is, however, considerably more vast, comprising North America, Europe, and Asia.

The wigeon (*A. penelope*) has a wide range in Asia and Europe, while in America the species is replaced by two similar species, the American wigeon (*A. americana*) and the southern wigeon (*A. sibilatrix*), inhabiting northern and southern regions respectively. Almost the opposite, ecologically, of the wigeons are the pintails, who possess long, narrow necks, heads and bills, and an equally narrow tail that terminates in a point. The pintails, in fact, frequent the same types of habitat as do the wigeons, enjoying a similar diet and finding their food down to a depth of some 16 in (40 cm) without submerging their body entirely. The best known and most widely distributed of the three species is the pintail (*A. acuta*), which breeds in North America and well as in Europe and Asia, flying to Africa and the more southerly parts of Asia in the winter months.

Among the ducks resembling the mallard, in addition to those already mentioned, is the spotbill duck (*A. poecilorhyncha*). This species, partially sedentary and with sexes that are much alike, is found in India, Indo-

Pintail
(*Anas acuta*)

Spotbill duck
(*Anas poecilorhyncha*)

Teal
(*Anas crecca*)

Baikal teal
(*Anas formosa*)

Wood duck
(*Aix sponsa*)

Flightless
steamer duck
(*Tachyeres
pteneres*)

Mandarin duck
(*Aix galericulata*)

The steamer ducks are the only ducks that are unable to fly. They flee by running across the water, flapping their wings, and by swimming underwater, likewise using the wings.

Muscovy duck
(*Cairina moschata*)

China, China, and Japan. Another fairly abundant group of dabbling ducks consists of the teals, the best known species of which are the teal (*Anas crecca*) and the Baikal teal (*A. formosa*).

The perching ducks (tribe Cairinini) include the highly unusual mandarin duck (*Aix galericulata*) and the wood duck (*A. sponsa*), renowned for the spectacular nuptial plumage of the males. In regions where they roam wild, these ducks prefer living on tracts of water bordered by tall stemmed plants in which they can lay their eggs, after lining the cavities densely with feathers. Many other representative species of the Cairinini live in the southern hemisphere. Among them are the extremely small and curious pygmy goose (genus *Nettapus*) and the Muscovy duck (*Cairina moschata*). The latter, originally ranging from South America to Mexico, is one of the few species to have been raised in captivity for several centuries.

Diving ducks are thought by many to include a variety of different duck tribes such as the Aythyini, Somateriini, Mergini and Oxyurini; others, however, prefer to restrict the term "diving duck" to the Aythyini alone. The Aythyini, nevertheless, are rightly differentiated by reason of the fact that they seek their food in deep water. Among the best known species are the pochard (*Aythya ferina*), the tufted duck (*A. fuligula*) and the scaup (*A. marila*). Of the three, the last is the least dependent upon fresh water, including a larger quantity of animal food in its diet during the winter.

The red-crested pochard (*Netta rufina*), a decorative species found throughout Asia and in southern Europe, is the only duck to adopt one aspect of behavior fairly common among other birds; the male of this species, during courtship, offers food (aquatic plants) to his mate.

Belonging to the tribe of Somateriini are the eiders, northern birds which during the winter months skim the sea surface and even dive below the water in search of food, consisting mainly of mollusks. The eider (*Somateria mollissima*) is well distributed and provides various northern populations with eggs, meat, and down. Even more spectacular is the male nuptial garb of the king eider (*S. spectabilis*) and of Steller's eider (*Polysticta stelleri*). Some of the species belonging to the Mergini tribe show

Goldeneye
(*Bucephala clangula*)

Pochard
(*Aythya ferina*)

Tufted duck
(*Aythya fuligula*)

Scaup
(*Aythya marila*)

Steller's eider
(*Polysticta stelleri*)

King eider
(*Somateria spectabilis*)

Common scoter
(*Melanitta nigra*)

Old squaw
(*Clangula hyemalis*)

certain affinities to the perching ducks of the Cairinini. The harlequin (*Histrionicus histrionicus*) generally nests beside rivers with strong-flowing currents, a habitat to which it is well adapted.

The old squaw (*Clangula hyemalis*) is a northern species with a number of notable peculiarities. It is, for example, the only duck which takes on three distinct forms of plumage successively in the course of a year. Furthermore, it is the best underwater swimmer of the lot, capable of diving deeper than 65 ft (20 m) and staying submerged for more than a minute as it hunts for small mollusks or crustaceans. The goldeneye (*Bucephala clangula*) is a widely diffused species, nesting mainly in the taiga and dependent on finding a suitable spot in a tree some way above the ground.

The common scoter (*Melanitta nigra*) is one of a group in which the male plumage is predominantly black. This duck nests in the north, at the extreme limits of tall vegetation, especially in a belt close to the Arctic Circle. It is easily distinguished from the similar white-winged scoter (*M. fusca*) which, as its name suggests, has white patches on the wings. These birds usually winter at sea, along the coasts, and are liable to suffer heavy losses as a result of oil pollution in waters where shipping traffic is becoming ever more busy.

In the merganser group, the smew (*Mergus albellus*) is one of the smaller species, notable for the male's elegant black-and-white plumage. The bird breeds in more or less the same areas as the black woodpecker and often commandeers the latter's nest for its own eggs. Similar in size is the hooded merganser (*M. cucullatus*), native to North America, closely related to two better known species, the goosander (*M. merganser*) and the red-breasted merganser (*M. serrator*).

The so-called stifftails belonging to the Oxyurini tribe are notable, as their name indicates, for having a long, stiff tail which functions as a rudder underwater as well as constituting a signal for courting males. The ruddy duck (*Oxyura jamaicensis*) has been imported from its original homes to some parts of Europe, especially Britain, and small populations are to be found even in the wild. The white-headed duck (*O. leucocephala*) is a Eurasian species, still fairly abundant in central and western Asia and in a few other places in eastern Europe.

Harlequin
(*Histrionicus histrionicus*)

Smew
(*Mergus albellus*)

Red-breasted merganser
(*Mergus serrator*)

Goosander
(*Mergus merganser*)

Hooded merganser
(*Mergus cucullatus*)

Ruddy duck
(*Oxyura jamaicensis*)

In general, ducks tend to be smaller and have a more varied range of beaks than geese. There are over 100 species, most of them migratory, meaning that they do not always have the same breeding grounds and winter quarters.

There are two principal groups, dabbling ducks and diving ducks, according to their manner of feeding. The two types differ partly in behavior and ways of flying as well as in outward appearance: color of plumage, foot structure (diving ducks have feet that are broadly webbed), and position (further back in diving ducks) and shape of bill.

Various species of diving ducks are shown on these pages, while a selection of dabbling ducks is illustrated on the previous pages.

FALCONIFORMES

The order Falconiformes comprises all diurnal birds of prey, notable for their particularly robust build, adapted to hunting and flying.

The mountain hawk-eagle (*Spizaëtus nipalensis*) belongs to the group of so-called "booted" eagles (family Accipitridae). The black bill is fairly solid. The legs are covered with feathers up to the joints; they are very strong and the feet are equipped with hooked black claws. The adult's overall length is about 27 – 35 in (66 – 86 cm). The bird performs rapid maneuvers among the trees of the forest when hunting prey, which includes young monkeys and other small to medium-sized mammals, as well as birds.

The mountain hawk-eagle lives in mountain forests at altitudes of 2,000 – 6,600 ft (600 – 2,000 m) and more in the Western Ghats, Sri Lanka, the Himalayas, Indochina, eastern China as far as the Yangtze-Kiang, the Korean peninsula, the Japanese islands, and Taiwan. Solitary by habit, it nests on trees. The female lays one egg, and the chicks are nidicolous.

The buzzard (*Buteo buteo*), also a member of the Accipitridae, measures 20 – 22 in (51 – 56 cm) in total length, has a wingspan of 46 – 56 in (115 – 140 cm) and weighs 1¼ – 3 lb (0.6 – 1.4 kg). This species is abundantly distributed in the wooded zones and taiga of the Palearctic region.

In many wooded areas bordering the cultivated steppes of central Europe, the buzzard is the commonest bird of prey. Although it nests in woods, it hunts in the open fields. The nest is generally situated in trees but also on rocks, especially in Mediterranean countries. The raptor feeds on small rodents and on other mammals up to the size of a small hare, on birds, reptiles, insects, and other invertebrates; nor does it refuse carrion in winter. One of its most typical hunting techniques is to perch in a tree or on a post, attentively watching for movement in the fields below. The buzzard has the ability to hover in midair, which greatly improves its hunting prospects.

The female usually lays 2 – 3 eggs, exceptionally 1 or 4 – 6. The chicks are nidicolous.

The osprey or fish hawk (*Pandion haliaëtus*) is the sole representative of

Mountain hawk-eagle
(*Spizaëtus nipalensis*)

Buzzard
(*Buteo buteo*)

Osprey
(*Pandion haliaëtus*)

Northern goshawk
(*Accipiter gentilis*)

Hen harrier
(*Circus cyaneus*)

Black kite
(*Milvus migrans*)

Secretary bird
(*Sagittarius serpentarius*)

Peregrine falcon
(*Falco peregrinus*)

Gray-faced
buzzard-e
(*Butastur*

Andean condor
(*Vultur gryphus*)

the family Pandionidae. It is the only diurnal bird of prey with a reversible toe and with nostrils that can be closed, perhaps as an adaptation to its technique of catching fish (its exclusive food), namely by diving into water.

Its total length is 22 – 24 in (55 – 60 cm), the wingspan 58 – 66 in (145 – 165 cm) and the weight 2½ – 4½ lb (1.1 – 2 kg). The legs are naked and covered with scales, and the feet are powerful; the scaled toes have their lower parts, especially at the joints, covered by pointed horny plates which, together with the long, curving claws, enable the bird to take a firm grasp of slippery prey.

The osprey ranges widely over Eurasia, Africa, North America, and central and coastal regions of Australia. It is not found in the polar regions or in South America. In temperate latitudes the bird frequents lakes and ponds with plenty of fish, as well as major rivers, especially in Asia, while in tropical and subtropical climes it is commonest along the coasts.

The osprey is a solitary species and only locally gregarious. The female lays, on average, 3 eggs; the chicks are nidicolous.

Another member of the Accipitridae, the hen harrier (*Circus cyaneus*) has a total length of 17 – 22 in (43 – 55 cm), a wingspan of 41 – 50 in (102 – 125 cm) and a weight of 10 – 22½ oz (290 – 700 g). It ranges over large tracts of central and southern Europe, as well as North America from Alaska to California, inhabiting natural and cultivated steppe-land, moors, and swamps. Its prey consists of small mammals and birds, reptiles, and amphibians. The nest may be situated on moors, in reafforested zones, in cornfields or in swampy areas among reeds and rushes. The species lays 3 – 6 eggs and the chicks are some time in the nest.

The gray-faced buzzard-eagle (*Butastur indicus*) (family Accipitridae), has a wide distribution through India, Southeast Asia, and central Africa. This is another raptor of a good deal smaller and slimmer than the buzzard, which it otherwise resembles. Its total length is 16 – 18 in (40 – 45 cm) and its wingspan 36 – 44 in (90 – 110 cm). It inhabits cultivated areas and woodlands interspersed with open spaces. Diet and hunting technique are similar to those of the buzzard.

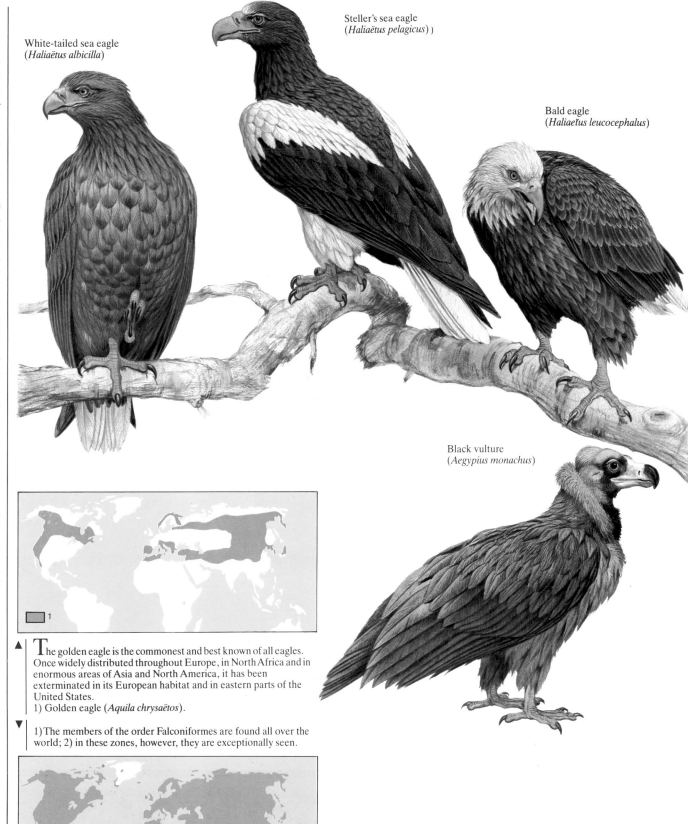

White-tailed sea eagle
(*Haliaëtus albicilla*)

Steller's sea eagle
(*Haliaëtus pelagicus*))

Bald eagle
(*Haliaëtus leucocephalus*)

Black vulture
(*Aegypius monachus*)

1

The golden eagle is the commonest and best known of all eagles. Once widely distributed throughout Europe, in North Africa and in enormous areas of Asia and North America, it has been exterminated in its European habitat and in eastern parts of the United States.
1) Golden eagle (*Aquila chrysaëtos*).

1) The members of the order Falconiformes are found all over the world; 2) in these zones, however, they are exceptionally seen.

1
2

On these pages some representatives of all the families belonging to the order Falconiformes are illustrated. The most primitive family, the Cathartidae, contains the Andean condor. The Pandionidae are represented by the osprey, which is also the only surviving species of the family. The Accipitridae comprise the majority of all living birds of prey, and the drawings show three species of a sea eagle, the black vulture, the hen harrier, the northern goshawk, the gray-faced buzzard-eagle, the common buzzard and the mountain hawk-eagle. The family Sagittariidae is constituted of the sole species, the secretary bird. Finally, the peregrine falcon, representing the most highly evolved family, Falconidae.

ANDEAN CONDOR

Vultur gryphus

Order Falconiformes
Family Cathartidae
Size Length about 3¼ – 4 ft (1 – 1.16 m)
Wingspan 9 – 10¼ ft (2.75 – 3.15 m)
Weight 20 – 26½ lb (9 – 12 kg)
Distribution South America
Habits Gregarious
Nesting In rock cavities
Eggs 1 (?2)
Chicks Nidicolous

Apart from their impressive size, adult Andean condors may be recognized by the color of their plumage, black with metallic reflections, and the wholly or partially white secondary remiges and greater coverts. The head is completely naked, and the male condor has a characteristic fleshy crest, some 4 in (10 cm) long and 1¾ in (4.5 cm) high; the female lacks both this crest and the male's lobe-shaped wattles. The color of the iris varies, too, that of the male being light brown and the female's reddish-brown.

The bill is solid and quite powerful, enabling the condor to tear strips of flesh from the carcasses of fairly large land and marine mammals. There is a white collar of down, slightly narrower in the female, at the base of the long, featherless neck.

The range of the Andean condor extends from northern Colombia along the line of the Andes south to Tierra del Feugo and then northward along the Atlantic coast of Argentina to the mouth of the Rio Negro, but in many regions the species has become rare or is already extinct. In the Andes the bird lives at heights of 10,000 to 16,500 ft (3,000 to 5,000 m), but in the southern part of its range, along the Atlantic and Pacific coasts, it also nests on high sea cliffs.

The condor is a social species as far as its scavenging habits are concerned, but does not nest in large colonies. Immature birds as well as non-breeding adults gather every evening on particular roosts situated on rock ledges, these being visible from afar by the white of the bird's excrement. More than 20 condors may assemble here for the night. Late in the morning, when the sun's heat has created rising thermal currents, the condors take wing

An adult Andean condor about to take wing. This bird's size is greater than that of all other birds of prey. The naked head and neck, with the collar of soft down, are special adaptations to a diet of carrion, the same features being present in many other vultures of the Old and New Worlds.

A fleshy crest and a light brown iris distinguish the male Andean condor from the female, the latter also being smaller.

and begin to soar, scanning the vast spaces below with their exceptionally keen eyes for carrion which may already have been discovered by other scavengers such as turkey vultures and caracaras. Apparently there is a social hierarchy among condors which is observed while they feed. Dominant individuals accept the presence of sub-dominants and "candidates," and it is rare for aggressiveness to culminate in outright struggles to establish a new hierarchy.

One white egg is laid on the bare ground inside a small cave in the rock wall, at altitudes varying from sea level to over 13,000 ft (4,000 m). Often several pairs will nest in the same rock face, each defending the surroundings of their little cavity. The nests, therefore, are extremely difficult to locate, not only because of the site but also because the condors are highly secretive while nesting. Incubation is carried out mainly by the female, although the male sometimes relieves her for a few hours a day. The young hatch after about 2 months and then remain in the nest for a further 6 weeks, depending upon the parents for food even after they begin flying. The entire breeding cycle may thus take more than a year, with the result that an egg is laid only every other year.

A related species, the California condor (*Gymnogyps californianus*), has a total length of about 3¼ – 4 ft (1 – 1.15 m) and a weight varying from 20 – 30 lb (9 – 13.5 kg). It nests in a rock cavity, laying one egg. The nidicolous chick stays for several months in the nest.

The plumage is black with bluish metallic reflections. The white wing bars, visible from beneath, are a certain means of identification when the bird is in flight, as is the huge wingspan, equivalent to that of the Andean condor.

Today the California condor's range is limited to a small region north of Los Angeles. During the first half of the present century the condor population was about 60 individuals, now reduced to less than 40 in spite of the conservation attempts of biologists and the American authorities.

▼ Male Andean condor gliding. The bird's wingspan may reach about 10 ft (3.15 m). The long, broad wings make it possible for the condor to utilize every rising air current without having to waste energy on flapping flight.

▼ Like the Old World vultures, the Andean condor and other New World vultures feed principally on the carcases of land and marine mammals.

▼ This aggressive behavior by two males is designed to establish a pecking order when feeding.

▼ Adult California condor, whose size is similar to that of the Andean condor. It is now one of the rarest birds in the world.

▲ The turkey vulture is the most abundant of all the New World vulture species.

▶ The king vulture is notable for the many vivid colors on its head.

◀ 1) The habitats of the king vulture (*Sarcorhamphus papa*) are savannas and the tropical forests extending from central Mexico to Paraguay and northern Argentina. 2) The Andean condor (*Vultur gryphus*) lives in northern Colombia along the range of the Andes southward to Tierra del Feugo, and along the Atlantic coast of Argentina to the mouth of the Rio Negro. 3) The California condor (*Gymnogyps californianus*) is today confined to a small area north of Los Angeles, represented by not more than 40 individuals.

1
2
3

GOLDEN EAGLE

Aquila chrysaëtos

Order Falconiformes
Family Accipitridae
Size Length 2½ – 3½ ft (75 – 90 cm)
Wingspan 6 – 7¼ ft (1.8 – 2.2 m)
Weight 6 – 15 lb (2.7 – 6.7 kg)
Distribution Europe, North Africa, Asia, North America
Habits Solitary
Nesting In rock cavities or trees
Eggs 1 – 3, normally 2
Chicks Nidicolous

The golden eagle may be distinguished from other eagles by its enormous size and its almost uniformly dark brown coloration, the nape and head of the adult tending towards golden-bronze or grayish. The bill is strong and fairly stout, tibia and tarsus are very large and "booted" to the joints. The toes are big and strong, with long hooked claws; the rear claw is far larger than the rear toe. In flight the golden eagle is easily recognized by its long but not unusually broad wings, narrower and trimmed toward the front, by the protracted head and by the long, slightly rounded tail.

Immature golden eagles are almost black with white spots on the wings and have a white tail terminating in a broad transverse black stripe. In the years following birth the white patterns on wing and tail gradually fade, disappearing completely in the fifth or sixth year of life as the bird attains sexual maturity. Except when in a family group, it is rare to see more than two golden eagles flying together.

This species was originally distributed all over Europe, in North Africa, over vast areas of Asia and in North America. In the course of history the species has been wiped out over much of its European range and in eastern parts of the United States as a result of human modification and transformation of the environment.

In central and southern Europe the species is relegated mainly to mountain regions with plenty of rocks and few trees, where there are deep gorges and inaccessible ledges for building the eyrie. In Scandinavia and the USSR, however, the bird also frequents areas of flat woodland devoid of human settlement. Here the nests

Immature golden eagle on a high vantage point, grasping a passerine in its claws. Of all present-day eagles, this is the most widely distributed and abundant.

are built chiefly in trees. Although the golden eagle has, in many regions, become a true mountain species, there are still zones where it breeds at low altitudes as in Scotland, Spain, Sardinia, and Crete. These are all hilly areas with broken terrain, very low population density and the minimum of human interference.

The density of the golden eagle population is restricted by the need for a large quantity of prey and the availability of suitable nesting sites. In places where human impact on the environment has been negligible, the species remains closely attached to its traditional habitats, utilizing the same sites from one generation to another.

Like many other large birds of prey, the golden eagle lives in couples, such pairs often being formed as early as the second year of life. During the "engagement" period until the attainment of sexual maturity in the fifth year, the two birds visit their chosen nesting site frequently, heaping up dry and leafy branches for the construction or repair of the nest. Each pair possesses several nests, often located on the same rock face or in the same wooded district. Some eyries are used for dozens of years and, according to the available space, may be up to 10 ft (3 m) high and more than 6½ ft (2 m) across. Male and female share in the building or repair work.

During courtship, the golden eagle performs nuptial flights, including one particularly spectacular display in which the male nosedives toward the female and she suddenly turns in midair onto her back, so that their claws touch.

As a rule 2 eggs are laid at an interval of 2 – 3 days, this occurring toward the end of February in southern parts of the range and near the end of March in central and northern zones. Incubation commences as soon as the first egg is laid. It is undertaken chiefly by the female, who is fed by the male, he briefly taking her place on the eggs as she feeds.

Initially the male brings food for the eaglets, but as they grow the female joins him in this task. Until they are about a month old, the young are fed by the mother on strips of meat that she has torn from the carcass with her beak. In due course, and not without some effort, the eaglets begin feeding on their own. At the age of about 3 months the eaglets have normally made their first flight.

▼ The vast wing surface with its trimmed primary remiges enables the golden eagle to use warm air currents and glide on high with the least expenditure of energy.

▲ The element of surprise is essential to the golden eagle's hunting technique, and prey is generally killed on the ground. Crows, small raptors, ducks, and other birds may also be caught on the wing, however, as the eagle suddenly and swiftly turns to attack.

▼ After hatching, the eaglets are covered with thick whitish-gray down.

◄ The golden eagle feeds principally on small and medium-sized mammals such as rabbits, hares, marmots, mice, etc. as well as birds. But it will not refuse carrion, especially in winter.

It nests as a rule on rock faces, usually situated at a lower altitude than its hunting territory; this makes it easier to carry heavy prey back to the eyrie. ►

BLACK VULTURE

Aegypius monachus

Order Falconiformes
Family Accipitridae
Length 42 – 45 in (106 – 114 cm)
Wingspan 105 – 113 in (265 – 287 cm)
Weight 17 – 27½ lb (7,000 – 12,500 g)
Distribution Europe and Asia
Habits Solitary
Nesting In trees
Eggs 1
Chicks Nidicolous

Apart from its impressive size, the black vulture (*Aegypius monachus*) is notable for the uniformly dark brown color of its plumage, the powerful black bill, and the large, light gray head, only partially covered with soft dark down. The naked parts of the head and neck are bluish, the eyes are fairly large and deep set, and the iris is almost black. A collar of brown feathers, longer at the sides, protects the bare neck from the cold.

The black vulture, a typical bird of Mongolia and Tibet, is present over vast areas of the southern Palearctic region. In many parts of its European range, however, it has become rare or even extinct. The vulture's Asiatic range comprises the whole of Turkey and the Caucasus range, western Turkestan, Iran, and Afghanistan, then east to inner Mongolia and Tibet and south to Hindustan and Assam. Of all the Palearctic vultures, none ranges farther north than this species, the northernmost limits being the Great Altai Mountains. In the Iberian peninsula and the Balkans the bird frequents hills and mountains covered by evergreen forests, as well as plains and high plateaus with extensive grazing for large herds of cattle and flocks of sheep and goats, whose carcasses are the basis of its diet.

It lives, like many other large raptors, in a permanent state of monogamy and may form pairs already before reaching sexual maturity, this occurring in the fifth or sixth year. The nest is a bulky construction of large branches, collected by the male and set in place by the female in a fork or at the summit of a tree, 6½ ft (2 m) to 65 ft (20 m) above ground level. A nest may be utilized for several years. Courtship flights, staged above the

The black vulture is the most impressive of all Old World vultures, being almost as big as the two American condors. When feeding around a carcass, it imposes its dominance over all other species even though tolerating their presence. The degree of competition depends on individual hunger and appetite. The hungriest birds, recognizable by their completely empty crops, in fact dominate the rest, but their aggressive instincts gradually dwindle until, in the final stages, all the vultures in the group end up feeding together.

The black vulture can easily be recognized in flight by its long, broad wings.

nesting site, are similar to those of the griffon vulture. One egg, white with reddish brown spots, is laid between mid February and end of March, being incubated by both sexes. The baby is born after 52-55 days.

Prey items of the black vulture, as of all other vultures, consists in the main of the carcasses of moderate-sized and large mammals, both domesticated and wild, though sometimes it will also hunt smaller mammals the size of hares. Vultures therefore perform a valuable ecological and hygienic function in eliminating carrion, a dangerous source of infection and epidemic disease, and speeding up the recycling of organic substances for the incessant flow of energy in the ecosystems of which they are part.

The griffon vulture (*Gyps fulvus*) is slightly smaller than the black vulture and also has much paler plumage. The griffon has a vast range over the southern Palearctic region, where two subspecies are identifiable. It is a highly gregarious bird, nesting in large colonies among rocks, the numbers sometimes reaching 150 pairs. The female lays one egg, and the chicks are nidicolous.

The distinguishing features of the white-headed vulture (*Trigonoceps occipitalis*) include a small crest of white down on the head and a broad red beak. The naked parts of the head are pale but may turn red when the bird is excited. The plumage of the back and collar is chocolate brown. The geographical range of the species extends in a wide belt from Senegal eastward to Nubia and Somalia, and comprises vast areas of eastern and southern Africa. It is absent, however, from the tropical forests in central and western parts. The habitat of the white-headed vulture is the savanna, where it lives in solitary pairs, building a large nest mainly in acacia trees. The female lays only one egg and the chick remains for some time in the nest. In addition to carrion, it also feeds on live prey up to the size of small antelopes.

The Egyptian vulture (*Neophron percnopterus*) is, along with the hooded vulture (*Necrosyrtes monachus*), the smallest of the Old World vultures. In the northern part of its range the vulture is migratory but in the central and southern parts sedentary. The bird frequents warm open terrain interspersed with rocky zones where it builds its nest. Two eggs are laid and the chicks are nidicolous.

▲ Griffon vultures feasting on the carcass of a zebra. The long neck is covered only by short, silky plumage, so that the head can be plunged deep into the anal opening and mouth of the dead animal for the extraction of the intestines and other organs.

▲ The white-headed vulture is the most colorful of the Old World species and is noted for its ability to capture live prey. It is less numerous than the two other African vultures and it is not usual to see more than one individual around carrion.

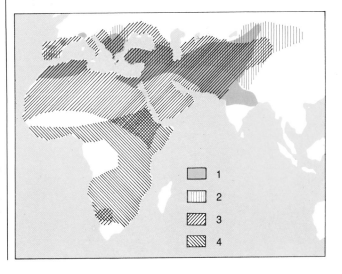

▢	1
▦	2
▨	3
▧	4

The small Egyptian vulture, in some parts of East Africa, has developed a singular method of eating ostrich eggs. In order to crack the thick shell, it picks up stones weighing up to 11 oz (300 g) and drops them hard and repeatedly on the egg.

◄ 1) The griffon vulture (*Gyps fulvus*) inhabits vast areas of the southern Palearctic region. 2) The black vulture (*Aegypius monachus*) lives in Europe and Asia; in many parts of its European range it has become rare or even extinct, as in Austria, Yugoslavia, and Spain. It ventures farther north than any other Palearctic vulture, the most northerly points of its range being in the Great Altai mountains. 3) The Egyptian vulture (*Neophron percnopterus*) lives in southern Europe, in Asia as far as India, and throughout North Africa. 4) The white-headed vulture (*Trigonoceps occipitalis*) is exclusively African, ranging across vast zones in the east and south of the continent.

GOSHAWK
Accipiter gentilis

Order Falconiformes
Family Accipitridae
Length 19 – 24½ in (47 – 61 cm)
Wingspan 40 – 45 in (100 – 115 cm)
Weight 1½ – 3 lb (670 – 1,350 g)
Distribution Eurasia and North America
Habits Solitary
Nesting In trees
Eggs 2 – 5
Chicks Nidicolous

The goshawk (*Accipiter gentilis*) is a raptor of average size with an accentuated sexual dimorphism, the female being considerably larger than the male. The head is dark brown and a contrasting broad white band breaks this uniform color above the eyebrows. The short, strongly curved bill is blackish. In flight the short, rounded wings, protractile head and long, rectangular tail are clearly visible.

A male goshawk may be mistaken for a large female sparrowhawk, although the wings of the former species are proportionately longer and the tail a little more rounded. The goshawk's flight consists of a series of rapid wingbeats followed by a glide with outstretched wings. The species is notable for an extensive geographical range, the birds tending to be heavier and with much paler plumage the farther north they roam.

Its distribution covers the northern Holarctic belt and the temperate zones of the Mediterranean region, ranging as far south as northern Morocco. The goshawk is mainly found in woods of tall deciduous or coniferous trees as well as in mixed forests, and it is here that it builds its nest. When hunting it also frequents clearings and open fields with thickets and hedges for cover.

Because of its elusive hunting technique and difficulty in locating its nest, built at a considerable height and often impossible to see from the ground, even the most attentive observer may sometimes be unaware of the goshawk's presence. The best time of year to keep watch on a pair of birds is in the spring when both partners appear high over the nesting site, indulging in nuptial flights. The birds mate on a tree close to the nest but seldom in the nest proper. Once a

▶| Flight silhouette as seen from below.

▼| Adult goshawk with a newly captured cock pheasant. Short wings and long tail permit the bird to execute rapid maneuvers within the woods where it finds a good part of its prey. The diet is highly varied and mainly comprises birds up to the size of a grouse or heron, but also mammals such as mice, squirrels, rabbits, and hares.

pair is formed, the male points out several sites to his mate and eventually she chooses the most suitable one. The pair will often make use of the same nest for several years.

The eggs are laid at intervals of 2 – 4 days, the period varying according to latitude, from mid March in the Mediterranean to mid April in Finland. The color of the eggs is an opaque white, sometimes speckled. Incubation may commence either before or after the last egg is laid, and is undertaken chiefly by the female. She is relieved for a few hours daily by her mate who spends time finding food. After 35 – 41 days the chicks are born, covered in thick white down.

The size of territory varies according to the amount of prey locally available. In central and northern Europe a pair of goshawks will occupy an area of 11 – 19 sq miles (30 – 50 km^2). Prey items of the goshawk consist predominantly of birds and a smaller quantity of mammals which vary in size according to the different dimensions of male and female as well as the area occupied by the goshawk population.

The sparrowhawk (*Accipiter nisus*) looks like a small goshawk and shares vast parts of the latter's Eurasian range. In this species, too, sexual dimorphism is very marked, the female being much larger than the male. The sparrowhawk is renowned for hunting small birds, catching them either by skimming low over the ground or by perching on the bottom branches of trees, body absolutely still and only the head moving in track of prey. In the nest, built on branches, the female lays 2 – 7 eggs, and the fledglings are nidicolous.

The honey buzzard (*Pernis apivorus*) is an average-sized bird of prey, more slender than the common buzzard. It has a highly specialized diet, consisting mainly of the larvae of wasps and other Hymenoptera, scooped out of nests that are usually situated on the ground but also in trees. The honey buzzard's range covers enormous areas of Europe and extends east to the Great Altai Mountains of central Asia. Favored habitats are wooded zones interspersed with open spaces. This is a migratory species that spends the winter months in equatorial Africa. Except when migrating, the bird is solitary by habit. The nest is built in a tree and the female lays 1 – 3 eggs. The chicks, like those of similar species, are nidicolous.

▲ Birds are caught on the wing, often after a long pursuit. The powerful talons guarantee a swift, accurate kill.

▲ The goshawk is often trained for falconry. Next to the peregrine falcon, it is the best adapted species for this kind of hunting which, in recent decades, has created vast problems for those concerned with rescuing from the wild young individuals of rare or endangered species.

▲ The osprey specializes in the capture of fish, seizing it with its talons. The outer toe of each foot is reversible so that it can firmly grasp the slippery prey.

Common buzzard (*Buteo buteo*)

Honey buzzard (*Pernis apivorus*)

Marsh harrier (*Circus aeruginosus*)

Gray-faced buzzard-eagle (*Butastur indicus*)

Sparrowhawk (*Accipiter nisus*)

African little sparrowhawk (*Accipiter minullus*)

◄ The goshawk's European range comprises the northern Holarctic belt and the temperate parts of the Mediterranean region. The Arctic taiga marks the northernmost limit and the southern boundary is a line extending from Turkey to northern Iran across to northern Mongolia, Manchuria, and Japan. It also has a wide distribution in North America. 1) Distribution of the goshawk (*Accipiter gentilis*).

BLACK KITE

Milvus migrans

Order Falconiformes
Family Accipitridae
Length 22 in (56 cm)
Wingspan 59 in (150 cm)
Distribution Eurasia, Africa, Australia
Habits Gregarious
Nesting On trees and rocks
Eggs 2 – 3, more rarely 1 or 4 – 5
Chicks Nidicolous

The black kite (*Milvus migrans*) is approximately the same size as a buzzard but looks more slender and is also distinguished by its dark brown coloration, its narrower wings and its forked tail. It is one of the most widely distributed and abundantly represented birds of prey in the world, displaying great flexibility in its choice of ecological niche. Given the vast extension of this global range, it is not surprising that there are 6 or 7 geographical subspecies, varying in the color of the plumage and the bill, as well as in dimensions, the smaller forms appearing in Australia and Indonesia, the larger ones in Eurasia.

The bird frequents wooded areas close to rivers, lakes, and other wet environments, both on level ground and up in the hills. In the Middle East it also finds its way into towns and villages, seeking contacts with humans who provide it with food and refuse. The black kite often nests in the neighborhood of heronries. In the mountains it soars to altitudes of 2,500 – 3,000 ft (800 – 1,000 m) but its densest populations are found on the plains and in the foothills.

The majority of European black kites migrate in autumn, flying south to tropical Africa for the winter. The various African subspecies likewise make periodic migrations from place to place, but little research has so far been done on this phenomenon, mainly because it is so difficult to distinguish these forms from wintering populations from Europe. The birds fly back to Europe across the Straits of Gibraltar as early as February, the biggest flocks appearing in March, and small contingents or single birds straggling through until May.

The black kite attains sexual maturity at the age of about three years. The nest in most cases is situated on a tree, either in a fork close to the trunk or on

The black kite (*Milvus migrans*) is an average-sized raptor which feeds principally on live and dead fish up to 12 in (30 cm) long, as well as small mammals, birds, reptiles, and amphibians, many of which are snatched from other birds of prey or picked up dead.

a lateral branch, at a height above ground level varying from 25 to 65 ft (8 to 20 m) or more. Whereas other raptors decorate their nest with green branches, the black kite lines the interior with rags, paper, pieces of plastic, and other objects, carried mainly by the male.

The female lays the eggs, which are greenish white with brown spots, at intervals of 1 – 2 days, over a period which varies according to latitude; this is March in North Africa and April-May in central Europe. Incubation, which often starts immediately after the laying of the first egg, lasts about 29 days; it is chiefly the responsibility of the female, who absents herself only to feed.

The Brahminy kite (*Haliastur indus*) is a raptor of medium size, distributed principally in India, north to the Himalayas, at altitudes up to 6,500 ft (2,000 m). Its range also includes Southeast Asia plus the islands to latitude 28°N, and finally New Guinea and the northern coasts of Australia. It is essentially a bird of wet zones such as rivers, lakes, shores, and marshes; and hundreds of the birds may often be seen milling around port areas. The species feeds on live and dead fish, caught with great skill on the surface, amphibians, lizards, mollusks, small birds and mammals, insects, carrion and, to a large extent, refuse of all kinds, thus performing a valuable sanitary and hygienic function.

In India the kite nests in December-January and has a second clutch in June. The nest is a modest structure, often situated in a palm or other tree surrounded by water; and it is similar to that of the black kite in being adorned inside with scraps of rag, bits of mud, pieces of paper, and other objects. The 2 – 3 eggs are incubated, almost wholly by the female, for about 28 days.

The red kite (*Milvus milvus*) is a large bird of prey with a majestic and elegant air, characterized by a long forked tail, long and narrow wings, and plumage of contrasting tones. The geographical range of the red kite is limited to continental and southern Europe, Turkey, and northwest Africa. Habitats most frequently associated with the red kite are woods of flat and hilly regions with plenty of open spaces, rivers, lakes, and ponds. In the Mediterranean it also lives in the mountains up to altitudes of 5,000 – 6,500 ft (1,500 – 2,000 m).

The bill is short and strongly curved, the upper mandible of the adult being furnished with a tooth-like projection.

From top to bottom: silhouette of goshawk, black kite, and red kite. In addition to its uniformly dark color, the black kite is smaller than the red kite and has a less prominently forked tail.

The black kite's nest is generally situated in a tree and is fairly small in size. It is often lined with rags, feathers, and other objects.

The Brahminy kite (*Haliastur indus*) is a species with a wide distribution in India and Southeast Asia, where it prefers to live in wet zones.

The red kite (*Milvus milvus*) is the largest of the kites, notable for its long, deeply forked red tail.

In zones where there is plenty of prey, black kites nest in colonies, especially near rivers and lakes.

The black kite's egg is creamy white, sometimes densely marked with reddish brown patches and spots.

The range of the black kite (*Milvus migrans*) (1)comprises much of Europe, Asia, Africa, and Australia. It is absent from the entire American continent, from the Sahara, Scandinavia, and the southern part of the Australian subcontinent (2).

WHITE-TAILED SEA EAGLE

Haliaëtus albicilla

Order Falconiformes
Family Accipitridae
Length 28 – 36 in (70 – 90 cm)
Wingspan 80 – 96 in (200 – 240 cm)
Weight 8½ – 16½ lb (4,000 – 7,500 g)
Distribution Eurasia
Habits Solitary, partly gregarious
Nesting On trees and rocks
Eggs 1 – 4, usually 2
Chicks Nidicolous

The eight species belonging to the genus *Haliaëtus* are large raptors distributed all over the world, except in Central and South America. The white-tailed sea eagle (*Haliaëtus albicilla*) is slightly bigger than the golden eagle, though not as handsome.

Formerly widespread throughout much of the northern Palearctic region, the white-tailed sea eagle is now extinct in many places, especially in Europe, as a result of large-scale human persecution and environmental changes that have occurred since the eighteenth century.

The species is fit to start breeding around its fifth year, living in a permanent state of monogamy. In central Europe courtship flights already begin in mid December, reaching a peak of intensity in February and March. The couple usually mate close to the nest but on rare occasions some miles away from it. The nests are usually built near the top of the tree, so that they are easily accessible to the eagles from above, and sometimes invisible from the ground; if used for several years in succession they can become very bulky.

The female lays her eggs at intervals of 2 – 5 days during a period which differs according to latitude. In the southern part of the range, such as in Greece, it begins as early as January, in East Germany from mid February to mid March, in Norway from mid to end April, and in Greenland from early May onwards. Incubation commences after the laying of the first egg in order for hatching to occur within 10 days.

The most northerly populations of the white-tailed sea eagle, especially those from Asia, set off on regular migrations southward in winter to escape from the ice-covered rivers and lakes that no longer afford them

▲ Juvenile white-tailed sea eagle with its prey, a dead seal. This large raptor ranges widely over the northern part of the Palearctic region, living close to the sea and along the banks of lakes and rivers swarming with fish and water birds.

P rey items include fish (cod, salmon, carp, pike, eels, etc.), birds (coots, ducks, swans, geese, grebes, gulls, etc.), and mammals (small rodents, hares, baby deer, reindeer, etc.), as well as carrion. ▶

...ient food. In other regions the species is more or less sedentary.

The African fish eagle (*Haliaëtus vocifer*) is about the size of a golden eagle. The female is slightly bigger than the male. It often lets out a characteristic cry, very like that of a herring gull, either when perching, head tilted upwards, or in flight. The range of the species extends from Senegal to Ethiopia and south to Cape Province. The bird mainly frequents lakes and rivers with an abundance of fish, but it also appears along the coasts where there are enough trees for it to build a nest. It is a fairly common species, particularly in the region of the great lakes of East Africa. Fish, which constitute the bird's principal form of food, are caught on the surface of deep or shallow water.

Steller's sea eagle (*Haliaëtus pelagicus*) inhabits a very restricted area of northeast Asia. Solitary by habit, it nests on rocks or on bare ground, the female laying 1 – 3 eggs and the fledglings remaining for a long time in the nest. Its present status is uncertain and it would seem that the species is rapidly declining because of pesticides which, in recent years, have had a markedly adverse effect on the birth rate.

The bald or American eagle (*Haliaëtus leucocephalus*) is the only representative of the genus to be found in America, where it is distributed from Alaska to California and Florida; it is absent from the northernmost regions of Canada. The nest is built in a tree and accommodates 1 – 3 eggs; the fledglings are nidicolous. The bald eagle frequents coasts, major rivers and lakes, but is also to be found in the mountains, such as the Yellowstone National Park. The eagle feeds chiefly on fish such as salmon and herring, and also on water birds, snakes, and carrion. This species often filches the prey of other raptors. In recent decades the bald eagle population has suffered a notable decline in numbers over vast parts of its range, due in the first place to systematic persecution because it is reputed to be a harmful species, particularly in sheep-grazing zones. Bald eagles nesting in the northern part of the continent migrate south in the autumn in preparation for the cold winter. Because the species is exclusive to North America, this very handsome bird of prey has been chosen as the symbol of the United States.

▲ Silhouettes of the white-tailed sea eagle (top) and Steller's sea eagle in flight. Both species have long, broad wings and a white, wedge-shaped tail.

▲ The white-tailed sea eagle often hunts by flying low over the water surface, feet extended for catching fish and birds.

Steller's sea eagle
(*Haliaëtus pelagicus*)

Bald eagle
(*Haliaëtus leucocephalus*)

African fish eagle
(*Haliaëtus vocifer*)

◄ 1) Steller's sea eagle (*Haliaëtus pelagicus*) inhabits a very limited area of northeast Asia. 2) The bald eagle (*Haliaëtus leucocephalus*) is widely distributed in North America from Alaska to California and Florida, but is not found in the northernmost parts of Canada. 3) The white-tailed sea eagle (*Haliaëtus albicilla*) lives in vast areas of the northern Palearctic region, though now extinct in many zones, especially in Europe. 4) The African fish eagle (*Haliaëtus vocifer*) is a bird of the African continent, from Senegal to Ethiopia and southward to Cape Province.

PEREGRINE FALCON

Falco peregrinus

Order Falconiformes
Family Falconidae
Length 15 – 19 in (38 – 48 cm)
Wingspan 31 – 45 in (80 – 115 cm)
Weight 19 – 46 oz (550 – 1,300 g)
Distribution Cosmopolitan
Habits Solitary
Nesting On rocks and trees
Eggs 2 – 5
Chicks Nidicolous

The peregrine falcon (*Falco peregrinus*) is a medium-sized raptor with a very compact, sturdy body. Sexual dimorphism is clearly marked, the dimensions of the female being almost one fifth bigger than those of the male. In flight clearly visible features are the pointed wings and the tail that tapers slightly towards the tip.

The peregrine falcon ranges far and wide over all the continents. The only parts where it is not found are the northernmost zones of the arctic region, the belt of desert stretching from the Sahara to China, broad areas of North America and South America as far as Patagonia, the dense tropical forests of central Africa, Southeast Asia, and many zones of Oceania. Because of this geographical variation the species appears in many different sizes and colors. The largest subspecies are to be found in North America and Siberia, the smallest in the Mediterranean and various island archipelagos (Cape Verde, Oceania).

It frequents many habitats, which in Europe include cliffs and rocks along the coasts and on the offshore small islands of the Atlantic and Mediterranean, rocky inland zones and wooded areas with wide open spaces. The species can even rest on rock faces.

The peregrine falcon is ready for breeding in its second year. In certain areas, when the population is fairly sparse, birds in juvenile plumage may also breed successfully. The species probably lives in a permanent state of monogamy. Having established their nesting sites, peregrine falcons stay put for some time, handing them down to successive generations.

Latitude plays an important part in determining the egg-laying period. The peregrine falcons of the Mediter-

▲ The adult peregrine falcon hunting white-fronted geese. This raptor is probably unrivaled for catching birds on the wing. Many populations have been gravely affected and their numbers much reduced in recent years because of the buildup in their bodies of pesticides ingested together with prey.

▲ Silhouette of peregrine falcon. The relatively long, pointed wings and the compact tail enable the bird to make rapid nosedives.

◄ Waders, passerines, doves, ducks, and also larger species such as geese, prairie chickens, and herons feature commonly in the peregrine falcon's diet.

ranean islands lay their eggs from mid February until the first ten days of March; in central Europe it is generally from the last ten days of March to the first ten days of April; and in Finland it is mid April in the south and the beginning of May in the north. The 3 – 4 eggs are laid at intervals of 1 – 3 days and incubation usually commences after the first or second. The female generally broods alone while the male finds food. The eggs hatch in 29 – 31 days, but the period may be extended for another week, depending on the size of the clutch.

The gyrfalcon (*Falco rusticolus*) is the largest representative of its genus. Solitary by habit, this bird lives in the tundras or arctic regions and the Far North of Eurasia and North America. The species nests mainly in the tundra, on rock ledges, but in some places on cliffs along the seashore. Food consists of small and medium-sized mammals, such as lemmings and hares, of marine and freshwater birds, but above all of grouse. The female lays 3 – 5 eggs and the chicks are nidicolous.

The hobby (*Falco subbuteo*) is a falcon of average size, slightly smaller than the peregrine, which it much resembles. The hobby ranges over the entire Palearctic region, with a northernmost limit of latitude 68°N; and it strays southward into the Oriental region to about 30°N. Its preferred habitats are wide open spaces on plains and hills, interspersed with wooded zones, often close to lakes and rivers. Swifts, swallows, larks, pipits, and other passerines make up most of its prey; and it also feeds on insects (dragonflies, grasshoppers, and termites), which it catches with the talons and often consumes in the air. The hobby settles in the old tree nests of rooks, magpies, jays, and other birds; in central Europe it begins nesting between the middle and end of May. The female lays 2 – 4 eggs.

In many parts of its range, the kestrel (*Falco tinnunculus*) is the best known and most abundant of all birds of prey. It roams the Old World, except for the Sahara and the tropical African forests. Solitary as a rule, the species nests on rocks and in trees, laying 4 – 6 eggs.

The American sparrowhawk (*Falco sparverius*) is the counterpart of the kestrel in the New World, being present from Alaska to Patagonia, with the exception of the central and southern tropical forests of America. It is considerably smaller than the kestrel.

The male, considerably smaller than the female, mainly hunts small and medium-sized passerines. At the climax of its dive the bird may reach a speed of 220 mph (350 kmh).

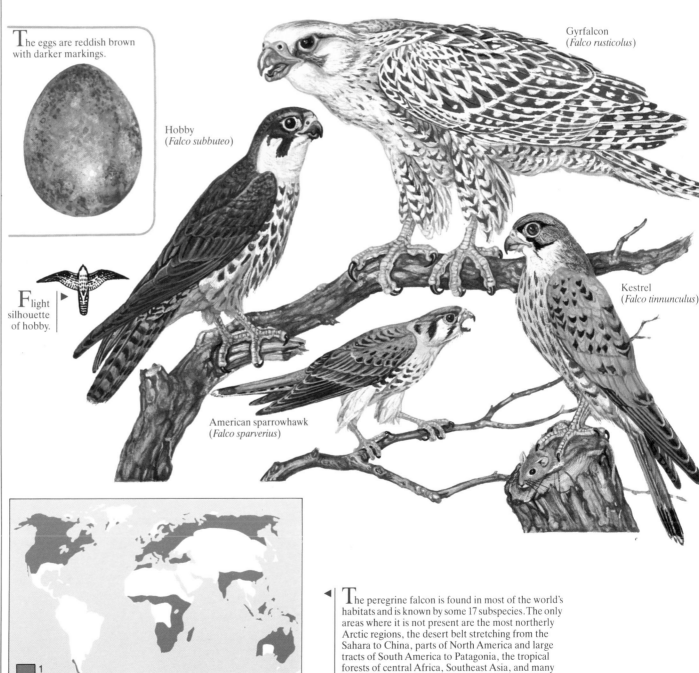

The eggs are reddish brown with darker markings.

Gyrfalcon
(*Falco rusticolus*)

Hobby
(*Falco subbuteo*)

Flight silhouette of hobby.

Kestrel
(*Falco tinnunculus*)

American sparrowhawk
(*Falco sparverius*)

The peregrine falcon is found in most of the world's habitats and is known by some 17 subspecies. The only areas where it is not present are the most northerly Arctic regions, the desert belt stretching from the Sahara to China, parts of North America and large tracts of South America to Patagonia, the tropical forests of central Africa, Southeast Asia, and many parts of Oceania. 1) Distribution of *Falco peregrinus*.

1

GALLIFORMES

This order comprises birds famed all over the world for the beauty of their plumage and valued, too, for their edibility. The majority of Galliformes are ground-dwelling species, nesting among shrubs, and the fledglings are nidifugous, soon leaving the nest to procure food for themselves; sexual maturity comes quite early and in many species there is a pronounced sexual dimorphism. They have a wide geographical distribution in a large variety of habitats, from arctic zones of rock and ice to the dense vegetation of the tropical forests. Their food consists in the main of vegetable substances.

The order Galliformes is subdivided into seven families: Megapodiidae, Cracidae, Tetraonidae, Numididae, Meleagrididae, Phasianidae, and Opisthocomidae. The family Phasianidae is subdivided into various subfamilies. The subfamily Perdicinae, comprises the quails and partridges, and is made up of many species with a wide distribution over nearly all the continents.

The gray partridge (*Perdix perdix*) exhibits most of the characteristics typical of the birds belonging to this subfamily. It lives in stubble on the fringes of cultivated land, in flat or hilly zones with mainly herbaceous and shrub vegetation, and sometimes in the mountains up to altitudes of over 3,300 ft (1,000 m). It is a typical ground-dwelling species; if compelled to take wing, after a hasty takeoff which involves a great deal of noisy fluttering, the bird settles into a glide (occasionally flapping its wings) and soon comes down to land a few hundred feet from its point of departure. The nest, dug in the bare ground, is lined with leaves and stems of dry grass, and is protected by a shrub, a root or a heap of twigs; in it are deposited ten or so eggs which are incubated by the female for 23 – 25 days.

The red-legged partridge (*Alectoris rufa*) lives chiefly in hilly regions on uncultivated land furrowed by gorges and rock ridges, but also frequents cultivated fields and vineyards. It is essentially a ground-dwelling species. The biological cycle is similar to that of the gray partridge but the period of incubation (23 days) is rather shorter.

▲ In early morning and late afternoon gray partridges forage among the bushes on the edges of cultivated fields; when it gets warmer they patrol beaten roads and paths, basking in the sun and taking dust baths.

◄ The food of partridges consists in the main of seeds, the dry fruits of cereals, leaves, and plant tops; in summer they feed quite substantially on animals, particularly invertebrates.

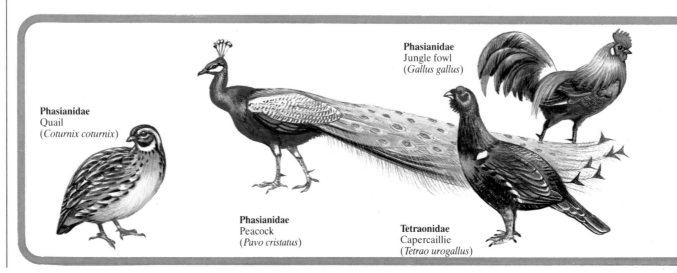

Phasianidae
Quail
(*Coturnix coturnix*)

Phasianidae
Peacock
(*Pavo cristatus*)

Phasianidae
Jungle fowl
(*Gallus gallus*)

Tetraonidae
Capercaillie
(*Tetrao urogallus*)

The rock partridge (*Alectoris graeca*) is usually identified by three subspecies: *A. g. saxatilis*, living mainly in the mountains, from the maritime Alps to Styria; *A. g. graeca*, inhabiting the Apennines, parts of Greece, and the Ionian Islands; and *A. g. whitakeri*, found only in the mountains of Sicily.

The Alpine rock partridge normally lives on grassy, stony slopes exposed to the morning sun at the foot of rock walls where the ground is uneven and pitted with pebbles, moraine deposits, and slabs of rock. In the mountains the breeding season of the rock partridge begins at the end of May, the female laying 8 – 12 eggs in June and incubating them for 24 – 25 days. The chicks are nidifugous and grow very rapidly.

In southern Asia, from Bangladesh to the southeastern coasts of China (and in southern Japan, where it has been successfully introduced), there is a related species known as the Formosan bamboo-partridge (*Bambusicola thoracica*). This bird has very colorful plumage and lives mainly in hills and on high plateaus on the edges of farmland where the dense growth of bamboo provides both protection and food. The latter consists of plant shoots, seeds, berries, and fruit; the biological cycle is similar to that of other partridges.

The cultivated or steppe-like prairies, well covered with shrub and dense undergrowth, that stretch from southern Canada to Brazil, are the haunts of the New World quails. The range of the bobwhite quail (*Colinus virginianus*) extends across the central–eastern United States from the borders with Canada to Mexico and the island of Cuba. Fairly abundant everywhere, the species has learned to reap full advantage from both cultivated farmland and grassland with plenty of herbaceous vegetation and low shrub growth.

The common quail (*Coturnix coturnix*) belongs, like the partridges, to the subfamily Perdicinae, and is the only migrating member of the Galliformes. In Europe it nests during the summer in cultivated fields and meadows from southern Italy to latitude 65°N. In autumn it migrates to central Africa and central to southern Asia. The quail's habitat is similar to that of the partridge, namely hedges, uncultivated fields, and rolling plains.

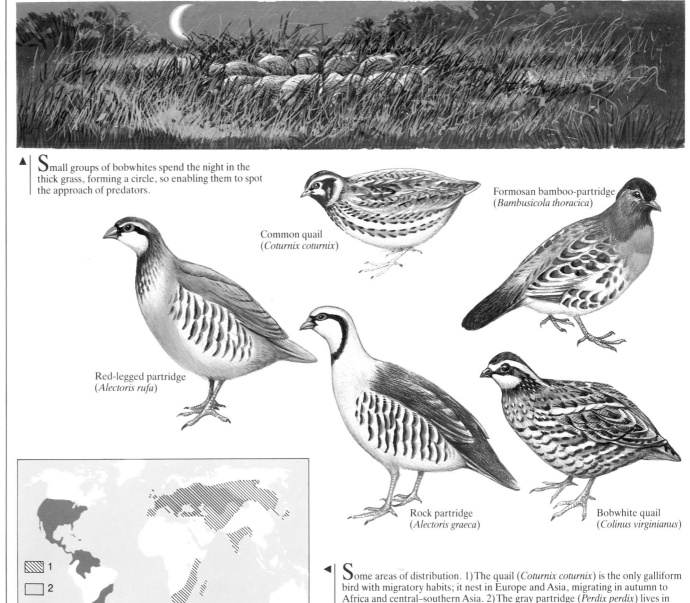

▲ Small groups of bobwhites spend the night in the thick grass, forming a circle, so enabling them to spot the approach of predators.

Common quail (*Coturnix coturnix*)

Formosan bamboo-partridge (*Bambusicola thoracica*)

Red-legged partridge (*Alectoris rufa*)

Rock partridge (*Alectoris graeca*)

Bobwhite quail (*Colinus virginianus*)

◄ Some areas of distribution. 1) The quail (*Coturnix coturnix*) is the only galliform bird with migratory habits; it nest in Europe and Asia, migrating in autumn to Africa and central–southern Asia. 2) The gray partridge (*Perdix perdix*) lives in Europe and parts of Asia. 3) The bobwhite quail (*Colinus virginianus*) is very abundant in the New World.

Principal families of the order Galliformes.

Megapodiidae
Mallee fowl (*Leipoa ocellata*)

Numididae
Vulturine guinea fowl (*Acryllium vulturinum*)

Cracidae
Great curassow (*Crax rubra*)

Meleagrididae
Wild turkey (*Meleagris gallopavo*)

MALLEE FOWL
Leipoa ocellata

Order Galliformes
Family Megapodiidae
Length 20 – 28 in (50 – 70 cm)
Distribution Southern and western Australia
Habits Monogamous
Nesting On ground. Embryonic development of the egg is assisted by heat generated from the decay of vegetation covered by sand
Eggs 10 – 12 (sometimes more), fairly large in keeping with body weight
Chicks Precociously nidifugous

The plumage of the mallee fowl (*Leipoa ocellata*) is mainly gray with varying darker tones. It lives in the interior of southern and western Australia and usually frequents arid regions with few trees and discontinuous herbaceous plant growth, interspersed with many bushes.

Along with all other representatives of the Megapodiidae, the mallee fowl utilizes the heat of the sun, the soil, and decaying plant matter to incubate its eggs. The female lays these eggs in a huge nest made from heaps of branches, grass, and other scraps of vegetation, all covered with soft sand. This conical structure acts as an artificial incubator. Every activity connected with breeding and birth of chicks involves the mallee fowl in long, painstaking work; and some ten months, in fact, elapse between the initial construction of the nest and the hatching of the eggs. All the preparatory work and later maintenance of the nest is done exclusively by the male.

In spring (September in the southern hemisphere) egg laying commences. The female places an egg in the hole that the male has prepared at the top of the mound, and he immediately covers it up when she has taken herself off. He then ensures embryonic development continues at a regular pace by removing sand or adding more to keep temperatures constant night and day, spring, summer, and autumn.

At the end of the fall the temperature has dropped still further but by this time the breeding cycle is complete, and the baby megapodes are born, a few days apart from one another.

Incubation mound of mallee fowl; in common with other megapodes, this species does not brood in the customary manner.

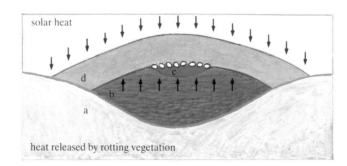

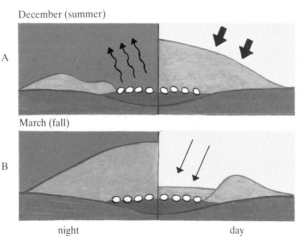

December (summer)

A

March (fall)

B

night   day

Cross-section of mound: a) soil excavated by mallee fowl; b) leaves, branches, and scraps of decaying vegetation; c) area for laying and incubating eggs; d) soft sand.
A) Summer: during the day the male protects the eggs from overheating by covering the mound with sand; at night he removes it so that the accumulated heat can be dispersed.
B) Winter: because of the drop in outside temperature, the process is reversed: in daytime the male uncovers the eggs and exposes them to the sun, and in the evening he covers them with sand to keep them warm.

The chicks, after hatching, have to dig a path through the soft sand to reach the surface of the mound.

GREAT CURASSOW

Crax rubra

Order Galliformes
Family Cracidae
Length 36 – 38 in (90 – 95 cm)
Distribution From southern Mexico to western Ecuador
Habits Gregarious for most of the year; monogamous in breeding season
Nesting In natural cavities of trees, at moderate heights
Eggs Usually 2, fairly large, with rough white shell
Chicks Precociously nidifugous

The great curassow (*Crax rubra*) inhabits the most northerly part of the geographical range of the Cracidae, from southern Mexico to western Ecuador. The customary habitats of the species are dense tropical or sub-tropical forests, which it frequents alternately in dry periods (winter) and wet periods (mainly in summer). Such habitats are therefore characterized by discontinuous belts of trees interspersed with a luxuriant growth of shrubs and extensive clearings.

The Cracidae, unlike the majority of Galliformes, are mainly arboreal by habit. The nest is built in the tallest trees, but not far from ground level, in natural cavities up the trunk or at the point where branches fork. The male initially chooses a suitable site and then brings the female to inspect it, and both birds line the bottom of the hole with leaves stripped from the surrounding branches. After a few days the female lays 2 eggs, a couple of days apart. During the period that precedes mating, the male behaves very aggressively towards conspecifics.

The eggs are quite large, and are incubated by the female alone for 28 – 29 days. The chicks are extremely lively and ready to make tiny leaps down to the ground almost as soon as their down is dry. They follow their mother all over the place as she seeks food, both on the ground and up in the trees; and at the least hint of danger they immediately take refuge beneath her body.

The great curassow's diet consists mainly of fruit, the tops of various plants, and large quantities of small invertebrates, especially arthropods.

▼| Female great curassow.

▲| The great curassow is essentially a tree-dweller, nesting in the natural hollows and usually decorating the nest with leaves and other plant substances.

◄| The long windpipe enables the bird to emit very loud noises which can be heard for quite a distance.

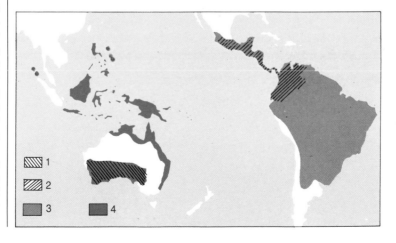

◄| The Cracidae live over much of Central and South America (3); the great curassow (*Crax rubra*) occupies the most northerly part of this range, a zone stretching from southern Mexico to western Ecuador (2). The Megapodiidae are Australian birds which live, as a rule, near the coast or in well vegetated zones (4). The mallee fowl (*Leipoa ocellata*), unlike other members of its family, prefers living in arid regions of grass and shrub in the interior of western and southern Australia (1).

TETRAONIDAE

The family Tetraonidae (grouse and ptarmigans) is represented by 11 genera with 18 species.

The members of this family are distinguished from other Galliformes in several ways. Stock and compact in build, they are medium to large birds, the tail being average or long, the bill short and curved, with feathered nostrils. Over the eyes are bare patches of red skin (caruncles), more developed in the males and becoming stiffer and larger during the breeding season. The legs and sometimes the feet as well are covered by feathers; the rear toe is shorter and higher positioned than the other three and at the sides of the toes are comblike horny appendages.

In some species there are air-sacs on the neck, identical in texture to the caruncles; in others there are, instead, tufts of erectile feathers on neck or crown.

In the past, the Tetraonidae inhabited large tracts of moorland and woodland in the northern parts of the northern hemisphere. After the advance and retreat of the glaciations they extended their range southward and eventually colonized the mountain systems of central and southern Europe, of North America and of southern Siberia. Present-day forms have evolved from an ancestral group of monogamous Tetraonidae living in wooded areas, and have branched off in two directions.

Some species have maintained monogamous courtship behavior; these are the so-called solitarily displaying species and are therefore regarded as being less evolved. Among the representatives of this group are the hazel grouse (*Tetrastes bonasia*), the ptarmigan (*Lagopus mutus*), the willow grouse (*Lagopus lagopus*), the ruffed grouse (*Bonasa umbellus*), and many other species. As a rule the courting pair takes over a territory and will seldom abandon it. The male assists the female in incubation and sometimes distracts the attention of possible predators. The sexes generally look similar. Species living in woodland have a fairly long tail and other very mobile structures; and apart from giving clear visual signals they emit loud, repeated calls (this being particularly characteristic of the ruffed grouse).

Other more highly evolved species have developed gregarious behavior during the breeding period and are known as

▲ A group of ptarmigans in winter plumage toward the e[nd] of fall. In the foreground on the left is an adult male, and [in] the center a female who has not yet finished her molt.

▼ A pair of ptarmigans with their brood high up in the mountain pastures at the beginning of summer.

▼ The nostrils of the ptarmigans are covered with feather[s] and there are red caruncles over the eyes, the latter bein[g] especially notable in the male, together with a band of black feathers extending from the base of the bill to the re[ar] of the eye. The tarsus and foot are covered in fine down which helps the bird to walk on snow; the rear toe is rais[ed] well above the level of the others.

collectively displaying species. Males tend to be fairly promiscuous, and each individual attempts, by displays, calls, and combats, to demonstrate his superiority over other rivals and thus earn the right to' establish ownership of a domain for singing.

Belonging to this group are the black grouse (*Lyrurus tetrix*), the capercaillie (*Tetrao urogallus*), the prairie chicken (*Tympanuchus cupido*), the sage grouse (*Centrocercus urophasianus*), and other species from North America and eastern Asia. Normally these species display a striking sexual dimorphism and for much of the year the sexes live separately. They tend to live in fairly open habitats, though an exception to this rule is exhibited by the capercaillie which displays in clearings, among snowfields and slopes inside the area of occupied territory. Each male, day after day, takes up his position inside the communal display ground and fiercely defends his little piece of territory. Individual areas toward the center of the display ground tend to be quite small but those nearer the outside are more extensive and occupied only by young males. A central position gives the male a better chance of mating because the females, when the moment is ripe, always head for the part of the territory where the greatest number of suitors are assembled. Combats between males are grimly selective, and the bird which emerges at the end to claim the center of the display ground is surely the strongest and cleverest fighter, exploiting to the full his knowledge of the terrain.

In all species the male exhibits characteristic behavior in the breeding season, performing a succession of actions that culminate in copulation. The females, on the other hand, all behave in the same manner when confronted by a male; when ready for the sexual act they lie flat on the ground, spread their wings slightly and prepare to receive their mate.

▲ When winter snowfall is heavy and the cold intense, the ptarmigan shelters at night by digging a hole in the snow.

▲ Phase of the spring courtship.

▼ A brooding female.

▼ An egg (natural size).

◄ Male ptarmigan in winter (left) and summer plumage.

Red grouse (*Lagopus lagopus scoticus*)

Greater prairie chicken (*Tympanuchus cupido*)

Black grouse (*Lyrurus tetrix*)

Ruffed grouse (*Bonasa umbellus*)

Hazel grouse (*Tetrastes bonasia*)

CAPERCAILLIE
Tetrao urogallus

Order Galliformes
Family Tetraonidae
Length Adult male 36 in (90 cm), adult
female 24 in (62 cm)
Weight Adult male 8½ lb (3,950 g),
adult female 4¾ lb (2,160 g)
Distribution Northern Europe and
Asia
Nesting On ground
Eggs 5 – 9, yellowish with brown spots
Chicks Nidifugous

The capercaillie (*Tetrao urogallus*) is the
largest European member of the family
Tetraonidae. The sexual dimorphism is
striking, for the male is much bigger
than the female and his plumage is more
vividly colored. The range of the capercaillie extends from Scotland to the
River Lena and Lake Baikal in eastern
Siberia; its northern boundary virtually
coincides with the Arctic Circle, and the
southern limit is latitude 50°N in
Siberia. Some populations, however,
live outside this vast area.

In spring, from early April till the
end of May, the capercaillie devotes its
activities to breeding and behaves in a
very characteristic fashion. The cock
takes up his position on a vantage point
in a tree when it is still dark, sometimes
settling there during the evening; and
the moment dawn breaks he begins to
sing. The song territory is always the
same, year after year, and the females
converge on it when the breeding
period is near. During the male's displays the females usually settle on the
branches of the conifers or at the foot of
the trees, listening to his song day after
day, both in the morning and evening,
and eventually mating with the cock on
the ground. He, because of mounting
excitement, sees and hears nothing during the final part of his song, but the
females are ever attentive, acting as sen-
tinels; and in the event of the slightest
noise or movement they fly far off in
alarm, clucking loudly and repeatedly.
This warns the cock, who immediately
follows them.

After mating, until the end of the
breeding season, each bird loses
interest in its companions and leads a
solitary life. The female lays 5 – 9 eggs,
at intervals of 24 – 48 hours, depending on weather conditions, in the nest,
which is a simple hollow in the ground.
The incubation period is 26 – 28 days.

▲ | Adult male capercaillie displaying in
courtship period.

▲ | Adult male and female on alert while feeding. Note the
horny, comb-like appendages on the toes which make it
easier for the bird to walk over snow, and the red caruncles,
better developed in the male.

◀ 1) The family Tetraonidae, widely distributed during the Cenozoic
era in the northern moorlands and woods of the northern
hemisphere, subsequently colonized regions farther south. Today it
also lives in the mountain zones of central and southern Europe, in
North America, and in southern Siberia. 2) Distribution of
capercaillie (*Tetrao urogallus*).

BLACK GROUSE
Lyrurus tetrix

Order Galliformes
Family Tetraonidae
Length Adult male 22 in (56 cm), adult female 16 in (42 cm)
Weight Adult male 2¾ lb (1,270 g), adult female 2 lb (890 g)
Distribution Northern Europe and Asia
Nesting On ground
Eggs 6 – 10, yellowish with a variety of dark brown spots and streaks
Chicks Precociously nidifugous

The black grouse (*Lyrurus tetrix*) is the best known of all Tetraonidae, above all for its lyre-shaped tail. The sexual dimorphism is marked both with regard to size and plumage coloration. The range of the black grouse extends, almost without any break in continuity, from the British Isles to the eastern shores of Siberia. As a rule, the species frequents forest fringes and clearings or open land close by.

At the end of winter the cocks return to the habitual zones where they assemble year after year in the breeding season, each establishing his own portion of territory or display ground, also known as a lek. Once settled on their display grounds, the cocks commence a whole series of ceremonial activities to the accompaniment of bubbling and crowing noises that can be heard for quite a distance, each trying to monopolize the central part of the lek. This is extremely important, for the females, once these disputes are terminated, soon arrive and show their readiness, according to well-defined rituals, to mate. The strongest males, with the greatest fighting experience and familiarity with the terrain, will by this time have taken possession of the central area of the display ground.

Following copulation, the females leave the lek and devote themselves to preparing the nest. This is, in effect, a shallow depression in the soil, hidden among bushes or well sheltered, eventually harboring an average of 7 – 8 yellowish, brown-speckled eggs. Incubation lasts 24 – 26 days.

The food of the adult varies considerably according to the surroundings, but consists basically of vegetation and small quantities of animal substances.

Combat between two male black grouse to demarcate display ground.

Courtship of the hen by the cock prior to copulation.

Nest and eggs of black grouse.

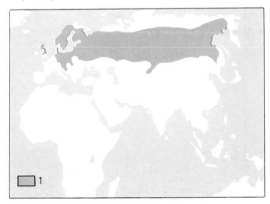
1) Distribution of black grouse (*Lyrurus tetrix*).

COMMON TURKEY

Meleagris gallopavo

Order Galliformes
Family Meleagrididae
Length Adult male 40 – 48 in (100 – 120 cm), adult female 32 – 34 in (80 – 85 cm)
Distribution North and Central America
Habits The male is polygamous
Nesting On ground
Eggs 8 – 10 (sometimes more), light yellowish brown with chestnut spots
Chicks Nidifugous

The common or wild turkey (*Meleagris gallopavo*) is the largest existing Galliforme of North and Central America. Sexual dimorphism is very noticeable both in respect of plumage and size, the male being much larger than the female. At one time it had a wide distribution across the United States and through Mexico. But by the end of the nineteenth century this range was already much reduced and nowadays it is even more restricted and fragmented, arousing fears for the future of the species.

The arrival of spring signals the start of the common turkey's breeding cycle. During the courtship parades, the naked, pimply areas of the cock's head and neck become inflated and turn light blue, in striking contrast to the fiery red warts and wattles. As he courts the female, the cock struts proudly along, swelling up and displaying the full splendor and magnificence of his nuptial garb.

Having mated, the females take their departure and the cock takes no interest whatsoever in the subsequent rearing of the brood. Scratching round the foot of a large tree with her strong claws, the hen scoops out a nest in the small hollow thus formed, preferably in the shelter of a bush, and roughly lines it with leaves, sticks, and stalks of dry grass. In it she lays 10 or so eggs, this operation normally taking about 20 days. At the end of this she commences incubation, which lasts 27 – 28 days.

The wild turkey's diet is constituted mainly of vegetation but during the summer the young also feed plentifully on arthropods and other invertebrates.

The wild or common turkey lives in the extensive woodlands of North America. This species is the ancestor of the domestic turkey, which was tamed long ago by the ancient tribes of Mexico.

Despite its considerable size, the wild turkey can fly quite well.

The head of the ocellated turkey is remarkable for numerous yellow and red warts sprouting from the naked, pimply skin of the forehead and above the eyes.

The wild turkey originated in North America and once ranged widely across vast parts of the central–southern United States and Mexico; nowadays this area is much broken up and reduced. 1) Wild turkey (*Meleagris gallopavo*); 2) Ocellated turkey (*Agriocharis ocellata*).

1
2

TUFTED GUINEA FOWL

Numida meleagris

Order Galliformes
Family Numididae
Length 20 – 22 in (50 – 55 cm)
Distribution Central and southern Africa
Habits Monogamous in breeding season, gregarious during rest of year
Nesting On ground
Eggs 8 – 15, variable in color from mustard yellow to reddish brown
Chicks Nidifugous

Known both to the ancient Greeks and Romans, guinea fowl (*Numida meleagris*) have in more recent times been introduced to Madagascar, western South Africa, America and many other places that are climatically similar to their countries of origin. The tufted guinea fowl normally lives in savannas or dry steppes dotted here and there with bushes and thorny shrubs, in sparse woodland or on rocky terrain. The only inhabitants of the African rain forests are a few species of the genus *Guttera*.

Tufted guinea fowl live in groups, sometimes very large, for most of the year. The start of the breeding period usually coincides with the onset of the rainy season. Within a short time the groups break up and individual pairs retreat to the wooded margins of the territory chosen for nesting and brood rearing. In the nest, which is a small hollow in the soil, the female lays a dozen or so eggs, which are fairly small but furnished with a thick, resistant shell. She incubates them for about 27 days.

Food consists of a huge and varied quantity of vegetation (leaves, buds, tubers, bulbs, fruit, berries, and seeds) and a large number of small invertebrates (insects, spiders, etc). Sometimes flocks even invade fields of cereal crops and plantations, doing damage which is often considerable.

Guinea fowl are essentially ground birds. When feeding or resting by day they stay on the ground and run rapidly away if disturbed, only taking wing when closely pursued. In the evening, however, they take refuge on the branches of trees to escape the attentions of many predatory mammals.

▼ Tufted guinea fowl, gathering in groups, spend much of the day searching for food in the arid zones of the savanna, on the borders of woodland.

▲ Food consists mainly of vegetation (seeds, plant tops, and the caryopses of various cereals); animal food is also important, particularly in the earliest months.

Vulturine guinea fowl (*Acryllium vulturinum*)

Kenya crested guinea fowl (*Guttera pucherani*)

◄ The guinea fowl came originally from Africa south of the Sahara; today they live throughout central and southern Africa to the eastern part of South Africa. 1)Tufted guinea fowl (*Numida meleagris*); 2) Zones in Africa to which the species has been introduced.

1

2

COMMON PEAFOWL

Pavo cristatus

Order Galliformes
Family Phasianidae
Size Length, adult male 44 – 48 in (110 – 120 cm); adult female 36 in (90 cm)
Distribution India and Sri Lanka
Habits Gregarious for most of the year
Nesting On ground
Eggs 4 – 8
Chicks Nidifugous

The common peafowl is the most spectacularly colored of all gallinaceous birds. The male's plumage is exceptionally brilliant. Head, neck and breast are blue-green and violet with metallic reflections. There is a patch of naked skin at the sides of the head around the eyes, and a crest of feathers with barbs only at the tip adorns the crown.

The fairly large beak is light brown and the iris of the eyes is also brown. The feathers of the back are greenish-gold with bronze edges, the tertiary wing coverts are white with closely ranged black bars, the secondary and primary coverts are blue-green with metallic tints, and both the remiges and rectrices are brown.

The upper tail feathers (of which there are 100 – 150) are very much longer than the rectrices and constitute the peacock's train. These feathers may grow to a length of 5 ft (1.6 m) – they continue growing up to the sixth year – but normally measure 4 – 4¼ ft (1.2 – 1.3 m). They possess long metallic-green barbs with blue and bronze reflections, and near the tips the barbs themselves merge to form an eyelike spot known as an ocellus, the bright blue center of which is surrounded by concentric brown, golden-yellow, and purple rings.

The peahen is smaller than the peacock. She has no train and her plumage is less gaudy.

The geographical range of the common peafowl comprises the whole of India and the island of Sri Lanka. It lives in forests and along river banks as well as on the edges of broad clearings, in warm, wet regions; and in the mountains of southern India it frequents open rainforests with sparse tree and shrub growth up to an altitude of 6,500 ft (2,000 m).

The common peafowl is a sedentary

During the breeding season, the peacock, in the presence of the hens, raises his tail, spreads out the magnificent, long upper tail feathers in a broad fan, and struts proudly in this display posture across his territory.

bird, living for the major part of the year in flocks of varying size. These large groups only disperse at the beginning of spring when each adult cock strays off, followed, as a rule, by 2 – 5 hens. The breeding period lasts throughout the spring. During the courtship parades, the male, watched by the females, raises the rectrices and spreads out the upper tail feathers like a fan. The hens in the group come running to his call and duly assume the postures that characteristically indicate readiness for mating, crouching on the ground in front of the male, wings half-open. At this signal the peacock quickly closes his magnificent train and mates with them in turn. After a while the hen prepares a rudimentary nest on the ground, usually high up in the shelter of a shrub or plant. In this crude nest she generally lays 4 – 5 eggs, but in the view of some authors there may be many more. When this activity is over she begins incubation, which lasts 28 – 30 days. In the wild, peafowl are omnivorous, feeding principally on vegetable substances (shoots, leaves, berries, seeds, etc.) but also on animals (snails, worms and, above all, insects).

Apart from the common peafowl, the subfamily Pavoninae comprises two other species, the green peacock (*Pavo muticus*), and the Congo peacock (*Afropavo congensis*).

The male green peacock is larger than his common relative. His plumage is predominantly green with metallic blue reflections and even more magnificent. The female, too, has bright green plumage but no train. The range of this species extends from Southeast Assam to Thailand and southern China, including the Malaysian peninsula and the island of Java.

The Congo peacock differs markedly from the two aforementioned species mainly by reason of its featherless neck and the absence of a train. The species was first described by the American ornithologist Chapin in 1936. He had seen, displayed in a case at the Congo Museum in Tervueren, Belgium, a pair of these stuffed Galliformes, wrongly described as young common peafowl. Having realized this classification error, Chapin planned to confirm the existence of a new species, and a year later, exploring the Ituri region of the Congo, succeeded in capturing seven specimens. The species was, in fact, known to the local population and to the whites living there.

◄ At night the bird takes refuge high up in the tree canopy.

▲ The peacock is essentially a ground-dwelling species but can, if forced, fly quite easily.

▲ The peahen accompanies her chicks in order to find food and sometimes, during their first few days, feeds them herself.

Green peacock
(*Pavo muticus*)

Common peacock
(*Pavo cristatus*)

Congo peacock
(*Afropavo congensis*)

◄ 1) The congo peacock (*Afropavo congensis*) lives in a fairly restricted area of the former Belgian colony, in the tropical rain forests. It was only recently discovered, in 1936. 2) The common peafowl (*Pavo cristatus*) lives throughout India and on Sri Lanka, in hill and mountain zones up to 6,500 ft (2,000 m), notably in wet woodlands with many clearings. Easily domesticated, it has been known in Mediterranean countries since antiquity and is nowadays widely bred for ornamental purposes. 3) The green peacock (*Pavo muticus*) is found in Southeast Asia and on the island of Java.

1
2
3

RING-NECKED PHEASANT

Phasianus colchicus

Order Galliformes
Family Phasianidae
Size Length, adult male 30 – 36 in (75 – 90 cm); adult female 22 – 25 in (56 – 63 cm)
Weight Adult male 2½ – 3½ lb (1.15 – 1.5 kg); adult female 2 – 2½ lb (0.9 – 1.1 kg)
Nesting On ground
Eggs 7 – 14, brown to bright green or pale olive, fairly rounded in shape
Chicks Nidifugous

The ring-necked pheasant (*Phasianus colchicus*) is notable for its beautiful plumage and characteristic long, pointed tail. There is marked sexual dimorphism, both as regards dimensions and coloration. The female's plumage is very drab whereas that of the male is extremely showy.

Ring-necked pheasants live freely wherever they find open woodland, hedges, and scrub, on the fringes of uncultivated land.

In winter they come together to form groups either of cocks and hens alone. At the beginning of spring these groups disperse and the cocks wander off to find suitable territories. Once in occupation of his zone, each male reinforces his claim by singing, and sometimes confronts rivals penetrating his domain. The area chosen is usually thickly covered with bushes, on the edges of a wood, including some open areas close to meadows or paths. The courtship period is fairly prolonged and the first mating activities take place, depending on the zone, from April onward.

The hens subsequently retire to their chosen nesting sites and begin laying their eggs. The nest is a hollow in the ground, lined with stems of dry grass and a few feathers dropped by the female; it is situated in the midst of fallen leaves, between two mounds of earth, under the branches of a small bush, on the edges of a field or in a hedge. The clutch usually consists of some 10 pale olive-green eggs; laying begins after the middle of April and the duration of incubation is 23 – 24 days. Normally there is only one clutch annually. After the eggs hatch, the hens remain where they are until the

▲ Male ring-necked pheasant in spring, busy patrolling the territory he occupies during the breeding period. A female is perched on the dead branch.

◄ This bird feeds principally on vegetation (seeds, plant tops, and fruit); in summer and fall there is also a large amount of animal food included in the diet, especially of the young.

◄ Cock pheasants have feet equipped with spurs.

chicks are fledged. After 4 – 5 months the young pheasants wear plumage similar to that of the adults.

Food varies considerably from season to season, but fundamentally it consists of herbaceous vegetation, seeds of gramineous species and other plants, berries, various fruits, and also animal substances.

There are many further species of pheasants living wild in Asia. The copper pheasant (*Syrmaticus soemmerringii*) is an inhabitant of the mountain forests of the Japanese island of Kyushu, above a height of 4,000 ft (1,200 m). Its typical habitat is dense brushwood and undergrowth, with small clearings close to streams and rivers. The golden pheasant (*Chrysolophus pictus*) and Lady Amherst's pheasant (*C. amherstiae*) are undoubtedly the most colorful and resplendent of all Asiatic pheasants. The former lives in the densest brushwood of the mountains of central and western China, up to an altitude of 8,200 ft (2,500 m) feeding principally on the leaves and buds of various shrubs and of dwarf bamboos.

Lady Amherst's pheasant is decked out with even more colors than the golden pheasant; the tail is longer and in the course of display stands out all the more prominently, together with the brilliant hues of the nuptial garb. This bird lives on the rocky slopes of the mountains of southwest China between 7,000 and 12,000 ft (2,100 and 3,600 m), and usually hunts for food among shrubs and stands of bamboo, consuming mainly buds.

The silver pheasant (*Lophura nycthemera*) lives in pairs or small groups in the mountain forests of Southeast Asia at altitudes between 2,000 and 7,000 ft (600 and 2,100 m). The vast geographical range comprises the whole northeastern part of the Indochinese peninsula to the Gulf of Tonkin, and all southeastern China.

The Himalayan monal pheasant (*Lophophorus impeyanus*) also has an extremely colorful plumage. The distribution of this species is vast, from Afghanistan and across the mountains of southern Asia to Tibet and Bhutan. The pheasant normally inhabits open coniferous forests or mixed forests of conifers and deciduous trees, usually settling on rocky slopes or deep ravines at heights of between 9,000 and 12,000 ft (2,700 and 3,600 m).

▲ A brooding hen blends with her surroundings.

▲ The unexpected flushing of a cock pheasant in spring gives away the position of its song territory.

◀ Chick aged a few days.

◀ Nuptial song of the male during spring.

Copper pheasant
(*Syrmaticus soemmerringii*)

Silver pheasant
(*Lophura nycthemera*)

Golden pheasant
(*Chrysolophus pictus*)

Himalayan monal pheasant
(*Lophophorus impeyanus*)

Lady Amherst's pheasant
(*Chrysolophus amherstiae*)

◀ Indigenous populations of the ring-necked pheasant are nowadays distributed over a discontinuous range from the southern and eastern shores of the Black Sea across central Asia to the east coasts of China. It was introduced in ancient times to Europe; it is not found in Iceland, northern Scandinavia, southern and western parts of the Iberian peninsula, the mainland of Italy, and southern Greece.
1) Distribution of ring-necked pheasant (*Phasianus colchicus*).

1

JUNGLE FOWL

Gallus Gallus

Order Galliformes
Family Phasianidae
Length Male 18 – 20 in (45 – 50 cm), female 16 – 17 in (40 – 43 cm)
Distribution Southeast Asia
Habits Gregarious, polygamous
Nesting On ground
Eggs 5 – 8, whitish
Chicks Nidifugous

The jungle fowl (*Gallus gallus*) is one of the most important species belonging to the order Galliformes because from it are derived all present-day species of domestic fowl. The cock's plumage is very bright and colorful. The hen, smaller than the cock, has virtually no comb or wattles, nor does she possess spurs; and her plumage is altogether duller than that of the male. During the summer the male livery or eclipse plumage is also quite drab.

The genus *Gallus* comprises only four species, living in Southeast Asia from India to the island of Java. The range of the jungle fowl extends from northeast India to the Sunda Islands. All four species normally frequent woodland zones with dense undergrowth where they can easily procure food and find suitable hiding places in the event of danger.

As a rule all the jungle fowl are polygamous, living gregariously for most of the year and moving about in groups of variable size to look for food on the ground, in clearings and open areas, often close to cultivated land. Towards the end of spring, when the breeding season commences, the strongest males (followed by a number of females) set out to demarcate their territories, defending them with determination and fighting bitterly with any males of the same species who dare infiltrate their domain. Some 3 – 5 hens establish themselves in each territory and after a while proceed to build their nests; the eggs are whitish with yellowish or pink tones, and are incubated for 20 – 21 days by the hens alone.

Foraging for food takes place mainly in the early morning and towards dusk. In the middle of the day the birds often bask in the sun and take "sand-baths" alongside a path or road, and at night they take refuge in trees.

▲ The jungle fowl has terrestrial habits, moving busily through the dense undergrowth in search of food.

▲ To escape predatory mammals, the jungle fowl flies off in the evening to shelter in the branches of a tree, where it spends the night.

The characteristic song of the cock in spring serves to mark out his territory and ward off all other males. ▶

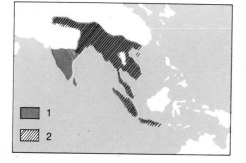

■ 1

▨ 2

◀ 1) The birds belonging to the genus *Gallus* live in Southeast Asia from India to Java. 2) The jungle fowl (*Gallus gallus*) occupies an area ranging from northeastern India to the Sunda Islands. All domestic fowl known and bred today throughout the world are derived from this species.

HOATZIN

Opisthocomus hoazin

Order Galliformes
Suborder Opisthocomi
Family Opisthocomidae
Size Length 24 in (60 cm)
Distribution South America
Habits Gregarious, arboreal
Nesting On branches low down on trees
Eggs 2 – 5, whitish with brown spots
Chicks Nidifugous and temporarily equipped with claws on tips of wings

The hoatzin has a fairly long body structure, and the upper-parts are mainly brown, with thin whitish streaks on the back; the feathers of the neck and breast are fawn, and the plumage of the abdomen, underparts, and remiges is reddish-brown.

It is interesting to note that the forelimbs (namely the wings) of newly hatched hoatzins are furnished with two well-developed, mobile claws, used for clambering about the branches. As the baby bird grows, these claws gradually atrophy and eventually disappear.

The hoatzin is distributed through the dense gallery forests and along streams and rivers in Colombia, Bolivia, Peru, and the Amazon basin. They are gregarious birds that live mainly in trees, where they find most of their food.

During the breeding season pairs do not move far apart and sometimes nest and brood quite close to one another in small groups. The nest is constructed on branches a little way above the ground or water surface; as a rule it takes the form of a large flattened basket, being made of interlaced sticks and dry scraps of vegetation. Both male and female collaborate in building the nest.

Incubation of the eggs is shared by both parents, and these hatch about 28 days after the last one is laid. At birth the chicks are totally naked but nevertheless able to move around quite nimbly, using their wing claws to climb, grip and transfer from branch to branch. During the first few days they are fed by the parents, but they grow very fast and soon become almost self-sufficient.

The most important sources of food for this species are the leaves of the arum plants and the fruits and leaves of other aquatic plants.

The hoatzin is basically an arboreal, gregarious member of the Galliformes. During the day it often lets out strong cries to keep in touch with other individuals of the group. It feeds on the leaves and fruits of various aquatic plants, but a large part of its diet is made up of the leaves of arum plants.

The forelimbs or wings of baby hoatzins are furnished with strong claws which help them to climb about in the trees.

The hoatzin is a South American species which lives in dense equatorial forests and along the banks of rivers in Bolivia, Colombia, Peru, and the Amazon basin.
1)*Opisthocomus hoazin.*

1

GRUIFORMES

The order Gruiformes (or Ralliformes) comprises 11 or 12 families and approximately 200 living or recently extinct species, all sharing common anatomical features but differing notably from one another in morphology and biology. The Gruiformes possess long legs and are familiarly known as waders, as are the representatives of the order Ciconiiformes. Yet certain characteristics of the bill and the feet as well as the development of the chicks show that these two orders are, in fact, markedly differentiated.

The birds belonging to this order are of variable size, usually with short, rounded wings not too well adapted for flying (except in the case of the cranes) but almost always with long legs for running rapidly on the ground. As a rule the Gruiformes have four toes on either foot, but the large toe is generally smaller and higher positioned than the others; for this reason the birds find it very difficult to grasp branches, seldom and most unwillingly perching in trees. The feet are not webbed but the coots and finfoots have membranous flaps (lobate webs) on their toes. The plumage is not, as a rule, brightly colored. The bill is normally strong, and the chicks have a thick layer of down and are nidifugous.

The family Gruidae contains 14 species. The sexes are generally similar, the color of the wings and body ranging from white to gray, with black remiges. Some species have a naked, bright red patch on the head.

Many species perform characteristic dances which are not necessarily confined to the breeding season. Monogamy is the rule, both parents building the nest and incubating the two eggs. Because of the special structure of the trachea, cranes have powerful voices that can be heard for several miles.

The demoiselle crane (*Anthropoides virgo*) is the smallest member of the family, measuring 38 in (95 cm), and displays typical tufts of white feathers on either side of the head. The whooping crane (*G. americana)* was once abundant over its entire range, which extended to Canada. In 1941, in spite of severe protective measures, only 23 birds were counted in the Aransas Wildlife Refuge, its restricted wintering zone on the coast of the Gulf of Mexico.

Some representatives of the family Gruidae.

Japanese crane
(*Grus japonensis*)

Sarus crane
(*Grus antigone*)

Siberian crane
(*Grus leucogeranus*)

Whooping crane
(*Grus americana*)

Demoiselle crane
(*Anthropoides virg*

Hooded crane
(*Grus monacha*)

White-naped crane
(*Grus vipio*)

The family Eurypygidae is represented by a single species, the sun bittern (*Eurypyga helias*) from the forests of South America.

The trumpeters (family Psophiidae) are represented by three species with similar habits, living in the forests of Brazil.

The family Aramidae is made up of only one living species, the limpkin (*Aramus guarauna*). About 24 in (60 cm) long, this bird is found in the southern United States.

The two constituent species of the Cariamidae are the crested seriema (*Cariama cristata*) and Burmeister's seriema (*Chunga burmeisteri*), inhabitants of the steppes and sparse forests of the high plateau regions of Brazil, Paraguay, and northern Argentina.

The family Mesitornithidae contains three small species, measuring 10 in (25 cm) living in Madagascar.

There are 15 species of hemipodes, or Turnicidae, looking somewhat like the common quail.

The three species of finfoots (Heliornithidae) are essentially aquatic by habit, shy birds living on the shores of rivers and swamps of tropical forests. Peter's finfoot (*Podica senegalensis*) is the largest, measuring 24 in (60 cm) long.

The family Rallidae is the largest family of the entire order, containing some 132 species generally known as rails. Some are terrestrial, others aquatic, and all are medium to small in size, perfectly adapted to living in thick marsh vegetation and on the banks of lakes and rivers. Many of the birds are active mainly at night and some, though common, are known almost exclusively by their calls.

The family Rhynochetidae only comprises the kagu (*Rhynochetos jubatus*), an inhabitant of the dense forests of New Caledonia.

The family Otididae consists of 22 species, typically adapted to life at ground level, with long, sturdy legs. The bustards live in semidesert zones, grassy savannas, and prairies with scattered tree growth. Many of these large birds are furnished with ornamental feathers on head, neck, throat and nape, displaying them to full advantage in the courtship period or using them as warning signals. The best-known species is the great bustard (*Otis tarda*).

White-winged trumpeter
(*Psophia leucoptera*)

Bustard quail
(*Turnix suscitator*)

Great bustard
(*Otis tarda*)

Limpkin
(*Aramus guarauna*)

Kagu
(*Rhynochetos jubatus*)

Water rail
(*Rallus aquaticus*)

Peter's finfoot
(*Podica senegalensis*)

▲ The order Gruiformes is subdivided into 11 (or 12, in the view of some authors) families, with a total of some 200 species, either living or recently extinct. Above, from left to right and from top to bottom, are representatives of some of these families: Psophiidae, Turnicidae, Aramidae, Otididae, Rallidae, Rhynochetidae and Heliornithidae.

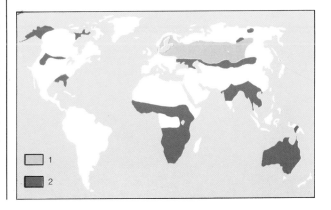

◀ The birds belonging to the family Gruidae are widely distributed throughout the world, except in South America, the Indo−Malaysian archipelago, New Zealand, and the Polynesian islands. The only species nesting in Europe is the common crane, which also ranges into Asia. 1) Common crane (*Grus grus*); 2) other members of the family Gruidae.

COMMON CRANE

Grus grus

Order Gruiformes
Family Gruidae
Male dimensions Length 48 in (122 cm); wing 23 in (58 cm); bill 4½ in (11 cm); tarsus 9½ in (24 cm)
Female dimensions Length 44½ in (113 cm)
Habits Migratory; nests on ground
Eggs 2, pale gray or olive

The common crane (*Grus grus*) is a large bird with long legs and an elegant drooping tail made up of very long inner remiges. Its flight is slow but powerful. As a rule the crane does not perch in trees but lives on the ground, walking with a slight swaying movement and occasionally breaking into a rapid run.

Both sexes are similar, the female being slightly smaller, and the plumage is uniformly ash gray with delicate bluish tints all over. The crown is red with two curving white bands extending from behind the eyes down the sides of the neck; the head is naked, the nape, throat, and legs are black, and the eye reddish. The young are darker than the adults and have a chestnut-brown neck and head.

In flight the birds hold their neck outstretched and the legs in a horizontal position; if it is very cold the legs are retracted and tucked into the abdominal feathers.

This widely distributed Palearctic species is found in northeastern Europe (Scandinavia, Poland, Russia, Hungary, Romania, and Yugoslavia) and in central Asia. East of the Volga the subspecies *G. g. lilfordi* inhabits Siberia to northern Manchuria, Turkestan, and Mongolia, ranging south to Armenia and Tien-Shan. Common in many places, these cranes occupy muddy terrain and swampland with few trees, on which they rarely perch. Gregarious, active by day, shy and suspicious by nature, they frequent open regions with plenty of water, slowly pacing and wading about in search of food. Both adults and young are excellent swimmers.

Cranes, by virtue of their sheer size, their habit of moving around in flocks, their long linear or V-shaped aerial formations, and their regular arrivals and

Common crane
(*Grus grus*)

departures in many regions, have for centuries fascinated and inspired naturalists and writers.

Most recent studies on the movements of birds indicate that they tend to fly faster in the course of migrating than at any other time, except when they are being hunted or pursued. If the wind is behind them, some species manage to reach a speed double that of flight in normal calm-air conditions. Migrating cranes, in especially favorable situations, have been observed traveling at very high speeds of over 62 mph (99 kmh).

The average altitude at which many birds fly varies considerably according to topography and atmospheric conditions. Ever since radar has been used as an auxiliary means of studying migrations, it has been shown that many species fly so high as to be invisible to the naked eye. Flocks of cranes have been identified on the screens at a height of about 16,500 ft (5,000 m) but it is important to note that this figure relates to equipment set up at ground level. In fact, many migrating birds are undoubtedly capable of flying much higher over mountain ranges; in the Himalayas large flocks of different species have been observed flying over passes more than 19,300 ft (5,800 m) up.

The food of the common crane consists mainly of plant substances such as seeds and shoots, twigs, berries, and leaves collected either from the water surface or by digging in the soil. It also hunts insects (crickets and grasshoppers, flies and mosquitos, dragonflies, butterflies, beetles, etc.), mollusks, worms, and small vertebrates such as frogs and lizards.

At the beginning of spring, the courtship season, flocks break up and pairs are formed, the birds remaining together for a long time. During courtship the birds perform characteristic dances which include huge leaps of 13 – 16 ft (4 – 5 m) into the air, runs in a circular, elliptical or figure-of-eight pattern, mutual bowing as small objects are picked from the ground, and the tossing of such objects into the air with attempts to catch them as they fall. The wings are fluttered as the cranes jump about, supporting themselves first on one leg and then on the other.

There are normally two eggs (often one in Sweden) laid in April or May, according to latitude, oval and elongated in shape, colored pale gray or olive.

Cranes in flight take up the characteristic V-formation.

Courtship ceremonies are unmistakable, with dances, high leaps first on one and then the other leg, and head-dips with half-opened wings.

The flat, broad nest is placed directly on the ground or on a small mound; the female lays 2 eggs.

Cranes at rest hide their head under the wing, standing balanced on only one leg.

The newly hatched chick has a thick cover of down. On the right is a juvenile.

WATER RAIL

Rallus aquaticus

Order Gruiformes
Family Rallidae
Length About 11 in (28 cm)
Wingspan 16 in (40 cm)
Weight Male 4½ oz (127 g), female 4 oz (111 g)
Distribution Europe, Asia, and Africa
Breeding period April – June
Incubation 21 days
Eggs 7 – 10
Chicks Nidifugous

Of several subspecies of water rail, the typical form nests in central and southern Europe, and in the north of the continent where it may be observed in the regions to the southwest of Siberia and in southern Scandinavia; it is also found in northwest Africa, lower Egypt, and Israel. One subspecies has been identified in Iceland and two more in central–eastern Asia to the Pacific. The bird is a partial migrant; as a rule, the more northerly populations winter in the south, settling along the Mediterranean and in southern Asia. Even so, there are many examples of flocks that spend the winter in their breeding grounds, bearing up against the worst the season can bring.

Like its relatives, the water rail migrates at night, covering considerable distances in uninterrupted flight at fairly low levels. It is given to concealment, and for this reason its natural habitat is a wet, marshy zone with plenty of vegetational cover. Rivers, canals, irrigation ditches, lakes, and ponds all offer suitable shelter, and the species is habitually found in such areas. It prefers shallow water in silty places, being little inclined to swim.

It is most active in the early morning and at dusk, resting at night or sometimes venturing out by moonlight. The water rail is unsociable, usually living in solitude and liable to turn aggressive, even towards birds of other species, particularly in the breeding season. It becomes more tolerant in winter, when it may be seen looking for food in company with others of its kind, probing in the mud with its long bill or dipping its head into the water. Food consists in the main of aquatic insects (diving beetles, water scavenger beetles, and mosquitos) as well as mollusks, worms, leeches, and crustaceans; it also hunts frogs,

▲| Shy and solitary by habit, the water rail often stands in the dense aquatic vegetation, identifiable by its characteristic voice. It is easily distinguished from other rails by its long, red bill, which gives it an unmistakable profile. Food consists in the main of animal prey (water insects, worms, mollusks, and crustaceans) which, particularly in winter, is mingled with seeds, berries, shoots, and other vegetable substances.

◀| The water rail's feet are furnished with long toes.

▼| The bird moves gracefully through the aquatic plants.

newts, and sometimes small fish.

During the courtship period the male performs a strange display in front of the female; flapping his tail, raising the wings and resting his bill against her breast, he circles around, showing off the bars of his flanks and the white feathers of the rump. This part of the ceremony is accompanied by characteristic cries which play an important role in pair forming.

The nest is a simple structure made of various water plants that are arranged so as to form a central cup, this being lined with dead leaves and scraps of dry or green vegetation. During the period from end April to end June, the female lays 7 – 10 eggs, creamy pink with brown spots. Incubation lasts three weeks and is carried out chiefly by the female, the male bringing her food and only replacing her now and then.

The spotted crake (*Porzana porzana*), with habits similar to those of the water rail, is olive brown above and dark gray with tiny white spots on the rest of the body, with brown, black, and white bands on the flanks; brighter patches of color are provided by the green bill with its red base and by the fawn rump. Similar to this species is the little crake (*Porzana parva*), slightly smaller and with a marked sexual dimorphism. This bird chooses to live in wet zones with plenty of floating vegetation, over which it hops rapidly and nervously, looking for insects.

Unlike the two preceding species, which are wholly aquatic, the corncrake (*Crex crex*) lives in the broad prairies with dense plant cover, and ideally where there are swampy areas and patches of low ground with scattered shrubs.

Similar in appearance to the moorhen, but smaller, is the black crake (*Limnocorax flavirostra*), an inhabitant of Africa and represented by one subspecies in South America.

One of the largest of the flightless rails is the weka or wood rail (*Gallirallus australis*), native to New Zealand. It has a stocky body and sturdy legs which enable it to run fast and, if need be, to swim strongly.

Protective measures are an urgent priority for many species of endangered rails, particularly those with a restricted distribution and those listed in the Red Data Books of the I.U.C.N.O. (International Union for Conservation of Nature and Natural Resources)

▲ Reluctant to take wing, when forced to do so it has to keep its legs dangling.

◄ Water rail sitting on its nest, built
▼ among tufts of sedge and generally in shallow water; the eggs are creamy-pink with brown spots.

Water rail chicks are covered in black down with greenish and violet tints; they are nidifugous. ►

Black crake
(*Limnocorax flavirostris*)

Moorhen
(*Gallinula chloropus*)

Other species of Rallidae

Little crake
(*Porzana parva*)

Corncrake
(*Crex crex*)

Spotted crake
(*Porzana porzana*)

Weka
(*Gallirallus australis*)

◄ 1) The water rail (*Rallus aquaticus*) nests in central and southern Europe, ranging northward as far as parts of Scandinavia and Siberia. It is occasionally seen in Africa. The species is partly migratory, and it is mainly individuals inhabiting the more northerly regions which tend to winter in the south, in Mediterranean lands and in southern Asia. Migrations take place at night; although they normally fly fairly low, water rails can, if need be, cross high mountain ranges. 2) The genus *Rallus* is found almost all over the globe.

1
2

MOORHEN

Gallinula chloropus

Order Gruiformes
Family Rallidae
Size Length 12½ – 14 in (32 – 35 cm)
Weight About 12 oz (320 – 330 g)
Distribution Europe, Asia, Africa, and America
Reproductive period March to April, with 2, rarely 3, clutches
Incubation 20 – 21 days
Eggs 5 – 11
Chicks Nidifugous

The moorhen is a water bird roughly the size of a pigeon. The wings are short and rounded, the body flattened from side to side, and the short tail flicks rhythmically up and down, especially when the bird is frightened. Adults have white stripes on the flanks, the white rump is divided in half by a black band, and the yellow-tipped red bill is surmounted by a bright red frontal plate. The legs are greenish with an orange or red "garter" on the lower part of the tibia, and the iris is reddish-brown.

The moorhen may be sedentary, a bird of passage or migratory, depending upon climatic conditions prevailing in breeding grounds. It usually frequents the banks of rivers and lakes, ditches and canals, swamps, marshes and cultivated land, particularly water-meadows and rice-paddies.

Not as shy and secretive as other Rallidae, the moorhen may often be seen swimming in open water or reconnoitring the banks, scuttling into vegetation at the slightest noise. Indeed, if disturbed, the moorhen immediately skitters across the water, wings beating rapidly, to find safety. It is reluctant to fly and if forced to do so rises heavily into the air, legs dangling. Very often, to escape danger, it will dive under the water and perhaps stay there for a couple of minutes, attached by feet and bill to aquatic plants and using both feet and wings for swimming. The bird resorts to diving more as a means of defense than as a way of finding food. The nest is built on the water or very close by, but sometimes it may be placed in a tree or bush or even borrowed from a crow, a rook or a magpie. Both sexes help to build it, the male carrying the materials, the female arranging them. In addition to this nest, used for depositing the eggs, the

Moorhen
(*Gallinula chloropus*)

Coot
(*Fulica*

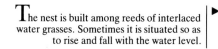
The moorhen is a familiar bird of different aquatic surroundings. The redbill a▸ frontal shield distinguish it at a glance from other Rallidae such as the coot, whic is bigger and has a white bill and frontal plate. Its food is varied, comprised chie of vegetation and, to a lesser extent, animal prey such as aquatic insects, worr snails, and small fish.

The nest is built among reeds of interlaced water grasses. Sometimes it is situated so as to rise and fall with the water level. ▸

moorhen builds other, more rudimentary nests that play their part in various stages of the courtship and in raising the young. The female lays 5 – 11 eggs, which are grayish-white with reddish-brown spots. Incubation by both sexes lasts 20 – 21 days.

A common bird of ponds and marshes, closely related to the moorhen, is the coot (*Fulica atra*). The adult measuring 15 – 18 in (38 – 45 cm) and weighing 25 – 35 oz (700 – 1,000 g), is easily recognized by its bill and frontal shield, which are both white, and stand out against the predominantly slate-gray plumage and shining black head and neck. The coot nests almost all over Europe, in North Africa, and in central-southern Asia; in Australia and New Guinea it is represented by similar species. Like the moorhen, it may be sedentary, a bird of passage or migratory. The bird spends much of its time in the water and swims jerkily, moving its head to and fro. It is in the habit of diving for food, sometimes to a depth of 26 ft (8 m). Besides eating large quantities of aquatic plants, the coot also consumes various species of mollusks, insects, larvae and, less frequently, worms and small fish. Both sexes collaborate in building their nest, which is generally made of aquatic vegetation, so interwoven as to make a floating platform. Incubation of the 7 – 12 eggs lasts 21 – 25 days and is shared by both sexes. The chicks are capable of diving at the age of 5 – 6 days, and are easily distinguished by their orange-red head.

An elegant member of the family, unmistakable by its splendid plumage, is the larger purple gallinule (*Porphyrio porphyrio*). The upperparts of the body are dark purple-blue, the breast is pale blue with metallic tints, and the pure white rump contrasts with the black abdomen; the bill, the long legs and the broad frontal plate are bright red. Some 20 species exist in various parts of the world.

A last mention should be made of the takahe (*Notornis mantelli*), a large flightless rail with brillant blue-green plumage, a massive beak, red at the base and pink at the tip, and a vivid red frontal shield. Nowadays it is a protected species in danger of extinction. The nest is a kind of tunnel between tufts of grass, containing 1 – 2 opaque, creamy, brown-speckled eggs.

◄ To take off, the coot gets a lift by skittering over the water for a short distance.

◄ When disturbed, the coot dives and swims underwater with rhythmical foot movements.

◄ The coot's foot is provided with toes enveloped in membranous webs.

The takahé (*Notornis mantelli*) is a flightless rail from New Zealand which is about the same size as a turkey. Thought to be extinct around the middle of the ninteenth century, it was accidentally rediscovered in 1948, but is obviously an endangered species, even if protected.

◄ Baby coot (orange-red head) and baby moorhen (red, yellow-tipped beak).

▲ Above, left to right: the rare crested coot (*Fulica cristata*) has characteristic fleshy red projections over its white forehead plate. The larger purple gallinule (*Porphyrio porphyrio*) has bright red legs, bill, and frontal shield, while the American purple gallinule (*P. martinica*) has its red, yellow-tipped bill surmounted by a light blue frontal plate, and pure yellow legs.

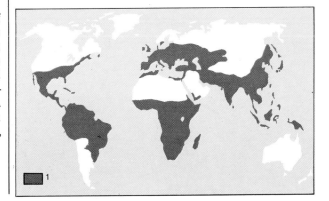

◄ The moorhen is distributed all over the world except for polar and desert regions; in Australia it is replaced by related species. Its habitats are wet places such as the banks of rivers, lakes, ditches and canals, swamps and marshes, water-meadows, and rice-paddies. 1) *Gallinula chloropus*.

GREAT BUSTARD

Otis tarda

Order Gruiformes
Family Otididae
Male dimensions Length 44 in (110 cm); wing 26 in (65 cm); tail 11½ in (28 cm)
Female dimensions Length 32 in (80 cm); wing 20 in (50 cm)
Eggs 2 – 4
Chicks Nidifugous

A large bird from the steppes, the great bustard (*Otis tarda*) is a sedentary species in southern regions and a partial migrant elsewhere when winter is especially cold. It frequents open plains with few trees, grassy steppes, and large fields of wheat, maize, rapeseed, and beet, using their mimetic coloration to escape the attention of predators. The European distribution of the species has been greatly reduced.

The great bustard is a bird of the wide open spaces and is normally a ground-dwelling species; it is extremely shy and walks warily with head held high. As a rule it gathers in small groups, which tend to be more numerous in winter, composed mainly of females. In case of danger the bird runs off rapidly, speeds of more than 22 mph (35 kmh) having been recorded, and takes wing only if compelled to do so, coming down as soon as possible after a brief flight. Now and then it lets out loud whistles that can be heard over a considerable distance.

The basic food of the adults consists of plant substances (tender shoots, stems, and flowers), and of the species consumed there is a preference for crucifers and legumes. The seeds of gramineous plants are much appreciated, as are insects (beetles, grasshoppers, etc.), larvae, mollusks, and small ground vertebrates. The birds spend the night in fields or hedgerows, gathering there as soon as it gets dark. At dawn they go foraging far from their nocturnal roosts. It seems almost certain that by nature the birds never drink.

Around the end of April, the bustard scoops out a hole in the ground and lines it with a few scraps of grass. The female lays 2–4 eggs, greenish with gray-brown spots. Incubation lasts about 4 weeks and is carried out by the females with the males being grouped around them.

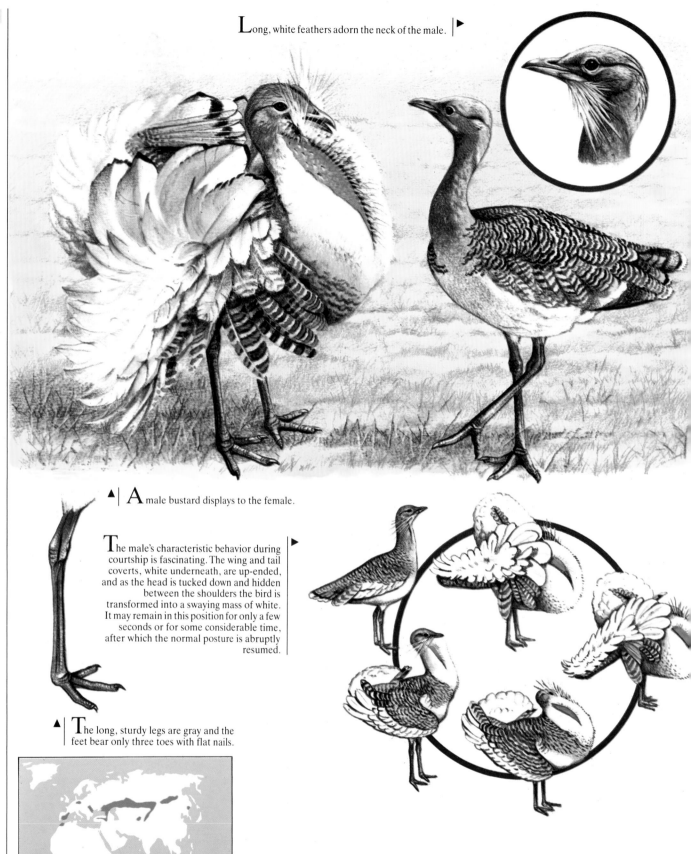

Long, white feathers adorn the neck of the male. ▶

▲ A male bustard displays to the female.

The male's characteristic behavior during courtship is fascinating. The wing and tail coverts, white underneath, are up-ended, and as the head is tucked down and hidden between the shoulders the bird is transformed into a swaying mass of white. It may remain in this position for only a few seconds or for some considerable time, after which the normal posture is abruptly resumed. ▶

▲ The long, sturdy legs are gray and the feet bear only three toes with flat nails.

◀ The great bustard is a bird of the steppes which winters in the south in Spain, Portugal, North Africa, and Asia from Syria to China. It nests in the Iberian peninsula, central and eastern Europe, Asia Minor, Siberia, and Turkestan. Formerly, the breeding grounds of the species covered a much wider area; at the beginning of the present century it was still nesting in France, Greece, Bulgaria, and the Ukraine.
1) Distribution range of the great bustard (*Otis tarda*).

SUN BITTERN

Eurypyga helias

Order Gruiformes
Family Eurypygidae
Dimensions Length 17 – 19 in (43 – 48 cm); wing 8½ in (21 – 22 cm); tail 6 in (15 – 16 cm)
Eggs Generally 2
Incubation 27 days

The sun bittern (*Eurypyga helias*) is a bird of medium size which has an unusually elegant arrangement of designs and colors. It lives in the forested zones of tropical America from southern Mexico to Peru, Bolivia, and central Brazil, frequenting the banks of streams and rivers shaded by the luxuriant vegetation.

The full splendor of the sun bittern's variegated plumage is seen during courtship displays as the male, in mounting excitement, performs fantastic dances, exhibiting the beautiful black, white, and chestnut mottling of his outspread wings, raising and fanning out his tail, and darting his neck back and forth. The delicacy and radiance of the wing and tail feathers are perhaps comparable only to the glistening hues of some of the huge nocturnal butterflies that inhabit these same tropical zones. The sun bittern, however, is not an accomplished flier, seldom perching on trees and generally to be seen patrolling muddy terrain, constantly on the move in search of food. It catches insects, small invertebrates and fish with great dexterity, impaling them with its pointed bill.

The nest is constructed by both sexes in the fork of two branches not high above the ground. The eggs are gray with red speckling. The chicks are born with a layer of down and do not leave the nest for several weeks. In self-defense the sun bittern bravely hurls itself into the attack, often challenging much larger predators.

The sun grebe (*Heliornis fulica*) frequents the banks of streams and rivers and the shores of lakes and ponds in the tropical forest zones of Central and South America as far as Peru, northern Bolivia, Paraguay, and northern Argentina. Timid and unsociable by nature, it lives alone or in pairs. It is an excellent diver and a fast swimmer, propelling itself with its powerful feet, with head partially submerged. Its guttural cries are similar to the yaps of a puppy.

During the courtship season the male sun bittern performs a fantastic dance, spreading his wings and showing off his splendid plumage.

Sun bittern
(*Eurypyga helias*)

The sun grebe or finfoot (*Heliornis fulica*) is a very agile swimmer and feeds mainly on fish caught by diving, sometimes to a fair depth. The yellow, black-barred feet are provided with webbed lobes which transform them into strong paddles.

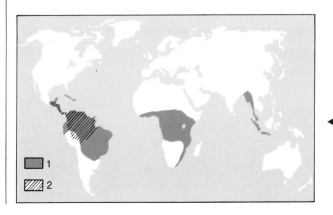

1) Distribution of the family Heliornithidae. Each of the three genera making up this family inhabits a distinct region but all are in the tropics: the genus *Heliornis* lives in America, the genus *Heliopais* in Indonesia, and the genus *Podica* in Africa.
2) The sun bittern (*Eurypyga helias*) is a bird of the intertropical forests of America from southern Mexico to Peru, Bolivia, and central Brazil.

JACANAS
Jacanidae

Seven species of jacanas make up this most unusual family of waders. Quite where they fit in the evolutionary pattern of the waders is not known. The one feature which immediately distinguishes them is the extraordinary long toes, ending in a huge hind claw. The legs, too, are long (a feature enhanced by bare tibia) but the bill is short, often with a fleshy frontal shield on the forehead and forecrown. Of the species, three are African, one American, one Australian, and two Asian.

The most numerous and widespread species in Africa is the African jacana (*Actophilornis africanus*). It is found south of the Sahara in all suitable localities. Almost twice the size of the lesser jacana, it can be immediately distinguished by its brownish upper and underparts which have a russet metallic tinge. The only contrast is with the brilliant white throat, sides of the neck and throat and the black eyestripe, crown and nape. In the breeding season it has a blue bill with a long blue frontal shield. There is little plumage difference between the sexes but the female is on average noticeably larger. Juveniles resemble the much smaller lesser jacana.

The pheasant-tailed jacana (*Hydrophasianus chirurgus*) has the most remarkable appearance of this family. It is the only species with distinct winter and summer plumages. In its summer breeding dress it has a white forehead, face, throat, and neck bordered by a thin black line merging on the breast into the very dark brown underparts. The nape is a brilliant golden yellow contrasting with the brown back. The wings and most coverts are white. It has a brown tail of up to 11¾ in (30 cm) long. In winter the crown and nape are brownish, slightly yellower on the latter. There is a black eyestripe which runs down the side of the neck and joins across the breast. The rest of the underparts are white. It has only a short brown tail.

The bronze-winged jacana is a slightly less widespread species. It is a very dark species, black and dark bronze-green, so that the white supercilia which meet on the nape are a striking feature. The sexes are similar in color but the female averages much larger than the male; there is a slight

Ringed plover
(*Charadrius hiaticula*)

Kentish plover
(*Charadrius alexandrinus*)

Killdeer
(*Charadrius vociferus*)

Gray plover
(*Pluvialis squatarola*)
summer

winter

Golden plover
(*Pluvialis apricaria*)
summer

winter

Dotterel
(*Eudromias morinellus*)

Turnstone
(*Arenaria interpres*)

Jacanidae
Pheasant-tailed jacana
(*Hydrophasianus chirurgus*)

Haematopodidae
Oystercatcher
(*Haematopus ostrale*)

Phalaropod
Northern phalarope
(*Phalaropus lobatus*)

Recurvirostridae
Avocet
(*Recurvirostra avosetta*)

Rostratulid
Painted snipe
(*Rostratula benghalensi*)

Scolopacidae
American woodcock
(*Philohela minor*)

Glareoli
Cream-
courser
(*Cursor cursor*)

▲ Some members of the Charadriidae family. The box illustrates some other mud-dwellers belonging to the order Charadriiformes with the names and respective families.

◄ The order Charadriiformes contains species very different from one another in structure and behavior, though most of them are aquatic. It comprises 16 families divided into about 334 species; of these the family Charadriidae groups together the majority of those species inhabiting marshes and wet regions in most parts of the world.
1) Little ringed plover (*Charadrius dubius*); 2) Family Charadriidae.

1
2

overlap of the wing lengths over the range of 6¾ – 7 in (172 – 180 mm).

The last species is the American jacana (*Jacana spinosa*). This is found widely from Mexico and Cuba south of Uruguay, and from the Atlantic west to the foothills of the Andes. The sexual dimorphism in size which is apparent throughout the family reaches its maximum here with females being larger than males (wing lengths 5 – 5½ in [130 – 140 mm] for females while only 4½ – 5 in [115 – 125 mm] for males). There is no difference, however, in coloration between the sexes.

Typically jacanas live on freshwater lakes, slow rivers or quiet backwaters for it is only here that the dense floating vegetation is commonly found. The areas of water are usually fairly shallow, often less than six feet deep, but need not be extensive – especially outside the breeding season. With their enormous feet and claws they are well adapted for walking on floating vegetation. They walk with a high stepping action to allow the feet to clear the vegetation, which is accompanied by a rail-like jerking of the tail. When pursued they are able to run quite quickly, preferring not to fly. Living in watery areas they are quite capable of swimming well if needed. Again, rail-like, they will take refuge by either submerging among vegetation with just their bill showing or diving and remaining completely submerged for several minutes. Diving is only resorted to when the bird is injured and cannot fly well.

They eat a wide range of items and most species are thought to concentrate on invertebrates. The breeding season is usually difficult to define since it varies annually with the timing of the rains. In countries, especially in Asia, where only one wet season is usual the season may only span four or five months but in places in Africa where there are long and short rains the jacanas may be found nesting in almost any month. The peak of egg laying takes place towards the end of the rainy season when water levels have reached the maximum and are relatively stable.

The nest is a very poor structure. Usually it is constructed on floating weed, and only a few extra strands of vegetation are included to prevent the eggs rolling over the side or falling through the bottom. Eggs, which almost invariably amount to four, are incubated by the male alone.

▼ The pheasant-tailed jacana (*Hydrophasianus chirurgus*) is the only member of the family Jacanidae exhibiting two plumage color phases, one in winter and the other in summer; its tail may measure up to 12 in (30 cm). The bird lives in zones of quiet, shallow water, forming flocks of up to a hundred or so individuals.

▲ The feet are particularly well adapted for walking on floating vegetation. As it moves, the bird raises its legs very high to shake off any grass that may be attached to them.

African jacana
(*Actophilornis africana*)

Bronze-winged jacana
(*Metopidius indicus*)

American jacana
(*Jacana spinosa*)

◄ Most of these birds live in tropical regions. They have not been subjected to intensive hunting, so that the main problem facing them is one of habitat. Over their range a decrease in the area of suitable wetlands has been recorded, and although the change does not appear to be very dramatic, it is doubtful whether future prospects are too good. 1) Distribution of family Jacanidae.

PLOVERS
Charadriidae

Plovers occur in an extremely wide range of habitats from tropical coastal salines to arctic mountains and to temperate grassland. They are able to utilize areas where few other waders can breed. In coastal salt pans the Kentish plover (*C. alexandrinus*) is found throughout the world, while on sandy beaches in temperate regions the ringed plover (*C. hiaticula*) is frequent. Around inland lakes and rivers and increasingly in gravel excavations occurs the little ringed plover (*C. dubius*). As we move into marshy areas long-legged species such as the Asiatic white-tailed plover (*Chettusia leucura*) have become adapted, while one stage further is reached by the long-toed lapwing (*Hemiparra crassirostris*) of East Africa; this has elongated toes to help it walk on water vegetation thus converging towards the lily-trotters (*Jacanidae*).

In temperate lowland grassland the lapwing (*V. vanellus*) is a typical breeder while as this grades into moorland it is steadily replaced by the golden plover. Further north again in the Tundra are found the lesser golden plover and some populations of the ringed plover. Isolated in mountain ranges throughout Europe the dotterel (*Eudromius morinellus*) occurs while some species have a very limited distribution on isolated islands in the southern hemisphere; typical of these is the shore plover (*Thinornis novaeseelandiae*) of the Chatham Islands off New Zealand.

One of the most obvious features of plovers is their feeding behavior. The clues to this come from the structure of the birds; the short bill and large eye indicate that they rely primarily on sight for detecting prey items. Virtually all species have a run–bobbing peck–stand still and upright pattern when feeding. They are able to see food at up to two feet away and they rush to gather it, then stop and wait for other items to show themselves. Grassland species such as the lapwing or golden plover additionally cock their head on its side as they listen for the sound of movement from invertebrates within the sward.

A wide range of prey items are gathered; the species and even the phylum of invertebrates depends on habitat and type of plover. However,

▼ The little ringed plover (*Charadrius dubius*) is often seen inland, living near lakes, along rivers and in gravel pits. In coastal zones it feeds mainly on marine worms, mollusks, and crustaceans; inland it eats earthworms and larvae of cockroaches, flies, and moths.

PAINTED SNIPE

Rostratula benghalensis

Order Charadriiformes
Family Rostratulidae
Distribution Africa, southern Asia, and Australia
Geographical range Tropical and subtropical regions
Wing length 4 ft – 5ft 4in (120 – 160 mm)
Sexual maturity Believed to be 1 year
Eggs 4, rarely 3 or 5 – 6

The Old World painted snipe (*Rostratula benghalensis*) has a very wide breeding distribution since it is found in Africa, southern Asia, and Australia. The species is thought to be non-migratory although it does move around locally depending on rainfall and subsequent ground conditions. Birds from Africa and Asia all belong to the race *R. b. benghalensis*. In all Old World painted snipe there is complete sexual dimorphism with the female being more brightly colored and larger than the male. The American painted snipe is superficially similar to *R. benghalensis* but with a less advanced sexual dimorphism.

Both species of painted snipe inhabit marshy areas; they show a wide tolerance of wetland types. Typically they are found in areas of dense growth, both grassy and in shrubs, but they can be found in rice paddies, lotus pools, salines, and areas where there are plenty of exposed patches of mud. On occasions they even penetrate into saline coastal zones.

Painted snipe run quickly with their head down and can swim well. In order to minimize predations they freeze and become motionless, relying on their camouflage. It is only in the last resort that they fly or run away from danger.

As in most species of waders in which the female is significantly larger and more brightly colored than the male, she carries out the most, if not all, of the display and territorial aggression. She is the one with the most penetrative call. In fact, the male's call is softer. On the ground the female has a most striking display. This is used both for sexual activities and as a threat display against other females invading the territory.

▲ Little is known about the feeding habits of the painted snipe (a female of which species is shown above). One difficulty is the fact that it is active from dawn to dusk and may continue feeding during the night. It obtains food mainly by pecking and stirring the mud with its beak. Sometimes it employs a more unusual method of moving the bill from side to side in shallow water. When drilling into the mud it can swallow food without lifting its beak, assisted by the tongue, which is almost as long as the beak itself; in fact, no other wader has a longer tongue. Prey includes a wide range of animals living in mud and water, such as mollusks, crustaceans, and worms; but the bird also feeds on many plant substances and has been seen to eat rice and grass seeds.

▲ The male incubates the eggs and apparently also rears the newly hatched chicks on his own.

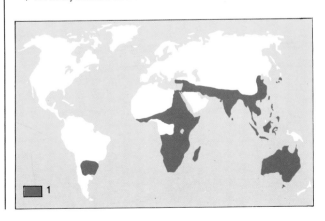

◄ 1) The painted snipe (*Rostratula benghalensis*) has a very extensive breeding range, being found in Africa, southern Asia, and Australia. With such a distribution it is surprising that there are not many differentiated subspecies. It is a gregarious species, forming groups of 50 – 60 individuals.

COMMON GULL

Larus canus

Order Charadriiformes
Family Laridae
Subfamily Larinae
Distribution Central and northern Europe, central Asia, northwestern America
Habits Gregarious
Nesting Mid May to early June. Single clutch
Eggs Usually 3, rarely 1–4, varying in color from brown to blue with dark spots
Chicks Born with gray-yellow marbled down. Semi-nidifugous

Gulls are distributed all over the world but most of them come originally from the northern hemisphere. By reason of their cosmopolitan habits and their ready adaptation to populated surroundings, they are certainly the best known of all marine birds, even if they actually frequent the coasts rather than the open sea; indeed, they seldom stray far from the shore and even visit inland areas provided there is some water available, such zones often being some way above sea level. Many species nest in circumpolar regions, leaving their breeding grounds at the approach of winter to seek out milder lands; others fly off on long migrations across the equator. Only the two kittiwakes are typically oceanic birds.

The common gull (*Larus canus*) is one of the most widely distributed species, for in addition to inhabiting the northern parts of the Palearctic region, it also frequents the northwest coasts of North America. Like almost all gulls, its habits are markedly gregarious and flocks of many dozens will often be seen flying over sandy beaches, river estuaries, and harbors; and in winter it is likely to be encountered, more than other gulls, inland around lakes, rivers, and marshes, often settling, too, on cultivated fields in its quest for food.

The gulls form a strikingly homogeneous group of some 45 species with well-defined characteristics. They are sturdy birds with pointed wings and a squarish tail. As a rule the body is white, but the upper parts of the wings may be all shades of gray, black, or pure white. Sometimes, for the sake of convenience they are divided into two groups, those

The common gull, like all gulls, is not averse to the presence of humans; it is a familiar bird of ports and harbors, perching for hours on posts and other vantage points. It feeds on fish, the eggs and young of other birds, small vertebrates, and waste matter of every kind.

Common gull
(*Larus canus*)

without hoods and those who, in nuptial habit, display a dark hood on the head, this disappearing quite frequently during the winter.

Gulls are equally at home on dry land, darting about and catching prey, and on water, where they come down to rest and feed. Unlike the majority of sea birds, however, they are unable to submerge themselves entirely. They are excellent fliers, and although their normal motion through the air is slow and powerful, they can, if need be, use gusts of wind to perform acrobatic maneuvers and soar upward on thermal air currents, gliding like birds of prey. Decidedly gregarious by habit, gulls display extremely complex social behavior which has an influence on all their activities. This is why famous scientists such as Tinbergen and Moynihan have found them so interesting to study. It is now clear, for example, that gulls communicate with one another by calls.

Gulls feed on more or less anything that attracts their attention, edible or not. Some species eat live fish or marine invertebrates, caught with the bill, but the majority consume small vertebrates, rodents, birds, insects, plants and, above all, refuse that can be picked up here and there. Certain gulls drop shells from a height on to the rocks, so as to break them open and feed on the mollusks inside; and some manage to waylay birds, often migratory species, near their colonies. The common gull frequently assumes the role of thief and parasite, filching food from other birds such as gulls, coots, and ducks, which learn to respect its strength and determination.

Gulls nest in colonies that sometimes number several thousand pairs and seldom in isolated couples. The density of nests in a colony is usually very high. Consequently the territory of a pair of gulls may consist almost entirely of the nest. Seacoasts are the favorite sites but inland bodies of water such as lakes, rivers, and swamps, as well as moors, are also frequented. Sometimes birds may stray far from shore, as happens with certain gulls which nest on the lakes of Tibet and the Andes at an altitude of about 16,500 ft (5,000 m).

The common gull nests on islets and along coasts with plenty of vegetation, but also on the banks of lakes and swamps close to the sea, streams, rivers, and heaths.

▼ It is always eager to pounce on fish and refuse thrown from ships.

▼ The black-legged kittiwake nests on the narrowest rock ledges.

▲ It skims the water surface, killing prey with its beak.

Ivory gull
(*Pagophila eburnea*)

Little gull
(*Larus minutus*)

Lesser black-backed gull
(*Larus fuscus*)

Herring gull
(*Larus argentatus*)

Black-headed gull
(*Larus ridibundus*)

Black-legged kittiwake
(*Rissa tridactyla*)

▲ Other species of gulls.

Black skimmer
(*Rynchops nigra*)

Great skua
(*Stercorarius skua*)

Inca tern
(*Larosterna inca*)

Crested auklet
(*Aethia cristatella*)

◄ Relatives of the gulls are, from left to right and top to bottom, the skuas, the skimmers, the terns, and the auks. All are members of the order Charadriiformes.

COMMON TERN
Sterna hirundo

Order Charadriiformes
Family Laridae
Size Length 14½ in (36 cm)
Distribution Throughout northern hemisphere, with cosmopolitan range
Habits Gregarious
Nesting From end of May to early June
Eggs 2 – 3, blue or brown with dark spots
Chicks Covered in yellow-gray or speckled brown down; semi-nidifugous

The common tern (*Sterna hirundo*) is the most typical member of the group of terns which contains another 20 or so related species. In this group there are larger birds such as the Caspian tern (*Hydroprogne caspia*), more than 20 in (50 cm) long; and the smallest of the lot is the least tern (*Sterna albifrons*), barely 9½ in (23 cm) in length. The common tern's average length is 14½ in (36 cm) and its wingspan is 31 in (79 cm). In the breeding season adults are completely black on top of the head, while in winter the crown is brown, streaked with white.

The common tern has a particularly wide distribution, its range embracing almost all continents apart from Antarctica. It is a migratory species. When winter approaches, groups of varying size fly off to winter quarters in the tropical belt, following the coasts or the beds of large rivers. At the onset of spring, in response to physiological mechanisms (the workings of which are still largely unknown) the birds resume their journey back to the regions where they were born. Such migration journeys may be very long; in fact, some populations of common terns nest at high latitudes, together with Arctic terns. The environments selected as nesting zones tend to vary. Like all terns, they frequent sandy coastlines, dunes, brackish marshes, river estuaries, and the like, but also nest in freshwater zones, on the banks of streams and rivers and along the shores of inland lakes.

It is undoubtedly in the air that terns show themselves to best advantage. Their flight pattern, with slow, regular wingbeats, is a picture of effortless grace, serving them well not only during migrations but also in everyday fishing activities. Much of their time

Although considered a marine bird, the common tern is not usually found out at sea, preferring to stick to the coasts, the mouths of rivers, and also inland waters. Large flocks are often encountered close to ports. This bird feeds principally on small surface fish but also consumes crustaceans and insects.

▶ Silhouettes of some sea birds in flight.

Shearwater   Skua   Gull   Tern

has to be spent in hunting for food, and they may often be seen in groups, skimming slowly over the water, head lowered to catch the least sign of movement on or beneath the surface. Having located their prey, they await the opportune moment to dive down and transfix it with their sharp bill. Such dives do not entail complete submersion nor do they swim underwater like other sea birds. Food consists in the main of small fish, crustaceans, and mollusks.

The common tern is a markedly gregarious species, nesting in colonies which, when situated near the seacoast, are likely to be very large. As soon as they arrive back at the breeding grounds after their tiring spring migration, these birds launch themselves into frenzied courtship flights. The aerial displays and pursuits continue without respite, the birds screaming noisily as they perform their incredible dives. Excitement dies down in the later phases of courtship as pairs are formed; and when each female has chosen her partner, couples fly off to find a suitable nesting site. This is simply a hole in the ground, lined with slivers of shell, grass stems, and scraps of seaweed.

Further courtship activities occur while the nest is being built, but most of these take place on the ground. In crowded colonies nests are situated very near one another, causing bitter territorial rivalry in the course of which the birds launch diving attacks and often peck viciously at invaders, including humans. Between April and May the female lays 2 – 3 blue-green, brown-spotted eggs, which are incubated in turn by both sexes for about 3 weeks. During this period the brooding bird is provided with food by its mate.

The breeding habits of the fairy tern (*Gygis alba*), a typical bird of small tropical islands, are quite different; it does not build a true nest but invariably lays its single egg somewhere above ground level, often in the fork of a tree trunk. For this reason its entire behavior pattern is unlike that of other terns. Both adults take turns in incubating at intervals of at least 2 – 3 days, thus reducing to a minimum the risk of their continual comings and goings dislodging the egg. The adult tern can catch and carry in its beak up to 15 fish at one time so it has to make only 2 – 3 journeys a day to provide the fledgling with sufficient food.

◄ ▼ The tern catches fish by plummeting down into the water and stabbing the victim with its sharp beak. Sometimes it hovers motionless in midair before nosediving on its prey.

▲ Nest building is preceded by courtship displays, in the course of which both birds, seated on the ground, symbolically exchange prey items.

▲ The chicks are born entirely covered in thick down.

Arctic tern
(*Sterna paradisaea*)

Roseate tern
(*Sterna dougalli*)

Sooty tern
(*Sterna fuscata*)

Least tern
(*Sterna albifrons*)

Black tern
(*Chlidonias niger*)

Fairy tern
(*Gygis alba*)

◄ The terns live practically all over the world. Most species are tropical but others have a cosmopolitan range and also nest in circumpolar regions. 1) Least tern (*Sterna albifrons*); 2) Common tern (*Sterna hirundo*).

153

ARCTIC TERN

Sterna paradisaea

Order Charadriiformes
Family Laridae
Subfamily Sterninae
Length 14½ in (36 cm)
Distribution Nests in Arctic regions; outside the breeding season it sets off on a very long migration, reaching Antarctica
Habits Gregarious
Nesting End May to early June. One clutch
Eggs Usually 2, sometimes 1 or 3, yellow or pale green speckled with brown
Chicks Like those of common tern, but with thicker dark markings

Much resembling the common tern, the Arctic tern (*Sterna paradisaea*) differs from the latter only in minute details. It is also very similar to another species, the roseate tern (*S. dougalli*).

As far as nesting is concerned, the Arctic tern's distribution is restricted to the Far North; and indeed, no other tern ventures for breeding to such high latitudes. Populations of the species that breed in more southerly zones of the range, not far below the Arctic Circle, often nest in colonies together with other terns, particularly the common tern, as well as with other species of sea birds. More than any other related species, too, the Arctic tern relies on the watery environment, frequenting coasts and also nesting on rocky and deserted islands. It is an exceptional migratory species. Covering about 24,000 miles (38,000 km) for its entire journey, the bird flies from the Arctic region to Antarctica and back every year.

The breeding period takes place between May and July. Both parents construct the nest, almost always without adornment. The 2 – 3 eggs are very similar to those of the common tern but with more conspicuous dark markings. Incubation lasts approximately 3 weeks and the newborn chicks can be distinguished from baby common terns by having a broader brown area on forehead and throat.

Gregarious throughout the year, terns are to be seen in flocks of varying size as they fly slowly over the water, often into the wind to slow their speed and improve their view of catch.

Arctic tern
(*Sterna paradisaea*)

▲ This bird is more typical of the high seas than are other terns; in fact, it often nests on small islands far from the shore. The breeding season is from May to July and incubation lasts about three weeks.

▲ From top to bottom: Roseate tern (*Sterna dougalli*), Arctic tern (*Sterna paradisaea*) and common tern (*Sterna hirundo*). These species are very similar: in flight it is often hard to distinguish them, but when perched there are several anatomical details which help to identify them.

◀ 1) Nesting grounds of the Arctic tern. This is a migratory species, flying away every year from the Arctic regions where it breeds to the Antarctic latitudes and back again, covering a distance of about 24,000 miles (38,400 km).

1

BLACK SKIMMER

Rynchops nigra

Order Charadriiformes
Family Rynchopidae
Length 19½ in (48 cm)
Distribution Coasts and inland waters of tropical America
Habits Gregarious
Nesting Late spring, in small colonies on banks and sandy coasts
Eggs 2 – 4, similar to those of terns
Chicks Covered in tawny down with dark spots. Nidifugous

The family Rynchopidae comprises three species: the black skimmer (*Rynchops nigra*), the African skimmer (*R. flavirostris*), and the Indian skimmer (*R. albicollis*). These birds are exclusively continental, inhabiting the tropical belts. The black skimmer lives in America; the populations breeding in zones farthest from the equator make short migrations to escape winter conditions. The African skimmer lives throughout tropical Africa and it, too, is partially migratory. The Indian skimmer, however, is limited to the coastal belt of India and Indochina. Skimmers have a preference for large rivers and lakes but also live on sandy seacoasts and particularly the mouths of rivers; they are seldom to be seen out at sea.

The unique structure of the bill is an adaptation resulting from the fishing techniques of these birds. All the skimmers fish by flying very low over the water with the lower mandible constantly cutting the surface. The submerged portion of the bill stirs up currents and eddies which drive all organisms living near the surface in the direction of the bird's mouth. When the tip of the bill strikes against a large-sized prey such as a fish, the skimmer reacts immediately by lowering its head and snapping the bill closed to grasp the victim.

As a consequence of this original fishing technique, these birds have also developed another less apparent but equally important adaptation, namely the capacity of flapping flight without the wings ever descending below the horizontal; this enables them to skim only a few inches above the surface of the water, never touching it with the wings.

▼ The black skimmer, flying low over the water, cuts the surface with its lower mandible which is much longer than the upper one, snapping up any fish which collides with the beak. Although it feeds mainly on fish, it also eats vegetable substances and small animals living on or near the surface.

Black skimmer
(*Rynchops nigra*)

African skimmer
(*Rynchops flavirostris*)

▲ The African skimmer lives along the banks of large rivers and lakes in tropical Africa; it is distinguished from the black skimmer by its yellow-tipped bill.

◀ The skimmers are birds of the tropical belts of various continents, inhabiting lakes and rivers and seldom venturing out to sea. 1) Black skimmer (*Rynchops nigra*); 2) African skimmer (*Rynchops flavirostris*); 3) Indian skimmer (*Rynchops albicollis*).

GREAT SKUA
Stercorarius skua

Order Charadriiformes
Family Stercorariidae
Size Length 23½ in (58 cm)
Distribution In the northern hemisphere it nests from the Scottish isles to Iceland. In the southern hemisphere it lives in the circumpolar regions of Antarctica. In the winter it ranges over the Atlantic to the tropic of Cancer.
Nesting End – May to early June. Single clutch
Eggs Usually 2, rarely 1, olive-brown or grayish-yellow with brown spots
Chicks Born with yellowish-brown down, paler on underparts. Semi-nidifugous

The plumage of the great skua (*Stercorarius skua*) is completely brown, except at the base of the primary flight feathers where white patches are visible on both sides of the wings. The dark bill, shorter and sturdier than that of gulls, is hooked, with an area of bare skin, the cere, at the base, and visible plates covering the zone of the nostrils. The dark feet are webbed and provided with strong claws which are indispensable to these predatory sea birds with their spectacularly piratical habits. The flight pattern, especially in the case of the great skua, may appear slow and ponderous, but it is swift and acrobatic whenever prey is sighted.

The skuas are noticeably aggressive towards other sea birds, pursuing them relentlessly until they drop or even regurgitate their prey, this often being snatched up before it hits the water. The parasitic skua prefers attacking terns, black-legged kittiwakes, and puffins, especially those carrying one large fish rather than several small ones. A single fish can be caught more easily before it touches the water or the ground, where it might be snapped up by competitors such as gulls and crows. This hunting strategy proves successful for this species nine times out of ten, whenever the victim is unable to find refuge in the sea or among rocks; it is called kleptoparasitism, and it is to be seen, though not so markedly, in young gulls. The great skua, although less prone to this type of activity than its relatives, will even take on the much larger gannets. The family name

Like all its relatives, the great skua is a kleptoparasite, feeding on the fish it steals from other sea birds. This aggressive habit partly explains their family name of Stercorariidae; it used to be believed that they ate the excrement emitted by the terrified birds they were pursuing, but skuas actually feed on birds, carrion, eggs and chicks, lemmings, and, of course, fish.

The bill of skuas (below) is fairly similar to that of gulls (above) but more prominently hooked at the tip, in keeping with its predatory habits.

Stercorariidae was, in fact, applied to them because of the mistaken belief that the skuas fed on the feces eliminated from fear by the birds they were chasing.

All skuas are highly skilled at capturing birds in the air, striking out so powerfully with feet and wings that the prey falls to the ground, where it is promptly finished off. Sometimes, however, these encounters are so ferocious that the skua is itself injured and eventually becomes the victim of other skuas, for cannibalism is a frequent practice among these species.

Skuas live for most part of the year at sea and settle on dry land only for breeding. The great skua usually nests close to the sea, on moors at varying altitudes, on bare ground or planted terrain, and in river estuaries. The parasitic skua also nests in these same surroundings but frequently ventures farther inland to the swampy tundra, habitats characteristic of the pomarine and long-tailed species. As is the case with all predators of the northern hemisphere, the breeding habits of skuas on the tundra are closely dependent upon the fluctuating populations of their prey, particularly of lemmings; it may, indeed, happen that skuas only succeed in raising an entire brood in those years when these rodents are abundant and may not breed at all when lemmings are scarce.

Skuas normally nest in small colonies or isolated pairs. Each nest, generally in an exposed spot, is surrounded by territory, varying in size, belonging to the breeding pair. Their aggressive instincts are so strong that in order to defend their territory and nest they will have no hesitation in attacking species much larger than themselves, even humans; the skuas dive from a great height and pull out only a few inches above the intruder's head, sometimes landing strong blows with a wing or foot. Colonies also accommodate nonbreeding individuals, who are all banished together to territories from which they can observe the activities of breeding pairs.

The nest is a small hollow dug in the ground by both members of the pair, who then line it with scraps of grass, moss, and other materials. Eggs are laid between the end of May and the early part of July and this is preceded by courtship parades. Incubation by both parents begins as soon as the first egg is laid, and after 23 – 30 days the first chick is born.

▼ Successive stages of an attack by a great skua: having sighted the victim, it follows the latter until it is forced to drop its food and then snaps the fish up before it can hit the ground or water.

▼ During the breeding season the great skua makes a special point of feeding on the chicks and eggs of other birds (in this case a gannet).

▼ In the Antarctic the skua plays a very important natural selective role in crowded penguin colonies.

Parasitic skua (*Stercorarius parasiticus*)

Pomarine skua (*Stercorarius pomarinus*)

Other skua species.

Long-tailed skua (*Stercorarius longicaudatus*)

◄ The skuas live for most of the year at sea and only visit dry land to nest. They all have a northern and Arctic distribution but outside the breeding season make long migrations that may take them into the southern hemisphere. 1) Parasitic skua (*Stercorarius parasiticus*); 2) Great skua (*Stercorarius skua*).

1
2

COMMON GUILLEMOT

Uria aalge

Order Charadriiformes
Family Alcidae
Size Length 16½ in (41 cm)
Distribution Northern coasts of the Atlantic and Pacific Oceans (North America, northern Europe, Greenland, Iceland)
Habits Marine, gregarious
Nesting In colonies on rocky islets and cliffs
Eggs 1, large and pear-shaped
Chicks Semi-nidicolous, venturing into sea before being able to fly

All the species in the family Alcidae have fairly similar plumage, black above and white below but sometimes completely black. Variation and contrast is effected by white patches and wing bands, distinctive patterns on the head (some species have tufts of colored feathers), naked skin on the beak and brightly colored legs and throat, all designed to help individuals of a species to communicate with one another. The basic black and white coloration clearly has a mimetic function. Aerial predators, especially sea eagles, are unable to pick out the black back of a bird floating on the dark sea surface, while underwater hunters such as whales and carnivorous fish cannot distinguish from below the bird's white belly against the dazzling light of the clear sky. Both sexes have similar plumage but may look very different at certain seasons; and both molt their wing feathers all together so that for a while thay are unable to fly. The sounds made by the birds are rudimentary, a blend of grunts, raucous cries, and whistles.

The alcids are ecological counterparts in the northern hemisphere of the penguins and diving petrels of the southern hemisphere. Auks and penguins represent a clear example of evolutionary convergence, that phenomenon whereby animals that are separately classified (penguins belong to the order Sphenisciformes and auks to the Charadriiformes) have come to look and behave alike because they live in the same environment and feed in the same way.

A typical representative of the family is the common guillemot (*Uria aalge*).

Guillemots nest on cliffs, crowding together on narrow rock ledges overlooking the sea. The clouds of birds wheeling over the cliffs as they return from fishing, the sharp, penetrating smell, the white excrement staining the rocks and the raucous cries emitted incessantly by adults and young, provide a spectacle of great beauty and animation.

Food consists of fish and, to a lesser extent, crustaceans, mollusks, and worms.

It looks much like a penguin, with its tapered body, long neck, conical and pointed bill, and feet positioned far back under the abdomen. The plumage is white on the belly, black or chocolate-brown on the back, head and neck. The feet and bill are black.

The guillemot is a sea bird which ventures onto dry land only for nesting; much of its life is spent on the high seas. It moves awkwardly on land and is forced to rest sitting upright on its tarsi. Nor is it notably versatile in the air; the short, narrow wings have to be kept fluttering rapidly to support the heavy body, the short tail precludes sudden changes of direction, and the webbed feet stick out widely from the sides of the body.

In the sea, however, the bird comes into its own, displaying its perfect adaptation to the element; the soft, thick plumage is covered by a layer of oil secreted by the uropygial gland and smeared over the feathers with the bill, protecting the body from the water and the cold. When the guillemot makes a brief dive underwater, it swims by beating its wings in paddlelike fashion and uses its feet as a rudder for changes in direction. It can dive to a depth of about 33 ft (10 m) and can go without breathing for more than a minute.

Toward the end of December the guillemots head for the shore, returning regularly to the sites used for breeding in the previous years. By April thousands of pairs have settled on the spots chosen for nest-building. The birds establish their colonies on the flat summits of rocky islands and on cliff ledges, precariously balanced as they defend the few square inches of space separating them from their neighbors. The egg is pale blue-green with brown and black marks; it is markedly pear-shaped so that if blown and buffeted by the wind it will roll about on the lighter pointed end and will be less likely to tumble off the narrow rock ledge. Both sexes share the incubation for 32 – 34 days.

By the time it is 3 weeks old the fledgling's plumage is already waterproof even though the feathers are hardly sprouting; urged on by the parents it hurls itself down from a few dozen feet into the sea, where it will learn to be an expert swimmer and diver before it can fly.

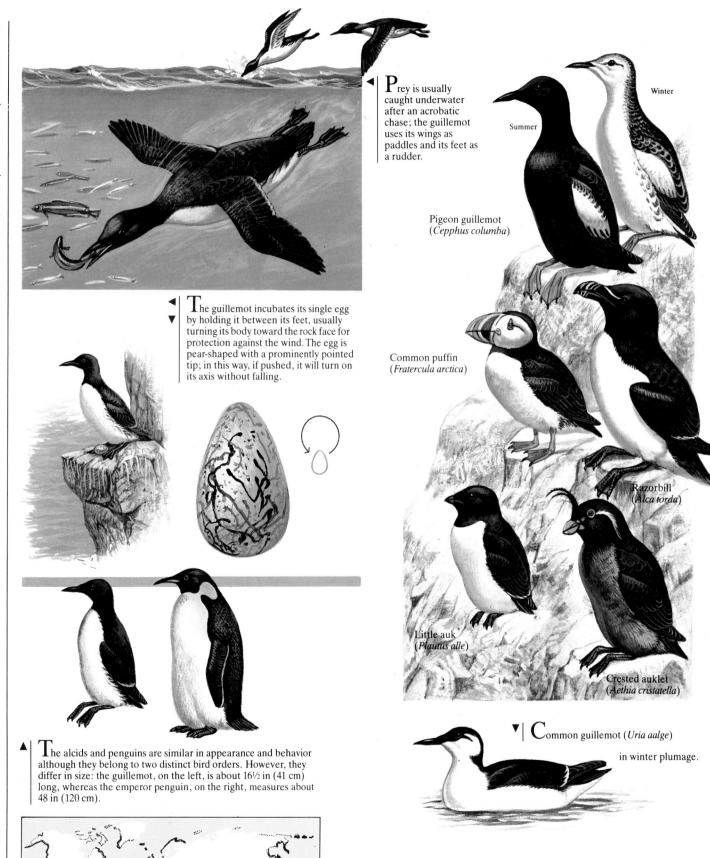

◄ Prey is usually caught underwater after an acrobatic chase; the guillemot uses its wings as paddles and its feet as a rudder.

Winter

Summer

Pigeon guillemot (*Cepphus columba*)

Common puffin (*Fratercula arctica*)

Razorbill (*Alca torda*)

Little auk (*Plautus alle*)

Crested auklet (*Aethia cristatella*)

◄▼ The guillemot incubates its single egg by holding it between its feet, usually turning its body toward the rock face for protection against the wind. The egg is pear-shaped with a prominently pointed tip; in this way, if pushed, it will turn on its axis without falling.

▲ The alcids and penguins are similar in appearance and behavior although they belong to two distinct bird orders. However, they differ in size: the guillemot, on the left, is about 16½ in (41 cm) long, whereas the emperor penguin, on the right, measures about 48 in (120 cm).

▼ Common guillemot (*Uria aalge*)

in winter plumage.

◄ The birds belonging to the family Alcidae are all marine species and are found in the cold zones of the northern hemisphere. After breeding they fly south into the Pacific and Atlantic: the guillemot's winter travels may take it as far as the Mediterranean, California, and northern Japan. 1) Family Alcidae; 2) Common guillemot (*Uria aalge*).

1

2

In returning to its nest on the cliffs the little auk skims over the surface of the sea, fluttering its wings rapidly. ▶

LITTLE AUK

Plautus alle

Order Charadriiformes
Family Alcidae
Length 8 in (20 cm)
Distribution North Atlantic and neighboring Arctic seas
Habits Gregarious
Nesting In colonies on small islands and cliffs
Eggs 1, sometimes 2
Chicks Semi-nidicolous, venturing into sea before being able to fly.

In the seas which are its home the little auk (*Plautus alle*) cannot be mistaken for any other bird. A little bigger than a starling, it has a plump, stocky body and a short bill. In summer the head, back, and breast are black and the underparts white. In winter all these parts turn white as do the ear coverts and the throat. The feet are gray, the bill is black, and the mouth is yellow. The bird does not weigh more than 5½ oz (160 g).

This is the most northerly species of the family, breeding in high arctic latitudes on cliffs and rocky islands off Greenland, Jan Mayen Island, Iceland, the Svalbard Islands, Novaya Zemlya, and Franz Josef Land. Outside the breeding season the little auks scatter over the oceans, often remaining near pack ice; some birds, tossed by storms, stray as far as the British Isles and the Mediterranean Sea. During the short nesting period this small bird is to be found on cliffs and stony seashores.

It feeds, principally on plankton (crustaceans, mollusks, and cephalopods) as well as worms and medium-sized fish. Because such prey abounds in surface waters, it does not need to stay submerged for more than 25 – 30 seconds and it dives only to about 8 ft (2.5 m). After swooping low over the sea, skimming the surface with its fluttering wings, the little auk snatches up its prey and flies back to the nest where its chick is waiting.

Nests are built in colonies containing thousands of breeding pairs on pebbly and rocky beaches or sometimes on mountain slopes 3 – 5 miles (5 – 8 km) inland. The single egg, blue-green with brown markings, is laid around mid June in a hole among the stones or in a rock cleft, and it is incubated by both adults for 24 days.

▲ This bird obtains food (crustaceans, small, fish, and mollusks) by diving under water and pursuing its prey, beating the wings in a paddle-like manner.

At times other than the breeding season, little auks spend most of the day out at sea, often close to pack ice where there is plenty of food. ▶

Rhinoceros auklet (*Cerorhinca monocerata*)

Parakeet auklet (*Cyclorrhynchus psittacula*)

Whiskered auklet (*Aethia pygmaea*)

▼ The little auk and the Adélie penguin, although far apart in classification and of different dimensions (the penguin is four times larger), are equally well adapted to life in the water.

COMMON PUFFIN

Fratercula arctica

Order Charadriiformes
Family Alcidae
Length 12 in (30 cm)
Distribution North Atlantic
Habits Marine, gregarious
Nesting In colonies on rocky islets and grassy slopes near seashore
Eggs 1
Chicks Semi-nidicolous

The puffin (*Fratercula arctica*) weighs 10½ – 16 oz (300 – 450 g). The body is stocky with broad webbed feet and the massive rounded head is furnished with a high, flattened bill, more conspicuous in the breeding season when it is adorned with horny plates of vivid hues (blue, red, and yellow) which disappear in winter. The back is black, the abdomen and cheeks are white, and the legs are orange.

Around the middle of March puffins return to the breeding grounds of former years, assembling at sea in huge flocks, within sight of the coast where nesting is to take place. The number of birds in the sea steadily grows and eventually a few individuals approach the land and start surveying the terrain, coming down to settle in suitable spots. Although some breeding pairs choose rock fissures and hollows for egg laying, most prefer to rear their chick in a grassy burrow in the soil. Both birds busy themselves with bill and feet to excavate a sloping tunnel about 8 ft (2.5 m) deep, ending in an incubation chamber where the female lays her single white, russet-speckled egg.

During the courtship ritual, which habitually precedes egg laying, both partners rub beaks, dip and toss their heads, and finally mate. Incubation, shared by both birds, lasts 40 – 43 days. The parents plunge into the sea and return to the nest with a mouthful of 15 – 20 fish, firmly clutched between the tongue and lower bill. Stocking up in this manner enables the puffin to continue fishing without being encumbered by the prey previously caught. By the beginning of August, with the departure of the last young puffins, the colony is once again silent and deserted. All the birds are now out in the open sea.

The common puffin grasps fish between its tongue and lower mandible; in this way it can continue fishing without having to return to the nest after each kill. This bird, like all other alcids, is seriously threatened by ocean pollution due to hydrocarbons. When the oil tanker *Torrey Canyon* was wrecked in the Channel, the puffin colony on Canada's Sept-Iles dwindled abruptly from 2,500 to 400 nesting pairs.

▼ Other puffin species living in the Pacific include the tufted puffin (*Lunda cirrhata*), above, and the horned puffin (*Fratercula corniculata*), below.

▲ The birds nest in large colonies on the grassy slopes of islands, which are often riddled with burrows excavated by the birds with bill and feet.

◄ Like all other alcids, the puffins are also typically found in northern waters of the northern hemisphere. 1) Common puffin (*Fratercula arctica*); 2) Horned puffin (*Fratercula corniculata*), which is the Pacific counterpart of the foregoing Atlantic species, the two being very much alike. To protect the nesting sites of alcids, many natural reserves have been set apart on cliffs; but in addition to this it is essential that the sea and its resources be sensibly exploited, prohibiting the indiscriminate discharging of hydrocarbons and toxic substances, and rigidly controlling oil tanker traffic to reduce the risk of accidents.

DOVES AND PIGEONS

Columbidae

There is no clear taxonomic distinction between doves and pigeons; both forms belong to the family Columbidae and are distributed almost everywhere, except in polar regions. Their sizes are very variable, some species being no bigger than a sparrow and others as large as a turkey; furthermore, the feeding habits of the 289 species of Columbidae range from those which are almost exclusively seed-eaters to those which feed basically on fruit. More than half these species live in the Indo-Malaysian regions or in Australia, while one small group inhabits the warm latitudes of America; six species are found in Europe.

Certain species, such as the rock dove (common or wild pigeon) display similar plumage in male and female; others exhibit colors designed to attract the opposite sex for breeding purposes, and this results in marked sexual dimorphism. All the Columbidae are monogamous, proverbially "loving" and loyal to each other. The nest is generally a roughly assembled structure, containing, as a rule, a couple of eggs, usually built by both parents who also collaborate in rearing the brood, taking turns to incubate. The incubation period varies from 12 – 30 days. Other common features are the nasal cere and the so-called "pigeon's milk."

The largest subfamily is that of the Treroninae or fruit pigeons, with a limited distribution over the tropical zones of the Old World, especially the Indo-Malaysian regions. All are essentially fruit-eating species and the majority show marked sexual dimorphism, the colors of the males often being vivid and spectacular.

One of the most typical representatives of the subfamily is the white-bellied green pigeon (*Sphenurus sieboldii*), a bird of southern Asia and Indonesia; it is about the same size as a common pigeon, the body yellowish-green with chestnut-brown upper parts, the legs being crimson and the eyes encircled with blue. Like almost all fruit pigeons, it moves about in groups, visiting trees heavy with ripe fruit. To find this food the colony shifts from

The family Columbidae contains a large number of species that vary greatly in size and choice of food.

Pallas's sand-grouse (*Syrrhaptes paradoxus*) belongs to the family Pteroclidae, which, together with the family Columbidae, makes up the order Columbiformes.

Stock dove
(*Columba oenas*)

European turtledove
(*Streptopelia turtur*)

EURASIA

Rufous turtledove
(*Streptopelia orientalis*)

Collared dove
(*Streptopelia decaoto*)

Wood pigeon
(*Columba palumbus*)

Japanese wood pigeon
(*Columba janthina*)

Green pigeon
(*Sphenurus sieboldii*)

SOUTHERN ASIA AND AUSTRALIA

Plumed pigeon
(*Lophophaps plumifera*)

Large green pigeon
(*Treron capellei*)

Elegant imperial pigeon
(*Ducula concinna*)

Red-breasted fruit d
(*Ptilinopus viridis*)

Emerald dove
(*Chalcophaps indica*)

Nicobar pigeon
(*Caloenas nicobarica*)

Bleeding heart pigeon
(*Gallicolumba luzonica*)

Yellow-bellied fruit pigeon
(*Leucotreon cinctatus*)

Green imperial pigeon
(*Ducula aenea*)

low-lying plains, where the fruit ripens earlier, to higher areas, so that each year there is a slow and gradual migration. Despite the bright colors, the bird is not easy to observe, because for most of the time it is well hidden high up in the fruit trees, capable of hanging upside-down, if need be, to reach the berries.

The largest group of Treroninae comprises the fruit doves of the genus *Ptilinopus*, the best known of which is the superb fruit dove (*P. superbus*), found in New Guinea, Tasmania, and Indonesia.

The imperial or nutmeg pigeons of the genus *Ducula* are notable for their brilliant metallic tints. One representative of the group is the green imperial pigeon (*D. aenea*), a very beautiful bird measuring almost 16 in (40 cm), with vivid metallic plumage.

The small subfamily Gourinae contains only three species, known as the crowned pigeons and occurring in New Guinea. Another important subfamily, the Columbinae, includes both seed-eating and fruit-eating species, along with some of the most markedly gregarious pigeons of the family.

The genus *Streptopelia* includes the African mourning dove (*S. decipiens*) and the European turtledove (*S. turtur*). Similar to them is the mourning dove (*Zeinadura macroura*) from Mexico and North America. About 12 in (30 cm) long, it has gray-brown plumage, the neck being a little darker with pink and violet tints on either side. It is the commonest American species, often nesting in cities.

One of the most decorative and vividly colored turtledoves is the emerald dove (*Chalcophaps indica*), a bird with terrestrial habits, found in the Indo-Malaysian forests and in Australia.

The genus *Columba*, in addition to the common pigeon (*C. livia*), contains two other European species, the wood pigeon (*C. palumbus*) and the stock dove (*C. oenas*).

There are two families of birds closely related to Columbidae. The first is the Pteroclidae family, just comprising 16 species known as the sand grouse, living in open and often desert regions of the Old World. The last family, the Rhaphidae, is presently extinct. It included a few flightless species, such as the dodo (*Raphus cucullatus*), which is now extinct. This was a gigantic flightless pigeon which measured more than 3 ft (1 m) in length.

AMERICA

Mourning dove (*Zeinadura macroura*)

The dodo (*Raphus cucullatus*) lived on the island of Mauritius and became extinct in 1680. It was as big as a turkey, with a plump body and a proportionately large head.

Blue-crowned pigeon (*Goura cristata*)

Magpie pouter

Fantail

Jacobin

Double-crested white trumpeter

1) The birds making up the family Columbidae live all over the world; about half of these species are concentrated in the Indo-Malaysian regions and the continent of Australia.
2) The Columbidae are very rare or absent in some areas, particularly the polar regions.

1
2

WILD PIGEON

Columba livia

Order Columbiformes
Family Columbidae
Length 12½ in (32 cm)
Distribution Europe, northern Africa and Asia, India
Habits Highly gregarious
Nesting Colonial, high on rocks or buildings
Eggs 2
Chicks Nidicolous

The geographical range of the wild pigeon (*Columba livia*) is vast, including almost the whole Palearctic region (Europe, North Africa, northern and western Asia) and part of the Oriental region (India). For thousands of years this species has played the role of parasite in towns and cities, and for that reason its range is steadily spreading, for it will nest in colonies wherever suitable buildings are erected. In urban areas already invaded by other birds, including some of the same family Columbidae, pigeons compete fiercely for food in town centers and surrounding zones. The wild pigeon, with such a huge area of distribution, is obviously represented by many geographical races; taxonomists, in fact, recognize about 15 subspecies, some of which are quite different in appearance.

The best guarantee of safety for the pigeon is its sociability. It is almost impossible to see a pigeon on its own and flocks of the birds, numbering thousands, are so constituted as to afford maximum security to each and every individual. Thus it is extremely difficult to get near a group of feeding pigeons in the wild, for there is always a "sentinel" ready to sound the alarm. Similarly, it is virtually impossible to approach a nest without being spotted. Despite the fact that the species is so highly sociable, each pair defends its nest against others, preventing almost any stranger from coming too close.

Nest building partly undertaken in the first stages of the courtship, is shared. It is a rough-and-ready structure, about 8 in (20 cm) across, made of twigs. The eggs are incubated for about 20 days and the chicks, born blind and covered sparsely with yellow down, are brooded for another few days after hatching. The two adults

▲ The wild pigeon (*Columba livia*) is a highly social species, living in flocks that sometimes contain thousands of individuals. Nests, situated very close to one another, often only a few feet apart, are usually found on inaccessible rocks overlooking the sea or a lake, safe from ground predators. The birds do not generally perch in trees and are most frequently seen on the ground collecting seeds, insects, or snails.

◄ Detail of the beak. One feature which distinguishes doves and pigeons from other birds is the presence of a nasal cere, a fleshy outgrowth covered with soft, shining skin, situated at the base of the bill, in which the nostrils open.

take turns on the nest, the male usually handing over to the female for a few hours after midday and never sitting at night. This behavior is the only activity which enables an observer to tell the sexes apart, for their plumage is absolutely identical.

The fledglings are fed on a special secretion known as "pigeon's milk," produced in the bird's gizzard as a result of the stimulation of a particular hormone, prolactin, very highly concentrated during this period. It is similar to human prolactin. In the first days after birth the chicks are fed exclusively on the milk from the crop of both parents. Later they are also given seeds, broken and half digested by the adults, until they are able to collect seeds themselves, usually when they are about a month old. Pigeon's milk is very similar in quality to mammal's milk and provides the brood with a rich source of protein; it is for this special reason that pigeons manage to produce a large number of broods annually, unlike other birds which, during periods when insects are scarce, do not raise any young.

Because the meat of the pigeon is so appetizing, because the various species are so prolific and by reason of other features of their behavior, such as their sociability, these birds have been bred since antiquity. The common street pigeon has come about as a result of certain populations of wild pigeon having gradually taken to living in cities; this process evidently started many centuries ago, as testified by the Latin generic name *Columba*, derived from *columna*, meaning "column," indicating that in olden times these birds habitually clustered on the roofs of houses and temples.

One of the most important groups of selectively bred pigeons is that of the carrier or homing pigeons. One mystery which has always fascinated scientists of every age is the amazing navigational capacity of the homing pigeon. Birds of this race are, in fact, able to find the way back to their loft or cote even if taken hundreds of miles from home; as soon as they are released, the pigeons head immediately in the direction of home, unerringly choosing the best route.

▼ During the breeding season, the male courts the female by cooing. When the links between the sexes are established the two pigeons exchange "kisses," introducing their beak into that of the partner.

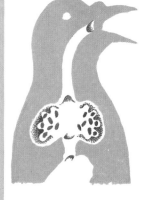

In the breeding period a special liquid known as "pigeon's milk" is secreted in the walls of the parents' gizzard. This milk, diluted with water, forms the sole food of the chicks in the days immediately following their birth. Later the diet is supplemented by half-digested seeds which the adults regurgitate into the crop of their fledglings. The addition of protein contained in the milk enables nestlings to be reared even at times when insects are scarce or absent; and it is for this reason that pigeons breed several times a year.

▼ The fidelity of pigeons is proverbial. Indeed, pairs that have once formed last throughout life, and the death of one partner causes obvious grief to the survivor.

◀ ▼ Pigeons roam freely in many cities. Originally pigeons were used to carry messages; nowadays they are usually bred for racing.

TURTLEDOVE
Streptopelia turtur

Order Columbiformes
Family Columbidae
Length 12 – 12½ in (30 – 32 cm)
Distribution Central and southern Europe
Habits Not markedly gregarious, except during migrations
Nesting High in trees
Eggs 2
Chicks Nidicolous

In body shape and flight silhouette the turtledove (*Streptopelia turtur*) much resembles a small pigeon; it is, however, more slender and has a noticeably longer tail. The European turtledove is a familiar bird of central and southern Europe. Almost entirely absent from Scotland, Ireland, and Denmark, it is seldom seen in the Scandinavian region. It is a species of the flatlands near woods and tall forests.

The Latin name of the turtledove is derived from the characteristic repetitive cooing noise made by the male and the species has, over the centuries, come to be the symbol of love and tenderness; such attributes are only partially merited in terms of the bird's actual behavior, for in some instances the birds can display notable aggressiveness and, in certain respects, real ferocity. Unhappily, the turtledove's gentle reputation has not prevented it from being hunted quite extensively, particularly in countries which are on its regular seasonal migration routes.

In the breeding season the male spends some time paying court to the female, attracting her by cooing and performing a series of displays similar to those of pigeons. During the whole phase of breeding he defends the area around the nest very fiercely, signaling his ownership of territory both with song and with special exhibitions of flying. If another male invades his territory, he will attack with single blows of the wing and powerful pecks aimed at the rival's nape. The calls signaling the "acoustic bounds" of territories are continued even through the night and, above all, just before and after dawn.

Once a relationship is formed, the birds construct a nest. This will hold 2 eggs, which are incubated for about 18 days.

The turtledove is a pleasingly attractive bird and a number of domesticated varieties have been bred for the aviary. It is often encountered in the country and on the fringes of a wood. A wary, timid bird, it can readily be identified during the breeding season when, perched on a high branch, it gives out its characteristic cooing call, audible hundreds of yards away. The turtledove feeds almost exclusively on small seeds, collected from the ground.

At night, when digesting or when the weather is especially cold, it fluffs up its feathers to increase the protective layer around its body, which in this way is warmly insulated.

Mating is preceded by a phase of courtship. In this illustration a male, in pursuit of a female, coos by filling his throat with air.

The turtledove, like the common pigeon, produces special milk for feeding the young. The fledgling stimulates the parents in this activity by repeatedly pecking at the sensitive areas of their head and neck with its beak.

BLUE-CROWNED PIGEON

Goura cristata

Order Columbiformes
Family Columbidae
Length 30 – 32 in (75 – 80 cm)
Distribution New Guinea and surrounding islands
Habits Gregarious, in small groups
Nesting Not too high up in trees
Eggs 1 (sometimes 2)
Chicks Nidicolous

The blue-crowned pigeon (*Goura cristata*) is the largest living pigeon, a real giant of the family, measuring up to 32 in (80 cm) long and weighing over 6½ lb (3 kg). The color of the plumage is violet-blue and it is an extremely beautiful bird. It lives in the wet zones of New Guinea, both in the north and south of the island; it is also commonly found in the adjacent islands. Although still fairly abundant in virgin forests, the species has practically vanished from areas around cities and villages. It nests close to rivers and swamps, especially in spots where the vegetation is most dense.

The blue-crowned pigeon, along with two other species, the Victoria crowned pigeon (*G. victoria*) and Sheepmaker's crowned pigeon (*G. scheepmakeri*), belongs to the genus *Goura*. About the size of a turkey, they make tasty eating, so it is not surprising that they constitute highly prized game for hunters; but perhaps even more interesting for trophy collectors are the feathers which form a spectacular crest on the head.

If a stranger approaches a group of the pigeons while feeding, they simply take refuge on a low tree branch and watch events from there. Because of this behavior, they are extremely easy to kill; and even after one of their number is shot, the other birds making up the group seem incapable of getting clear away, merely moving off a few yards. The reason why crowned pigeons behave in this apparently stupid manner is, probably, that they have no natural predators. This means they have not been compelled, as it were, to develop a more effective escape response, as has happened among the vast majority of birds, by getting off the ground and well out of range.

Two species of crowned pigeon are shown in the picture; in the foreground is the blue-crowned pigeon (*Goura cristata*) and behind it the Victoria crowned pigeon (*G. victoria*), recognizable by the white patch on the wings.

The very beautiful crest feathers have been used, particularly in the nineteenth century, as personal ornaments. Because of these highly valued plumes and the trusting habits of the blue-crowned pigeon, the species has been brought to the brink of extinction.

The birds feed exclusively on fruit that has dropped to the ground. When they sense danger, their only reaction is to perch on the low branch of a tree or bush, so becoming an easy target for the hunter's gun.

Detail of leg and foot. As is the case with other species of pigeon, the legs of the two crowned pigeons illustrated on this page are not covered by scales but with a kind of tiled epidermis.

167

PALLAS'S SAND GROUSE

Syrrhaptes paradoxus

Order Columbiformes
Family Pteroclidae
Length 14 in (35 cm)
Distribution Central and southern Eurasia, Africa
Habits Gregarious
Nesting In small colonies on ground
Eggs 2 – 4
Chicks Nidicolous

Pallas's sand grouse (*Syrrhaptes paradoxus*) is found throughout central and southern Asia and much of Africa, with the exception of the central–western sector, Madagascar, and the extreme southeast. In Europe it appears each year regularly only in the south of the Iberian peninsula, although it makes frequent incursions elsewhere. Such appearances are not usually on a large scale, involving a small number of birds that fly comparatively short distances to settle in sandy zones of eastern Europe; but sporadic invasions of larger proportions are sometimes recorded, with thousands of birds reaching Denmark and the Färoes, the last of them having occurred in 1908, when a few nesting pairs were even seen in the British Isles.

The habitat of this species, as it is for the great majority of Pteroclidae, is typically restricted to arid zones, mainly sandy, with little or no plant growth. These birds have evolved so as to live in arid or semi-arid regions by making use of a whole range of special anatomical, physiological, and behavioral adaptations. The term "hyperspecialization" is applicable to species living in particularly unfavorable habitats (in this case deserts, where finding water is a problem and where extremes of temperature are the rule); and this is one of the main reasons why such species are driven to pay regular visits to new areas on the fringes of the zones where they are habitually found.

In the desert where it spends most of its life, the fundamental problem for the sand grouse is to obtain a daily supply of drinking water. This is why, every day at dawn and sunset, with amazing regularity, flocks consisting of several dozen birds assemble

▲ Pallas's sand grouse (*Syrrhaptes paradoxus*) is a typical bird of arid zones with little or no plant growth. Its mimetic coloration is essential for escaping the notice of predators in this type of terrain. It is a highly social species, with groups regularly assembling, at dawn and dusk, around the rare desert water holes.

◄ It feeds on seeds and insects (grasshoppers, spiders, etc.) found in the desert.

◄ The foot is short and robust, completely covered by feathers; the rear toe is missing.

The lower surface ▶ of the foot is flat and covered by thick scales. This and other adaptations help to insulate the bird from the scorching desert sand during the day.

round one of the rare water holes in the desert, often flying long distances to get there. During these journeys they utilize a complex range of acoustic signals (twittering and whistling sounds) to keep the flock together in the semi-darkness.

Whereas mimetic plumage and complicated behavior patterns serve to protect the adult sand grouse, other equally remarkable adaptations come to the assistance of immature birds and help them survive in their hostile surroundings. The chick is born in a nest hastily dug in the sand, no more than a simple hollow lined with a few scraps of straw. The eggs, a little larger than those of a pigeon, are greenish-brown with a scattering of darker spots, blending well with the sand. The female incubates by day and the male by night; by taking turns on the eggs there is less risk of the more brightly colored male being spotted from afar during the day and thus putting the entire brood in danger. In the daytime the male assists the brooding female by occasionally bringing her food and water regurgitated from his beak.

Pallas's sand grouse have semi-colonial habits, with pairs nesting close to one another but each remaining absolutely monogamous. When a predator approaches the nest, the parents put on a diversionary performance, pretending to be injured and unable to fly, thus drawing the enemy away from the brood. This behavior is, of course, typical of many other birds that nest on the ground.

The only other genus of the Pteroclidae is *Pterocles*, the representatives of which are notable for their particularly short feet and feather-covered toes; there is no large toe and the others are linked by a web. Altogether there are 14 species in the genus. The pin-tailed sand grouse (*P. alchata*) shows marked sexual dimorphism; and the spotted sand grouse (*P. senegallus*) is found in North Africa. The largest species in the genus and, indeed, the whole family, is the black-bellied sand grouse (*P. orientalis*). This species, together with the pin-tailed sand grouse, is the only one to be found in Europe. The black-bellied species ranges over southern Europe but its habitat is now disturbingly limited.

When the birds move about in flocks they take up the classic V-formation, similar to so many other medium- and large-sized birds which migrate in groups.

▲ The sand grouse, along with pigeons, are the only birds to drink by sucking water.

▼ When a possible predator approaches the nest, the parents flutter about pretending to be injured or sick so as to distract attention.

▲ The chicks, from the moment they hatch, wear a sand-colored, perfectly mimetic plumage.

Black-bellied sand grouse (*Pterocles orientalis*)

Pin-tailed sand grouse (*Pterocles alchata*)

In the early hours of the morning the adults fly off to get water. They allow their plumage to become soaked, immersing themselves to the abdomen and teetering up and down a few times; then they fly back to the nest, where the fledglings take hold of the wet feathers in their beak to squeeze out the moisture.

◀ Pallas's sand grouse is distributed through central and southern Asia and over much of Africa, except for the central–western sector and the extreme south east as well as Madagascar. In Europe it makes an appearance every year in the south of the Iberian peninsula. Like the majority of Pteroclidae, it is particularly well adapted to inhospitable habitats such as deserts and savannas. 1) Distribution of Pallas's sand grouse (*Syrrhaptes paradoxus*).

PARROTS AND ALLIES
Psittaciformes

The strongly hooked beak, with both jaws markedly hinged, the feet with two toes turned forwards and two backwards, the striking colors, predominantly green, red, yellow, and blue, and the distinctive cries, almost always loud and raucous, are just a few of the more obvious characteristics that make the parrots so easily identifiable.

Most parrots live in the tropical regions of the southern hemisphere, especially in South America, Australia, and New Guinea. There are relatively few species in Africa, and Madagascar, southern Asia, the Philippines, the Sunda archipelago, New Zealand, Micronesia, Melanesia, and Polynesia. With the disappearance of the Carolina parakeet (*Conuropsis carolinensis*), which until the end of the nineteenth century still lived in the southeastern part of the United States, the highest northern latitude is now reached by the Himalayan slaty-headed parakeet (*Psittacula himalayana*), which ranges to northwestern Afghanistan at latitude 36°N. In the southern hemisphere the austral parakeet (*Microsittace ferruginea*) is found at the southernmost tip of Tierra del Fuego, a record that until the beginning of the present century was shared with the red-fronted parakeet (*Cyanoramphus novaezelandiae erythrotis*), from the desolate Macquarie Islands, which was exterminated by cats imprudently brought into the small archipelago by penguin hunters.

Many species have remarkable powers of adaptation, inhabiting vast areas and continually expanding their range even into city centers. The most typical example of this is the African ring-necked parakeet (*Psittacula krameri*), inhabiting the Cape Verde Islands in the Atlantic and distributed across equatorial Africa and parts of the Middle East as far as southeast China. Yet other parrots may have an extremely restricted range, even when there are no impassable natural barriers such as mountain chains and oceans. The species which probably has the most limited range is the Antipodes Islands parakeet (*Cyanoramphus unicolor*) from the archipelago of that name, a tiny group of rocks barely 25 sq.

One of the most striking features of all parrots is their brightly colored plumage. Broadly speaking, the principal color is green, but there are parrots which are completely white, blackish, pink, yellow, blue or red. The last color predominates in the scarlet macaw (*Ara macao*), illustrated here.

miles (38 km²) in area, lying to the southeast of New Zealand. In the case of others, such as the indigo macaw (*Anodorhynchus leari*) and the little blue macaw (*Cyanopsitta spixi*), the geographical distribution is practically unknown, for there have been only a few uncertain reports of their presence in eastern Brazil.

Although the majority of parrots live in the tropical jungle, it is fair to say that there is hardly any habitat they do not occupy. Some species are found in grassy and wooded savana, in semi-desert and desert regions, in cultivated zones, in high mountains where the ground is covered by snow for most of the year, in mangrove swamps, on cliffs, and in salt lagoons along the seashore. Certain parrots are closely associated with particular vegetable substances, as is the case in Australia with the glossy cockatoo (*Calyptorhynchus lathami*) and the casuarina, or in America with the red-spectacled parrot (*Amazona pretrei*) and the araucaria, and the thick-billed parrot (*Rhynchopsitta pachyrhyncha*) and various pines.

The largest representative of the order is the hyacinthine macaw (*Anodorhynchus hyacinthus*) from Brazil, which is nearly 39 in (1 m) in length and weighs 3 lb (1,500 g), while the smallest is the buff-faced pygmy parrot (*Micropsitta pusio*) from New Guinea, which is barely 3½ in (8.5 cm) long and only weighs about ½ oz (15 g).

The principal and most striking aspect of the parrots, nevertheless, is their range of colors, usually very vivid, with a predominance of green. Green, of course, is not a pure color but the result of mixing yellow and blue. Among parrots the range from yellow to red is due to the presence of a pigment not yet exhaustively studied but with a biochemical structure analogous to the carotenes; it has provisionally been called psittacin.

The phenomenon of sexual dimorphism, namely a difference in color between the male and female, is fairly widespread among parrots from Australia, New Guinea, and Asia, but less so among those from Africa and America. Normally it is the male who boasts the more brilliant colors but the opposite is true of the eclectus parrot (*Eclectus roratus*) of New Guinea and neighboring regions, for the female is red and blue and the male mainly green. This dimorphism in reverse is

They probe into tree bark to find insect larvae on which to feed.

As a rule parrots feed on seeds, berries, fruit, grass, leaves, tender slivers of bark, buds, shoots, and roots. Some species grasp food with the claw in order to eat it.

Besides being employed for eating, the beak is also used as an additional point of support when moving around in trees and over rocks; the larger species utilize it, too, as a balance when they are on the ground.

The main enemy of the scarlet macaw is the harpy eagle (*Harpya harpya*).

Both members of a pair, which remain together for years, will frequently peck each other on head and neck as signs of affection.

exceptional, found only (and to a lesser degree) in two other African parrots of the genus *Poicephalus*, namely the brown-necked parakeet (*P. robustus*) and Rüppell's parrot (*P. rueppellii*). In some species the dimorphism affects, in addition, the color of the beak, the iris, and the cere, the last being the small fleshy projection at the root of the upper mandible on which the nostrils open.

The wings of a parrot, with ten primary and ten secondary remiges, have no special characteristics. Some are long and narrow, as in the genera *Nymphicus*, *Polytelis*, *Melopsittacus* or *Lathamus*, others fairly short and rounded, as in *Amazona*, *Nestor*, *Probosciger* or *Strigops*, this last genus being incapable of sustained flight but only short glides. The only real anomaly is to be found in the adult male princess parrot (*Polytelis alexandrae*), which has a strange drop-like appendage, of unknown significance, at the tip of the third primary flight feather.

All the cockatoos bear mobile crests of varying shapes, the functions of which are uncertain. Crests are used nowadays for sending signals, especially during courtship, but certainly they did not develop for this purpose, which is only a secondary function. One author suggests that these crests constitute a kind of sham elongation of the head, thus in some measure blunting the attacks of falcons who, in aiming for the nape, may find themselves left with a clawful of feathers. This is an ingenious theory but not very plausible. It is more likely that the crest serves as a sort of parasol or turban giving better protection from the sun, especially in the arid stretches of Australian hinterland where most cockatoos live. Almost all parrots are capable of moving the feathers on the lower part of their cheeks forward so that they cover much of the bill and thus help to limit heat loss while they are resting.

Molting is associated with the breeding cycle and may occur early or late according to seasonal weather conditions. It generally commences during incubation and after the birth of the chicks, taking some 3 – 4 months to complete. The presence of naked zones on the head, sometimes colored (white, black, gray, blue, yellow, brown, red, or pink), is a phenomenon that is particularly evident among macaws and certain cockatoos.

In spite of a superficial resemblance

Hyacinthine macaw
(*Anodorhynchus hyacinthinus*)

Blue and yellow macaw
(*Ara aracauna*)

Red and green macaw
(*Ara chloroptera*)

Carolina parakeet
(*Conuropsis carolinensis*)

Sun parakeet
(*Aratinga solstitialis*)

AMERICA

Military macaw
(*Ara militaris*)

Yellow-headed amazon
(*Amazona ochrocephala oratrix*)

Salmon-crested cockatoo
(*Cacatua moluccensis*)

AUSTRALIA AND NEW ZEALAND

Leadbeater's cockatoo
(*Cacatua leadbeateri*)

Sulfur-crested cockatoo
(*Cacatua galerita*)

Palm cockatoo
(*Probosciger aterrimus*)

Gang-gang cockatoo
(*Callocephalon fimbriatum*)

to that of birds of prey and especially owls, a parrot's beak, as can easily be observed, functions in quite a different manner. Here both mandibles are fully articulated and can simultaneously be opened wide to their fullest extent. While eating, the two parts of the bill operate somewhat like the jaws of ruminants, the cutting edges of the lower part moving rhythmically against the grooved roof of the upper part, shelling or grinding food with the aid of the tongue. It is common to see a parrot at rest rubbing the two bill sections against each other; this not only keeps the edges sharp but also prevents excessive growth. In addition to eating, the beak is also used as an extra point of support as the parrot moves through the branches and as a possible prop (for large species only) when on the ground.

The shape and size of the bill vary according to the food normally eaten. They range from black, gray, and white to brown, red, orange, yellow, and greenish. Sometimes the two sections of bill are differently colored.

The large, fleshy tongue of parrots helps to grasp morsels of food against the roof of the mouth while the cutting edge of the lower bill does the necessary shelling or grinding. It also gets rid of food particles lodged in the throat, and in the latter context is particularly important for Pesquet's parrot which swallows large pieces of banana and other soft fruits; these are directed properly through the mouth by the retracted rear portion of the tongue. It is generally blackish, brown, bluish, or flesh-pink, but in some instances it may be more curiously colored: black and yellow in the hyacinthine macaw; red and black in the palm cockatoo.

All parrots are zygodactylous, their feet having two toes facing the front and two facing the rear, this structure being typical of climbing birds.

The majority of parrots feed on seeds, berries, fruit, grass, leaves, tender slivers of bark, shoots, buds, and roots. The strictly arboreal Loriini feeds almost exclusively on nectar, pollen, and sweet pulps. Insects are included, to some extent, in the diet of almost all species, but some, such as the black cockatoos of the genus *Calyptorhynchus* and in particular the kaka or southern nestor (*Nestor meridionalis*), are markedly insectivorous and spend most of the time ripping away old bark to find larvae, to some extent

Gray parrot
(*Psittacus erithacus*)

Nyasa lovebird
(*Agapornis lilianae*)

AFRICA

Masked lovebird
(*Agapornis personata*)

Plum-headed parakeet
(*Psittacula cyanocephala*)

African ringed-necked parakeet
(*Psittacula krameri*)

Red-faced lovebird
(*Agapornis pullaria*)

Paradise parrot
(*Psephotus pulcherrimus*)

Budgerigar
(*Melopsittacus undulatus*)

Scarlet-chested parrot
(*Neophema splendida*)

Himalayan slaty-headed parakeet
(*Psittacula himalayana*)

Cockatiel
(*Nymphicus hollandicus*)

Rainbow lorikeet
(*Trichoglossus haematodus moluccanus*)

Kakapo
(*Strigops habroptilus*)

Ground parrot
(*Pezoporus wallicus*)

SOUTHERN ASIA

Kea
(*Nestor notabilis*)

◀ The majority of parrots are distributed through the tropical regions of the southern hemisphere, especially in South America, Australia, and New Guinea. Comparatively few species live in Africa and Madagascar, southern Asia, the Philippines, the Sunda archipelago, New Zealand, Micronesia, Melanesia, and Polynesia. The farthest point north is reached by the Himalayan slaty-headed parakeet (*Psittacula himalayana*) which, in Afghanistan, is found in the region of latitude 36° N; and in the southern hemisphere its counterpart is the austral parakeet (*Microsittace ferruginea*), which reaches the southernmost tip of Tierra del Feugo. 1) World distribution of the order Psittaciformes.

1

replacing woodpeckers, which are not found either in Australia or New Zealand. It is possible that small vertebrates are also included in the diet of more parrot species than is generally believed. Certainly the kakapo or owl parrot (*Strigops habroptilus*) of New Zealand, a nocturnal species almost incapable of flight, also feeds on lizards. Among the mainly vegetarian species, some are highly specialized in cracking open nuts and fruit stones.

Most parrots move around in groups which range from small families to flocks comprising thousands of individuals. The flight pattern, particularly of the smaller species, is swift, low and undulating, a series of high-speed wingbeats being followed by a brief pause for losing height. The larger species flap their wings more slowly and regularly, but their flight, at high altitude, is, with a few exceptions, equally fast and agile. A notable exception is the palm cockatoo, with short, rounded wings proportional to its body weight, which differs from all other parrots by flying with its head bent downwards, the enormous beak resting on the breast.

Many parrots, as stated, cover long distances every day to get to and from their feeding grounds; others are nomadic, moving about here and there to take fullest advantage of the sporadic rainfall in the dry Australian interior. Still others set out on genuine seasonal migrations, such as many Loriini of New Guinea, various Ariini from the southeastern parts of South America, the blue-winged parrot (*Neophema chrysostomus*) and the orange-bellied parrot (*N. chrysogaster*), these last two crossing the Bass Strait separating the Australian continent from Tasmania, in a two-way journey. As they fly, many parrots utter loud, discordant cries, repeating them in rapid succession; these calls help flocks to keep together in the course of their evening and nightly journeys.

Separate populations of the same species may have slightly different vocal repertoires because of their inborn gift of imitating the sounds of other birds. Because of this capacity for mimicry, some species, such as the gray parrot and the yellow-headed amazon (*Amazona ochrocephala*), have unhappily become the special target of dealers, and every year large numbers of adult and young birds are captured.

Comparatively little is known about the varied courtship behavior of

The palm cockatoo (*Probosciger aterrimus*), with its characteristically sharp-edged beak, is able to crack open the hardest nuts. Having done this, it scoops out the contents, bit by bit, with the point of the lower mandible and conveys them to its mouth with the sucker-like tip of the red and black tongue.

The yellow-tailed black cockatoo (*Calyptorhynchus funereus*) feeds plentifully on insects and spends much time in trees stripping off bark in search of larvae. The fallen leaves are eaten by sheep and it is thought that the animals follow the birds around for this purpose.

Some parrots are noted for their inborn ability to imitate noises made by other animals and also the sound of the human voice. Among such species is the gray parrot (*Psittacus erithacus*), which, because of this aptitude, is in great demand commercially, entailing the periodic capture of both adults and fledglings. In the home the gray parrot is a popular, easily tamed pet.

parrots in the wild, for most observations have tended to apply to individuals bred in captivity. Allowing for the fact, therefore, that many exceptions exist, there are two principal types of courtship: first, that typical of species that are prevalently dimorphous (particularly in the Australasian and Oriental regions), among which relationships between the sexes are normally confined to the breeding season, and, secondly, that which is characteristic of species lacking secondary sexual features (mainly from the Neotropical region) which usually remain together all year round and often for an entire liftetime.

In its early phases courtship tends to be more varied and balletic, and the prerogative of the male who dips his head repeatedly, contracts his pupils, erects the head feathers, spreads out his tail, lowers the wings, gives out cries that are sometimes quite musical, and (except in the case of cockatoos) offers food to the female after a series of headpumping movements to stimulate regurgitation.

In the next stages links between the pair are frequently reinforced, all the year through, by reciprocal displays, almost identical in both sexes, during which the iris is strongly contracted, the feathers of the cheeks, nape, neck, and whole body are erected, the tail is spread, and slow, measured steps are taken, head lowered and body horizontal, towards the partner. Each bird often scrutinizes the other's neck and head for parasites, while offerings of food are restricted to the periods immediately before and during mating.

Mating takes place in two different ways: either the male mounts with both feet on the female's back or (among the American parrots only) the male places one foot on a branch and the other on the back of his partner.

In nature most parrots lay their eggs in the hollow of a tree, but many also nest in the cavity of a rock or wall, under the eaves of a roof, in a hole on the ground, among tufts of grass or piles of stones, in tunnels dug on a slope or in a termite mound. The eggs, invariably white, measure about ⅝ in (16 mm) in the case of the buff-faced pygmy parrot, ranging to 2 – 2¼ in (50 – 55 mm) for the palm cockatoo and big macaws. As a rule it is the female who incubates, but pairs of white cockatoos (*Cacatua, Nymphicus*) and gang-gang cockatoos take turns on the eggs.

Typical of southern Asia and the adjacent islands are the hanging parakeets of the genus *Loriculus* which have an altogether curious way of sleeping; like bats, they hang from slender branches, head downward, and they gather the fruit on which they feed suspended in the same position.

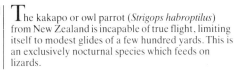

The kakapo or owl parrot (*Strigops habroptilus*) from New Zealand is incapable of true flight, limiting itself to modest glides of a few hundred yards. This is an exclusively nocturnal species which feeds on lizards.

The kea (*Nestor notabilis*) is an inhabitant of the New Zealand mountains. It is alleged that it attacks and kills sheep to devour their fat and kidneys, but there is no positive proof of this accusation. Dead animals, however, may be partially consumed.

COMMON CUCKOO

Cuculus canorus

Order Cuculiformes
Family Cuculidae
Subfamily Cuculinae
Length 12½ – 14½ in (32 – 37 cm)
Weight 5½ oz (150 g)
Distribution Europe and Asia
Habits Parasitical
Nesting In nests of passerines
Breeding period Spring
Incubation 12½ days
Eggs 12 (exceptionally up to 26)
Chicks Inept
Sexual maturity Probably at age of 2 years

The common cuckoo (*Cuculus canorus*) is the only parasitical bird which chooses hosts that are unrelated to it, mostly insect-eating passerines, but sometimes seed-eaters as well, such as the buntings of the family Emberizidae. The parasitical instinct is evidently deep rooted, for it is immediately noticeable that baby cuckoos open their beaks wide to show the red palate which is larger than that of their siblings (so attracting greater attention from the adoptive parents). Another adaptation pointing to remote ancestry is the fact that the droppings of the baby cuckoo, like those of passerines, are enveloped in a gelatinous substance, and so easily removable. There can be no doubt that the cuckoo is an extremely specialized bird in its choice of brood and that its survival is intimately linked with that of its host.

The species forms no fixed pairs, and partners may meet by chance as they move about daily; but they remain loyal to one territory and may return there year after year. One portion of territory may partially overlap those of others, even of the opposite sex; this is why two males can sometimes be seen with one female, and polyandry, as well as polygamy, may occur.

The mature female chooses her territory according to the number of nests available for parasitizing, and if these are scarce she will fly off elsewhere. She begins to ovulate at about the time when the host species builds its nest. Eggs are laid at intervals of a couple of days (there are usually 12 but some-

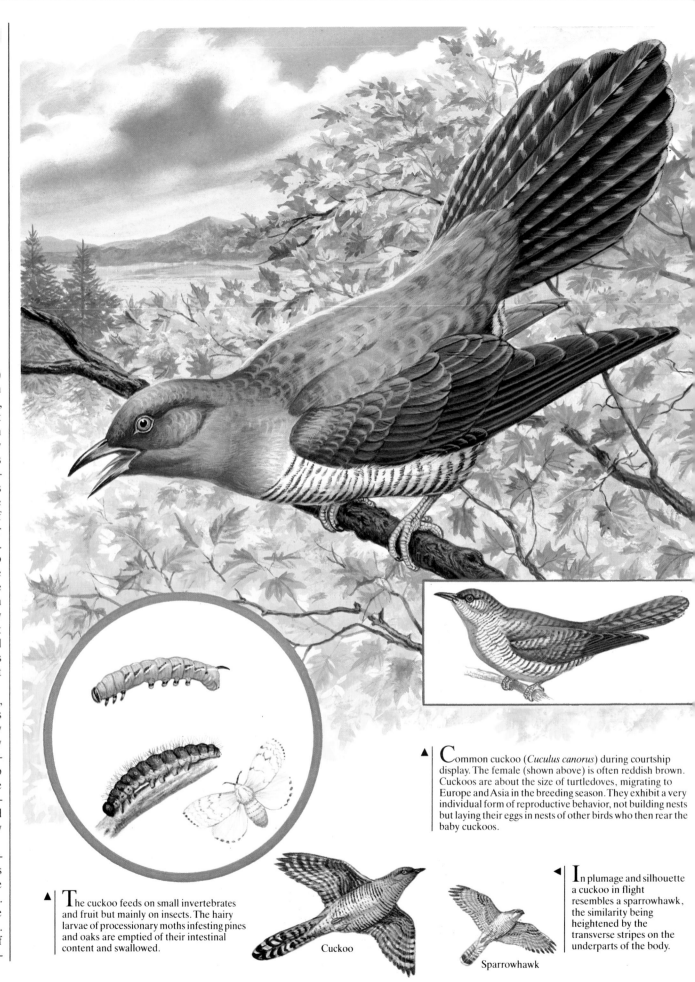

▲ Common cuckoo (*Cuculus canorus*) during courtship display. The female (shown above) is often reddish brown. Cuckoos are about the size of turtledoves, migrating to Europe and Asia in the breeding season. They exhibit a very individual form of reproductive behavior, not building nests but laying their eggs in nests of other birds who then rear the baby cuckoos.

▲ The cuckoo feeds on small invertebrates and fruit but mainly on insects. The hairy larvae of processionary moths infesting pines and oaks are emptied of their intestinal content and swallowed.

Cuckoo

Sparrowhawk

◄ In plumage and silhouette a cuckoo in flight resembles a sparrowhawk, the similarity being heightened by the transverse stripes on the underparts of the body.

times up to 18 or even, exceptionally, up to 26) in different nests, but always belonging to the same species. In this way the possibilities of individual babies surviving to become independent are increased. Should nests be few and far between, two eggs may be laid in the same nest, and cases have been recorded of nests containing the eggs of two different cuckoos.

The cuckoo's eggs are generally laid before the host birds have finished laying their own. Incubation lasts 12½ days, this period being shorter than that of any passerine, which incubate for at least 13 days. This, too, is a remarkable adaptation to a parasitic type of life.

It has been observed that the skin on the flanks and back of baby cuckoos is highly sensitive from about 10 hours after birth to the time they are four days old, and sometimes until the end of their first week. Almost anything that brushes against the baby's body irritates it to such an extent that the fledgling does all it can to keep it away. By means of this sophisticated evolutionary mechanism the newborn chick hoists eggs and the babies that hatch on to its back and heaves them right out of the nest. Two special anatomical features assist it to accomplish this feat: the somewhat concave back which easily accommodates a small egg, and the fairly strong wings which help it to clamber around the nest. In those exceptional circumstances when two cuckoos' eggs are laid in the same nest, each chick may try to remove the other; observations have shown that it is usually the stronger one which wins, but in rare instances both may survive. After about four days the sensitivity of the skin on sides and back disappears and the baby feels no urge whatsoever to eject any object from the nest. So the small parent bird may now be faced with the problem of feeding not one but two large baby cuckoos.

In the light of information assembled, there is nothing to indicate that any other chick will survive in the nest; the baby cuckoo, stronger and more enterprising, may well grab all the food for itself, causing the others to die of hunger. The host bird is therefore compelled to fly continually to and fro with food, especially arthropods, for its disproportionately large foster child. The cuckoo seems insatiable, endlessly demanding food by opening its enormous mouth wide, an effective stimulus for its adoptive parents.

▲ Cuckoos migrate southward in May and June; because they fly like sparrowhawks they often terrify other birds.

▲ The eggs of the host bird need 13–15 days to incubate while a cuckoo's egg takes only 12½ days. In this way the baby cuckoo, blind and naked, is first to hatch.

▲ The host bird accepts the cuckoo and rears it lovingly as its own baby. Within about three weeks the young cuckoo fills the nest.

▲ When a small passerine leaves its nest for a moment, the cuckoo filches an egg, lays one of its own, and flies away, the whole operation lasting only about a minute.

▲ After a couple of days the baby cuckoo heaves other eggs and chicks out of the nest, balancing them on its concave back and using its wings to help.

▲ Eventually, unable to stay in the nest any longer, the fledgling perches on a branch and the small foster-parent stands on its back to feed it.

Red-backed shrike

Cuckoo's egg

Shrike's egg

◀ The eggs of the cuckoo are roughly the same size as those of its host; the shell color is also very similar, increasing the likelihood that the latter will not notice the difference. On the left are the eggs of a cuckoo and of a parasitized bird, in this case a red-backed shrike (*Lanius collurio*).

CUCULIDAE

The representatives of the family Cuculidae are small to medium-sized birds with an elongated silhouette, a slightly curved bill, fairly rounded wings and a long tail with quite large covert feathers. The legs are short and rather weak in those species that live in trees, whereas those of ground species are longer and fairly sturdy. The latter species also have an elongated fourth toe.

The true cuckoos (Cuculinae) are arboreal birds of medium dimensions, very soft skin, a voice with typically two-toned modulations and dark plumage with irregular sexual dimorphism. They are rapid fliers, have migratory habits and travel long distances, chiefly at night. Cuckoos can adapt marvelously to their surroundings. Despite their innate shyness of people, they have succeeded very well in establishing themselves in populated areas. Their characteristic call can be heard not only in dense woodland but also in town gardens and orchards. Because of this adaptive capacity they have settled almost everywhere in the world.

The 50 or so species of parasitic cuckoos choose hosts that vary in size from a wren, weighing ¼ oz (7 g), to a crow, weighing about 2¼ lb (1,000 g). These host birds, regardless of their size, are left to rear foster babies weighing between ¾ oz (25 g) and 2¼ lb (1,000 g), depending on species, when ready to fly. Almost all passerines may find a cuckoo's eggs in their nest. At least 20 regular hosts and some 70 occasional hosts rear chicks of the common cuckoo but another 200 or so have at one time or another been added to this count. The cuckoo may lay about 20 different types of egg, but each female lays only one form and thus makes use of a regular host.

The female cuckoo is known to lay her eggs in the nest of the species that has reared her; this adaptation has led to the appearance of genuine oological races, each behaving differently in relation to the species it parasitizes, being wholly familiar with the latter's habits. Thus in Finland there are cuckoos which lay only blue eggs in the nests of the European redstart (*Phoenicurus phoenicurus*), Hungarian cuckoos, which lay them in the nests

Redstart
(*Phoenicurus phoenicurus*)

Great reed warbler
(*Acrocephalus arundinaceus*)

Robin
(*Erithacus rubecula*)

Whitethroat
(*Sylvia communis*)

Willow warbler
(*Phylloscopus trochilus*)

Gray wagtail
(*Motacilla cinerea*)

Wren
(*Troglodytes troglodytes*)

▲ Some of the habitual hosts of the common cuckoo. The egg on the left is that of the parasitized species and the one on the right (larger) that of the cuckoo, which imitates it.

The toes of the Cuculiformes are arranged two to the front and two to the rear. This zygodactylous structure is evidently useful for climbing on trunks, as is the custom among woodpeckers, but cuckoos, oddly enough, do not climb.

▼ Other members of the order Cuculiformes.

Cuculidae
Roadrunner
(*Geococcyx californianus*)

Musophagidae
Violet touraco
(*Musophaga violacea*)

Cuculidae
Giant coua
(*Coua gigas*)

of the great reed warbler (*Acrocephalus arundinaceus*), African cuckoos which, choose the nests of the Algerian redstart (*Diplootocus moussieri*), and so on. The cuckoo's eggs often match those of the host so perfectly that even an expert may have difficulty in recognizing them.

The most frequent hosts of cuckoos are: passerines such as the wagtails and pipits (Motacillidae), particularly the pied wagtail (*Motacilla alba*), the gray wagtail (*M. cinerea*), the tree pipit (*Anthus trivialis*), and the meadow pipit (*A. pratensis*); and warblers of the family Sylviidae, especially wood warblers of the genus *Phylloscopus*, but also redstarts and the robin (*Erithacus rubecula*). Other frequent hosts include the hedge sparrow (*Prunella modularis*), the wren (*Troglodytes troglodytes*), and the shrikes. From time to time cuckoos parasitize other species belonging to different families; in every region particular hosts are preferred. In Spain the great spotted cuckoo (*Clamator glandarius*) lays eggs in the nests of the common magpie (*Pica pica*).

The eggs laid by cuckoos are either very small or very large in relation to those of their hosts. The former is true of those laid by the Eurasian little cuckoo (*Cuculus poliocephalus*), which are about the same size as those of the wren chosen as host. The latter applies to the eggs of the great spotted cuckoo, similar in size and design to those of the magpie in whose nests they are deposited.

Brood parasitism depends for its success basically on the homochromous nature of the cuckoo's eggs; the passivity of the host is an additional factor working in favor of the baby cuckoo's survival. This passivity, however, which causes the host to incubate strange eggs, is unconscious. Cases have been observed in which the host has reacted in an unexpected way when making the discovery that such eggs are not its own. A shrike, for example, has been seen destroying its nest and a great reed warbler covered its entire nest with additional building material. This is why some 35 per cent of all cuckoos' eggs are laid in vain. They are by no means accepted by all species, particularly smaller ones whose nests may be damaged by the female cuckoos and who therefore refuse to continue incubating. Furthermore, small passerines display marked dislike for cuckoos in hostile reactions, particularly among groups.

Oriental cuckoo
(*Cuculus saturatus*)

Fugitive hawk cuckoo
(*Hyerococcyx fugax*)

Red-throated bluethroat
(*Cyanosylvia svecica*)

Crowned willow warbler
(*Phylloscopus occipitalis*)

Great spotted cuckoo
(*Clamator glandarius*)

Eurasian little cuckoo
(*Cuculus poliocephalus*)

Tawny prinia
(*Prinia subflava*)

Magpie
(*Pica pica*)

Yellow-billed cuckoo
(*Coccyzus americanus*)

Koel
(*Eudynamis scolopacea*)

Emerald cuckoo
(*Chrysococcyx cupreus*)

▲ The great spotted cuckoo is unusual in choosing a host on the basis of food preferences. In fact, while the adult feeds mainly on the hairy larvae of the pine and oak processionary moths, the young eat a much more varied range of food, made up principally of insects and mollusks.

▲ Other species of cuckoos. Some are shown next to the birds they often parasitize; the cuckoo's egg is the larger.

◄ Thanks to the manner in which they adapt so easily, cuckoos are found all over the world, including the islands of Polynesia. The parasitic species, however, inhabit only those regions where the suitable host species live.
1) Distribution of the genus *Cuculus*.

ROADRUNNER

Geococcyx californianus

Order Cuculiformes
Family Cuculidae
Size Length 23 in (58 cm)
Weight 18 oz (500 g)
Distribution Southwestern parts of North America
Habits Solitary
Nesting On bushes or cactuses
Reproductive period Spring
Incubation 18 days
Eggs 2 – 12
Chicks Inept
Sexual maturity 1 – 2 years

The roadrunner (*Geococcyx californianus*) is a well-known bird featured in many a comic strip and animated cartoon. It is medium-sized, chestnut-brown and dirty white in overall color, with a blue eye ring that is much broader at the rear. The large, powerful bill is hooked at the tip and is capable of disposing of prey such as snakes. There is a small crest on the head, the neck is moderately long and the tail as long as the rest of the body.

Speed is typical of birds that live on steppes and savannas but this is gained at the expense of flight capacity. The roadrunner, although a very fast runner, is an extremely awkward flier, and in any event the small wings only carry it short distances. It scampers nimbly over rocky and sandy terrain, accomplishing leaps of up to 10 ft (3 m). Maximum running speed is about 15 mph (24 kmh) but as a rule the average rate is 10 mph (15 – 6 kmh).

The roadrunner eats grasshoppers, snails, birds, mice, lizards, and snakes, including venomous species such as young rattlesnakes. It also has a habit of heaping up snail shells, and this activity often signals its presence.

The species is found in southern California, Texas, and central Mexico. It nests on cactuses, trees, and tall bushes to a height of up to about 17 ft (1 to 5 m); the female lays 2 – 12 dirty white eggs at intervals of alternate days.

Incubation, unusually, begins soon after the first egg is laid, and it is possible to find eggs and chicks together in the same nest. Incubation lasts 18 days and the babies, although helpless at birth, are able to walk about on the ground and perch on bushes at the age of 7 – 8 days.

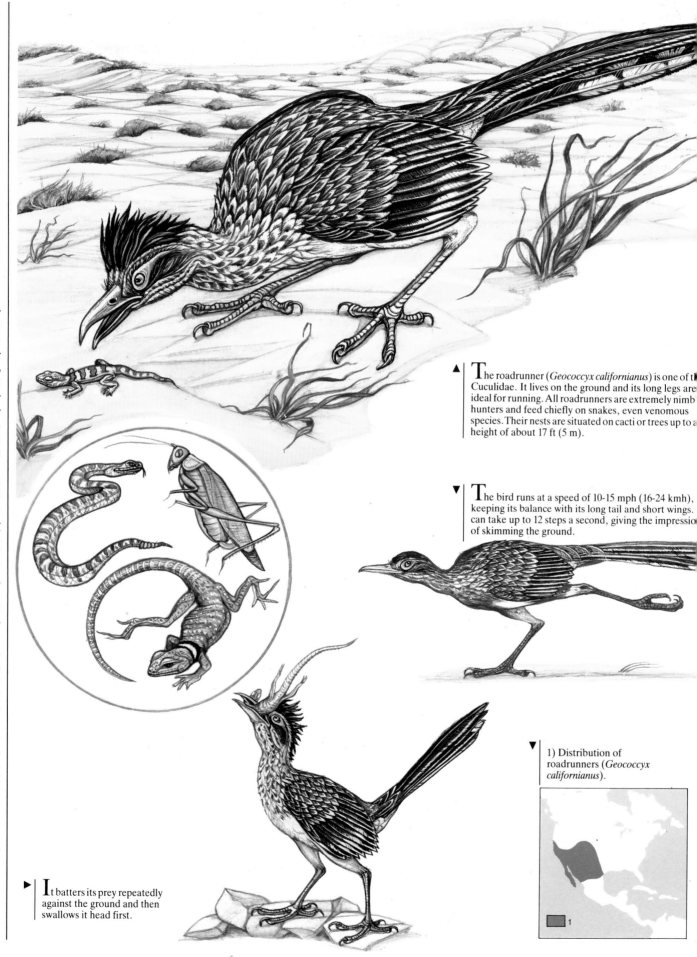

▲ The roadrunner (*Geococcyx californianus*) is one of the Cuculidae. It lives on the ground and its long legs are ideal for running. All roadrunners are extremely nimble hunters and feed chiefly on snakes, even venomous species. Their nests are situated on cacti or trees up to a height of about 17 ft (5 m).

▼ The bird runs at a speed of 10-15 mph (16-24 kmh), keeping its balance with its long tail and short wings. can take up to 12 steps a second, giving the impression of skimming the ground.

▼ 1) Distribution of roadrunners (*Geococcyx californianus*).

► It batters its prey repeatedly against the ground and then swallows it head first.

KNYSNA TOURACO

Tauraco corythaix

Order Cuculiformes
Family Musophagidae
Length 16 – 28 in (40 – 70 cm)
Weight 7 – 32 oz (200 – 1,000 g)
Distribution Southeast Africa
Habits Not markedly gregarious, very timid
Nesting In trees
Breeding period Throughout year
Incubation 16 – 18 days
Eggs 2 – 3
Chicks Inept
Maximum age 20 years

The touracos have semi-zygodactylous feet, the third toe capable of being turned forwards or backwards; the short bill is convex, sometimes hooked and sometimes sharp along the edges, and the color of the plumage is very beautiful. Touracos derive their coloration from substances that they alone secrete. The green color is produced by turacoverdin and the red remiges of many species by turacin. This latter pigment is partly composed of copper and is soluble in alkaline dilutions. It dissolves slightly when mixed with water.

Little is yet known about the ecology of the different species. Hartlaub's touraco (*Tauraco hartlaubi*) was studied in the 1950s by Van Someren in Kenya. The bird emits its short cry mainly in the morning and at dusk, triggering off a vocal response from other individuals. It is a very timid bird which usually stays hidden in the foliage and remains quite motionless if discovered. It feeds abundantly on berries, buds and fruit.

During his courtship display the male emits calls, ruffles his crest, raises the tail and slightly spreads his wings to show off the red feathers. He pursues the female, repeating the display many times and offering her food. She lays 2 eggs between April and July or between September and January. Incubation lasts 16 – 18 days.

The Ruwenzori touraco (*T. johnstoni*), which lives from 6,500 to 13,000 ft (2,000 to 4,000 m) above sea level, has been studied by Chapin who noted that the sounds it makes are like the chattering of monkeys and that it may breed throughout the year.

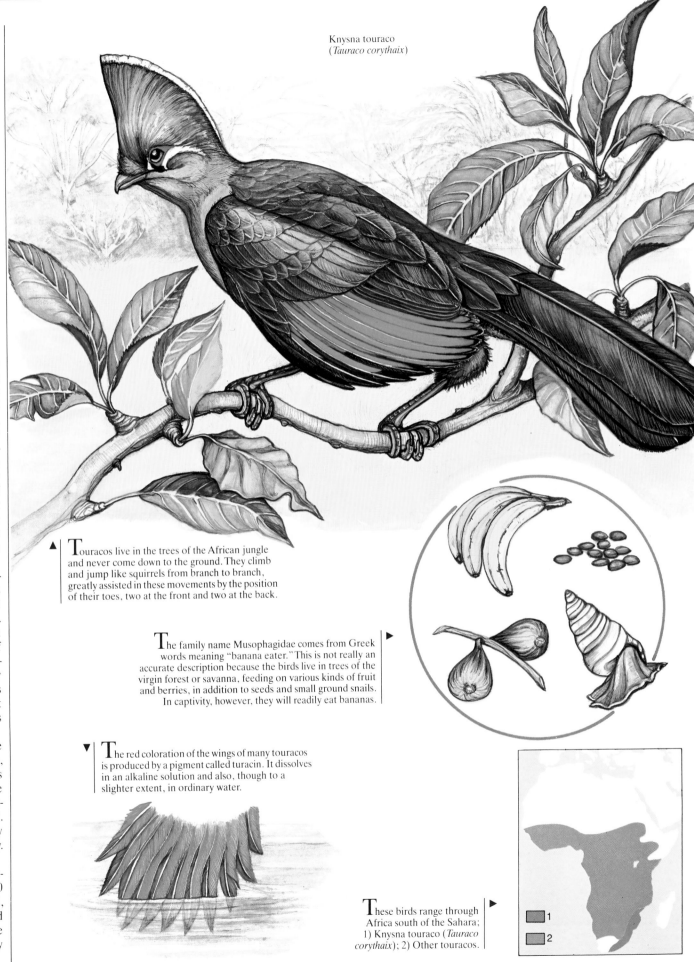

Knysna touraco
(*Tauraco corythaix*)

Touracos live in the trees of the African jungle and never come down to the ground. They climb and jump like squirrels from branch to branch, greatly assisted in these movements by the position of their toes, two at the front and two at the back.

The family name Musophagidae comes from Greek words meaning "banana eater." This is not really an accurate description because the birds live in trees of the virgin forest or savanna, feeding on various kinds of fruit and berries, in addition to seeds and small ground snails. In captivity, however, they will readily eat bananas.

The red coloration of the wings of many touracos is produced by a pigment called turacin. It dissolves in an alkaline solution and also, though to a slighter extent, in ordinary water.

These birds range through Africa south of the Sahara; 1) Knysna touraco (*Tauraco corythaix*); 2) Other touracos.

1
2

OWLS

Strigiformes

The owls or nocturnal raptors (Strigiformes) are an order of birds comprising only two families, the Tytonidae, with just over 10 species, best known of which is the barn owl, and the Strigidae, with more than 120 species, further divided into two subfamilies, Bubonirae and Striginae.

Owls have large, relatively immobile eyes situated at the front of the head and encircled by large concave zones known as facial disks. All this gives them a most distinctive appearance. The feathers that grow inside the disks are soft, with few barbs and lacking barbules, while those on the edges, forming a kind of border, are small, stiff and slightly curved. In the center of the face there are two areas shaped like a half-moon, usually white, which touch each other to form the inner margin of the eyes. The beak is strongly curved, quite large and fairly broad at the base. The head of an owl, as a rule, is large and rounded, and in certain species adorned with special feathers which form hornlike tufts, that have a mimetic function. The claws are always powerful in proportion to the size of the species. The fourth toe is opposable both to the rear toe and the front ones.

Broadly speaking, an owl's plumage consists of neutral, mimetic colors, mainly gray or chestnut-brown, its uniformity broken by varied streaks and spots. Little noise is made when flying because of the very soft extensions of the barbules, which form a kind of velvety cushion for the feathers.

Sight is one of the keenest senses of nocturnal birds of prey, as is evident from the exceptionally large dimensions of their eyes; those of the tawny owl are, in fact, bigger than human eyes. Furthermore, owls' eyes are furnished with a highly developed crystalline lens, a markedly convex cornea and an opaque nictitating membrane or third eyelid, a unique feature among birds. Their overall field of vision ranges virtually through 180° and a third of this is made up of binocular vision. Thus an owl is readily able to distinguish reliefs in the terrain and to estimate distances. In total or almost total darkness even these birds are unable to distinguish anything and rely wholly on their hearing to locate and

Little owl
(*Athene noctua*)

Scops owl
(*Otus scops*)

Ural owl
(*Strix uralensis*)

Short-eared owl
(*Asio flammeus*)

Tengmalm's owl
(*Aegolius funereus*)

Long-eared owl
(*Asio otus*)

Snowy owl
(*Nyctea scandiaca*)

Oriental hawk owl
(*Ninox scutulata*)

Barn owl
(*Tyto alba*)

Eagle owl
(*Bubo bubo*)

Blakiston's fish-owl
(*Ketupa blakistoni*)

The Unseen World --Heyoka
A Proposal for an Animated Multiplatform digital Series
By Loretta Antonell

Tag line: Teen Spirit saves the world

This story takes place today, though in the mythic realms our stories traverse, time is non-existent.

OVERVIEW

"The Unseen World" will be a unique animated adventure series, building an ongoing storyline of unusual depth and intrigue. The heroes; a young American girl named Tara McKenna and her companions, the incredible Heyoka, all young mortals drawn together from difficult times and places attend St. Rita's high school in the Hollywood Hills. Their mission: attend high school, get good grades, go to the prom and in their spare time, travel within the worlds of myth and legend -encountering fabulous and fearsome beings drawn from every tradition - and gather up the pieces of the powerful Spear of Destiny, all while dodging the constant efforts of a malevolent dragon race to stop them and capture Tara. This demonic hoard and their allies are determined to tip the scales from light to darkness, both in the Unseen world and our own.

Format
After the initial discovery of Tara's destiny and the nature of the two worlds, each episode will involve the two worlds in interweaving stories. Tara has been given a quest - to recover the broken pieces of her spear of destiny -, which was scattered across time and mythic space! Many of the adventures involve Tara and her newfound Heyoka friends making just such journeys; other will involve the relentless attempts of the evil Mares to capture Tara. Episodes will feature both action and cosmic adventure and more typical school intrigue and interactions here on earth.

- **Competition: All forms of Media**
- **Target demographic:** Tweens --Mass appeal. This commodity has the ability to plug into any demographic and top-selling story line, making this project extremely unique in its ability to continue to produce future revenue.
- **Competition: All forms of Media**

catch prey. Being long-sighted, they have difficulty in seeing nearby objects, so when tearing up food they use their sense of touch, bringing into play the long whiskers growing from the base of the beak.

Owls are not exclusively nocturnal, especially in the Far North where species such as the snowy owl spend the summer in conditions of almost perpetual light. All species hunt, if they can, around dusk and dawn, in the semi-darkness. During the night they alternate active periods with intervals of song and rest; but it is generally during the day that they satisfy the latter need, retreating to remote, shady spots in order to sleep, safe from the attacks and clamor of other birds who normally display hostility toward them. Owls probably require such long periods of quiet and immobility to regulate their metabolism properly.

Food for many species consists principally of rodents, but owls hunt many other small animals including tiny mammals, birds, reptiles, amphibians, fish, insects, and various invertebrates. The largest types of prey may weigh 6 – 8 lb (3 – 4 kg) but only the eagle owl and other Strigidae or similar size can cope with victims of such dimensions. Victims are usually swallowed whole, and only when they are too big are they ripped to pieces.

Calls play an important part in the life of nocturnal birds of prey. As a rule the male emits a cry of one or more notes, repeated at regular but varying intervals. This has territorial significance and serves to entice the female, who is normally less vocal than her mate, giving out similar sounds but with different tonalities. Most of the singing occurs in the breeding season. The syrinx (vocal organ) consists only of bronchi and vibrates under the impulse of two pairs of muscles, which sometimes come into hard contact with the jaws, producing a characteristic sound.

Owls generally breed in isolated pairs and not in colonies, but they may display gregarious habits when migrating and in winter quarters. With the exception of a few species, such as the short-eared owl, they build no nest, contenting themselves in some cases with a small hollow in the ground, but generally laying their eggs and rearing their young in rock fissures, tree hollows, burrows, and nests of other animals. Many species habitually make use of buildings for these purposes.

Spectacled owl
(*Pulsatrix perspicillata*)

Pygmy owl
(*Glaucidium passerinum*)

Saw-whet owl
(*Aegolius acadicus*)

Great horned owl
(*Bubo virginianus*)

Ferruginous pygmy owl
(*Glaucidium brasilianum*)

Elf owl
(*Micrathene whitneyi*)

Barred owl
(*Strix varia*)

Hawk owl
(*Surnia ulula*)

Pell's fishing owl
(*Scotopelia peli*)

Great gray owl
(*Strix nebulosa*)

Brown wood owl
(*Strix leptogrammica*)

The Strigiformes have morphological features in common, thus differentiating them from other orders of birds. Their eyes are situated at the front of the head and are surrounded by broad concave facial disks. Some species have two hornlike ear-tufts on the head, which have a mimetic function. Because of the abundant fluffy plumage, owls typically have a stocky, rounded shape. The smallest, such as the elf owl, weigh little more than 1¾ oz (50 g), the largest such as the eagle owl, weigh around 8¾ lbs (4 kg). These nocturnal birds of prey comprise 130 different species divided into 28 genera and two families. 1) Distribution of the tawny owl (*Strix aluco*); 2) distribution of the Ural owl (*Strix uralensis*); 3) the birds belonging to the order Strigiformes are distributed in all continents, except Antarctica.

1
2
3

TAWNY OWL
Strix aluco

Order Strigiformes
Family Strigidae
Length 14½ – 18 in (37 – 46 cm)
Wingspan 36 – 40 in (90 – 100 cm)
Weight Male 11¾ – 17¼ oz (331 – 490 g), female 12 – 24½ oz (336 – 695 g)
Distribution Northwest Africa and Eurasia, except for most northerly zones and much of southern Asia.
Habits Solitary or in pairs
Nesting In tree hollows, rock clefts, on ground, in other birds' nests or in buildings
Eggs 2 – 6 on average
Chicks Nidicolous

The tawny owl (*Strix aluco*) has a vast range which embraces almost the whole of continental Europe, with a northern limit in Norway around latitude 64°N, the British Isles, Sicily, northwest Africa, and Asia from Turkey to Korea, including the island of Taiwan but excluding the more northerly zones, southern Arabia and the southeastern regions. Thus its distribution is mainly Palearctic. Semi-wooded areas are preferred, where glades, meadows, cultivated fields, and other types of open ground alternate with deciduous forests. The species has no difficulty in adapting to rocky zones and built-up areas as well, finding shelter and breeding in caves, barns, ruins, etc. It hunts equally readily in meadows, cultivated fields, and other kinds of open terrain, woods, thickets, and so forth. In general the tawny owl is more common at low and medium altitudes, reaching up to 5,000 ft (1,500 m) in mountainous regions but seldom going higher.

For much of the day the tawny owl settles in sheltered, shady places such as rock clefts, caves, large trees with dense foliage, tree hollows, barns, lofts, ruins, and other types of building. Here, the large body with its big rounded head is well camouflaged, thanks to the mimetic plumage, against the background. Indeed it is difficult to see the bird at all unless one is very close. By day it generally sleeps, with one or both eyes closed, apparently heedless of anything going on around it. Its activities commence soon after dusk and continue until shortly before dawn. During the night it intersperses its bouts of hunting with rest periods of song, mainly emitting

Tawny owl
(*Strix aluco*)

▲ This owl lives in semi-wooded regions and generally shelters either on a branch or a rock. From such a perch it can survey the surrounding terrain when night comes, waiting in the faint light of the stars or moon for its prey. The tawny owl's plumage is fairly mimetic, with neutral colors ranging from gray to reddish brown: the individual shown here is of the latter type. The eyes are dark streaks both on the upper and lower parts of the body. The eyes are dark with bluish or orange reflections, and encircled by rounded facial disks with faint concentric rings. The legs and feet, with black claws, are covered with feathers.

its unmistakable three-note call, the first being short and sharp, followed 2 – 7 seconds later by a kind of modulated double hoot. This distinctive cry can be heard almost a mile away, and is the best clue to the whereabouts of this elusive bird of prey. These calls may be heard all year round, but are most frequent in the breeding season and, at intervals, in full daylight.

When hunting, the tawny owl flies 6 – 10 ft (2 – 3 m) above ground level, carefully scrutinizing those areas where prey is most likely to be found. More often it settles on a suitable perch from which it can survey an area sufficiently open as not to offer any concealment for potential victims. In this manner it captures mainly small mammals such as field mice, wild mice, rats, shrews, moles, leverets, rabbits, and squirrels, these animals weighing around 11 – 14 oz (300 – 400 g). Thanks to its silent flight, the owl can drop down on its prey from a height, claws extended, without the victim having any hint of its approach. Other food items comprise amphibians, fish, and many invertebrates such as mollusks and insects, including beetles and grasshoppers. Like other owls, it locates its prey both by vision and hearing.

Courtship may begin as early as mid winter, the male marking out his territory and singing for increasingly long periods in order to attract his partner. Furthermore he offers prey to her as an inducement to coupling. She, in turn, chooses the place to lay the eggs and rear her brood, such a site often being used year after year. As a rule it is a tree hollow, either in the trunk or at the foot among the roots; alternatively it may be the old nest of another bird of prey, a squirrel's drey, a rock fissure, a cave, a hole, the roof or steps of a building such as a granary, stable or cottage, a pile of ruins, or even the burrow of a mammal. An artificial nest, preferably placed on a trunk a few meters above the ground, is readily acceptable. The eggs are laid mostly at the end of winter or the beginning of spring, between January and April, according to latitude and altitude. There are generally 2 – 6 spherical white eggs but sometimes more, each weighing about 1½ oz (40 g). They are laid at intervals of several days and are each incubated by the female for about a month so that they also hatch some days apart. During incubation the male procures food for his partner as well, bringing prey to the nest.

To compensate for the relative immobility of the eyes, the tawny owl, like other species, can revolve its head through at least 180°.

Approximately 75 per cent of prey taken by this species consists of moles, field mice, wild mice, shrews, passerines, and beetles; the rest is made up of small hares and squirrels.

The bird's field of vision is relatively restricted because the eyes face forward. To compensate for this, there is an almost total overlapping of the visual fields of either eye, so that the bird has excellent perception of the lie of the land and an accurate gauge of distance.

During the day the owl risks being mobbed by other birds, especially passerines.

It often nests in tree hollows and rears its brood there. The adults feed the owlets with animals they have caught.

The tawny owl catches birds which it flushes by swooping low over the bushes.

The fledgling is covered in gray down with darker markings.

SNOWY OWL

Nyctea scandiaca

Order Strigiformes
Family Strigidae
Length 22 – 26 in (56 – 65 cm)
Wingspan 60 – 63 in (150 – 160 cm)
Weight Male 2¾ – 4½ lb (1,300 – 2,000 g); female 3¼ – 5¾ lb (1,500 – 2,600 g)
Distribution North America and Eurasia, between latitudes 60° and 80°N
Habits Solitary or in pairs
Nesting In small hollows on ground
Eggs 3 – 10
Chicks Nidicolous

Being adapted to arctic conditions of extreme cold, and blending with the predominant whites and grays of snow and ice, the plumage of the snowy owl (*Nyctea scandiaca*) is thick and soft.

It has a circumpolar distribution, nesting in arctic regions, both continental and insular, of Eurasia and North Amercia, its southern limit being in Norway around latitude 60°N and its extreme northern boundary in Greenland around 82°N. In winter it may find its way to more southerly areas, reaching the United States and central Europe. But the usual habitat of the species is the arctic tundra and its surroundings; it is in these zones that it normally lives, hunts, and breeds.

This raptor is one of the most redoubtable predators of arctic zones. It hunts either by making exploratory flights or by lying in wait, both by night and day, having adapted to the extremely long periods of light in the northern summer. When perched, as often happens, on a rock spur or other prominent spot, the color of its plumage provides effective camouflage with the surroundings. It is much easier to pick it out when flying, for it can be recognized by its characteristic wing movements, lazy and slow when descending, more rapid and urgent when gaining height.

The territory occupied by a pair of snowy owls usually covers several square miles. The female, in May – June, scoops out a shallow hole in the still frozen ground and lays 3 – 10 (and sometimes up to 14) eggs there, at intervals of a couple of days, starting to incubate as soon as the first is laid. Each egg weighs about 2 oz (60 g) and is incubated for about 34 days, so that hatching is staggered.

Snowy owl
(*Nyctea scandiaca*)

The plumage of the snowy owl is chiefly white except for a few dark spots and streaks. These markings are more numerous in the female, as shown in the individual here brooding her chick. The male, illustrated with a field mouse in his beak, is generally lighter in color.

The flight silhouette much resembles that of a buzzard, because the primary flight feathers appear separated at the tips.

The fledglings are fed by the female. If the large chick attempts to grab the whole prey, she tugs it in order to rip it up and divide it among all the babies.

The snowy owl is a mighty hunter, whose diet includes lemmings, field mice, ptarmigans, varying hares and even arctic fox cubs.

BARN OWL

Tyto alba

Order Strigiformes
Family Strigidae
Length 13 – 15½ in (33 – 39 cm)
Wingspan 36 – 38 in (91 – 95 cm)
Weight 10¼ – 12½ oz (290 – 355 g)
Distribution Almost cosmopolitan.
Absent from Antarctica and cold
regions
Habits Solitary or in pairs
Nesting In rocks clefts, on buildings or
in tree hollows
Eggs 2 – 8, exceptionally up to 18
Chicks Nidicolous

The barn owl (*Tyto alba*) is virtually cosmopolitan in its range, being found in the warm and temperate regions of Eurasia, Africa, the Americas, and Australia. Its distribution, therefore, is somewhat irregular; by and large, it is absent in northern zones, deserts and equatorial forests. As a rule it is sedentary. Barn owls originally inhabited rocky or semi-wooded zones adjacent to wide open spaces such as prairies and steppes; in due course they adapted very successfully to built-up areas, nesting in ruins, granaries, barns, and bell towers, and hunting in cultivated fields, meadows, etc. To day, therefore, it is a bird of plains and hills, generally venturing not higher than 3,300 ft (1,000 m).

The barn owl spends the day sleeping in semi-darkness in some well-sheltered hollow or inside a barn or cave. At nightfall it sets off on the hunt, flitting over field and meadow. Every now and then it hovers but more often it perches on a fence, a post or some other suitable vantage point in order to scrutinize the surrounding territory, tracing its prey by sight as well as hearing and eventually diving down silently and swiftly for the kill.

The female lays her eggs on a loose bedding of straw, fluff or other available material. Because of the fairly flexible breeding behavior of the species, this may occur in almost any month and there may be two broods a year.

The whitish eggs weigh about ¾ oz (20 g) and range in number from 2 to 8, but up to 18 in very exceptional cases. They are laid at intervals and incubated by the female for approximately 35 days. In this way the chicks hatch in relays and differ in size at any given point.

D roppings pile up around the roosts most frequently used by the owl. They are composed of hairs, bones, feathers, and other inedible parts of prey which, having been swallowed during the meal, are later regurgitated as small pellets.

A t one time barn owls lived only in rocky zones, nesting in caves, cracks or tree hollows; in due course they also adapted themselves to areas taken over by man, sheltering and breeding in huts, barns, bell towers, and other types of building.

A t night, because of the pale coloration of its underparts, the barn owl looks like a flitting white ghost in the dim moonlight.

1) The barn owl (*Tyto alba*) has an almost cosmopolitan range, inhabiting warm and temperate regions of all continents, except for Antarctica.
2) The snowy owl (*Nyctea scandiaca*) nests in the Arctic zones of Eurasia and America, its southern limit being around latitude 60°N.

The chicks trot away from the nest, location permitting, before they have learned to fly. They are covered in thick white down, have dark eyes and already display the typical heart-shaped face.

OILBIRD

Steatornis caripensis

Order Caprimulgiformes
Family Steatornithidae
Length About 18 in (45 cm)
Weight About 14 oz (400 g)
Distribution Northern and western regions of South America
Nesting In colonies on rock ledges inside caves
Eggs 2 – 4, white speckled with brown
Incubation 33 – 34 days
Chicks Inept (unable to fly for 90 – 125 days)

The oilbird (*Steatornis caripensis*) is the only representative of the family Steatornithidae, and lives on the island of Trinidad, in Venezuela, Colombia, Ecuador, and Peru. In these countries the bird inhabits forests but only where it can also find the caves essential for its safety and for breeding; so this necessity restricts it to mountain zones and rocky coastlines. The species was discovered in 1799 by the German naturalist and explorer Alexander von Humboldt in the Caripe Cave, located in the coastal mountain range of northwest Venezuela. Nowadays this site is reserved as a national park.

Because of the oilbird's particular biological adaptations, it leads a most unusual life, spending the entire day inside huge caves, perched on outcrops or ledges of the rock wall. Colonies of hundreds of birds are to be found deep inside such caves, sometimes hundreds of yards from the entrance. Towards evening, led by a few exploratory individuals, they emerge from the caves, and fly distances of up to 50 miles (80 km), if necessary, to find food. They stay outside for the whole night and although not hunting in compact groups, keep in touch with one another by emitting loud cries. At the first light of dawn they make their way back through the forests and eventually disappear inside their caves once more.

Oilbirds feed mainly on the fruits of palms and laurels, never perching on the trees and plants but hovering in midair to rip off the fruit with their hooked beak. It is likely that in their search for food they use their particularly well-developed sense of smell. Seeds, of course, are not digested but regurgitated when back inside the

Oilbird
(*Steatornis caripensis*)

Common potoo
(*Nyctibius griseus*)

Tawny frogmouth
(*Podargus strigoides*)

Owlet-nightjar
(*Aegotheles cristatus*)

▲ The oilbird belongs to the order Caprimulgiformes, and the family which it constitutes differs from others by dint of various anatomical, biological, and ecological characteristics. Its wholly vegetarian diet is based on palm and laurel fruits.

◄ The order Caprimulgiformes comprises five families: in addition to Caprimulgidae and Steatornitidae, they are Podargidae (left), Nyctibiidae (center), and Aegothelidae (right).

cave, often germinating on the floor. The plantlets so formed, lacking the necessary light for survival, die and thus, along with the birds' droppings, help to form a thick layer of humus.

The method whereby the oilbird manages to move about so freely and confidently in an environment that is totally without light was only revealed as recently as 1954 by the biologists Donald R. Griffin and William H. Phelps Jr. The mechanism is based on echoes, like that already known to exist among bats; but whereas the latter animals give out ultrasounds, inaudible to the human ear, the sounds emitted by oilbirds have a frequency of about 7,300 cycles per second and can thus be heard as metallic clickings which are overlaid by their more obvious sharp, raucous cries. The birds produce these sounds more frequently when actually flying and more particularly when they come up against an obstacle, which is identified and measured by reflected sound waves. As far as is yet known, the oilbird is the only species of bird endowed with such a "sonar" system.

Breeding, too, always takes place inside the cave. Using the humus from the cave floor, the oilbird builds a solid nest, some 12 in (30 cm) in diameter, in the shape of a truncated cone, placing it on a ledge or in a cleft, usually quite high above ground. Such a nest may be utilized by the same pair of birds for several consecutive years. Both parents share in the incubation of the 2 – 4 eggs for 33 – 34 days.

The Spaniards called this bird *guacharo*, which literally means "the crier and wailer," because of its distinctive calls. The English vernacular name, for its part, alludes to the long-established custom of the local Indians of obtaining oil suitable for cooking from the plump fledglings. It was inevitable that sooner or later the enormous quantity of fat accumulated in the body of these baby birds would be put to some profitable use. The Indians therefore gathered during the birds' breeding season, exploring the dark caves with torches, and armed with long poles set about capturing as many nestlings as they could, sometimes in thousands. The chicks were eviscerated and the oil, melted out by heating, was stored in earthenware jars. This oil is fluid, odorless and transparent, and it can be stored without becoming rancid, for many months and often more than a year.

Fruits are ripped off with the hooked beak, without the bird having to settle.

Tawny frogmouth (*Podargus strigoides*) in characteristic posture.

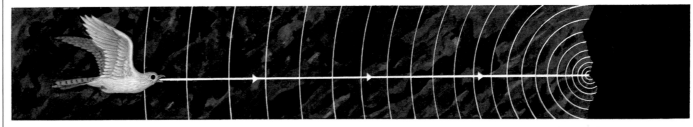

Oilbirds spend the day crouching in rock clefts inside large caves.

In their completely dark subterranean world, the birds use an echo-location system based on sound waves (unlike bats, who rely on ultrasounds).

The chick, fed on oily fruits, gets enormously fat, until it becomes much heavier than the adults.

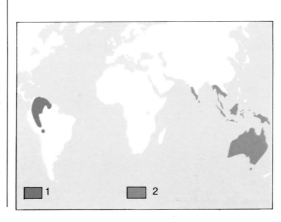

1) The oilbird (*Steatornis caripensis*), only member of the family Steatornitidae, lives on the island of Trinidad, in Venezuela, Colombia, Ecuador, and Peru. 2) The family Podargidae is distributed in Australia, Tasmania, and New Guinea; it is made up of the genera *Podargus* and *Batrachostomus*, containing 12 species.

NIGHTJAR

Caprimulgus europaeus

Order Caprimulgiformes
Family Caprimulgidae
Length 10¼ in (26 cm)
Wingspan Male 7¼ – 7⅞ in (184 – 198 mm); female 7⅛ – 7¾ in (183 – 195 mm)
Tail 5 – 5½ in (128 – 138 mm)
Weight 2 – 3¼ oz (58 – 89 g)
Distribution Europe, western and central Asia, northwest Africa. Winters in east and central Africa and India
Nesting On ground. Normally two annual broods
Eggs Generally 2, sometimes up to 4, elliptical, gray-white or cream with brown or gray marbling
Incubation 18 days
Chicks Inept (able to fly within 16 – 18 days)

The nightjar (*Caprimulgus europaeus*) as a nesting species with various sub-species, is distributed over a vast part of the Palearctic region, including Europe as far as latitude 64° – 65°N, northwest Africa and temperate Asia to Lake Baikal and Afghanistan. The bird's habitats are fairly well varied but generally comprise areas with tree growth. In the breeding season its nesting zones are mainly woods of conifers (pines) or deciduous trees which do not grow too densely, especially where the terrain is rocky or sandy but not high up in the mountains; and it is also to be found on moors and heathland, among dunes and in parkland. In winter it visits savannas, shrubby steppes, and wooded tablelands.

The nightjar flies silently, with sudden changes of direction and swift gyrations, but not high above ground level. It may be seen chiefly around dusk and on clear nights, for it emerges by day only if disturbed where roosting. During the day it crouches lengthwise on a branch or on the ground, perfectly camouflaged, its eyes half closed. At sunset the nightjar then commences hunting.

Although the nightjar may also collect ground insects such as beetles, grasshoppers, cockroaches, etc., it depends mainly upon insects that fly around dusk, namely moths, mosquitoes, gnats and flies, various kinds of beetle, bugs, etc. These are all caught in the bird's gaping mouth but also with the aid of the bristles

▲ Nightjar incubating on the deciduous forest floor, well camouflaged with the surroundings. It feeds wholly on insects, including flies, butterflies, and beetles.

◀ The structure of the mouth and the bristly feathers around it indicate that the bird is highly specialized in hunting on the wing.

The nightjar hunts only at dusk and on moonlit nights. With its long, powerful wings, the bird flies with great agility and in complete silence. ▶

surrounding the mouth. If weather conditions (cold and rain) restrict the normal activities of such insects, the nightjar is compelled to go without food, perhaps for several days. It gets through this period by falling into a sort of lethargy, during which its temperature drops to near that of the surroundings, the body becomes stiff and motionless, and both heartbeat and respiration rates are reduced to a minimum.

In late spring the males return from winter quarters before the females and immediately take possession of their breeding sites, signaling their arrival with a buzzing song which may go on for several minutes. This song becomes more lively and noisy when the females join them. Both sexes then proceed to their elaborate courtship display which culminates in their mating. They build no nest but simply select and prepare a hole on the bare ground of a woodland clearing. The female generally lays 2 eggs at intervals of about 36 hours, these being incubated for approximately 18 days, mainly by the female but also, during the early hours of the night, by the male.

The family Caprimulgidae is very uniform and almost all its representative species have the same morphological features as the European nightjar. The whip-poor-will (*Caprimulgus vociferus*) is a species from the eastern parts of North America which winters in the southern United States, Mexico, and Central America. It lives in forest regions. The poor-will (*Phalaenoptilus nuttallii*) comes from the western regions of North America and is distinguished by a white half-collar on the throat. The most interesting aspect of this bird is that it was the first to be proved to actually hibernate, this being a rare occurrence among birds, though common in other classes of vertebrates.

The standard-winged nightjar (*Macrodipteryx longipennis*) inhabits a belt of African territory north of the equator, migrating to regions farther north. It lives in zones with dense vegetation. It flies with irregular, jerky movements. A characteristic feature of the male, in the breeding season, is that the ninth primary flight feather, consisting of a long bare rachis and a vane only towards the tip, reaches a length of 18 in (45 cm).

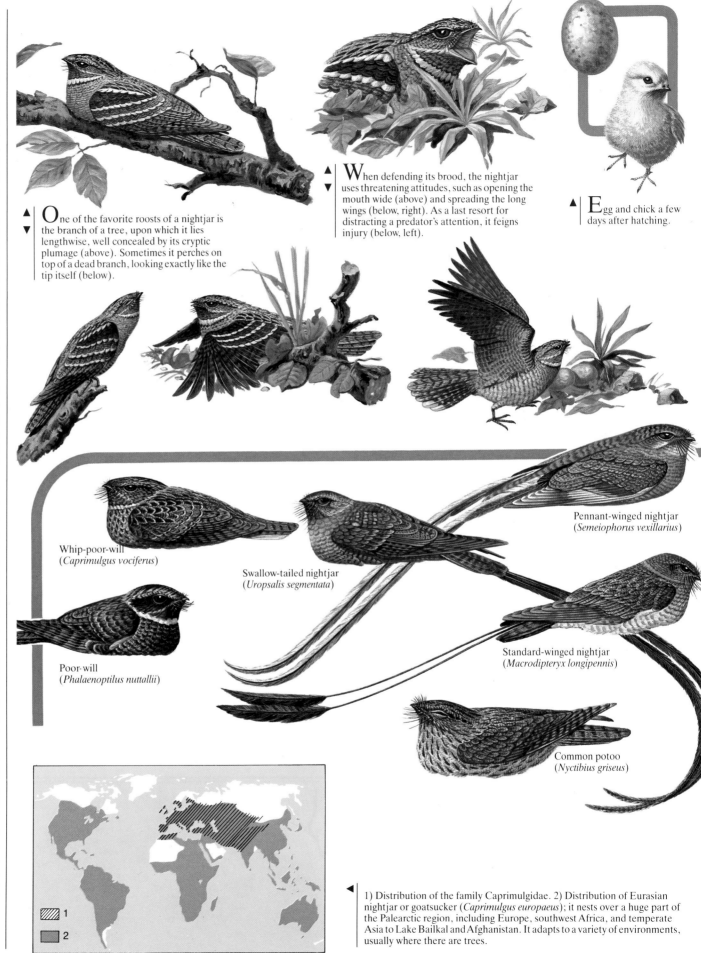

▲▼ One of the favorite roosts of a nightjar is the branch of a tree, upon which it lies lengthwise, well concealed by its cryptic plumage (above). Sometimes it perches on top of a dead branch, looking exactly like the tip itself (below).

▲▼ When defending its brood, the nightjar uses threatening attitudes, such as opening the mouth wide (above) and spreading the long wings (below, right). As a last resort for distracting a predator's attention, it feigns injury (below, left).

▲ Egg and chick a few days after hatching.

Whip-poor-will (*Caprimulgus vociferus*)

Poor-will (*Phalaenoptilus nuttallii*)

Swallow-tailed nightjar (*Uropsalis segmentata*)

Pennant-winged nightjar (*Semeiophorus vexillarius*)

Standard-winged nightjar (*Macrodipteryx longipennis*)

Common potoo (*Nyctibius griseus*)

◀ 1) Distribution of the family Caprimulgidae. 2) Distribution of Eurasian nightjar or goatsucker (*Caprimulgus europaeus*); it nests over a huge part of the Palearctic region, including Europe, southwest Africa, and temperate Asia to Lake Baikal and Afghanistan. It adapts to a variety of environments, usually where there are trees.

1
2

191

SWIFT
Apus apus

Order Apodiformes
Family Apodidae
Size Length 6 – 7 in (16 – 18 cm)
Distribution Old World; absent from polar regions and South Africa
Habits Markedly gregarious
Nesting In colonies on high rocks and buildings
Eggs 2 (rarely 3)
Chicks Nidicolous

The swift (*Apus apus*) has a stream-lined body with long, slender wings and a relatively short, forked tail. The mouth, when open, is squarish in shape, with a very wide gape; the bill is rather short and strongly hooked. When the bird is perched, the wings, much longer than the tail, cross each other above the upper tail.

The swift is easy to identify, for it nests, winters and migrates in flocks that often contain hundreds of individuals. The flight silhouette is distinctive, too, with long, thin, gracefully curving wings and forked tail. The bird is also mistaken for a swallow, but its resemblance to the latter is merely due to evolutionary convergence, for it is quite distinct from the phylogenetic viewpoint. Swifts and swallows evolved from very different ancestors but have developed similar structures performing identical functions.

The swifts are found all over the world, except for the polar regions, New Zealand, South Africa, and certain island groups. Habitats are extremely varied, and they are to be seen equally commonly in cities, up in the mountains and along the seashore. Food consists of a vast range of insects, from flies and gnats to small butterflies.

The swift is one of the most perfectly formed of all flying birds. Its normal speed through the air is 38 – 56 mph (60 – 90 kmh) and at times it reaches up to 125 mph (200 kmh). Swifts, in fact, spend roughly half their life in the air, accomplishing most basic activities, hunting insects, courting and mating, on the wing. From time to time they engage in short but violent aerial flights, to the accompaniment of sharp, shrill cries: several males will compete for a female or a complex social pecking order will be established at the beginning of the breeding

▲ Swifts normally fly at about 35-55 mph (60-90 kmh) but can for short distances reach a speed of over 125 mph (200 kmh). The varied flight pattern alternates periods of flapping with glides and wheeling movements. Thanks to certain structural adaptions which they have in common, swifts and hummingbirds are unsurpassed in performing complex aerial maneuvers.

▼ Insects are caught in the air as the bird flies with mouth agape.

▲ The swift is one of the most specialized hunters of flying insects, and because it destroys a large number of harmful insects it is protected in many lands. The small creatures on which it feeds, such as flies and butterflies, make up the so-called aerial plankton.

season, with birds of many species staking out invisible but inviolable boundaries to territories reserved either for pairs or groups.

The material for building a nest (feathers, bits of straw, hair) is likewise snatched up on the wing; and even when drinking, swifts merely skim the water surface and make off. The only occasions when the birds remain perched for any length of time is at night and when incubating their eggs.

As a rule, swifts experience great difficulties in taking off when they accidentally come to rest on a horizontal surface. If one of these birds is encountered on the ground, it is a good idea, having made sure that there are no breaks or other injuries, to help it to get away by assisting it to some vertical takeoff point. The swift can sustain its characteristically rapid, darting flight for considerable periods without evidence of physical effort. It is believed that at least two species of swifts actually sleep on the wing, and pilots of aircraft have reported sighting these birds, outlined against a full moon, at unbelievable altitudes. There is no certain proof of the theory, but swifts that live at sea are often observed flying out at sunset and returning to dry land at dawn.

These birds, perfectly streamlined for catching insects in midair, possess a variety of special structures which enable them to fly very fast, for long periods and with the sudden changes of direction that are vital for capturing any insects trying to escape pursuit. The mouth, so extraordinarily large, is held wide open during flight and can thus easily trap the tiniest insects, which are helped on their way by an encircling "funnel" of hairs.

The swift is one of the most typical migrating species, traveling from its breeding grounds to its wintering quarters and back again with astonishingly precise timing, returning every year to the same nest it occupied the previous season, as verified by recoveries of ringed birds. Indeed, the regularity of the departure and return dates is proverbial, narrowed down to almost the same days each year. This habitual pattern does not seem to be related to the local weather conditions, but is explained by the fact that in "deciding" the day of departure, the swift is guided not by temperature or availability of food, but by the varying length of the period of daylight. In other words, the swift does not leave

Despite spending up to half their life in the air, swifts are sometimes compelled, as during periods of violent rainstorms, to grip rock faces for shelter. ▶

◀ **W**hen grasping a vertical surface, the swift turns its head upward. The feet are so adapted that the four toes can entirely support the weight of the body. The fourth toe is mobile and can be rotated through 180°.

▼ **T**he swift can wash itself in flight, without coming down to rest.

▲ **I**t builds a semicircular nest of flimsy materials collected during flight, all stuck together with their particularly adhesive saliva. The most common building materials are wisps of straw, dead leaves, petals, feathers, and tiny scraps of paper.

▼ **C**omparison of flight silhouettes.

Swift

Swallow

Nightjar

Falcon

▼ **A**ccording to airplane pilots' reports, the outlines of swifts, silhouetted against the moon, have been sighted at unbelievable heights. These and other observations support the theory that swifts are capable of sleeping in the air.

Europe at the end of summer because it senses the approaching cold or the imminent scarcity of insects but because the shortening days trigger off processes inside its brain which cause changes of a hormonal, somatic (feather molt, gonad recession) and behavioral nature.

The swift, strictly "programed" for its two annual migrations, may occasionally encounter serious problems when, in the course of its long and exhausting journey, it has to face disturbances and obstacles such as heavy rain, snow, a strong headwind or a local shortage of insects. In such cases the bird can bring another special mechanism into play, namely hibernation. This reduces it to a state of passivity, entailing a range of modifications which affect physiology and behavior. The former changes are manifested in a lowering of body temperature and reductions in the rates of heartbeat and respiration, the latter in the urge to crowd together in caves and fall into lethargic sleep there. Hibernation will continue until conditions once again become favorable enough for the journey to be resumed. Swifts have a highly sophisticated sense of orientation: when taken from their nests and transported over 60 miles (100 km) away, they are able to make their way home.

The large brown-throated spine-tail swift (*Hirundapus giganteus*), which has a wingspan of 18 in (45 cm), lives in flocks composed of thousands of birds. These swifts nest frequently among rocks behind waterfalls. The chimney swift (*Chaetura pelagica*) is a small, blackish North American species. It migrates in huge flocks of hundreds of thousands, wintering in South America. Typical of these birds during migration is their habit of sleeping together inside natural cavities, where they take shelter every evening at twilight.

The alpine swift (*Apus melba*) is slightly larger than the common swift and is distinguished from the latter by its gray-brown plumage, the throat and abdomen being whitish and a darker band running across the breast. Its habitats are the mountain regions of southern Europe and the Mediterranean zone, and migrations take it as far as the Himalayas. Colonies of these swifts visit cities, usually flying at a greater height than common swifts. Some authors maintain that this species is actually capable of sleeping

Northern white-rumped swift
(*Apus pacificus*)

Chimney swift
(*Chaetura pelagica*)

Large brown-throated spine-tail swift
(*Hirundapus giganteus*)

Illustrated on this page are some of the more interesting species of swifts. Particularly fascinating is the edible-nest swiftlet which produces the celebrated "bird's nests" so appreciated by gourmets in many parts of the world, consisting of the bird's dried saliva. The crested tree swift is the only non-colonial swift; equipped with sturdy legs, it uses them to grip the branches on which it perches.

Alpine swift
(*Apus melba*)

Crested tree swift
(*Hemiprocne longipennis*)

Great swallow-tailed swift
(*Panyptila sanctihieronymi*)

Pallid swift
(*Apus pallidus*)

Palm swift
(*Cypsiurus parvus*)

Edible-nest swiftlet
(*Collocalia inexpectata*)

on the wing, too.

The pallid swift (*Apus pallidus*) looks much like the common swift and is similar in size; and the two species often live together. The only difference in plumage, hard to discern in flight, is the paler overall color and whitish throat. It nests very often in cities and on sea cliffs.

The great swallow-tailed swift (*Panyptila sanctihieronymi*) builds a very unusual nest, consisting of a long vertical tunnel that measures 8 – 24 in (20 – 60 cm), made from feathers stuck together with saliva. The entrance to the nest is at the base of the tunnel, while the eggs are incubated in a chamber at the top end, which is slightly enlarged. The nest is placed high up under a roof or projecting rock.

The palm swift (*Cypsiurus parvus*) is a bird of the tropical zones of the Old World. Its nest is a small cup-shaped structure stuck with saliva to the lower surface of a palm leaf; the eggs are glued to the bottom of the leaf forming the nest wall.

The edible-nest swiftlet (*Collocalia inexpectata*), from the Indo-Australian region, has salivary glands which secrete an astonishingly plentiful quantity of saliva; and it is, in fact, the only bird capable of constructing a nest exclusively from its own saliva. This is the species which produces the celebrated "birds' nests" beloved of Oriental gourmets. Around the colonies of these swifts a flourishing industry collects and consigns these highly prized edible nests to markets throughout the Orient and, to a lesser extent, to the West. Each pair of swiftlets actually builds three nests in succession: the first, of the highest quality and therefore fetching the highest price, is made wholly of dried saliva, whereas the other two contain reinforcing materials, since the birds no longer produce enough saliva for the purpose.

The crested tree swift (*Hemiprocne longipennis*), unlike other Apodidae, has legs sufficiently sturdy for grasping branches, so that the bird can perch in trees. The markedly forked tail is a clear means of identification in flight. Both sexes have an erectile crest of feathers, but the male is adorned with brighter plumage. The swift lives on the fringes of tropical forests in groups of two or three individuals, hunting in the glades. In contrast to other swifts, this species nests in pairs rather than colonies.

Swifts have a remarkable sense of orientation. Experiments in which birds have been removed at night and transported more than 60 miles (100 km) from their nest have proved their ability to find the way home.

▲ The nests of certain swifts. Top to bottom: great swallow-tailed swift (a vertical tube of feathers stuck with saliva, with an upper chamber for incubation); palm swift (a cup fixed to the lower surface of a palm leaf; the eggs are also stuck to the leaf); Cuban palm swift (the nest is shaped like a bag, likewise stuck to a leaf; edible-nest swiftlet (the only bird capable of building a nest wholly from its own saliva); crested tree swift (the nest is built by binding strips of bark with saliva; the single egg is stuck to the bottom).

▼ Swifts live all over the world, except for a few zones that include Australia and New Zealand. They can adapt to the most varied habitats. 1) The common swift (*Apus apus*) can be seen in summer in the countryside and towns of Europe. 2) Distribution of the order Apodiformes.

1

2

HUMMINGBIRDS
Trochiliformes

The family Trochilidae, comprising the hummingbirds, contains not only the smallest living bird but also the smallest warmblooded animal, namely the bee hummingbird (*Mellisuga* [*Florisuga*] *helenae*), scarcely 2 in (5 cm) long, half of this length being made up of tail and bill. At the opposite extreme is the giant hummingbird (*Patagonia gigas*), as big as a starling and weighing about ¾ oz (20 g), roughly ten times heavier than the bee hummingbird.

With 315 – 320 species, divided into some 120 genera, the family Trochilidae is the second largest in the New World. The majority of these species are concentrated into a narrow equatorial belt, extending no more than 10° in breadth; in fact, more than half of the known hummingbirds live there. The numbers drop sharply as one moves north, with 51 species in Mexico, 13 in the United States (below latitude 50°N), four in Canada and one in Alaska. Southwards the same situation prevails, with only 20 or so species below latitude 30°S and one, the green-backed firecrown (*Sephanoides sephanoides*), crossing the Magellan Strait to nest in Tierra del Fuego. About 19 species are to be found in the West Indies, and two have colonized the distant island group of Juan Fernandez some 440 miles (700 km) off the Chilean coast.

There are many reasons why the hummingbirds come in so many shapes and sizes. The main cause is polygamy, which permits the best endowed or most adaptable males to attract more females and thus produce numerous descendants who will in turn develop and pass on the paternal characteristics. Then comes their great capacity of adaptation, enhanced by nocturnal lethargy, which enables many species to derive maximum benefit from flowers growing at latitudes bordering on regions of perennial snow, areas where other birds cannot venture because of low temperatures that drop to several degrees below zero. The isolation provided by the deep valleys of the Andes has also helped the species to multiply.

Some hummingbirds live exclusively in the lower stratum of the

Ruby-throated hummingbird (*Archilochus colubris*)

The future of the hummingbirds looks somewhat gloomy. Most of them live in tropical forests which are fast disappearing, and this directly threatens the survival of many species. Yet they have an advantage over many birds from the same regions. Because of their natural lack of fear, their comparative intelligence, and their ability to adapt, various species have been able to make the most of parks and gardens in and around the villages and towns that are gradually springing up in place of the primary forests.

primary forest, others in the upper stratum. There are those adapted to arid regions, where the vegetation consists principally of flowering cactus, and those that regularly visit parks and plantations.

Whereas some species have a local and fairly restricted distribution, others have developed nomadic or migratory habits, and by exploiting the natural resources of diverse, widely separated zones, have given rise to new species and races. Species such as the white-necked jacobin (*Florisuga mellivora*) are continuously on the move from one area to another, according to the flowering seasons of particular plants; others, such as the sparkling violet-ear (*Colibri coruscans*), make vertical migrations, nesting at great heights along the Andean range and descending to lower altitudes at the start of the rainy season. Anna's violet-ear (*Calypte anna*) moves in the opposite direction, nesting in the plain and climbing higher at the end of the wet season.

When hummingbirds hover motionless, the wings move forward and backward as well as up and down, and the tips trace a flat, horizontal figure-of-eight pattern. The speed of a hummingbird's flight does not normally exceed 30 mph (50 kmh), but under certain stimuli, as when courting or defending territory, some species, although only for brief moments, reach 60 mph (100 kmh). The vast majority of hummingbirds can neither walk nor jump. They seldom perch on the ground and even when moving along a branch only a few inches in length are forced to fly.

Apart from their tiny dimensions and flight capacities, hummingbirds are, of course, notable for their vivid, shining colors, the iridescent effect being produced in much the same way as in a soap bubble or blob of oil on a road surface. The beak, whether black, reddish, or yellowish, is always slender and delicate, but size and curvature vary enormously. Thus the tiny beak of the purple-backed thornbill (*Ramphomicron microrhynchum*) is not more than a centimeter in length, while that of the sword-billed hummingbird (*Ensifera ensifera*) is about 4 in (10 cm), virtually the same length as body and tail combined. As regards curvature, the beak may be upturned at the tip as in the fiery-throated awlbill (*Opisthoprora euryptera*) and mountain avocetbill (*Avocettula*

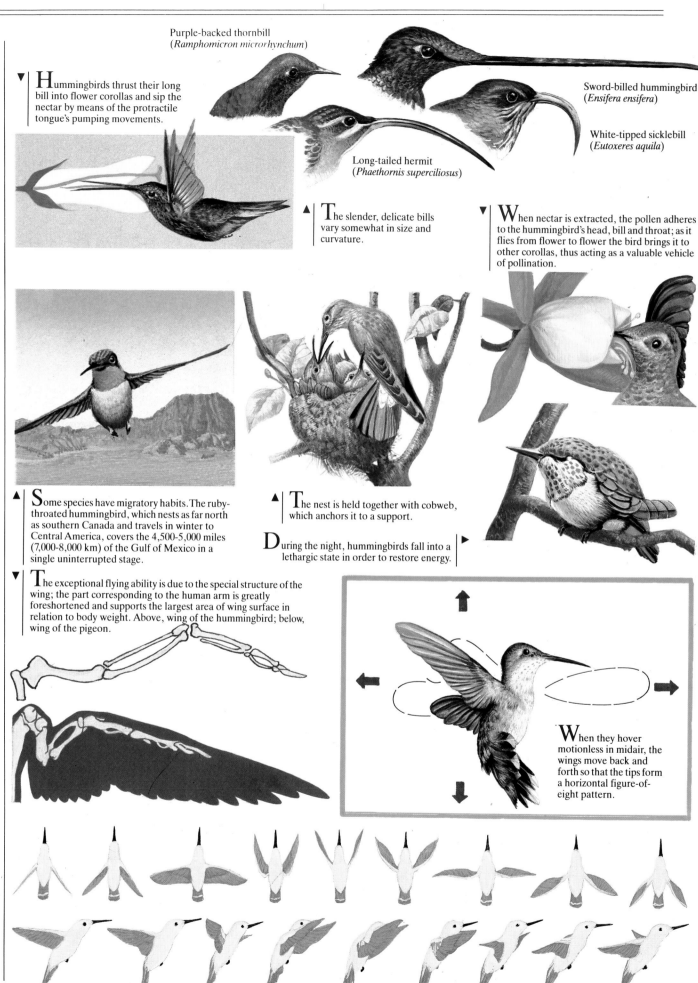

Purple-backed thornbill
(*Ramphomicron microrhynchum*)

Sword-billed hummingbird
(*Ensifera ensifera*)

White-tipped sicklebill
(*Eutoxeres aquila*)

Long-tailed hermit
(*Phaethornis superciliosus*)

▼ Hummingbirds thrust their long bill into flower corollas and sip the nectar by means of the protractile tongue's pumping movements.

▲ The slender, delicate bills vary somewhat in size and curvature.

▼ When nectar is extracted, the pollen adheres to the hummingbird's head, bill and throat; as it flies from flower to flower the bird brings it to other corollas, thus acting as a valuable vehicle of pollination.

▲ Some species have migratory habits. The ruby-throated hummingbird, which nests as far north as southern Canada and travels in winter to Central America, covers the 4,500-5,000 miles (7,000-8,000 km) of the Gulf of Mexico in a single uninterrupted stage.

▲ The nest is held together with cobweb, which anchors it to a support.

▶ During the night, hummingbirds fall into a lethargic state in order to restore energy.

▼ The exceptional flying ability is due to the special structure of the wing; the part corresponding to the human arm is greatly foreshortened and supports the largest area of wing surface in relation to body weight. Above, wing of the hummingbird; below, wing of the pigeon.

When they hover motionless in midair, the wings move back and forth so that the tips form a horizontal figure-of-eight pattern.

197

recurvirostris), or curved sharply downward as in the white-tipped sicklebill (*Eutoxeres aquila*).

Just as the hummingbirds were evolved to extract nectar from flowers in the most efficient manner, so many plants in their turn were gradually modified in order to attract the birds and encourage pollination. The favorite flowers of hummingbirds are those with a narrow funnel, blossoming freely and abundantly without any constricting leaves or twigs. The anthers are so situated as to allow pollen to be deposited liberally on head, throat or beak, and the stigma is structured in such a way that it comes easily into contact with such pollen. Furthermore, there is a precise link between the shape of the beak and the structure of particular flowers so that nectar can be extracted in the simplest possible way. The consequence is that hummingbirds of different species can live harmoniously together in the same area, each feeding mainly on distinct plants. Some short-billed species, such as the purple-crowned fairy (*Heliothryx barroti*), have the habit of perforating the base of the corollas from the outside, sucking out the nectar but not contributing to the process of pollination.

Hummingbirds manage to conserve energy, in some measure, by falling into a miniature state of lethargy in the course of the night. Like other birds, but in contrast to mammals, their body temperature varies, depending on whether they are at rest or fully active, from 102° to 108°F (39° to 42°C). During this phase of torpor this may drop to almost the same level as the outside temperature, but never down to freezing point, with heart rate falling to around 40 per minute from the normally active 500 – 1,300 per minute.

Hummingbirds do not form pairs. Relations between the sexes are usually limited to copulation and from then on the female assumes all responsibilities from nest building to rearing the brood. Males of some species sing all day long, with brief intervals for feeding, while others sing mainly in the morning or evening. Most hummingbirds merely produce a few sharp, shrill notes, tirelessly repeated, but the males of the little hermit (*Phaethornis longuemareus*), the wedge-tailed saberwing (*Campylopterus curvipennis*) and the wine-throated hummingbird (*Atthis ellioti*) all have a decidedly varied and harmonious song.

Tufted coquette
(*Lophornis ornata*)

Vervain humming
(*Mellisuga minimo*

Red-tailed comet
(*Sappho sparganur*

Rufous hummingbird
(*Selasphorus rufus*)

Ruby-topaz hummingbird
(*Chrysolampis mosquitus*)

Streamertail
(*Trochilus polytmus*)

Bearded helmetcrest
(*Oxypogon guerinii*)

Shallow-tailed hummingbi
(*Eupetomena macroura*)

Giant hummingbird
(*Patagona gigas*)

Ruby-throated hummingbird
(*Archilochus colubris*)

Violet saberwi
(*Campylopterus
hemileucurus*)

Purple-throated carib
(*Eulampis jugularis*)

Marvelous spatuletail
(*Loddigesia mirabilis*)

Long-tailed hermit
(*Phaethornis superciliosus*)

White-tailed
goldenthroat
(*Polytmus
guainumbi*)

Long-tailed sylph
(*Aglaiocercus kingi*)

Wire-crested thornbill
(*Popelairia popelairii*)

Hummingbirds of the tropical regions, limited by lack of adequate space amid the dense vegetation, have fairly simple courtship displays. As a rule the male makes jerky movements of the body as the female sits motionless on a twig or branch. In more open temperate regions or at greater heights along the Andes, males do not normally need to join together to attract notice and both sexes will perform series of aerial acrobatics, in perfect unison, hovering opposite each other at intervals. The brighter the male's colors and appendages, the more he relies on aerial dancing for his courtship; if he belongs to a species not so well endowed with secondary sexual adornment he will concentrate almost wholly on song.

Although some observers claim to have seen hummingbirds coupling in midair, the possibility cannot be ruled out that these activities are really aerial tussles between two males for possession of a flowering plant. As far as is known, copulation takes place with the female motionless on a branch; and the mating act generally represents the only occasion when the sexes meet. In temperate latitudes most courtship displays occur in spring and summer, but in tropical zones the breeding season tends to be more irregular, linked as it is to the flowering periods of the various plants on which the different species feed. The female usually builds a nest on her own, far removed from the sight and sound of the congregated males.

Almost all species lay only two white eggs, noticeably elongated in form. The smallest eggs are probably those of the calliope hummingbird (*Stellula calliope*), which measure barely ½ × ⅓ in (12 × 8 mm), and the largest belong to the giant hummingbird (*Patagonia gigas*), which often lays only one, measuring ¾ × ½ in (20 × 12 mm). The interval between the laying of the two eggs is generally two days, rarely one and exceptionally three. Should four eggs be found in a nest this indicates that they have been laid by two females, one of whom (the more aggressive) will be left to incubate them and rear the young. In spite of their small dimensions, hummingbirds' eggs take quite a long time to hatch. The period varies, according to species, from 14 to 23 days, but if the weather is bad the process may last one or two days more.

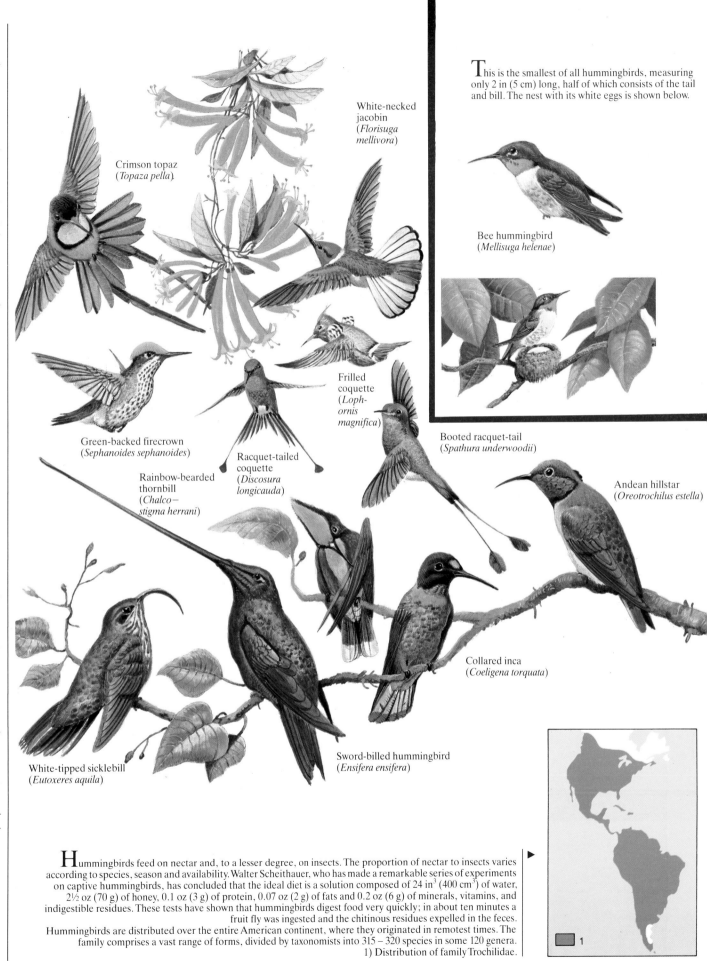

Crimson topaz
(*Topaza pella*)

White-necked jacobin
(*Florisuga mellivora*)

Frilled coquette
(*Lophornis magnifica*)

Green-backed firecrown
(*Sephanoides sephanoides*)

Racquet-tailed coquette
(*Discosura longicauda*)

Rainbow-bearded thornbill
(*Chalcostigma herrani*)

Booted racquet-tail
(*Spathura underwoodii*)

Andean hillstar
(*Oreotrochilus estella*)

Collared inca
(*Coeligena torquata*)

White-tipped sicklebill
(*Eutoxeres aquila*)

Sword-billed hummingbird
(*Ensifera ensifera*)

This is the smallest of all hummingbirds, measuring only 2 in (5 cm) long, half of which consists of the tail and bill. The nest with its white eggs is shown below.

Bee hummingbird
(*Mellisuga helenae*)

Hummingbirds feed on nectar and, to a lesser degree, on insects. The proportion of nectar to insects varies according to species, season and availability. Walter Scheithauer, who has made a remarkable series of experiments on captive hummingbirds, has concluded that the ideal diet is a solution composed of 24 in³ (400 cm³) of water, 2½ oz (70 g) of honey, 0.1 oz (3 g) of protein, 0.07 oz (2 g) of fats and 0.2 oz (6 g) of minerals, vitamins, and indigestible residues. These tests have shown that hummingbirds digest food very quickly; in about ten minutes a fruit fly was ingested and the chitinous residues expelled in the feces.
Hummingbirds are distributed over the entire American continent, where they originated in remotest times. The family comprises a vast range of forms, divided by taxonomists into 315 – 320 species in some 120 genera.
1) Distribution of family Trochilidae.

QUETZAL

Pharomachrus mocino

Family Trogonidae
Size Total length of male 40 – 47 in (100 – 120 cm), tail up to 41½ in (105 cm); female 16 in (40 cm)
Weight 5½ – 6¼ oz (160 – 180 g)
Reproductive season April – August
Incubation period 17 – 18 days
Eggs 2, sky-blue
Sexual maturity Probably at 3 years old
Maximum age 22 years

The quetzal has conspicuous plumage, glossy green above, and red below. The upper tail coverts in the male are lengthened, forming plumes of up to 3 ft (1 m) long.

The quetzal is found only from Mexico to Panama. It lives in the dark mountain forests up to an altitude of 10,000 ft (3,000 m) but comes down to 3,500 ft (1,000 m) in the rainy season.

Adult quetzals feed mainly on fruit, which they pluck in flight. They require large amounts of food, consuming on average 3¾ oz (105 g) per day, or more than half their own body weight. They swallow whole fruits as large as cherries, and fruit 1¾ in (4.5 cm) long has been found in a quetzal's crop. The young birds are fed chiefly on insects during their first few days, and later supplement their fruit diet with small vertebrates such as frogs and lizards, as well as snails. Other members of the family live mainly off butterflies and their larvae.

Outside the breeding season, quetzals frequently live in small groups. Only older males are seen alone in winter. They mostly stay in the treetops of tropical forests, 160 ft (50 m) or more above the ground, and in spite of their conspicuous plumage, they are hard to see, especially as they often sit quietly on a branch for long periods. Occasionally they betray their presence by their call, which is most frequently heard during the breeding season.

The male quetzal has an impressive mating flight. It soars above the jungle treetops and flies in circles, uttering a call of several notes. The birds then make their breeding holes, which resemble those of woodpeckers, high up in the soft wood of rotten tree trunks. Males and females share the incubation of the eggs, and bring up the young birds together.

The very beautiful iridescent green feathers of the quetzal were used by Pre-Colombian civilizations of Central America to adorn the head-dresses of kings an chieftains. After the European invasion of the continent, intensive hunting decimated the species so that nowadays the bird is very rare, an additional reaso being deforestation which has destroyed much of its traditional habitat.

It feeds principally on large amounts of fruit, daily equivalent to about half its body weight. The bird also eats small vertebrates and snails. Some species of the family mainly consume butterflies and their larvae.

It scoops out a nest in the soft wood of rotting treetrunks, high above the ground. Both male and female (shown here) share incubation and rear the chicks together.

The Trogonidae live in the primary forests of Central and South America, Africa and southern Asia. 1)The quetzal (*Pharomachrus mocinno*) lives only in America, in a zone that includes southern Mexico and Panama.

BAR-BREASTED MOUSEBIRD

Colius striatus

Family Coliidae
Size Full length 9¾ – 14¼ in (25 – 36 cm); tail 6¼ – 9¾ in (16 – 25 cm)
Weight 1½ – 2½ oz (42 – 71 g)
Reproductive season During a large part of the year
Incubation period 10½ – 14 days
Eggs 1 – 6 eggs, usually 2 – 3
Sexual maturity 6 – 10 months
Maximum age 11 years

The mousebirds owe their name to their unremarkable gray-brown plumage, which looks like fur underneath, and their long tails, giving them the look of mice. They have strong feet with very mobile toes, and their strong claws are very well adapted to climbing trees.

The bar-breasted mousebird is found in Africa south of the Sahara from Nigeria to the Sudan and from Ethiopia down East Africa and southern Africa to the Cape. It is found on the edges of forests, in forest galleries beside the rivers, and in the savanna, but not in dense tropical jungles of the Congo basin or in dry and treeless zones.

Mousebirds are overwhelmingly vegetarian, and live off fruit, young shoots, leaves, and flowers. They are social birds, and live in family groups and larger parties outside the mating season. They prefer to sit in the branches of leafy trees and bushes, which they are well adapted to climbing. They shoot like tiny arrows from one bush to another, but never fly far at a time. They come only rarely to the ground, to take a dustbath or eat some earth.

The male has no song, but flies and hops back and forth like a tiny ball of feathers, until the female is ready to mate. They build open, bowl-shaped nests in the trees and bushes of small twigs and roots, lined with kapok and green leaves. The 2 – 4 white eggs are incubated by both sexes from the moment the first egg has been laid, so that the young chicks hatch one after another. The chicks are blind at first, and nearly naked, but their first quills grow and their eyes open after only a few days.

Blue-naped mousebird
(*Colius macrourus*)

Red-faced mousebird
(*Colius indicus*)

The birds derive their name from the gray-brown color of their plumage. Mainly vegetarian, they feed on fruit, leaves, and flowers in large quantities, often raiding orchards. Now and then they also catch insects.

They live in Africa south of the Sahara to Cape Province, but are not found in the dense jungles of the Congo basin or in arid treeless zones. 1) Distribution of order Coliiformes.

During the night they roost on branches, tail perpendicular to the ground, clustering close to each other.

EUROPEAN BEE-EATER

Merops apiaster

Order Coraciiformes
Family Meropidae
Length 11 in (28 cm)
Distribution Southern Europe, North Africa, western Asia
Habits Arboreal, terrestrial when breeding, gregarious
Nesting In burrows on ground
Eggs 4 – 10, usually 5 – 7
Chicks Nidicolous

The European bee-eater (*Merops apiaster*) has reddish brown upperparts with ocher and blue green tones below. The throat is yellow, the forehead white and the iris scarlet. A black band separates the yellow throat from the blue breast, and another black stripe runs from the beak through the eye to the nape. The two central tail feathers project far beyond the rest of the tail.

It breeds in northwest and southern Africa, in western Asia to Kashmir and Baluchistan, and in the Mediterranean region of Europe, putting in occasional appearances farther north (in Germany, where it has nested, and in Scandinavia). The European bee-eater lives in arid surroundings such as sandy and clay terrain near seacoasts and salt lakes, creeks with sparse herbaceous cover, and rugged cliffs overlooking water. It is very reliant, mainly for feeding purposes, on warm climatic conditions and either natural or artificial roosts from which it can swoop on prey.

Bee-eaters are sociable by nature, flocking in zones where insects swarm abundantly and adopting two distinct hunting techniques, depending on the nature of the surroundings. When they cannot find suitable vantage points for observing prey, they fly tirelessly, swooping low over cultivated fields, flowering meadows, the Mediterranean maquis and ponds rich with animal life, accompanying such aerial maneuvers with characteristic guttural cries, sometimes harsh and raucous, sometimes twittering and more melodious.

They are capable of astonishing feats as they pursue their prey. Smaller insects are swallowed in midair but larger ones have to be consumed while

European bee-eater
(*Merops apiaster*)

The European bee-eater's plumage is multicolored. In the breeding season birds form large colonies in steep sandbanks which are creviced with tunnels. These long burrows are excavated with beak and feet. They do not always nest in vertical walls, and where it proves impossible they will adapt to fairly level ground, preferably sloping slightly downward, without too much grass.

Representatives of some of the families of the Coraciiformes.

Alcedinidae
Black-capped kingfisher
(*Halcyon pileata*)

Todidae
Jamaican tody
(*Todus todus*)

Bucerotidae
Rhinoceros hornbill
(*Buceros rhinoceros*)

Meropidae
Red-bearded bee-eater
(*Nyctornis amicta*)

Upupidae
Hoopoe
(*Upupa epops*)

standing still on a perch. Branches and electric wires make suitable observation points, as they do for flycatchers. They keep a close watch on the surrounding air space and eventually pounce on their insect victim, closing the beak round it with a loud snap and returning to their starting point for the meal. If the prey is of fair size they first batter it against a branch, eyeing it attentively until certain it is stunned and helpless, the sting of venomous species projecting harmlessly from the abdomen. Then they toss the insect high in the air and swallow it, head first.

Male and female conduct their courtship on a branch or perch close to the place selected for building the nest, defending this territory from neighboring pairs by ruffling the feathers of back and nape and giving out menacing cries. The male hops sideways to his partner, performing a few twists and turns, and offers her an insect, fluttering his tail. This offering is a prelude to copulation, and this is followed by the digging of a tunnel some 2 – 3 in (5 – 8 cm) wide and 28 – 100 in (70 – 250 cm) deep. A successful dig may take from 10 to 25 days. The two birds, frequently changing places, break up the soil with their beak and kick it backwards with their feet. The burrow is almost always dug in a vertical wall (such as a river bank), but when this proves impossible a flat piece of ground is chosen, without too much grass and sloping gently downward. At the end of the tunnel is a large hole where the remains of insects are heaped. Here the female lays 4 – 8 eggs, incubated by both birds for 20 – 22 days.

The carmine bee-eater (*M. nubicus*), with red abdomen and blue head, nests in colonies containing thousands of pairs on the steep river banks of central and western Africa. This bird is attracted by savanna fires and by the hordes of small creatures which are flushed out at such times, and it often pursues swarms of locusts and flying ants. The southern carmine bee-eater (*M. nubicoides*) is an inhabitant of southern Africa. Both the above-mentioned species are migrants but whereas the former flies south, the latter journeys farther north. The red-throated bee-eater (*M. bulocki*), green above and red below, lives in flocks which hunt flying insects in the treetops, and it nests in central–western Africa, often together with the carmine bee-eater.

The blue-naped bee-eater hunts insects by chasing them acrobatically through the air. Alternatively, it will perch on a high branch until a prey passes close by and will then swoop.

Bee-eaters pursuing insects trying to escape from a fire.

In order not to be stung by venomous wasps and hornets, the bee-eater grasps the insect by the thorax and batters it against a branch, squeezes the body and then, before swallowing it, forces out the limp sting from the abdomen.

Carmine bee-eater (*Merops nubicus*)

Little green bee-eater (*Merops orientalis*)

Red-throated bee-eater (*Melittophagus bulocki*)

Sometimes the bird dives into the water to capture tiny aquatic animals.

Prey includes wasps, hornets, bees, bumblebees, and dragonflies.

The third and fourth toes of the foot are partially fused.

The bee-eaters inhabit tropical, subtropical and warm-temperate zones of Africa, Eurasia, and Australia.
1) The European bee-eater (*Merops apiaster*) is a bird of arid regions; 2) Overall distribution of the family Meropidae.

1
2

BLUE ROLLER

Coracias garrulus

Order Coraciiformes
Family Coraciidae
Length 12 in (30 cm)
Distribution Central and southern Europe, North Africa, Asia
Habits Arboreal, solitary
Nesting In tree trunks, among rocks and on buildings
Eggs 4 – 7
Chicks Nidicolous

The blue roller (*Coracias garrulus*) is unmistakable, prominent features of its silhouette being the stocky body, the square tail, the short legs and the heavy bill. The bird is nut brown on the back, blue on the head and under-parts, dark blue on flight feathers and base of tail.

This species formerly inhabited a large part of Europe, but for various reasons (not least climatic changes and resultant alterations in environment) their range has slowly dwindled in Europe and shifted to the East. Today the blue roller lives in northwest Africa, central–southern Europe, and western Asia, but its distribution is often irregular and broken. It nests in deciduous and coniferous woods with plenty of clearings, in evergreen forests along the Mediterranean coasts and in parkland and hilly country.

At the end of April the blue roller returns to its breeding grounds. Much of its day is spent perched on a branch or telegraph wire, from which it can get a good view of the surroundings. Once a victim is sighted, the bird launches itself into the air; the blue wings flash in all their splendor, and in an instant it is on the ground with the prey in its powerful, hooked beak. Back it flies to its original vantage point, battering the animal until it is stunned and then gulping it down.

The blue roller is highly expert in hunting a variety of victims, many caught on the wing. Even the most strongly armored insects such as long-horned wood borers and stag-beetles are regularly captured, such species usually providing food only for a few birds of prey. The principal part of the diet consists of insects such as grass-hoppers, mantises, rose chafers and other beetles; the balance is made up of ground invertebrates, lizards, tiny mammals, and small birds.

The courtship parade includes periods of diving and soaring flight, punctuated by midair hovering. After this ceremony male and female perch alongside each other on a branch, dipping the head and letting out raucous cries.

The blue roller is the size of a pigeon and its plumage is brilliant blue and fawn. The head is large and the bill sufficiently stout to cope with armored beetles and venomous wasps and bees, disdained by other birds. It lies in wait for its victims on tree branches and telegraph wires and, after the kill, returns to its roost to make a meal of them. In autumn it flies off to winter in the African savannas, where it encounters local species of crows, vying with them for food and roost.

The blue roller and other members of the family have two of their toes linked at the base. This makes life in the trees easier but is a disadvantage for moving about on the ground. Food consists of small vertebrates and insects such as beetles, cicadas, dragonflies and grasshoppers.

Pairs remain somewhat isolated and roam vast territories, although in some regions where conditions are particularly favorable they may form small colonies.

The male's courtship flight is extremely graceful and interesting, with the dual purpose of signaling occupation of territory and wooing the female. From his perch he soars, wings beating powerfully, to a height of about 250 ft (70 m) and then goes into a glide. Suddenly he closes his wings and plummets down like a bomb; but near the ground he straightens out and climbs once more, circling in a slow glide and gaining sufficient altitude to dive again, repeating the whole performance. Eventually he perches and awaits his partner, croaking and dipping his head in preparation for mating.

The nest is situated in a tree hollow, a hole in a building, or in the sand or clay of a river bank, at heights varying from a few inches to some 30 feet above ground level. There is no special lining material for the nest, apart from bits and pieces of half-digested prey, some feathers or a few blades of grass. In Europe the bird lays 4 – 5 (sometimes up to 7) white eggs, at intervals of two days, in early May. Some ornithologists believe that incubation begins when the last egg is laid, others think it starts with the first. Both sexes share incubation, which lasts 18 – 19 days. The parents take turns in looking after the brood and fly off to hunt within a radius of several miles from the nest.

The short-legged ground roller (*Brachypteracias leptosomus*) has a red head, a blue nape, a green back, and a white belly with red marks. It lives in primary forests and hops nimbly about on the ground among the bushes, seldom taking to the air. Hardly anything is known about the reproductive behavior of the bird, except that the eggs are laid inside a burrow previously dug in the soil.

The courol (*Leptosomus discolor*), 18 in (45 cm) in length, inhabits Madagascar and the Comoro archipelago. Its plumage is notable for sexual dimorphism. The back of the male is dark gray with green and purple tints, while the rest of his body is ash gray. The female is reddish brown, with a fawn, black-streaked abdomen. The species lives in rain forests and spends much time up in the treetops hunting large beetles and hairy caterpillars.

Lilac-breasted roller
(*Coracias caudata*)

Dollar bird
(*Eurystomus orientalis*)

Courol
(*Leptosomus discolor*)

Short-legged ground roller
(*Brachypteracias leptosomus*)

◀ The flight pattern of this bird is sustained and powerful.

◀ It constructs a nest in the hollow of a tall tree from 32 to 50 ft (10 to 15 m) above ground. While rearing the young it becomes highly aggressive and will attack any animal that ventures too close, including humans.

▨ 1 ▨ 2 ▨ 3

◀ The rollers have a wide distribution, 11 species inhabiting the warm, dry regions of Europe, Asia, Africa, and Australia. Habitats include Mediterranean-type scrub, parkland, and woods well provided with glades. 1) The blue roller (*Coracias garrulus*), originally from the Orient, is found in northwest Africa, central and southern Europe, and western Asia; for various reasons its range has been progressively broken up and reduced. 2) The broad-billed roller or dollar bird (*Eurystomus orientalis*) comes from eastern Asia, Australia, and the chains of islands linking the two continents. 3) Many other species of the family live in Africa.

KINGFISHER

Alcedo atthis

Order Coraciiformes
Family Alcedinidae
Length 6½ in (16 cm)
Distribution Africa, Europe, and Asia
Habits Aquatic, solitary
Nesting In burrows on ground
Eggs 4 – 10, usually 6 or 7
Chicks Nidicolous

The common kingfisher (*Alcedo atthis*) is stocky in build, with a short tail and a large head. The head is made to appear even bigger by the long pointed bill which measures over 1½ in (4 cm) and is thus a quarter of the whole body length. The plumage is bright and glittering. Head, back, and tail are blue with metallic reflections, the underparts are reddish fawn, the throat and ear patch are white, and the legs are red.

The kingfisher's geographical range extends from North Africa, across Europe (northward to central Sweden) and much of central–southern Asia to Japan, Malaysia, and many of the island groups of Oceania. There are nine separate subspecies. Its food is all found in the water and it therefore lives along the banks of rivers, lakes, and fresh ponds among reeds, tree thickets, and steep embankments of sand or soil. It seldom climbs to great heights and has been observed at about 6,000 ft (1,800 m) alongside mountain streams.

The common kingfisher, fluttering its tiny wings rapidly, flies fast and in a straight line. Complex maneuvers are ruled out by the shortness of the tail, and it generally skims the surface, announcing its presence with sharp, shrill cries, only gaining altitude in order to avoid an unexpected obstacle. Perching on a reed or branch jutting out over the water, it surveys its territory, upright and attentive, moving its head imperceptibly to scan the water below, which should ideally be clear, calm, and free of any floating vegetation. As soon as it spies something of interest, it plummets down into the water and immediately reappears, prey clutched in beak, to return to its vantage point. Sometimes the victim will vanish a few moments before the kingfisher dives, in which case the bird soars gracefully upward, hovers immobile for a second or two

Common kingfisher
(*Alcedo atthis*)

▲ The kingfisher feeds mainly on small fish and, to a lesser extent, on aquatic insects and their larvae, small frogs, crustaceans, and mollusks. The three front toes of the feet are joined at the base, so that the bird cannot walk but makes use of them in shoving away the soil when digging its nest.

◄ The family Alcedinidae contains a large number of species: the small European or common kingfisher is here seen beside the large kookaburra or laughing jackass, a kingfisher with a thick, broad bill, which lives in wooded districts.

until it again locates its prey and then swoops down. The victim is pierced with the beak and battered against the branch until stunned; any sharp parts are removed in this way and the fish is then thrown into the air and swallowed head first so that opened fins do not damage the bird's throat. Most of the fish eaten are about 3 in (7 – 8 cm) long but others are smaller. In Europe fish tend to be mainly surface species, including minnows, bleak, chub, trout, and mullet, and to a lesser extent aquatic insects and their larvae, small frogs, crustaceans, and mollusks.

The common kingfisher is a solitary and strictly territorial bird. Each has its own stretch of bank, both at times of reproduction and wintering (the two sometimes coinciding as the species is only partly migratory), measuring about a hundred yards with its habitual rest places from which it will chase away any intruders.

Pairs form as early as January, but later in zones where the birds are migrants. Male and female, linking territories for the entire summer, pursue each other with trilling song through the reeds and bushes and along the banks, skimming low over the water. While she looks on from a branch, he engages in an undulating nuptial flight like that of a butterfly, singing all the while with a succession of sharp, piercing trills. Then he lands beside her, points his bill in the air, opens his wings to show off the brilliant blue of his back and offers her a fish. The pair exchange gentle beak tappings and prepare to mate.

The nest is built in the steep banks of lakes and rivers, at a height varying from 24 in (60 cm) to 25 ft (8 m) above the water. The operation begins as both birds fly towards the chosen wall of sand, clay or soil, testing it with their beak and scraping their feet against the surface, but always remaining in the air. Having scooped out a small hole, they then begin to excavate a proper tunnel at a slight upward slope. Both birds break the earth with their beak and push it away with the feet. The burrow, from 16 in (40 cm) to 39 in (1 m) in length, terminates in a wider incubation chamber, which is lined with the friable white scales and skins of half-digested fish. The female usually lays 7 eggs which are incubated by both birds in turn for 19 – 21 days.

It is obviously impossible to list here all the 86 species making up the family Alcedinidae, so just a few of the more

The small, handsome common kingfisher lives beside streams and rivers and on the shores of freshwater and brackish lakes. It is a solitary bird which spends much of its time on a branch or reed, scanning the water for prey.

The members of the family living in forests and savannas feed on almost all kinds of small animals (snakes, rodents, shrewmice, frogs, crustaceans, and large insects), waiting perched on dead branches.

When it sights prey on the surface it makes a plunge-dive into the water, emerging with its victim and returning to its perch.

The nest is in the form of a long burrow, widened at the end to make a chamber suitable for incubating the eggs. As a rule the adults do not line the nest, but simply heap up the semi-digested remains of meals. The layer of fragmented fish scales and skins gives off a foul smell. The smooth eggs are glossy white.

interesting ones will be mentioned.

One of the smallest is the African pygmy kingfisher (*Ispidina picta*), measuring 4½ in (11.5 cm) and found throughout central and southeastern Africa. This is a typical land bird from tree and bush savanna, capturing small insects on the ground. It breeds at different months of the year, according to the dry and rainy seasons.

The white-breasted kingfisher (*H. smyrnensis*) is one of the most beautiful species; its back is blue, the abdomen and head are brown, there is a large white patch on the breast, and the bill is red. The bird ranges from Turkey to Vietnam and the Philippines, across the whole of southern Asia. It lives in virgin forests close to water and feeds on insects and small vertebrates, caught equally dexterously in water and on land.

The gray-headed kingfisher (*H. leucocephala*) lives in dry zones, although it is not uncommon to see it close to ponds and lakes. Its favorite habitat is tree and bush savanna where it hunts a variety of ground-dwelling animals such as invertebrates and reptiles by swooping on them from the branches.

The ruddy kingfisher (*H. coromanda*) is an Asiatic species, frequenting the river banks and mangrove swamps of Southeast Asia. The belted kingfisher (*Megaceryle alcyon*) lives in the central and southern regions of North America; each pair of birds scoops out a nest from steep river banks, laying 5 – 8 eggs.

The lesser pied kingfisher (*Ceryle rudis*) has a range from Asia Minor to southern China and Africa. This species inhabits wetlands and pinpoints fish by hovering for a moment over the water surface and then diving. After the breeding season, the lesser pied kingfisher gathers with companions in small flocks which often perch on branches overhanging the water.

Among the four members of the long-tailed genus *Chloroceryle* is the Amazon kingfisher (*C. amazona*).

The kookaburra or laughing jackass (*Dacelo gigas*) lives in Australia, Tasmania, and New Guinea. It feeds on snakes, including venomous species, small mammals, insects, and marine crabs, which it cracks open with its powerful bill. The 2 – 4 white eggs are incubated for 25 days by both sexes. The kookaburra is a noisy bird, its call being loud and strident, very like human laughter.

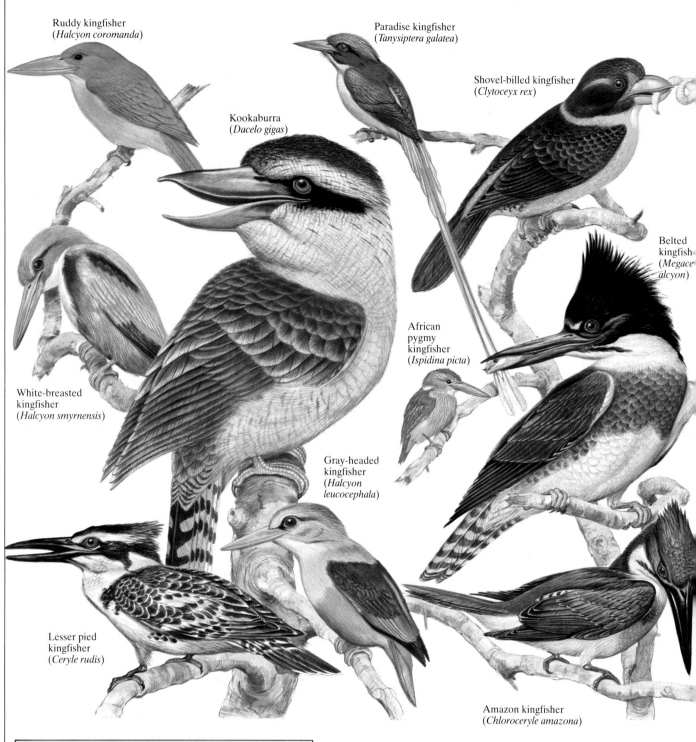

Ruddy kingfisher
(*Halcyon coromanda*)

Paradise kingfisher
(*Tanysiptera galatea*)

Shovel-billed kingfisher
(*Clytoceyx rex*)

Kookaburra
(*Dacelo gigas*)

Belted kingfisher
(*Megaceryle alcyon*)

African pygmy kingfisher
(*Ispidina picta*)

White-breasted kingfisher
(*Halcyon smyrnensis*)

Gray-headed kingfisher
(*Halcyon leucocephala*)

Lesser pied kingfisher
(*Ceryle rudis*)

Amazon kingfisher
(*Chloroceryle amazona*)

1
2

▲ The kingfishers of the family Alcedinidae come in a great variety of shapes and colors. The structure of the bill accords with the diet: long and pointed in fishing and hunting species; broad in the kookaburra, which crushes animals with tough skin; shovel-shaped in *Clytoceyx rex*, which feeds on worms pulled from the soft earth.

◄ 1) The members of the family Alcedinidae live in tropical, subtropical and temperate zones throughout the world. 2) Distribution of the common kingfisher (*Alcedo atthis*).

BLUE-CROWNED MOTMOT

Momotus momota

Order Coraciiformes
Family Momotidae
Length 18 in (45 cm)
Distribution Central and South America
Eggs 3 – 4
Chicks Nidicolous

The blue-crowned motmot (*Momotus momota*) is the largest member of the family, measuring 18 in (45 cm) in length. It lives in Central America and Costa Rica down to northern Brazil, food consisting of large insects, invertebrates, and fruit. It spends a great deal of time perched on branches so as to catch any passing prey. The bird nests in tunnels dug into the steep banks of rivers, but sometimes it takes advantage of holes already excavated by other animals. The adults change places on the eggs only twice a day and after about three weeks the chicks hatch.

Green species of motmots include the turquoise-browed motmot (*Eumomota superciliosa*), 12 in (30 cm) long, with its black throat edged blue, and the small tody motmot (*Hylomanes momotula*) from Mexico and Central America, the only species with a short tail and probably the most primitive member of the family. Its plumage is green, the crown of the head is ruddy, and there are two bright blue patches above the eyes.

The todies of the family Todidae, native to the West Indies, are related to the kingfishers, motmots and bee-eaters. The Cuban tody (*Todus multicolor*) lives in the woods of Cuba; its upperparts are green, the feathers around the eyes are yellow, the cheeks blue, the flanks and throat red. The Puerto Rican tody (*T. mexicanus*) has a red throat and yellow sides, while the Jamaican tody (*T. todus*) has a green breast and pink flanks. The broad-billed tody (*T. subulatus*), from the mountains of Hispaniola, and the narrow-billed tody (*T. angustirostris*), from the same island but frequenting areas below an altitude of 5,000 ft (1,500 m) are almost alike. All five species are more or less similar from the ecological viewpoint, but these two are distinct in that, by occupying territory at different altitudes, they do not compete with each other.

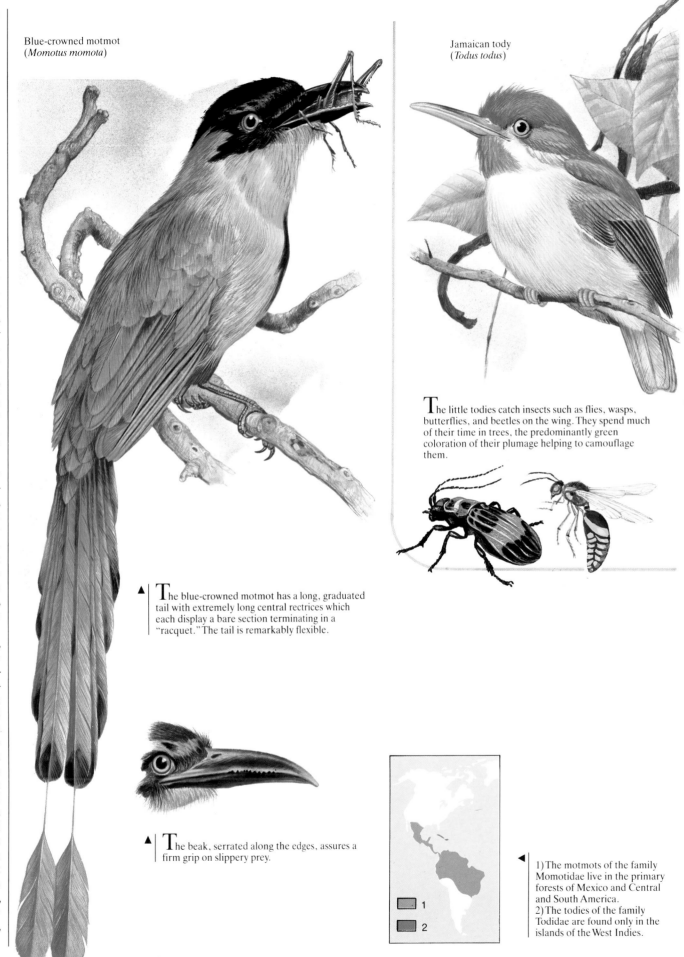

Blue-crowned motmot
(*Momotus momota*)

Jamaican tody
(*Todus todus*)

The little todies catch insects such as flies, wasps, butterflies, and beetles on the wing. They spend much of their time in trees, the predominantly green coloration of their plumage helping to camouflage them.

▲ The blue-crowned motmot has a long, graduated tail with extremely long central rectrices which each display a bare section terminating in a "racquet." The tail is remarkably flexible.

▲ The beak, serrated along the edges, assures a firm grip on slippery prey.

◄ 1) The motmots of the family Momotidae live in the primary forests of Mexico and Central and South America.
2) The todies of the family Todidae are found only in the islands of the West Indies.

1
2

209

RHINOCEROS HORNBILL

Buceros rhinoceros

Family Bucerotidae
Size Full length 48 in (120 cm)
Weight Male 5½ – 6½ lb (2.5 – 3 kg);
female 4½ – 5 lb (2 – 2.3 kg)
Reproductive Season January – April
Incubation period 30 – 40 days
Eggs 1 – 2 white eggs, exceptionally 3
Maximum age 33 years

The plumage of the rhinoceros hornbill is almost entirely black, only its tail being white with a black band. It has an enormous yellow beak tinged with red on the base, with a prominent casque, which reaches the tip of the beak in some subspecies. As with all the hornbills, with the exception of the helmeted hornbill (*Rhinoplax vigil*), which has a solid casque, the casque is hollow so that the beak is relatively light in spite of its size. Hornbills also have extremely aerated bones in their extremities, so that they are lighter than their size would suggest. The plumage of both sexes of the rhinoceros hornbill is alike, but the female is a little smaller. The iris of the eye is also red in the male, and white in the female. Other species of the hornbill family are distinguished by differentiation of the plumage between the sexes, and in the coloring of the bald patches around the eyes and throat.

The hornbills are found in Africa, southern Asia and across the neighboring archipelagos as far as New Guinea. However, the rhinoceros hornbill is found only from the Malacca peninsula across Sumatra and Borneo as far as West Java. It inhabits the great primeval forests, but does not live higher than 4,000 ft (1,200 m) up its native mountains. Forest clearance is threatening the species since they require undisturbed woodlands with large trees in which to find the holes they will nest in, in order to survive. Only the smaller species of the family, such as the tokos, inhabit the African savannas and similar habitats in India. Other representatives of the hornbills live in tropical forests on the slopes of the African volcanoes up to a height of more than 6,500 ft (2,000 m) above sea-level.

Hornbills live in pairs, or in small

Rhinoceros hornbill
(*Buceros rhinoceros*)

◄ The most spectacular feature of the rhinoceros hornbill is the enormous beak, surmounted by an equally remarkable casque. The latter is a horny sheath supported inside by spongy bone, so that in spite of appearances it is fairly lightweight. The presence of a casque distinguishes hornbills from toucans, whose bills are otherwise slightly similar.

▼ Most of the hornbill's food consists of fruit but sometimes it also eats animal prey.

Toucan

Rhinoceros
hornbill

parties outside the breeding season. They prefer to sit in treetops 150 – 200 ft (50 – 60 m) above the ground. They require a large amount of food, and so seek out the fruit-bearing trees over a large surrounding area, often flying in from all directions. Their wings are rounded, making their flight difficult, and unusually noisy for a bird. Many species call continuously while they are in the air. The rhinoceros hornbill has a resonant call like a goose which the two partners of a pair emit alternately while they are in the air, and this is one of the most characteristic bird calls of the Borneo forest. The pairs stay very close together throughout the year, and the females are often fed by their mates even outside the breeding season.

Hornbills have very remarkable breeding behavior. All species breed in holes in trees, but the special feature of the rhinoceros hornbill's behavior is that it fills up the entrance of the hole with droppings and bits of food until only a narrow slit remains. The female remains in the hole throughout the incubation period and even after her young are hatched, and is fed during the whole of this period by the male. When the young hatch, the male must provide food for them as well. The rhinoceros hornbill needs a large hole to nest in, and these can measure up to 20 in (55 cm) long, 15 in (40 cm) wide, and 50 in (120 cm) deep.

Generally, 2 eggs are laid. These are incubated for more than a month, and the young need another 2½ – 3 months before they can leave the nest. The female leaves the hole somewhat earlier however, after molting her wing and tail feathers. If anything should happen to the male during this period, then both the female and her young will die. It has been observed, however, that other unmated males will then start to tend the birds in the nesting-hole. After the female has left the hole, the young close up the entrance again to the size of a narrow slit. They continue to be fed by their parents for a long time after leaving the nest, and remain in the family group until the next breeding season. They can be distinguished for a long time by their smaller casques. Those species which inhabit the tropical forests and can find sufficient food throughout the year breed more or less all year round. A single breeding-hole may be used for several broods, or else used by different pairs in alternation.

▼ The edges of the bill are serrated so that food can be tightly gripped. The bird tosses fruit in the air and then catches and swallows it.

The nest is situated in the hollow of a trunk and the entrance is so narrow that only the beak can be poked through. The female incubates inside, literally sealed up in the nest, and is fed through the entry slit by the male. Because she is so cramped she has to hold her tail vertically, this characteristic position being imitated by the fledglings. ▶

▲ Section of spongy bone tissue of the casque, consisting of extremely delicate combs of cells.

Helmeted hornbill (*Rhinoplax vigil*)

Red-billed hornbill (*Tockus erythrorhynchus*)

Abyssinian ground hornbill (*Bucorvus abyssinicus*)

Trumpeter hornbill (*Bycanistes bucinator*)

Yellow-casqued hornbill (*Ceratogymna elata*)

◀ 1) The members of the family Bucerotidae are found all over Africa, southern Asia, and neighboring islands as far as New Guinea, living in forests with the tall trees necessary for nesting.

HOOPOE

Upupa epops

Order Coraciiformes
Family Upupidae
Length 10½ in (26 cm)
Weight 1¾ – 2¾ oz (50 – 80 g)
Wingspan About 18 in (45 cm)
Distribution Europe, Asia, and Africa
Nesting In cavities of trees and buildings
Eggs 5 – 7 (rarely up to 10 or 12)
Chicks Nidicolous

The hoopoe (*Upupa epops*) is virtually cosmopolitan, with nine subspecies in central and southern Europe, Africa (apart from the central regions), and Asia as far as eastern Siberia and Malaysia. Populations are subject to irregular fluctuations, the causes of which are unknown.

In flight the hoopoe looks like a huge black and white butterfly, following an erratic, undulating course as the broad wings sweep down at every beat to touch each other below the body. Then, when at rest either on the ground or in a tree, it almost vanishes from sight, the immobile pink silhouette blending with the background, its presence given away only by the nervous spreading and closing of the long crest, a sign of excitement or alarm. It is never a very common bird, by reason of the fact that pairs live some distance from one another and are rather unsociable. Only when breeding is finished will small family groups of six or seven birds be seen flying silently among the trees. It feeds on insects, mainly beetles (scarabs and chafers, burying beetles and dung beetles), caterpillars, and ants. The diet is supplemented, too, by invertebrates (worms, snails, and centipedes).

The presence of the hoopoe on its nesting sites (occupied as early as March in the Mediterranean) is announced by its monotonous three-syllabled uh-pu-pup, given out by the male on the ground. In the course of courtship display the two partners adopt a series of postures that show off the brilliant colors of the wings, also raising and lowering their crests. The male, with wings and tail outstretched, offers the female food; this offering is a prelude to copulation, which takes place close to the site chosen for the nest.

The hoopoe looks for food on the ground, trotting about on its short legs, head swaying at every step. Prey is purposefully seized and killed, either in the grass or just beneath the surface, with the long beak. Favorite feeding grounds are the edges of woods and meadows enriched by animal excrement and thus swarming with coprophagous insects. Prey items include worms, spiders, insects, and larvae. Larger victims are battered against a hard surface to stun them and get rid of the inedible chitinous parts, then tossed in the air and swallowed. Undigested bits are eliminated in the form of tiny pellets.

The splendid head crest can be opened and closed like a fan.

The nest is usually placed in a tree hollow but sometimes in a wall cavity. It is extremely foul smelling because of the excrement and malodorous secretions of the fledglings, designed to keep predators at bay. During incubation, the female is fed by the male at least eight or ten times daily. Sometimes the pair rears a second brood.

GREEN WOOD-HOOPOE

Phoeniculus purpureus

Order Coraciiformes
Family Phoeniculidae
Length 13½ in (34 cm)
Distribution Central and southern Africa
Habits Arboreal, gregarious
Nesting In tree hollows
Eggs 2 – 5, usually 2 or 3
Chicks Nidicolous

The green wood-hoopoe (*Phoeniculus purpureus*) is slimly built, its plumage is black with green and purple tints, and the curved bill is red. In flight the white marks on the short, rounded wings are clearly visible and there are white bands on the tail.

This is a localized species, although well distributed over a vast area extending from South Africa to Sudan and to Lake Tanganyika. It inhabits tropical savannas with much tree growth and also dense rain forests.

The green wood-hoopoe's presence in the dense tree canopy is given away by the sharp, metallic calls emitted, often in chorus by several individuals. They are, in fact, gregarious birds who explore the forest in chattering groups and are continually on the move. They climb treetrunks with great agility, descending head downwards, hanging from branches and thrusting their long, powerful beak into bark and cracks to get at the small animals on which they feed, especially insects, spiders, and also to a lesser extent, berries and seeds.

When the breeding season approaches, each pair of wood-hoopoes looks for a suitable nesting site, generally a split in the trunk at varying heights above ground level. A heap of wood chips is assembled inside the hole and this serves as a bed for the 2 or 3 white eggs which are incubated only by the female.

The white-headed wood-hoopoe (*Phoeniculus bollei*) is black with metallic tints; the bill and feet are red and the head is white with fawn shading. It lives in the rain forests of West Africa. The forest wood-hoopoe (*P. castaneiceps*) is rare and restricted to the mountain forests of the Gulf of Guinea. It is a small bird with a russet head.

Green wood-hoopoe
(*Phoeniculus purpureus*)

▲ The wood-hoopoes can be seen as a link between the hoopoe and the hornbills, for they have features in common with both families. They live in trees and clamber along the trunks to extract tiny animals such as grubs, beetles, termites, and ants from the bark. They also eat small quantities of berries and seeds.

▲ The nest, which stinks like that of the hoopoe, is situated in a hollow or hole made by a woodpecker. The eggs are laid on wood shavings.

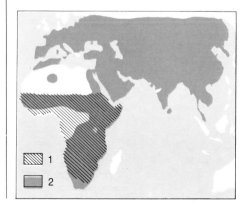

1) All six species belonging to the family Phoeniculidae come from Africa, being found in tree savannas and rain forests. 2) The hoopoe (*Upupa epops*) is, however, an almost cosmopolitan species, their populations being subject to irregular fluctuations, for reasons still unknown. Thus in western Europe between 1910 and 1940, according to the reports of the ornithologist P. Geroudet, numbers declined strongly and then recovered. Hoopoes are migrants, those from Asia overflying the high mountain ranges, having been sighted in the Himalayas at about 26,000 ft (8,000 m), on their way to tropical Africa.

WOODPECKERS
Piciformes

There are some 210 species of woodpeckers, all very agile tree-climbers. Ecologically speaking, there are three types: the tree woodpeckers, easily the most numerous and highly specialized (as, for example, the great spotted woodpecker and the three-toed woodpecker), who spend virtually their whole life on the trunks and branches of trees; then come the ground woodpeckers (such as the green woodpecker), finding most of their food on the ground; and finally the large woodpeckers that occupy an intermediate position (such as the black woodpecker). Measurements vary from 3¼ in (8 cm) for the tiniest piculets to 22 in (56 cm) in the case of the imperial woodpecker from Mexico.

The woodpeckers inhabit every continent except Antarctica; nor are they found in the Arctic, on the island of Madagascar, in Australia, New Guinea, New Zealand, and throughout Oceania. The eastern limit of their distribution is to the east of Celebes and Alor, these being the last islands where the family is present. In the northern hemisphere woodpeckers range to the northernmost limits of the coniferous forests (the taiga); and in the southern hemisphere they extend to the forests of false beech (*Nothofagus*) in Patagonia. The majority of species live in Southeast Asia and tropical America.

The coloration of woodpeckers' plumage ranges from black, mingled in varying measure with white and red, to green and to chestnut with red or yellow patches. Males and females often differ by virtue of the presence or absence of small colored marks, usually on the head; for example, the mustaches of the male green woodpecker are red with black borders, whereas those of the female are black. Various anatomical modifications provide evidence of the birds' climbing capacities, and other physical changes have come about because all woodpeckers, apart from the wrynecks, nest in cavities which they drill themselves in hard or rotting wood. Among such features are: a strengthening of the neck muscles; the presence of special mechanisms designed to deaden the repercussions caused by the hammering

Male great spotted woodpecker (*Dendrocopos major*), recognizable by the red patch on the nape, here shown feeding one of his babies. The young remain in the nest for 20-23 days. Below, some of the insects eaten by the great spotted woodpecker: beetles, ants, and their larvae.

of the bill against wood, so as to avoid possible damage to the brain; a lengthening of the projections of the hyoid bone supporting the tongue, so that it can be fully extended from the beak to capture prey; and a modification of the structure of the tail feathers, so that the tail can be used as a prop whenever they interrupt their climbing activity.

Woodpeckers are closely associated with environments such as woods and forests. A few take up residence in parks, gardens, thickets, copses, and orchards in open country; but three species are notable for managing to live in surroundings where there are no trees. Feeding basically on insects, which they are able to find all year round because they capture them beneath the bark and in the wood, the woodpeckers of cold and temperate zones apparently have no need to migrate. An exception is the wryneck (*Jynx torquilla*) which winters in Africa south of the Sahara. The other markedly migratory woodpeckers live in North America. They are the common flicker (*Colaptes auratus*), the red-headed woodpecker (*Melanerpes erythrocephalus*) and the yellow-bellied sapsucker (*Sphyrapicus varius*), one subspecies of which is a migrant.

Apart from the wrynecks, all woodpeckers nest in holes which they dig, with a few exceptions, in wood. Sometimes several weeks are required for excavating a nest, and sometimes (as in the case of the larger species) it is a more gradual process, especially when the hole is in a living tree. The birds cling to the bark until the cavity is deep enough; then they venture inside and carry on excavating, tossing out the shavings with the beak; these pile up at the foot of the tree. The nest cavities all have the same shape inside; a horizontal opening leads to a vertical shaft with more or less parallel walls, and this is gradually widened. Only some shavings and sawdust remain at the bottom of the hole. No other nesting material is brought in and the eggs are laid directly on this bed of wood. The depth of the hole varies according to whether it is being used for the first time or has been occupied for some years and thus been enlarged. Woodpeckers do not necessarily dig out a new nest every year, but clearly show their need to drill wood and improve an old nest by making it deeper and broadening the entrance hole which, if the tree is living, tends to close up

◀ The great spotted woodpecker can extend its tongue several inches beyond the tip of the beak in order to capture insect larvae concealed in the wood.

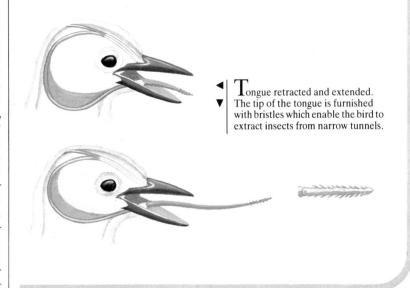

◀ Tongue retracted and extended. ▼ The tip of the tongue is furnished with bristles which enable the bird to extract insects from narrow tunnels.

▲ Pair of great spotted woodpeckers (male on left, female on right) exchanging places to incubate the eggs.

▼ Some North American woodpeckers. The acorn woodpecker is noted for its habit of stocking acorns in single cavities along the treetrunk.

◀ Great spotted woodpeckers keep their nest very clean; after each feed, the adult waits for the chick to produce its droppings (wrapped in a kind of capsule) and then carries them away.

Acorn woodpecker (*Melanerpes formicivorus*)

Yellow-bellied sapsucker (*Sphyrapicus varius*)

Common flicker (*Colaptes auratus*)

F light trajectory of a woodpecker. Because the bird beats its wings intermittently, this tends to be undulating.

again until there are merely scarred outgrowths on each side.

Tropical woodpeckers most often lay 2 or 3 eggs while those from temperate regions lay from 4 to 7. Incubation normally lasts from 12 or 13 days (lesser spotted and black woodpeckers) to 16 days. This is the shared responsibility of male and female, who change places regularly, but among European species it has been observed that it is always the male who sits on the eggs first during the night. When the eggs hatch, the chicks are naked and pinkish. The fledglings, according to species, take 3 or 4 weeks to grow.

Almost all the woodpeckers are solitary by habit and, except in the breeding season, males and females live separately. Woodpeckers announce their presence and communicate with one another by giving out sharp call notes and also by tapping their bill repeatedly and very rapidly against the dead wood of a tree, producing a drumming sound which can be heard for quite a distance. This drumming can be regarded as the equivalent of a passerine's song, because it also serves to demarcate territory. Since it varies in duration, rhythm, and frequency according to species, it can be used for identification purposes. Furthermore, it may also help to synchronize the behavior of the male and female just before they mate. The drumming has nothing to do with feeding, because it continues for a fixed period, whereas when a woodpecker is trying to extract an insect from the trunk, its tapping is irregular and will often go on for a long time.

Woodpeckers are insectivores, but many species also feed generously on seeds or fruits. Ants and termites make up an important proportion of the diet in numerous cases, but the birds also hunt insects that live in the wood or beneath the bark of trees. The great spotted woodpecker feeds both on insects and seeds.

In North America the acorn woodpecker (*Melanerpa formicivorus*) is celebrated for its habit of "stocking up" acorns which it places in small holes drilled into the bark. Because these "larders" are used for years on end, the acorns are collected in enormous numbers, literally in hundreds or even thousands (up to 50,000).

At the end of winter and beginning of spring some woodpeckers dig overlapping rows of more or less horizontal holes in the bark of young trees, sucking

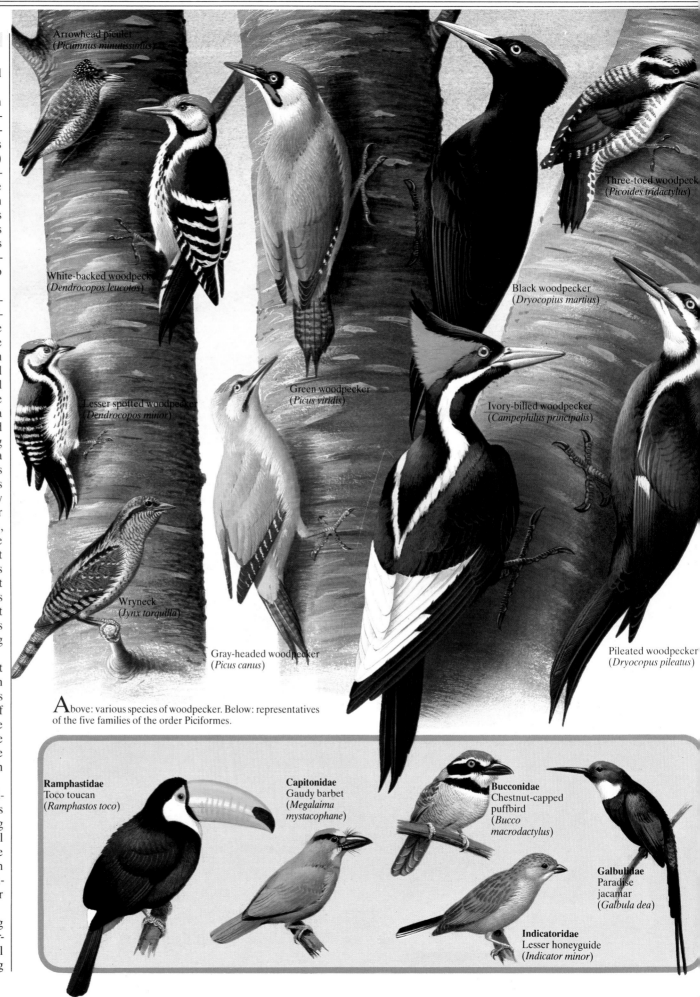

Arrowhead piculet (*Picumnus minutissimus*)

White-backed woodpecker (*Dendrocopos leucotos*)

Lesser spotted woodpecker (*Dendrocopos minor*)

Wryneck (*Jynx torquilla*)

Green woodpecker (*Picus viridis*)

Gray-headed woodpecker (*Picus canus*)

Black woodpecker (*Dryocopius martius*)

Three-toed woodpecker (*Picoides tridactylus*)

Ivory-billed woodpecker (*Campephilus principalis*)

Pileated woodpecker (*Dryocopus pileatus*)

Above: various species of woodpecker. Below: representatives of the five families of the order Piciformes.

Ramphastidae Toco toucan (*Ramphastos toco*)

Capitonidae Gaudy barbet (*Megalaima mystacophane*)

Bucconidae Chestnut-capped puffbird (*Bucco macrodactylus*)

Galbulidae Paradise jacamar (*Galbula dea*)

Indicatoridae Lesser honeyguide (*Indicator minor*)

the sap that flows out and also removing slivers of wood. This behavior is typical, for example, of the yellow-bellied sapsucker (*Sphyrapicus varius*) of North America.

Because of their feeding habits and the fact that they provide nesting places and shelter for other animals as well (especially insect-eating passerines), woodpeckers have an important part to play in forests. They hunt a large number of insects (in Europe the black woodpecker includes at least 70 in its diet) and the species most vigorously hunted are also the most abundant. Like many other animals (birds, predatory and parasitic insects, mammals) they help, therefore, to maintain populations of their prey within acceptable, fairly constant limits. By excavating hollows for their own nests they also provide tits, nuthatches, and flycatchers with ideal nesting sites. In Europe the presence of Tengmalm's owl depends in large measure on that of the black woodpecker, for this small nocturnal bird of prey almost invariably nests in the abandoned cavity of a woodpecker. The same thing happens in some places with certain ducks, such as the smew. Among other animals making free use of such cavities are bees, wasps and hornets, certain bats, and some rodents.

Lastly, woodpeckers speed up the transformation of dead trees into humus because, in order to reach wood-eating insects, they shatter the wood itself. The splinters, exposed to the elements, are attacked more quickly by fungi than is the untouched part of the trunk. Woodpeckers which drill holes in healthy trees do relatively little harm because they tend to occupy the same cavity for several years in succession. Instead of immediately chopping down such trees, it is better to leave them standing because they attract woodpeckers which simply renovate and enlarge the old cavity; otherwise the birds would be forced continually to attack new trunks.

The paradise jacamar (*Galbula dea*) has blue-black plumage, the throat being white; its tail measures 6¾ in (17 cm) long. Like other jacamars, it lives in thick lowland forests but often frequents open spaces such as river banks, glades, and plantations, where it can catch large quantities of insects.

▲ The jacamar perches on a branch, swoops like lightning and catches its prey after a rapid chase. It then returns to its perch. The species feeds on insects of all sizes, mainly dragonflies and butterflies.

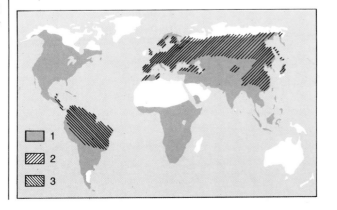

◀ 1) The birds belonging to the order Piciformes are found all over the world except for Australia, New Zealand, the polar regions, and almost all oceanic islands.
2) The great spotted woodpecker (*Dendrocopos major*) inhabits Eurasia and some parts of Mediterranean Africa. It generally lives in woods and forests. During winter, individuals from northern and central Europe feed largely on conifer seeds, especially those of the pine; and because seed production of such trees fluctuates from year to year, when supplies are scarce the woodpeckers have to move from one zone to another to avoid dying of hunger.
3) The Galbulidae are South American birds, living in Venezuela and Bolivia eastward to Guyana.

BLACK-THROATED HONEYGUIDE

Indicator indicator

Order Piciformes
Family Indicatoridae
Size Length 8 in (20 cm)
Distribution Africa
Nesting Brood parasite, in nest hollows of other birds
Chicks Nidicolous

The family Indicatoridae contains 15 species of medium-sized birds, measuring 5 – 8 in (12 – 20 cm) long, with fairly drab plumage, distributed over the tropical regions of the Old World. All seem to be sedentary, living in forests or more open terrain.

Honeyguides practice brood parasitism: the female lays the eggs in the nests of other birds. At least 30 species of birds are selected as hosts, and they belong to very different families.

It is not known how many eggs the honeyguides lay. Incubation varies in duration from 11 to 21 days. The baby, when hatched, is blind with naked pink skin. It is often the sole remaining occupant of the nest, for the hosts will have thrown out their own eggs; alternatively, their babies, deprived of food by the greedy honeyguide fledgling, will have died of hunger and likewise been ejected from the nest. In one case a baby honeyguide has been seen to remove the host's brood by itself. The chick will be reared for 35 – 40 days, much longer than for the host species.

Honeyguides are long famous for their habit of guiding men and the mammals known as ratels or honeybadgers to the nest of wild bees. Confronted by a man, the bird starts calling, unless it has previously been calling and is awaiting the latter's arrival. As soon as the man approaches, it flies off and repeats the process a little further on, perching on a tree. Eventually the bird halts close to a colony of bees. There it sometimes ceases to call and waits in a tree for up to one and a half hours; then it eats the wax and, more especially, the bees and larvae.

Black-throated honeyguide
(*Indicator indicator*)

▲ Honeyguides are noted for their habit of guiding humans and honey badgers or ratels (*Mellivora capensis*) to the hives of wild bees. Actually this behavior has been clearly observed only in two species, one of them being the black-throated honeyguide, and it is uncertain whether other members of the family act in this manner. As a result of detailed study, it has been established that the bird does not point the way directly to the bee colony but only to its vicinity, and evidently it does not always know exactly where the hives are situated. Despite a liking for wax, honeyguides do not feed exclusively on this substance; actually they eat all kinds of insects, as well as honey and pollen.

▼ The birds making up the family Indicatoridae (1) are found in the tropical regions of the Old World. The African species live south of the Sahara; of the Asiatic species, one lives in the Himalayas, another in Burma, Thailand, Malaysia, Sumatra and Borneo.
2) The toucans of the family Ramphastidae are birds of tropical America, from southern Mexico to southern Brazil and from Paraguay to northern Argentina.

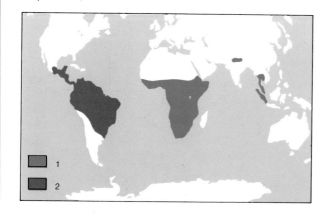

1

2

▲ A honey badger ripping open a nest of wild bees. The honeyguide awaits its turn to feed.

▼ The bird now consumes the larvae and wax left by the honey badger.

TOCO TOUCAN

Ramphastos toco

Order Piciformes
Family Ramphastidae
Size Length 24 in (60 cm)
Distribution South America
Nesting In tree cavities
Eggs 3 – 4
Chicks Nidicolous

There are about 40 species of toucans, which measure 12 – 24 in (31 – 60 cm). Toucans range from the Mexican state of Vera Cruz through Central America into South America as far as southern Brazil, Paraguay, and northern Argentina.

Toucans are poor fliers and essentially tree-dwellers. The majority of species have very bright, contrasting colors, with yellow, orange, red, blue or white zones on the underparts. There is no noticeable difference between males and females. The bill is both very long and very large, but, despite its enormous size, being largely hollow, is light in weight. The inside is honeycombed, with thin walls, yet is also remarkably solid. The precise function of such a huge bill is not known.

Most toucans are forest birds living on plains and in mountains, up to an altitude of 12,500 ft (3,800 m) in the Andes. Apart from rainforests they also inhabit wooded savannas, sparse woodland and river banks, provided there are trees.

The birds are monogamous and form permanent pairs. They nest in tree hollows, either natural cavities or holes drilled by woodpeckers and large barbets. The nest is generally situated high up, between 65 and 100 ft (20 and 30 m), but sometimes quite low. The floor is either bare or lined with a few shavings. Females lay 3 – 4 fairly rounded eggs. Both male and female take turns to incubate them.

Toucans feed mainly on fleshy, juicy fruit (bananas, guavas, etc.) and on the berries of wild or cultivated trees, but they also eat insects and the eggs of other birds.

▶ Toco toucan (*Ramphastos toco*). Like all toucans, this bird is essentially arboreal and not well suited to flying. Its bill, enormous but fairly lightweight because most of it is hollow, is 8¾ in (22 cm) long.

Keel-billed toucan
(*Ramphastos sulfuratus*)

Cuvier's toucan
(*Ramphastos cuvieri*)

Emerald toucanet
(*Aulacorhynchus prasinus*)

▲ Toucans' bills are brightly colored and have tiny teeth along the edges.

▶ In order to eat, the birds tear off fruit and sometimes toss it in the air so that it drops into the open beak. They drink like most birds, raising the head after each gulp.

PASSERINES

Passeriformes

The Passeriformes (perching birds) constitute by far the largest and most cosmopolitan order of birds, containing as it does some 5,110 species. The birds vary considerably in size, although none are very big, their length ranging from 3 to 38 in (7 to 95 cm); and they are fairly uniform in structure. They are distributed all over the world except for the polar regions and the great expanses of ocean, although they often cross the seas in the course of their migrations and erratic journeys.

Their life is mainly spent in trees, but some groups have become accomplished fliers as well. Many species settle close to water but avoid actual physical contact with it; exceptions to this rule are the dippers of the family Cinclidae, comprising four species with a mainly Holarctic distribution.

There is still much disagreement concerning classification into families and suborders. Among the many morphological criteria applied are the position of the tendons of the toes and the number of muscles in the lower portion of the larynx. Some authors distinguish the following four suborders: Desmodactylae, in which the flexor tendons of the third and rear toe are linked, the front toes also being joined at the base; Tyranni, with independent flexor tendons, and 1 – 2 pairs of muscles in the lower larynx; Suboscines, with independent toe tendons and 2 – 3 elastic muscles in the lower section of the larynx; Oscines, also with free tendons and 4 – 9 pairs of elastic muscles inserted into the two ends of the tracheal half-rings (these, also known as Passeres, are the so-called songbirds).

The distinctive song of the Oscines is produced by the vocal organ or syrinx and is usually very resonant, audible, in fact, for up to several miles. Its chief function is undoubtedly to mark out the bounds of personal territory; and as a rule, it is the male who sings. Among many species the capacity to sing is inborn and birds such as the warblers, the pipits, and the redstarts can sing perfectly without ever having heard a note uttered by one of their kind. Other species only manage to sing properly after listening to another

The nest of a passerine (order Passeriformes) is usually circular and made of blades of grass, rootlets, and leaves, all mixed together. It is placed at varying levels above the ground, depending on the family, and it is always kept tidy and clean. The chicks, born naked and blind, instinctively open their beaks wide, impelled by vibrations of the nest caused by the parents perching on it or singing in it. The inside of the mouth, depending on species, shows bright or contrasting colors designed to stimulate the feeding activities of the parents.

Willow warbler
(*Phylloscopus trochilus*)

individual of that species, as is the case with the greenfinches, the Old World warblers, the finches, etc. Still other species are able to imitate, with varying degrees of success, the calls and songs of other birds; they include those of the starlings, the blackbirds, the melodious warblers, etc. According to the geographical distribution of the various populations, there are also distinctive dialects which are learned by the young who live in a particular region. Typical examples include different finch and blackcap populations which can produce songs that vary surprisingly depending on the locality.

The majority of passerines are territorial. This territory can be defined as the space surrounding a nest or breeding site, which is defended mainly against other individuals of the same species. Birds which nest in cavities lay claim to a much smaller territory, usually the area immediately adjacent to the nest. The territory has a number of functions, and the main one, unquestionably, is to ensure that too many individuals do not assemble in the same area when breeding is in progress. Another purpose is to guard against predators; indeed, no matter how well concealed the nest, nor how cryptic the coloration of the eggs, these would not be sufficient precautions unless the nest were surrounded by ample space. Size of territory varies according to how much or how little food is available. As a rule the domain is defended by the male, who proclaims his ownership by singing and patrols it continuously, attacking any potential intruders.

The passerines generally build a tree nest, round in shape, from materials such as blades of grass, rootlets and interlaced leaves. Families such as the Hirundinidae (swallows) mix mud with saliva and attach the nest to rock faces or the walls of buildings. Species like the nuthatches and tree-creepers nest in tree cavities, which may either be natural or drilled by woodpeckers. The eggs of those species using these hollows, as well as those in closed nests such as the wrens and dippers, are usually white. A passerine nest may sometimes serve as a refuge outside the breeding season, especially during the night. The best known of these are the nests of the wren and of many members of the weaver family.

▼ Passerines mark out a territory of varying size around their nesting site. Some species, such as the robin, also fiercely defend their portion of winter territory.

▼ Typical bands of color on the head of certain passerines.

▲ Structure of the vocal mechanism or syrinx, situated at the point where the two bronchi join to form the trachea or windpipe.

trachea

lung

bronchus

air sacs

clavicular sac

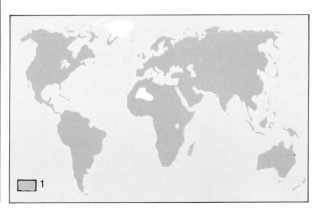

1

Desmodactylae
Lesser green broadbill
(*Calyptomena viridis*)

Suboscines
Superb lyrebird
(*Menura novaehollandiae*)

Tyranni
Vermilion flycatcher
(*Pyrocephalus rubinus*)

Oscines
Bullfinch
(*Pyrrhula pyrrhula*)

▲ Classification of this large and complex order still arouses controversy. The four suborders generally distinguished are: Desmodactylae, Tyranni, Suboscines, and Oscines, the last being the so-called songbirds.

◄ The Passeriformes constitute the largest and most cosmopolitan order in the bird kingdom. They are distributed everywhere, apart from the polar regions and the broad tracts of ocean, although the birds often cross these seas during migrations or erratic wanderings. 1) Distribution of the members of the order Passeriformes.

BROADBILLS
Eurylaimidae

WOOD-CREEPERS
Dendrocolaptidae

The broadbills of the family Eurylaimidae are divided into 8 genera and 14 species, all of which live in the tropical regions of the Old World. Difficulties in classifying this group of birds are such that they were once considered not to belong to the order Passeriformes at all. The family Eurylaimidae is composed of genera without any common relationship, including species which are clearly relics of a much bigger group ancestral to the Suboscines of South America and of which the Oscines of the Old World are counterparts.

General characteristics of the group are the following: body length varying from 5½ to 11 in (14 to 28 cm); a very large head and bill in relation to the rest of the body; 15 cervical vertebrae, one more than in all other passerines; and short, rounded tail and wings; vividly colored plumage (green, red, blue, and black). Their food is greatly varied according to species and dimensions. As a rule they feed on insects and small vertebrates such as fish, amphibians, and reptiles, as well as fruit. The birds live in the secondary tropical forests of Africa (four species) and of Borneo and Indochina. Normally they settle along the banks of rivers.

Little or nothing is known of their biology and behavior. Their voice is very loud and unmistakable. Thus Delacour's broadbill (*Smithornis capensis*) gives out a deafening croak quite unlike any sound normally associated with a bird; and the wattled broadbill (*Eurylaimis steerii*), inhabiting the Philippine Islands, lets out a shrill cry accompanied by a penetrating whistle. Some species, during the courtship ceremony, reveal areas of the back adorned with brightly colored feathers.

The birds build a characteristic pear-shaped nest which is suspended from a branch and may measure up to 6½ ft (2 m) in length. This nest has an opening at the side and is situated at some height above ground in a shady spot. It is constructed of interlaced scraps of grass, leaves, and rootlets, lined with lichens. The 3 – 5 eggs are uniformly

Lesser green broadbill
(*Calyptomena viridis*)

▲ Very little is known about the biology
◀ and behavior of the wood-creepers of the family Dendrocolaptidae, which live on the banks of streams and rivers in the heart of tropical forests. Food varies according to the species and dimensions of the birds, but consists principally of insects, small vertebrates, and fruit.

◀ Broadbills build a pear-shaped nest which is hung from a branch in a shady spot. The nest is made from interwoven scraps of grass, lined with lichen, and it has a side opening.

Banded broadbill
(*Eurylaimus javanicus*)

Long-tailed broadbill
(*Psarisomus dalhousiae*)

▲ Other members of the
family Eurylaimidae.

◀ 1) The family Eurylaimidae (broadbills) lives in the tropical regions of the Old World. The subfamily Eurylaiminae inhabits central and southern Africa and Asia from the Himalayas to Borneo; the subfamily Calyptomeninae is typical of eastern Asia, from Malaysia to Sumatra and Borneo.

pinkish-white, with red or purplish spots.

The family Dendrocolaptidae, from Central and South America, consists of small birds known as wood-creepers, which resemble tree-creepers and woodpeckers in appearance. There are about 47 species, with well-defined and fairly uniform characteristics. In shape these birds look much like the Oscines but this is simply a matter of convergence. The body is slender and the long tail is notable for its stiff-shafted rectrices, similar in appearance and function to those of woodpeckers. The plumage is usually highly cryptic and the birds are difficult to observe, not so much because of their nature, for they are fairly unafraid of humans, but because they blend so well with the trunks on which they are perched. Dominant colors of the plumage are brown and olive green.

The wood-creepers are adept in catching insects both on the surface and in the cracks of trees. Unlike woodpeckers, they do not ever use their bill to dig beneath the bark for food or to excavate a nesting cavity. The birds methodically explore the treetrunks, generally starting at the bottom and working their way up spirally. They may also hunt for food on the ground, especially on stumps and dead trees. They feed on a large variety of insects, and often make a meal of those fleeing from the relentless advance of army ants.

Wood-creepers do not normally form flocks but live alone or in pairs throughout the year. They are sedentary by habit, but may sometimes move about from one zone to another. Their voice is not particularly melodious and their vocal range not very extensive; but they are fairly noisy and in the breeding period produce drumming sounds on the trunks, like woodpeckers, although not at regular intervals.

These birds nest in natural cavities or the abandoned holes of woodpeckers. As a rule they choose a cavity with a very narrow entry so as to keep out any possible arboreal predators. They lay 2 or 3 circular eggs which are white, sometimes tinged with green. Among many species they are incubated by the female alone for about two weeks. The chicks hatch naked, with a tuft of feathers on the back. They stay in the nest for some 20 days, and the task of feeding is shared by both parents.

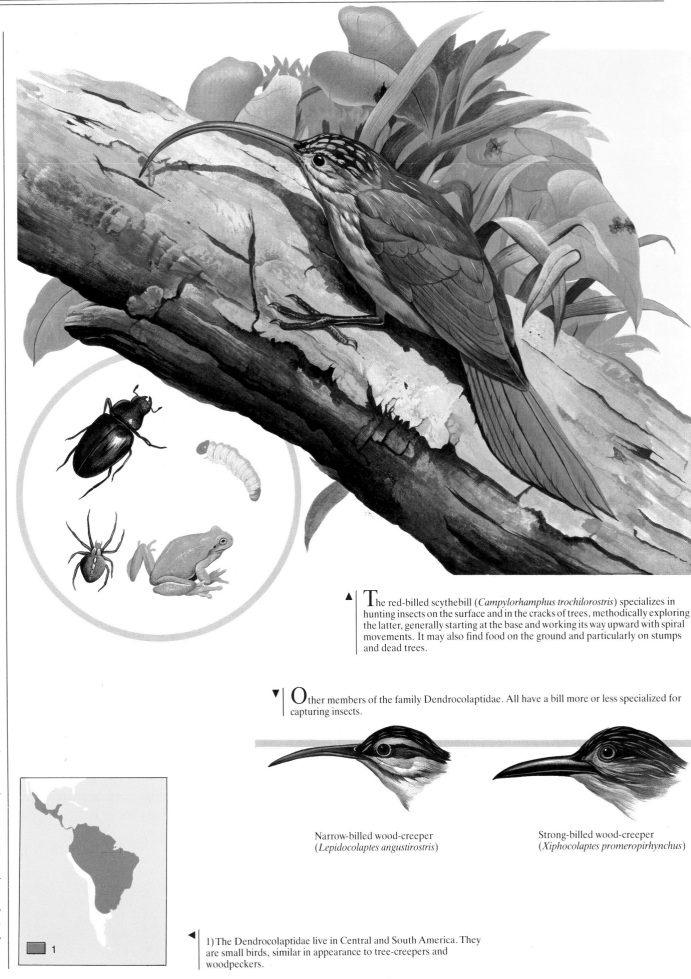

▲ The red-billed scythebill (*Campylorhamphus trochilorostris*) specializes in hunting insects on the surface and in the cracks of trees, methodically exploring the latter, generally starting at the base and working its way upward with spiral movements. It may also find food on the ground and particularly on stumps and dead trees.

▼ Other members of the family Dendrocolaptidae. All have a bill more or less specialized for capturing insects.

Narrow-billed wood-creeper (*Lepidocolaptes angustirostris*)

Strong-billed wood-creeper (*Xiphocolaptes promeropirhynchus*)

◄ 1) The Dendrocolaptidae live in Central and South America. They are small birds, similar in appearance to tree-creepers and woodpeckers.

1

OVENBIRDS

Furnariidae

TAPACULOS

Rhinocryptidae

The ovenbirds form part of the large New World suborder of Tyranni. They are all quite small, measuring between 4¾ and 11 in (12 and 28 cm), and the plumage is generally brown above and a paler tone, even white, depending upon species, below. The shades of brown vary, too, being tinged quite brightly with red in the rufous ovenbird, as its name suggests. Apart from size and color, the members of the family have little in common, their habits being enormously varied.

By and large, the greater number of Furnariidae live in areas of dense woodland growth. Some spend their entire life up in the highest strata of the tropical forests. Others, such as the leaf-scrapers, stick to the thick undergrowth where, by rummaging through the bushes and fallen leaves, they find all the food they need throughout the year. The true ovenbirds, along with some others, prefer parkland or even open country with few and scattered trees.

The ovenbirds are distributed almost continuously from southern Mexico to Tierra del Fuego, with outposts, occupied by a very few species, in the Falkland Islands and on Trinidad and Tobago, but not elsewhere in the West Indies.

Where breeding habits are concerned, information is available only for a comparatively small number of species, mainly those that nest in relatively open zones or build up their nests in places where they are clearly visible. Here again, behavior varies so much that it is only possible to select a few of the more striking examples. The one common characteristic is the white coloration of the eggs which, except in a very few instances, are free of marks and patterns. The number of eggs per brood is, as happens among tropical birds, fairly limited, normally 3 to 5.

Species with terrestrial habits, like the miners and earth-creepers, lay their eggs in holes in the ground, either natural cavities or pits dug by themselves. The incubation chamber is often situated at the end of a long tunnel. Some species, including some

Rufous ovenbird
(*Furnarius rufus*)

▲
▼ The mud nest of the rufous ovenbird, seen in cross-section, is shaped like a snail's shell of variable regularity. The internal incubation chamber is reached through the upper edge of the entrance corridor, which does not come in contact with the roof. Because of the poor air circulation inside, the nest really becomes an oven, and when it is time for them to leave, the fledglings are literally forced out so as not to be suffocated by the heat and the unbearable stench of the excrement.

◀ Food consists mainly of insects and spiders.

These birds have an almost continuous range from southern Mexico to Tierra del Fuego. The Neotropical regions offer an extraordinary number and variety of microhabitats and ecological niches; this fact, as well as the relative antiquity of the family, which has enabled the ovenbirds to stake first claim in many areas, accounts for their remarkable diversity. 1) Distribution of the family Furnariidae.

leaf-scrapers, nest in banks of earth along rivers; others use natural cavities in trees or nests abandoned by different species of the family. The spinetails build nests which are disproportionately large for their size, often high above the ground, consisting of huge piles of twigs. The most curious and elaborate nests, much more sturdy and secure, are those of the true ovenbirds. All species are capable builders but the most familiar and famous is the rufous ovenbird.

The 28 species of tapaculos making up the family Rhinocryptidae, wholly Neotropical in distribution and probably in origin, have a range extending to the southernmost parts of South America. They, too, belong to the suborder Tyranni, which are noted for certain rather primitive anatomical features, especially with regard to the vocal apparatus or syrinx.

The tapaculos vary in length from 4½ to 10½ in (11 to 26 cm), so that the smallest individuals are the size of a sparrow and the largest the size of a thrush. The scientific name of the family is derived from a strange anatomical characteristic, namely a movable flap or operculum which wholly covers the nostrils. Rhinocryptidae, therefore, stems from the Greek for "hidden nostrils."

Although they are not rare, the tapaculos are difficult to observe in the wild because they spend their whole life in the heart of dense vegetation. Those species that live in the dry grass of the vast expanses of pampas tend to be rather lighter in color, similar to many larks; and this cryptic coloration makes them additionally hard to see. The presence of these birds is generally given away by their voice, the typical song being a monotonous repetition of a few loud notes of varying tones.

Food consists mainly of insects but also spiders and other invertebrates; and plant substances have been found in the stomachs of some species. The birds nest on the ground, in excavated burrows, or in tree cavities, but certain species, such as the ocher-flanked tapaculo (*Eugralla paradoxa*), build a spherical nest with a side entrance, on a bush quite close to the ground. Materials are blades of grass, twigs, leaves, etc. Normally 2 to 4 eggs are laid; they are fairly large and completely white, although they may collect so much dirt that they appear to be spotted.

Ocellated tapaculo
(*Acropternis orthonyx*)

Crested gallito
(*Rhinocrypta lanceolata*)

The South American nickname tapaculo is derived from the bird's habit of holding its tail upright (somewhat like the European wren), boldly displaying its rump. Food consists chiefly of insects but may also include spiders, other invertebrates, and plant substances.

The scientific name of the family stems from a curious detail of anatomy: the mobile operculum or flap which wholly covers the nostrils. Rhinocryptidae is derived from the Greek words for "hidden nostrils."

Distribution is South American and exclusively Neotropical, even though some species reach the southernmost limits of the continent.
1) Distribution of the family Rhinocryptidae.

1

PITTAS

Pittidae

PHILEPITTIDAE

The 25 species of pittas making up the family Pittidae are birds which vary in length from 6 to 11 in (15 to 28 cm). Seen at close hand they look much like short-tailed thrushes, their plumage very often being quite colorful and the sexes sometimes looking alike and sometimes very different. Some of the birds are brilliantly colored, though a few are quite drab.

Rather wet undergrowth with plenty of rotting leaves and broken branches and twigs is the favorite habitat of the pittas, and this is typical of the tropical forests of Southeast Asia and the hotter parts of India and Africa. The birds live on or close to the ground, clambering about in the lower branches of trees and in bushes, avoiding flying, darting and hopping around in the leaf litter in search of food. As far as is known, this consists almost entirely of small animals, most of them invertebrates.

The fairly vivid coloration of many pittas might suggest that these plump little birds are easy to see in the uniform darkness of the tropical undergrowth; actually the contrasting tones of their plumage, set against the shimmering lights and shadows of the forest surroundings, make it all the more difficult to pick them out, so that they are almost invisible. It is their voice that most often gives them away, for the calls, though not markedly varied, are very resonant.

For much of the year pittas live separately or in pairs, and the infrequent groupings of a few individuals are probably due to the concentration in the same zone of single birds attracted by a local abundance of food. It is less likely that these are birds gathering together in preparation for migration, although some species do, in fact, migrate every year from breeding grounds to winter quarters, traveling surprisingly long distances for birds that have little capacity and hardly any inclination to fly.

The pittas build a bulky nest, circular or oval in shape, with the entrance to the incubation chamber situated at the bottom or the side; materials

Blue-winged pitta
(*Pitta brachyura*)

Scientists have borrowed the name pitta, which probably has an onomatopoeic significance from the Telegu language of Malaysia. Alternative vernacular names do these birds more justice, for they are variously known as jewel thrushes, resplendent thrushes, etc., because of their beautiful multicolored plumage, or ground thrushes, ant-eating thrushes, etc., referring to their habits.

The nest is a circular or oval structure of leaves, rootlets, and other plant matter. The inner chamber is neatly lined with a layer of mixed material. The nest is placed on the ground, on a low plant, at the base of a stump or among the roots of tall trees.

They live mainly on the ground in the dense wet undergrowth with its rotting leaves and broken branches, typical of the tropical forests of Southeast Asia and the torrid zones of India and Africa. Pittas avoid flying, being content to hop about and rummage in the litter for food, consisting of small vertebrates and, above all, invertebrates.

include leaves, rootlets, and other soft plant substances, and the inside is lined with mixed vegetation. It is placed on a plant close to the ground, at the base of a stump, among the roots of a big tree or, more simply, on the ground itself. The eggs have a very strong shell and look as if they were glazed, the basic color varying from cream to buff, with an overlaid, delicate pattern of violet or russet flecks and spots, often highlighted by grayish shading. As regards the number of eggs per brood, it is worth mentioning that in the Indo-Malaysian region there are 4 – 5, in Australia 3 – 4, and in Africa 2 – 3.

Pittas certainly appear to be birds with a strong territorial instinct, at least during the breeding season. This varies from region to region, although where climatic conditions are fairly constant this behavior pattern does not fluctuate much. Probably the territorial instinct is also exhibited when reproduction is over, but judging from reports there is no great display of aggressive behavior, with rare hostile encounters between individuals and birds sometimes assembling into small groups.

The Philepittidae are part of that large assembly of primitive passerines with a simple, distinctive arrangement of syrinx muscles, most of them having evolved and diversified in the New World, but represented in the Old World by the pittas, by the two genera of New Zealand wrens (variously known as Xenicidae and Acanthisittidae) and by these asities and false sunbirds.

The asities measure about 6 in (15 cm) long, with a rather squat body, a very short tail, a tiny bill, medium-sized wings and sturdy legs for gripping branches but also for moving about on the ground. The velvet asity lives in the rain forests of eastern Madagascar. Male and female have olive-green upperparts and are lighter green, with a darker scaly pattern, below. Solitary by nature, this bird gives out a loud whistling call every so often as it bustles around for small animals and berries in the thick undergrowth. Information is sparse concerning the two false sunbirds. The wattled species has iridescent upperparts and a long curving beak. The small-billed false sunbird is known only from a few stuffed specimens in museums, apparently collected from the eastern part of Madagascar.

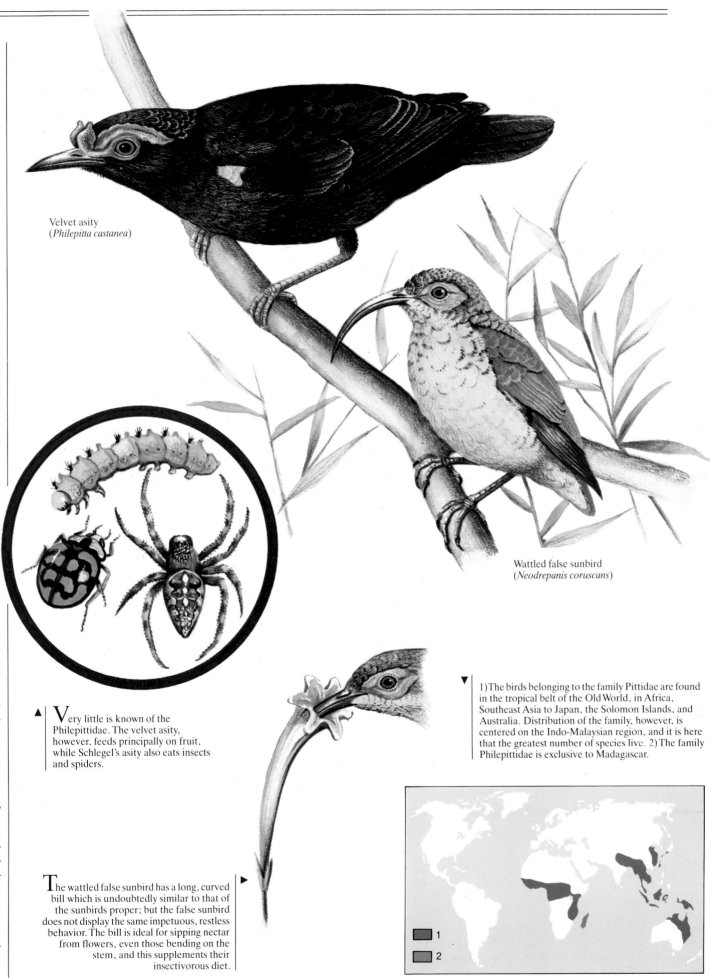

Velvet asity
(*Philepitta castanea*)

Wattled false sunbird
(*Neodrepanis coruscans*)

▲ Very little is known of the Philepittidae. The velvet asity, however, feeds principally on fruit, while Schlegel's asity also eats insects and spiders.

The wattled false sunbird has a long, curved bill which is undoubtedly similar to that of the sunbirds proper; but the false sunbird does not display the same impetuous, restless behavior. The bill is ideal for sipping nectar from flowers, even those bending on their stem, and this supplements their insectivorous diet. ▶

▼ 1) The birds belonging to the family Pittidae are found in the tropical belt of the Old World, in Africa, Southeast Asia to Japan, the Solomon Islands, and Australia. Distribution of the family, however, is centered on the Indo-Malaysian region, and it is here that the greatest number of species live. 2) The family Philepittidae is exclusive to Madagascar.

■ 1
■ 2

TYRANT FLYCATCHERS

Tyrannidae

MANAKINS

Pipridae

The family Tyrannidae, with between 362 and 384 species (the experts do not entirely agree), is by far the largest American family of birds and one of the biggest in the world.

The majority of tyrant flycatchers are concentrated in the tropical zones of America, including the West Indies and other Atlantic and Pacific islands; but at least 31 species travel in spring beyond the northern bounds of Mexico and seven fly as far as Alaska. The Tyrannidae are found in every kind of environment, from mangrove swamps, along the seacoasts up to the mountain snowlines, and from tropical forests to deserts. Nevertheless, most of the birds occupy secondary forests, the fringes of primary forests or open terrain, irregularly strewn with shrubs, and never too high above sea level. Only a few species venture deep into the jungle, but many can be seen in the tangled plant growth along the banks of rivers, lakes, and swamps.

Almost all members of the family live on their own or in pairs, but the fork-tailed flycatcher (*Muscivora tyrannus*) gathers in large flocks in the late afternoon, before settling for the night in one particular spot in the forest or mangrove swamp which offers the best protection.

Because of the simplified structure of their syrinx, the Tryannidae are not greatly gifted singers. Some, neverthe-less, give out quite a pleasant song, consisting of a few tirelessly repeated notes, heard mainly towards evening. Others emit loud and distinctive, but mostly unmusical, calls.

Courtship, in addition to vocaliza-tion, entails the display of colored zones of the body, especially on the head and rump, revealed by ruffling the feathers and lowering the wings.

Most of the species which nest in cavities lay white eggs, but those of the other species are varied, with reddish, brown or lilac spots on a white, cream, pale gray, or yellowish ground. Birds breeding in tropical regions lay 2, sometimes 3, and rarely 4 eggs,

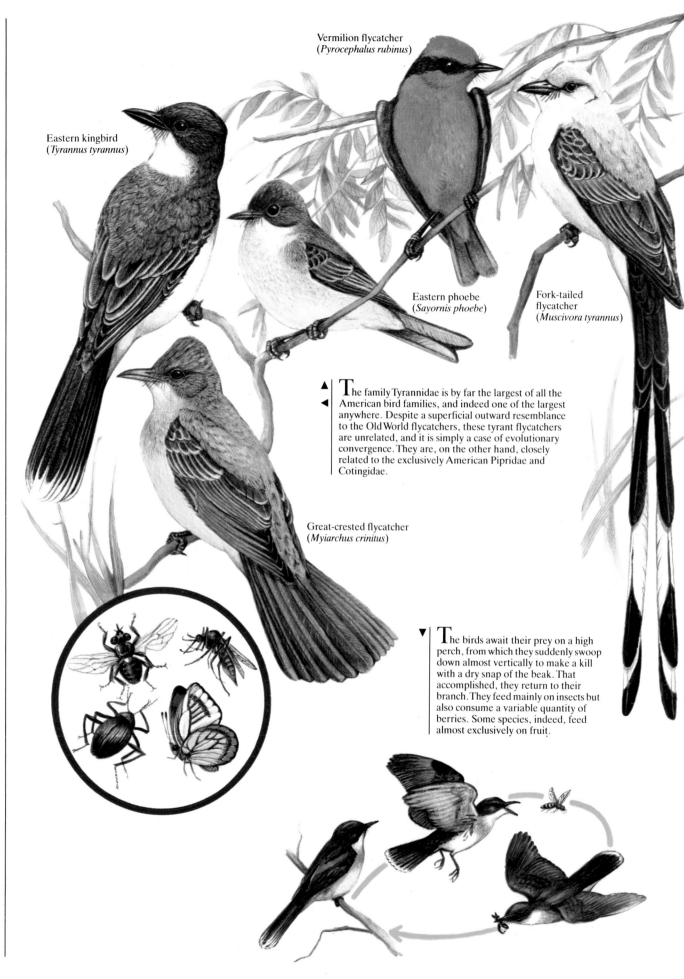

Vermilion flycatcher
(*Pyrocephalus rubinus*)

Eastern kingbird
(*Tyrannus tyrannus*)

Eastern phoebe
(*Sayornis phoebe*)

Fork-tailed flycatcher
(*Muscivora tyrannus*)

Great-crested flycatcher
(*Myiarchus crinitus*)

The family Tyrannidae is by far the largest of all the American bird families, and indeed one of the largest anywhere. Despite a superficial outward resemblance to the Old World flycatchers, these tyrant flycatchers are unrelated, and it is simply a case of evolutionary convergence. They are, on the other hand, closely related to the exclusively American Pipridae and Cotingidae.

The birds await their prey on a high perch, from which they suddenly swoop down almost vertically to make a kill with a dry snap of the beak. That accomplished, they return to their branch. They feed mainly on insects but also consume a variable quantity of berries. Some species, indeed, feed almost exclusively on fruit.

whereas those nesting at higher latitudes, whether north or south, lay between 2 and 6, usually 4 eggs.

Incubation appears to be the responsibility of the female on her own. Duration varies from genus to genus, but especially according to latitude. In temperate regions it fluctuates from 12 to 14 days and in tropical zones from 14 to 23 days.

The manakins of the family Pipridae are stocky birds, not much bigger than sparrows. The males of most species have glossy, brilliant colors, in which the predominantly black plumage is punctuated with precise red, white, blue, yellow, and orange markings. The females are mainly olive green with paler green and yellowish underparts.

The 53 – 56 species making up the family are irregularly distributed over the tropical zones of Central and South America, including the islands of Trinidad and Tobago, but most of them are concentrated in the basin of the Amazon and its tributaries. The manakins live in the dense undergrowth and in the forest canopy far above, generally only a little above sea level. They feed mainly on berries and small fruits, which they usually grip and tear off with a quick thrusting movement and then swallow whole. It is hard to say how much live food is included in the diets of different species, because of insufficient observations in the wild.

Females live a solitary existence, whereas almost all males exhibit social behavior in which they indulge in fantastic courtship displays, combining visual and acoustic signals, for much of the year. Such sounds comprise rattles and buzzes, produced by the very rapid vibrations of flight and tail feathers as well as snappings of the bill; by contrast, the calls emitted by the primitive vocal organs are simple, sharp chirps. Only among a few species in which there is no sexual dimorphism is there a real song, quite pleasant on the ear but rudimentary and very subdued.

Female manakins of species showing sexual dimorphism build a cup-shaped nest of moss, lichen, leaves, and other scraps of vegetation, with the edges barely raised, which is situated in the horizontal fork of a branch at a height varying from 5 to 70 ft (1.5 to 22 m). Two eggs only, with uneven cheshnut streaks on a gray-blue or light brown ground, are laid in the nest and incubated for 17 – 19 days.

▶ The Pipridae (manakins) are stocky birds, not much bigger than sparrows. They feed principally on berries, and small fruits, grasping them and breaking them off with a short leap and then swallowing them whole. Even the tiniest fruit flies are occasionally caught on the wing.

▼ During courtship, males of the genus *Manacus* set up little display grounds in forest clearings, all close together. When a female approaches, they begin to dance madly back and forth, producing a kind of buzzing noise, until the female chooses the individual whose performance has most pleased her.

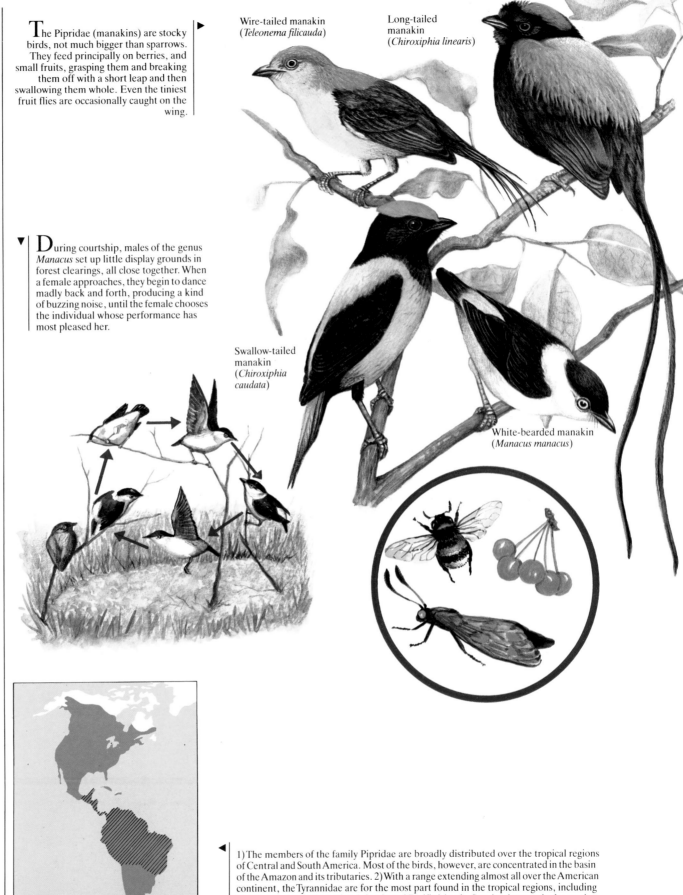

Wire-tailed manakin
(*Teleonema filicauda*)

Long-tailed manakin
(*Chiroxiphia linearis*)

Swallow-tailed manakin
(*Chiroxiphia caudata*)

White-bearded manakin
(*Manacus manacus*)

◀ 1) The members of the family Pipridae are broadly distributed over the tropical regions of Central and South America. Most of the birds, however, are concentrated in the basin of the Amazon and its tributaries. 2) With a range extending almost all over the American continent, the Tyrannidae are for the most part found in the tropical regions, including the West Indies, and on other Atlantic and Pacific islands. Species that nest in the tropics generally tend to be sedentary, but many of those breeding in the Andes migrate downward, the distances covered being variable but sometimes exceeding 13,250 ft (4,000 m).

1

2

PLANTCUTTERS

Phytotomidae

LYREBIRDS

Menuridae

The three species of plantcutters comprising the family Phytotomidae are small South American passerines grouped in a single genus (*Phytotoma*). The bill has serrated edges, making it particularly suitable for grasping buds, shoots, young leaves, and fruits, which are the principal constituents of the diet. Indeed, the parts actually consumed by these birds are severed so neatly that there is comparatively little harm done to the plants themselves.

The rufous-tailed plantcutter (*Phytotoma rara*) is found only in central and southern Chile. The bird frequents orchards, gardens, and open shrubland. During the southern spring pairs may also be encountered in the wooded valleys of the Andean foothills, up to an altitude of over 6,500 ft (2,000 m).

The male launches his territorial singing towards the end of winter, giving out a monotonous succession of totally unmusical croaks. Nesting begins in October and may continue until late December. The rufous-tailed plantcutter's nest is a flat, roughly assembled structure of twigs and rootlets, heaped together without much planning to form an open, shallow bowl. Such a flimsy construction would be too exposed at the top of a fruit tree or bush, so it is usually situated in spots where it is sheltered from wind and rain. The female lays 2 – 4 eggs, their color being blue-green with a scattering of brownish or blackish spots.

In Argentina, Uruguay, the Chaco region of Paraguay, and a part of Bolivia there is another species, the white-tipped plantcutter (*P. rutila*) which greatly resembles the rufous-tailed species. This bird is a fairly familiar inhabitant of the vast prairies of Patagonia. The third and last member of the family is the Peruvian plantcutter (*P. raimondii*), which only lives in the coastal areas of central–northern Peru.

One of the most familiar of all Australian birds, at least in appearance, is the lyrebird. Yet despite this, remarkably little is known of its habits

White-tipped plantcutter
(*Phytotoma rutila*)

▲ The bill of the plantcutters, short, strong and conical, has finely serrated edges, which enables the birds to take a firm grasp on the plants which are the main constituents of their diet; the edible parts are, in fact, sliced off so neatly that minimum damage is done to the rest of the plant.

◄ The nest is an open, shallow cup of roughly prepared vegetation and it stands up well to bad weather. The female lays 2 – 4 blue-green, brown-spotted eggs.

◄ 1) The Phytotomidae are distributed in the central–western parts of South America.

and origins. There are, in fact, two lyrebird species, making up the family Menuridae; and these birds, together with the strange little scrub-birds, likewise Australian, of the family Atrichornithidae, comprise one of the four suborders of the Passeriformes, the Menurae. The two species of Menuridae are the superb lyrebird (*Menura novaehollandiae*) and Albert's lyrebird (*M. alberti*). The birds are confined to eastern Australia, and with the exception of the scrub-birds, to which they may be related, they have no close links with the birds of any other countries.

The superb lyrebird builds a very bulky, dome-shaped nest with interlaced twigs and branches. It is placed on the ground, on a rock ledge, on a tree stump or even in the main fork of a tree. The female lays a single egg, brownish violet with gray-blue markings. For many years this was all that was known of the lyrebird, plus the fact that the male performs extraordinary courtship displays, showing off his tail and singing melodiously in the heart of the forest. Only recently, since the lyrebird has been afforded official protection and accommodated in two nature reserves near Melbourne and Sydney, has it become less shy and retiring, affording students the opportunity to observe its activity in all seasons and thus to reach important conclusions about its reproductive and general behavior.

Lyrebirds can certainly not be described as good fliers, and their aerial displays are confined to glides over the hillsides or awkward fluttering movements from branch to branch or rock to rock. But although most of their food is collected on the ground, among the dry leaves of the underbrush, the birds are quite at home in the trees and sometimes build a nest about 65 ft (20 m) up. Food, mainly animal, consists of worms, insects, crustaceans, and mollusks. The breeding season occurs in winter when there is evidently a plentiful and varied supply of such creatures. The courtship ceremonies begin in mid autumn and the nest is completed by May or June, built entirely by the female and insulated with feathers from her own breast. Constructed of interwoven branches, it has a roof of moss and a large, high incubation chamber in which the growing chick can stand upright. The whole period of incubation lasts about 6 weeks.

From the early years of the nineteenth century, lyrebirds were ruthlessly and senselessly hunted merely to satisfy the whims of feminine fashion and to adorn the walls of many an austere Victorian home. There were real fears for the survival of the species which, as the great naturalist and painter John Gould pointed out in 1840, ought to be regarded as the national emblem of Australia.

Food is found mainly on the ground among the dry leaves of the undergrowth. It consists principally of worms, insects, crustaceans, and snails.

Superb lyrebird
(*Menura novaehollandiae*)

The lyrebirds nowadays live in confined zones of Australia, their habitats being so inaccessible that they are very difficult to observe in the wild. 1) Distribution of the family Menuridae.

SKYLARK

Alauda arvensis

Order Passeriformes
Family Alaudidae
Length 7 in (18 cm)
Distribution Europe, Asia, North Africa
Nesting On ground
Eggs 3 – 4, occasionally 1 – 6
Chicks Nidicolous

The lark family is made up of approximately 70 species belonging to 15 genera, distributed all over the globe with the exception of South America and the islands of Oceania. They are birds of medium size, about 8¾ in (22 – 23 cm) on average, rather stout and often ungainly. Their sturdy legs are well suited for running. The feet are equipped with long claws, the rear toe in particular bearing a characteristically straight, long claw. The larks walk but never hop, and as a rule they are good runners.

The plumage is fairly modest and common to almost all species, the dominant color being light brown with darker streaks in varying number. The sexes do not differ, except for the black lark (*Melanocorypha yeltoniensis*) and the horned lark (*Eremophila alpestris*). Almost all larks are accustomed to living in arid regions of desert, subdesert or tundra; and they can endure long periods of drought without drinking water. The birds feed on a variety of wild and cultivated plant seeds, and offer insects to their young during the breeding season.

Virtually all the larks are sedentary and often territorial. They generally move about within their living area, according to the season. There are, nevertheless, some species, such as the short-toed lark (*Calandrella cinerea*) and the eastern calandra lark (*Melanocorypha bimaculata*), which are genuine migrants.

Males defend a well-marked territory and their song, heard both on the ground and in flight, is varied in tone but somewhat repetitive. Many detailed studies have been carried out with the skylark as central subject, especially in the breeding season, and various behavior patterns have been analyzed.

Larks are territorial birds and the early part of the breeding period is spent, especially by the males,

▲ During the breeding season the male skylark (*Alauda arvensis*) can be heard singing as he flies in circles, often at a great height, over his territory.

▶ Silhouette of the skylark in flight.

▼ The skylark has long, sturdy legs and long claws, suited both for walking and running. Food consists of seeds and insects collected from fields.

232

marking out and defending territory. Once pairs are formed, the birds restrict their activities to the bounds of their own domains. Pairs of larks generally return to the same areas occupied in previous years, and this applies also to the young who come back to their birthplaces. They emit at least three types of song during the reproductive period: one can be heard as the birds circle above their territory, often at a considerable height; a second is produced on the ground at various stages of courtship and territorial defense; and the third occurs when the birds are following each other around.

The males sing more frequently and for longer periods in the air while they are courting the female and when she is sitting on the eggs; frequency and duration do not appear to vary much at different times of day. Females can sing as eloquently as the males, but do so only now and then, when mating and building the nest.

The courtship behavior of the male in the female's presence is particularly fascinating. When he meets a female on his own territory, the male stages an exhibition, usually consisting of a series of small hops on the spot, head held vertically with beak pointed upward. Apart from this attitude, he may display other courtship movements, perhaps turning his back on her and fluttering his slightly outspread wings. The female's courtship attitudes are far less varied than those of the male. All she does is to invite him to copulate by turning towards him; and this invitation is extended repeatedly as the nest approaches its completion.

Neither member of the pair plays a clearly dominant role, and duties tend to be delegated. Having copulated, the female builds the nest, busying herself with this task mainly during the morning. Choosing a hollow in the soil, she smooths and shapes it with her body, then lines it with blades of grass. Egg laying begins early in the morning and continues at intervals of 24 hours. As a rule 3 or 4 eggs are laid, these being whitish gray, streaked with brown. Each female has 2 or 3 broods per season, and the number of eggs may vary from one clutch to another. The brooding female has well-developed incubation patches and instinctively assembles the eggs close together beneath her. The chicks hatch after 11 days without any assistance from her, and the shells are removed by both parents.

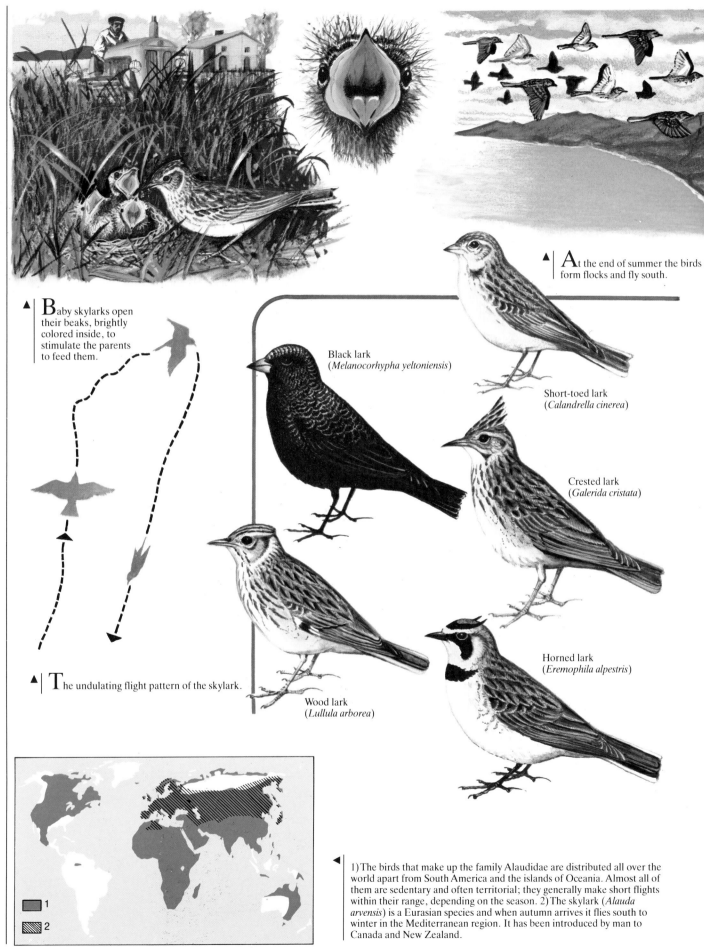

▲ Baby skylarks open their beaks, brightly colored inside, to stimulate the parents to feed them.

▲ At the end of summer the birds form flocks and fly south.

▲ The undulating flight pattern of the skylark.

Black lark
(*Melanocorhypha yeltoniensis*)

Short-toed lark
(*Calandrella cinerea*)

Crested lark
(*Galerida cristata*)

Horned lark
(*Eremophila alpestris*)

Wood lark
(*Lullula arborea*)

◄ 1) The birds that make up the family Alaudidae are distributed all over the world apart from South America and the islands of Oceania. Almost all of them are sedentary and often territorial; they generally make short flights within their range, depending on the season. 2) The skylark (*Alauda arvensis*) is a Eurasian species and when autumn arrives it flies south to winter in the Mediterranean region. It has been introduced by man to Canada and New Zealand.

SWALLOWS
Hirundinidae

The Hirundinidae family comprises species that are ideally adapted for life in the air. Swallows are elegant birds with long, pointed wings and a more or less prominently forked tail. The very compact plumage is usually dark and glossy. Highly skillful hunters of insects on the wing, they have a short, triangular-shaped bill. Most of their time is spent flying and chasing insects at various altitudes. When at rest on the ground, they move about awkwardly because of their short legs.

Swallows are very widely distributed all over the world, being absent only from the Arctic, Antarctic, and New Zealand. The family is, in turn, subdivided into two distinct subfamilies: Pseudochelidoninae and Hirundininae. The former group is represented by two species only, the African river-martin (*Pseudochelidon eurystomina*), from the river regions of Zaïre and Gabon, and the white-eyed river-martin (*P. sirintarae*), which has been sighted only in central Thailand during the winter. The other subfamily groups together a number of genera that all look much alike.

The genus *Hirundo*, which contains the largest number of species, comprises birds which build an open cup-shaped nest; one of the best known of these is undoubtedly the barn swallow (*Hirundo rustica*), an inhabitant of both the Old World and the New. It is a bird which has learned to live in town and country, and has, in fact, always followed in the wake of human expansion and settlement. The favorite habitat is open cultivated land. It nests inside buildings (stables, sheds, barns) but also in places much frequented by people, such as station entrances, subways, etc. Nevertheless, the barn swallow is not so commonly seen in large cities because of air pollution and the absence of places suitable for hunting insects.

Another very familiar bird in Europe and Asia is the house martin (*Delichon urbica*), which has shown itself to be the commonest and best adapted species to urban surroundings. It is recognized by its short tail, dark plumage on the back, and white on abdomen and breast. Among other swallows visiting Europe in the breeding season are the red-rumped swallow

The barn swallow (*Hirundo rustica*) adapts well to the presence of humans and has always followed in the wake of man's expansion and settlement. It finds many nesting sites in built-up areas but nowadays tends to shun cities because of pollution and lack of insects.

The feet, not very strong, are suited for gripping.

The bill is short and triangular, but the mouth opens very wide to capture insects in flight.

The silhouette of the swallow differs from that of a swift by virtue of the tail, which is made up of 12 feathers and is typically divided into two parts.

(*H. daurica*), the crag martin (*H. rupestris*), and the bank swallow (*Riparia riparia*).

Swallows are inevitably associated with migrations. In recent years, thanks to the increased practice of ringing, ornithologists have been able not only to track the migration paths but also to observe the movements of most species in their winter quarters. For the European and Asiatic swallows, Africa is the final destination when breeding is over.

The American swallows display equally marked migratory tendencies. In North America, for example, there are eight species and only three of these do not fly farther south for the winter than Mexico. The tree swallow (*Iridoprocne bicolor*), for example, winters in the southern parts of the United States, Central America, and the West Indies. The cliff swallow (*Petrochelidon pyrrhonota*), widespread all over the United States and Canada in the breeding season, chooses restricted wintering zones in Brazil and Argentina. The purple martin (*Progne subis*), distributed throughout North America, spends the winter in Brazil. But the longest migration, by far, is that of the American barn swallow (*Hirundo rustica erythrogaster*), which nests in all parts of North America and flies south to winter in South America from Colombia to Venezuela and from Chile to Argentina, sometimes reaching Tierra del Fuego.

Swallows have many natural enemies such as falcons, rats, snakes, etc., and to protect themselves against these they build nests sheltered by rock walls or eaves, or alternatively in natural cavities and, as in the case of the bank swallow, in burrows excavated by themselves. The sandy banks of rivers are the favorite sites for this last species to dig its long tunnels. In America the bank swallow is hunted extensively by birds of prey such as the American sparrowhawk (*Falco sparverius*), which takes its victim either on the wing or on the ground and steps up its predatory activities mainly when the baby swallows are about two weeks old. This is the time when the chicks come out to the tunnel entrance to receive food from the parents. When a sparrowhawk approaches a colony, the social call of the swallow in flight changes abruptly to an alarm cry, which immediately carries to the fledglings, who all retreat back into the tunnel.

▲ ◀ In spring, having just arrived at its nesting site, the swallow collects mud and grass for its nest, this being the only occasion when it perches on the ground. Construction of the nest takes from eight days to four weeks, depending on weather conditions.

Purple martin (*Progne subis*)

House martin (*Delichon urbica*)

Red-rumped swallow (*Hirundo daurica*)

Bank swallow (*Riparia riparia*)

▲ Top: the purple martin nests among rocks. Center: the bank swallow nests in colonies, building its nest inside horizontal tunnels dug into steep embankments. Bottom: the barn swallow builds a mud nest, shaped like a bowl, and sticks it to some natural or artificial projection; the nest is used for many years in succession.

◀ Swallows are famous for their seasonal migrations. The ringing technique enables ornithologists to study the routes which take the birds north to nest and south to spend the winter. 1) World distribution of the family Hirundinidae; 2) Breeding grounds.

235

MOTACILLIDAE, CAMPEPHAGIDAE

The family Motacillidae, comprising the wagtails and pipits, contains some 50 species, arranged in six genera, distributed nearly everywhere except for the Pacific islands and circumpolar regions. They are elegant, slim birds, usually with a long tail which is flicked rhythmically up and down.

Typical birds of watery environments, they can move fast over the ground, sometimes running long distances. Normally they walk but do not hop. The bill is long and thin, and the legs are well developed with fairly long claws on the toes. Some of the secondary flight feathers are almost as long as the primary remiges.

The birds feed, as a rule, on insects which are caught on or near the ground; but they also eat smaller quantities of vegetation (shoots, seeds, etc.).

Nesting is at ground level in natural cavities. The nest is fairly shallow and in it the female lays from 3 to 8 eggs, these being brown or gray with a sprinkling of spots.

The genera most common to Europe are *Anthus* and *Motacilla*. The first has a wide range and includes species such as the tawny pipit (*A. campestris*), the tree pipit (*A. trivialis*), the meadow pipit (*A. pratensis*), the water pipit (*A. spinoletta*), and the red-throated pipit (*A. cervinus*). All of these are birds with modestly colored and decidedly cryptic plumage. They live in open zones of grassland, uncultivated terrain and subdesert, from sea level up to high mountain regions. Territorial during the breeding season, they become gregarious in autumn and winter, forming large flocks. The song, similar in all species, is heard only in the breeding period.

Some species are regular migrants. One of these is the tawny pipit, which winters either in western or southern Africa, depending on populations. The species nests in North Africa. In winter it settles on the savanna, similar in composition to its breeding grounds. It is generally encountered in very dry regions. The tree pipit winters in tropical Africa, preferring open terrain with plenty of trees. The meadow pipit and the water pipit spend the winter in

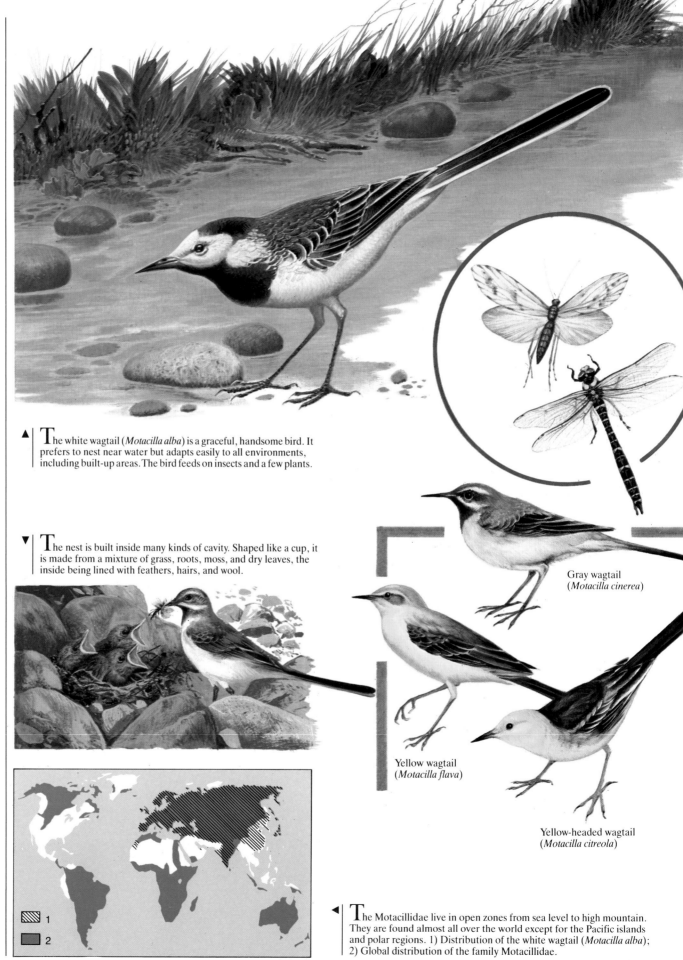

▲ The white wagtail (*Motacilla alba*) is a graceful, handsome bird. It prefers to nest near water but adapts easily to all environments, including built-up areas. The bird feeds on insects and a few plants.

▼ The nest is built inside many kinds of cavity. Shaped like a cup, it is made from a mixture of grass, roots, moss, and dry leaves, the inside being lined with feathers, hairs, and wool.

Gray wagtail
(*Motacilla cinerea*)

Yellow wagtail
(*Motacilla flava*)

Yellow-headed wagtail
(*Motacilla citreola*)

◄ The Motacillidae live in open zones from sea level to high mountain. They are found almost all over the world except for the Pacific islands and polar regions. 1) Distribution of the white wagtail (*Motacilla alba*); 2) Global distribution of the family Motacillidae.

North Africa and the Mediterranean region.

The second genus, *Motacilla*, contains the wagtails, graceful little birds brightly colored in yellow, white, and black tones, with fairly obvious sexual dimorphism. They are inhabitants of wet zones and stream and river regions. All are migratory, the species from Europe and Asia traveling long distances to Africa and the southern parts of Asia. The gray wagtail (*M. cinerea*), for example, winters in Africa north of the equator, although it is also encountered farther south. The same behavior is true of the white wagtail (*M. alba*). But the species which journeys farthest is undoubtedly the yellow wagtail (*M. flava*). Represented by some 11 subspecies, it spends the breeding period in Europe and Asia; then in autumn it flies to many parts of Africa south of the Sahara. During the winter large flocks may be seen around Lake Chad and Lake Edward. This species, so particular about its breeding habitat, adapts to other surroundings in Africa and is likely to be encountered almost anywhere, from city parks and gardens to cultivated areas.

The family Campephagidae comprising cuckoo shrikes and minivets, is made up of 70 species in eight genera. They are birds which live in the tropical parts of Africa, southern Asia, Malaysia, Australia, and the islands of the western Pacific. They generally live in primary and secondary forest zones. Strictly arboreal by nature, they prefer the upper parts of trees, where they perch and hunt insects. An exception to the rule is the ground cuckoo shrike, an Australian bird which lives on open terrain and moves freely about on the ground and hunts insects on the wing, in the manner of swallows and swifts.

Sedentary as a rule, the birds may fly short distances from season to season; but the ashy minivet (*Pericrocotus divaricatus*), a well-distributed species from northeastern Asia to Borneo and the Philippines, is a genuine migrant, flying towards the southeast.

Members of the family build a cup-shaped nest high in a tree, made of moss, lichen, roots, and dry grasses, all woven together. From 2 to 5 eggs are laid, according to the species, and these are usually whitish or greenish.

Cuckoo shrikes and minivets live in the treetops, flying around in search of the insects on which they feed.

Sexual dimorphism is marked: whereas females are gray-yellow, males boast bright colors, either red and black or orange and black.

Rosy minivet
(*Pericrocotus roseus*)

Scarlet minivet
(*Pericrocotus flammeus*)

1) The members of the family Campephagidae are widespread through the tropical regions of Africa, southern Asia, Malaysia, Australia, and the islands of the western Pacific. Sedentary as a rule, they make short seasonal migrations.

CINCLIDAE, TROGLODYTIDAE, MIMIDAE, PRUNELLIDAE

The dippers of the family Cinclidae are the only wholly aquatic Passeriformes. Their plumage is waterproof, a nictitating membrane keeps the eyes clear, the outer ear can be sealed by a fold of skin, and the nostrils are covered by membranous flaps. All these features, plus the thick plumage, help to protect and insulate the birds in the water. Furthermore, their bones are not very pneumatic, and this increases the specific weight, a great advantage under water.

This family is represented by four species belonging to a single genus. Two species inhabit the Palearctic region, the Eurasian dipper (*Cinclus cinclus*), found throughout Europe, North Africa, and Asia, and the brown dipper (*C. pallasii*) from central and eastern Asia. The other two species are American: the American dipper (*C. mexicanus*) lives in the western parts of North America and Central America, and the white-capped dipper (*C. leucocephalus*) is an inhabitant of the Andean range from Venezuela to Bolivia. All of them live in streams and rivers, feeding on aquatic insects and larvae which they often capture by diving under water. They build a circular nest of mosses near waterfalls. The birds defend their territory, sometimes outside the breeding season as well.

The wrens of the family Troglodytidae are distributed almost wholly in America. These little birds have plain plumage, usually chestnut brown with darker streaks. In shape they are much like dippers, although they do differ from these in certain important respects.

The song is very loud, has territorial significance, and can be heard throughout the year. In certain species, such as the common wren (*Troglodytes troglodytes*) and the bay wren (*Thryothorus migricapillus*), it can be heard above the sound of rushing water.

The wrens live in many different habitats and have truly exceptional ability to adapt to all environments.

The Eurasian dipper (*Cinclus cinclus*) lives beside mountain rivers and feeds on aquatic insects and larvae, as well as amphipods caught on the wing. It can swim very rapidly with the aid of its short, powerful wings. ▶

◀ The loud song of the wren (*Troglodytes troglodytes*), heard even over the roar of a waterfall, is surprising for such a tiny, inconspicuous bird. The wren feeds mainly on arthropods but often supplements this diet with vegetable substances and the eggs of other birds.

▲ Like all other representatives of the family Mimidae, the mockingbird (*Mimus polyglottus*) is a remarkable mimic and can imitate the song of many birds.

Their diet consists basically of arthropods, hunted on the ground, among bushes, along trunks, and in rock clefts. Some species also feed on vegetation and may consume the eggs of other birds. They are not normally migratory, but move about, according to the season, inside their territory.

The Mimidae family of mockingbirds is found only in the New World, from southern Canada to Tierra del Fuego, including the Galapagos Islands. Similar in shape and habit to thrushes, they measure from 8 to 12 in (20 to 30 cm). The body is slender and the tail long and rounded. The bill is curved. Plumage is not brightly colored, mainly reddish brown above and whitish below. Nor is there any evident sexual dimorphism.

The birds generally live in bushy zones and, in the case of the *Toxostoma* species, in subdesert regions. The species inhabiting more northerly parts of the range are migrants, moving south in the winter. The song is easily recognizable and many mockingbirds, particularly those of the genus *Mimus*, are, as their name suggests, in the habit of imitating other birds.

Mockingbirds are, as a rule, territorial. They build, sometimes in the space of a couple of days, a cup-shaped nest in the bushes. Only a few eggs are laid (2 – 3) and are brooded mainly by the female.

The accentors of the family Prunellidae represent 12 species in a single genus, and they live in Europe, temperate parts of Asia, and North Africa. They are birds of medium size, from 6 to 7 in (15 to 17 cm), with a stout body and strong legs. The bill is straight, fairly slender but sturdy. The wings are generally short and rounded, and as a rule the birds pursue an undulating flight near ground level. The plumage is drab with colors ranging from dark brown to gray.

Accentors are to be found in plains and mountains, even above the tree line, whether in wooded or open regions. The nest is a tidy cup, situated close to the ground. Depending on populations and zones, accentors may be either sedentary or migratory. Thus the hedge sparrow or dunnock (*Prunella modularis*) stays put over much of Europe but there are some populations which migrate for the winter to southwest Asia. Among sedentary populations there are also local movements down to the plains.

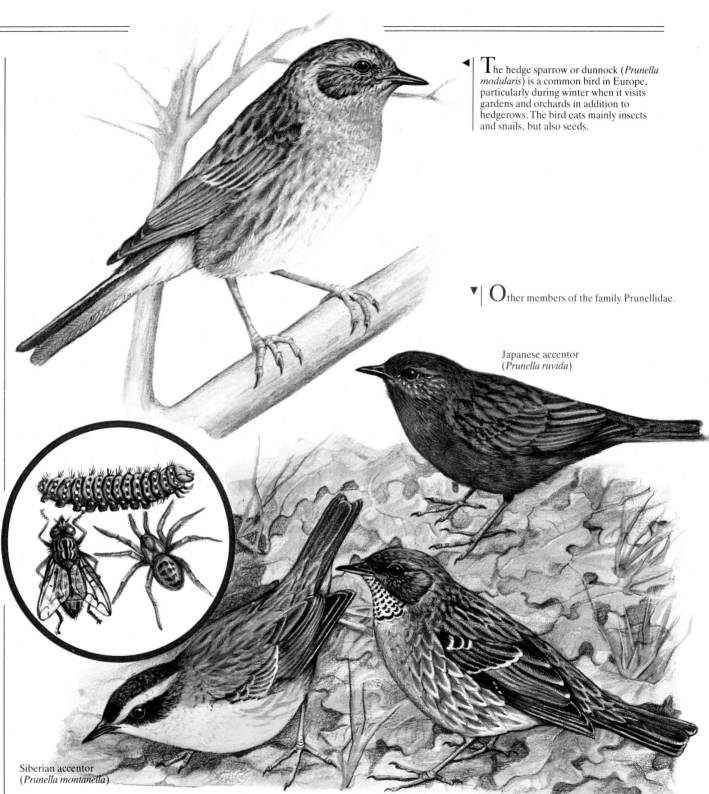

The hedge sparrow or dunnock (*Prunella modularis*) is a common bird in Europe, particularly during winter when it visits gardens and orchards in addition to hedgerows. The bird eats mainly insects and snails, but also seeds.

▼| Other members of the family Prunellidae.

Japanese accentor
(*Prunella ruvida*)

Siberian accentor
(*Prunella montanella*)

Alpine accentor
(*Prunella collaris*)

1) The family Prunellidae is found in Europe and temperate parts of Asia. 2) The family Mimidae is exclusive to America, from southern Canada to Tierra del Fuego, including the Galapagos Islands. 3) The range of the Cinclidae comprises Europe, North Africa, Asia, and the Americas. 4) The family Troglodytidae is almost wholly American, with a few representatives in Europe and North Africa.

PYCNONOTIDAE, LANIIDAE, VANGIDAE, PTILOGONATIDAE

Along with the cuckoo shrikes and minivets of the family Campephagidae, the bulbuls of the family Pycnonotidae are the most primitive of the songbirds. Their range extends from the intertropical belt of Africa south of the Sahara to Madagascar, Asia Minor, Iran, and eastwards to Japan and some of the Pacific island groups (Philippines, Moluccas, Indonesia, etc.).

The body is quite stout, the tail fairly long, the wings short and rounded, the legs small. Measurements vary from about 6 to 12 in (15 to 30 cm). The bill is slim and curved. Bright colors are mostly absent from the plumage, green, brown, and yellow predominating, and there is no marked sexual dimorphism. The song is not greatly varied but carries a long distance.

The diet consists in the main of fruit; and being gregarious by habit, when they invade cultivated areas in large flocks, the birds may cause much damage to orchards. Some species mix this diet with animal prey. Thus the yellow-crowned bulbul (*P. zeylanicus*) also feeds on freshwater snails, while the slender-billed greenbul (*P. gracilirostris*) includes ground arthropods in its diet. The nest is built at varying heights, from low bushes to the canopy of tall trees.

The shrikes of the family Laniidae are sturdy birds with a specialized bill.

The Laniinae (true shrikes) are inhabitants of Africa and Eurasia. There are 25 species which belong to three genera (*Lanius, Urolestes* and *Corvinella*). Most of them live in open tree country such as the African savannas and Eurasian steppes. Their favorite type of habitat is open terrain with plenty of natural vantage points such as hedges, small trees, and bushes, where they can perch and keep a close watch on the surroundings, like falcons, for prey. Food consists of insects, small rodents, reptiles, and sometimes birds. These miniature birds of prey often create "larders" by impaling

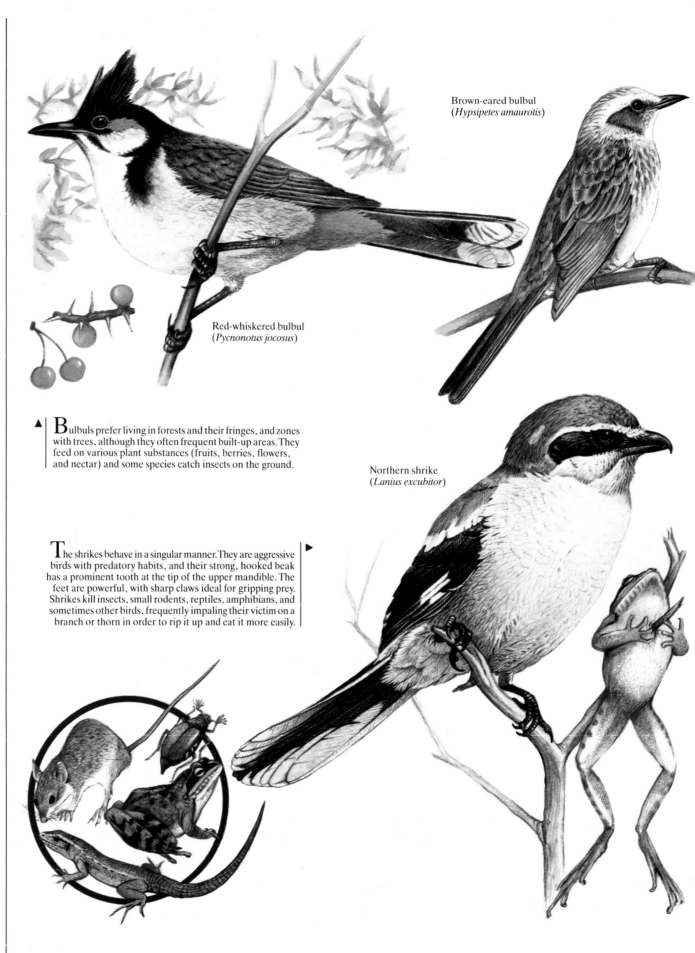

Brown-eared bulbul
(*Hypsipetes amaurotis*)

Red-whiskered bulbul
(*Pycnonotus jocosus*)

▲ Bulbuls prefer living in forests and their fringes, and zones with trees, although they often frequent built-up areas. They feed on various plant substances (fruits, berries, flowers, and nectar) and some species catch insects on the ground.

Northern shrike
(*Lanius excubitor*)

The shrikes behave in a singular manner. They are aggressive birds with predatory habits, and their strong, hooked beak has a prominent tooth at the tip of the upper mandible. The feet are powerful, with sharp claws ideal for gripping prey. Shrikes kill insects, small rodents, reptiles, amphibians, and sometimes other birds, frequently impaling their victim on a branch or thorn in order to rip it up and eat it more easily. ►

their victims on thorns, sometimes sticking more than one animal on a single plant.

Although all shrikes which nest in Europe show a preference for open country, some have ecological niches which enable them to coexist without competition. The red-backed shrike, for instance, lives in sparse forest with an undergrowth of thorn bushes, and on the fringes of sunlit woods. It is also encountered in roadside hedges. The northern or great gray shrike (*L. excubitor*) prefers even more exposed terrain with an abundance of thorny plants. The woodchat shrike inhabits warm, dry regions with little forest cover, frequenting olive groves, orchards, and Mediterranean scrubland with isolated trees and plenty of free space. In central Europe this bird is often seen along tree-lined roads and on telegraph wires.

The lesser gray shrike prefers to nest in zones where there is more tree cover, in contrast to the northern shrike, and the trees it selects are taller than those frequented by the woodchat shrike. So it tends to choose surroundings with thicker vegetational growth and is less reliant than other shrikes on the presence of thorn bushes.

The family of vangas or vanga shrikes (Vangidae) is native to Madagascar, with one species also found in the Comoro group. Altogether there are 13 species. There is much variation in the color of plumage within the family. The white-headed vanga is blue above and white below, and the helmet bird has a reddish back and very dark tips to the flight feathers. Vangas live in groups and build low, cup-shaped nests in trees, at varying heights. The females lay 3 – 4 whitish or greenish eggs. Very little, however, is known about these birds.

The members of the subfamily Ptilogonatinae (silky flycatchers) are American in distribution, living in the western part of North America and in Central America. They inhabit wooded mountain zones and have fairly vivid plumage, especially when flying. Measurements vary little. The birds generally feed on insects, but supplement this diet with small fruits. Insects are caught in flight, as among the true flycatchers, after a swoop from a high vantage point. The nest is a shallow cup in which 2 – 4 greenish eggs are laid, depending on species. Often the female incubates them alone.

The Bohemian waxwing is a characteristic bird of the taiga with conifers, birch, and poplars. Populations move about in various ways, either making short journeys in small numbers (sometimes reaching Hungary) or full-scale migrations which may take them to North Africa, though usually occurring at ten-year intervals. Such invasions are generally preceded by an enormous increase in the numbers of sexually mature individuals and an expansion of breeding grounds.

Japanese waxwing
(*Bombycilla japonica*)

Bohemian waxwing
(*Bombycilla garrulus*)

Woodchat shrike
(*Lanius senator*)

Phainopepla
(*Phainopepla nitens*)

Lesser gray shrike
(*Lanius minor*)

The members of the family Vangidae are found on the island of Madagascar, where they live in social groups. They also inhabit the Comoros.

Four-colored bush shrike
(*Telophorus quadricolor*)

White-headed vanga
(*Leptopterus viridis*)

Other species of birds belonging to the family Laniidae.

Red-backed shrike
(*Lanius collurio*)

MUSCICAPIDAE, TURDINAE

Modern taxonomists tend to assemble about a thousand species in the family Muscicapidae, although previous classifications allotted them to a number of separate families. However, for the sake of convenience, we shall list and describe separately the most important subfamilies.

The subfamily Turdinae is the largest group in the family, with more than 300 species, belonging to many genera, distributed almost everywhere, except for Antarctica. They live in many different surroundings, including desert and tundra, displaying their great adaptability. By and large they are terrestrial birds although some are strictly arboreal. Indeed, much of their food, consisting mainly of earthworms, grubs, grasshoppers, and snails, is found at ground level. In autumn and winter they feed freely on berries and all kinds of fruit, often collecting such food, where abundant, in large groups.

Although the birds behave quite sociably in winter, when spring returns there is open hostility among individuals of the same species, particularly the males, each of whom eventually acquires territory which is defended against all other male intruders.

The members of this subfamily are incomparably rich in vocalization, and no other group can boast so many genuinely musical singers; two of the most celebrated are the nightingale (*Luscinia megarhynchos*) and the white-rumped shama (*Copsychus malabaricus*). These and other species generally communicate two types of message through song, one to drive away rival males from their territory, the other to attract a female seeking a partner for nest building.

Once the pair is formed, the female takes the initiative in building the nest and preparing to incubate the eggs. The situation of the nest is a further indication of the thrushes' remarkable powers of adaptation, for it may be found on the ground, among the lower branches of a bush, high up in a tree, in a rock cleft, or in a natural cavity. Species which are most accustomed to human presence, such as the American robin (*Turdus migratorius*) and the black

Thrushes are sturdy, undemanding birds. They originally inhabited woodland zones but have since learned to adapt to all kinds of man-made transformations, so that nowadays they are very familiar visitors to parks and gardens, enlivening the scene in spring with their melodious songs. They find food mainly on the ground, this being comprised of worms, snails, and insects. In autumn they consume large quantities of berries and wild fruits.

Dusky thrush
(*Turdus naumanni*)

Wood thrush
(*Hylocichla mustelina*)

Mistle thrush
(*Turdus viscivorus*)

Blackbird
(*Turdus merula*)

Song thrush
(*Turdus philomelos*)

American robin
(*Turdus migratorius*)

1) The subfamily Turdinae contains a fairly large number of birds found almost everywhere, apart from Antarctica.
2) Distribution of the robin (*Erithacus rubecula*). 3) Distribution of the nightingale (*Luscinia megarhynchos*).

1
2
3

bird (*T. merula*), place their nest in the most unlikely spots, not necessarily quiet and undisturbed. The nest is always compact and well made, the materials including grass, moss, lichens, and often clay.

The 2 – 6 eggs are light in color, often green or blue, with variable speckling. After about two weeks of incubation the chicks hatch, and they stay in the nest for another couple of weeks, fed by both parents.

Given the large number of species, this subfamily has of late been divided into several homogenous smaller groups; but again for the sake of convenience, we shall restrict these to two only: one containing the true thrushes; the other, more varied, comprising the wheatears, the robins, the nightingales, etc.

The true thrushes are the largest members of the entire family Muscicapidae, and the 60 or more species are fairly uniform in appearance. The majority belong to the genus *Turdus* which is the most widely distributed of all genera in the subfamily. In recent times many of these birds have become part and parcel of the daily scene. Originally they only inhabited wooded areas, but nowadays, particularly in the more industrialized countries, they have adapted to life in towns and cities.

The second major grouping of the subfamily Turdinae contains genera that are highly diversified, indicating the addition of many newly evolved species, yet also including some very primitive relict forms. Apart from leading a secluded life, these birds are all melodious and versatile singers. The most notable among them is the nightingale, celebrated by poets and composers, and regarded throughout the western world as the very symbol of natural song. Were it not for its voice, the nightingale would surely go unnoticed. The uniformly brown plumage and shy habits make it a difficult bird to observe, but from April to June its whereabouts are given away by its unrivaled singing.

Even better known and more friendly is the robin, a tiny bird which has become highly popular because of its cheerful appearance and merry song as it boldly hops and flutters around the garden. This happens particularly in winter, when strong curiosity and a complete lack of fear encourage the robin to come looking for food, often venturing as far as the windowsills.

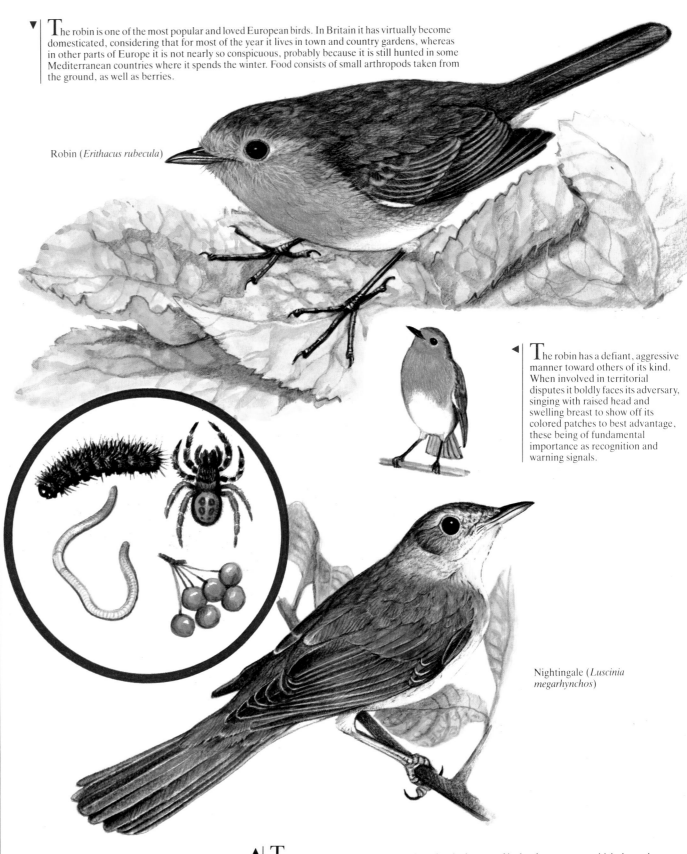

▼| The robin is one of the most popular and loved European birds. In Britain it has virtually become domesticated, considering that for most of the year it lives in town and country gardens, whereas in other parts of Europe it is not nearly so conspicuous, probably because it is still hunted in some Mediterranean countries where it spends the winter. Food consists of small arthropods taken from the ground, as well as berries.

Robin (*Erithacus rubecula*)

◀| The robin has a defiant, aggressive manner toward others of its kind. When involved in territorial disputes it boldly faces its adversary, singing with raised head and swelling breast to show off its colored patches to best advantage, these being of fundamental importance as recognition and warning signals.

Nightingale (*Luscinia megarhynchos*)

▲| The nightingale is known everywhere for the beauty of its loud, pure song, which the male even produces during the night from his tree or bush. His repertory consists of simple phrases or even one repeated note steadily increasing in strength, punctuated by short periods of silence. Harsh and sharp notes are included but the sharp ones are so pure and clear that they can often be heard a mile away. As he concludes his song, the male stakes his claim to individual territory against all rivals.

BABBLERS
Timaliinae

With some 280 species, the babblers and their relatives make up one of the largest groups of Passeriformes. As might be expected in such a big subfamily, there is a marked difference in morphological features. Some birds are the size of a wren, others as large as a magpie; and the plumage may either be plain brown or brightly colored in red, green, and yellow. The shape of the bill varies, too, among the many species; it may be very short and feeble, long and curving, short and heavy, or long and straight. Nevertheless, there are certain physical characteristics which are common to almost all these birds, sufficiently to typify the entire group. Thus the plumage is long and soft, especially in the rear part of the body; the fairly short, rounded wings are held slightly away from the body; and the tail, which may be quite long, is left drooping. The birds tend, therefore, to be poor fliers, preferring to hop about on the ground on their thick, sturdy legs.

The babblers are chiefly found in Eurasia, but the group has also colonized Africa, Madagascar, Indonesia, New Guinea, and Australia.

These birds feed on insects and, in some measure, on fruit. Their typical habitat is the dense forest undergrowth, and here they dart about, usually near the ground, hopping and scurrying around with brisk flicks of wings and tail to find shelter among the fallen trunks, lianas, and dead leaves. As they go, they emit a continuous series of noisy cries.

In the breeding season most of the birds build a cup-shaped nest or one formed more like a dome, with a side entrance, usually placed on trees or bushes, but sometimes on the ground, in tufts of grass or among reeds; more rarely, a mud nest is attached to a rock ledge or outcrop. Eggs, too, vary greatly in appearance and may be white, green, blue or pink, often with streaks or spots. The 2 – 7 eggs are incubated either by both parents or by the female alone, while rearing the young is also a joint responsibility.

Red-capped babbler
(*Timalia pileata*)

◄ **A**ppearance and size vary considerably among the various species of babblers. These highly gregarious birds live all year round in small groups which chatter noisily in thickets and undergrowth. The red-capped babbler, in particular, frequents bamboo thickets, feeding on insects and often seeds and fruits as well.

▼ **O**ther representatives of the subfamily Timaliinae.

Large scimitar babbler
(*Pomatorhinus hypoleucos*)

White-eyed quaker babbler
(*Alcippe nipalensis*)

White-crested laughing thrush
(*Garrulax leucolophus*)

Peking robin
(*Leiothrix lutea*)

Jungle babbler
(*Turdoides striatus*)

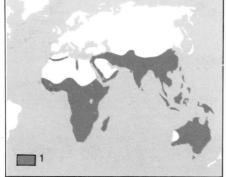

◄ **M**ost of these birds are found in Eurasia but they have also widely colonized Africa, Indonesia, Australia, and New Guinea. One species, the bearded reedling (*Panurus biarmicus*), has crossed Europe and reached the British Isles, having expanded its range steadily since taking refuge in tropical climes during the Pleistocene glaciations. An even stranger case is that of the wren-tit (*Chamaea fasciata*) from the western coasts of North America, for this is the only member of the group to be found in the New World, where the subfamily's ecological niche is occupied by the antbirds (Formicariidae), very different in structure but similar in appearance and habits as a result of evolutionary convergence. 1) Distribution of the subfamily Timaliinae.

MUSCICAPINAE, PACHYCEPHA-LINAE

The birds of the subfamily Muscicapinae, collectively known as flycatchers, make up a large assembly of more than 300 species living in the three continents of the OldWorld. The European flycatchers, being birds of temperate and northern latitudes where habitual prey, in the form of flying insects, is only abundant in summer, are all migratory.

The species whose breeding behavior has probably been studied in greatest detail is the pied flycatcher (*Ficedula hypoleuca*), a common bird of central–northern Europe. When the males return from their winter quarters, they immediately look for a suitable nesting hole. Females, who arrive afterwards, are attracted here by his singing and special postures.

One of the most brilliantly colored species is the black-and-yellow flycatcher (*Ficedula narcissina*), an Asiatic bird from China and Japan which winters in the Philippines and Indonesia. It lives in all kinds of forest and its song is one of the most melodious of the entire subfamily. Another gifted singer is the blue and white flycatcher (*Cyanoptila cyanomelaena*), which inhabits the thick vegetation of valleys and mountain slopes in eastern Asia, migrating to Indochina and Indonesia.

Fairly similar to the flycatchers, the birds of the subfamily Pachycephalinae have a sturdier body, a rounded head and a hooked beak rather like that of a shrike. They are known both as thickheads and whistlers, the latter name being derived from their shrill calls. The basic colors of the plumage are yellow, green, and black, and as a rule there is no sexual dimorphism.

Whistlers live in the bush and forests of Australia, New Guinea, Malaysia, the Philippines, and many oceanic islands. Food consists principally of insects but some species also feed on berries. The large, roughly constructed nest is situated close to the ground, being built almost wholly by the female, who also incubates the 2 or 3 eggs.

Pied flycatcher
(*Ficedula hypoleuca*)

▲ Like the other flycatchers, the pied flycatcher has a broad, flattened bill, encircled by hairs. The male is notable for his conspicuous black-and-white plumage. Particularly skillful hunters on the wing, flycatchers are very common in central and northern Europe. Their food consists in the main of flying insects, chiefly flies and small butterflies.

B efore taking wing, the bird waits for its prey motionless on a branch. Another characteristic attitude is the nervous, rapid fluttering of tail or wing. ▶

Asian paradise flycatcher
(*Terpsiphone paradisi*)

Blue and white flycatcher
(*Cyanoptila cyanomelaena*)

Rufous-bellied niltava
(*Niltava sundara*)

Red-breasted flycatcher
(*Ficedula parva*)

Yellow-bellied fantail
(*Rhipidura hypoxanta*)

Narcissus flycatcher
(*Ficedula narcissina*)

WARBLERS
Sylviinae

Containing approximately 340 species, this is the largest and apparently the least heterogeneous group in the whole family Muscicapidae. Whereas the other major subfamily, that of the thrushes, is represented in all five continents, thus proving their antiquity, the warblers of the subfamily Sylviinae are not found in America, except for one species confined to Alaska and two members of the genus *Regulus*, often treated as a separate group.

The huge subfamily Sylviinae can be further divided into groups which contain genera resembling one another partly in physical features but even more by virtue of common ecological needs. There is, for example, the group of aquatic warblers, represented most typically by the genera *Cettia* and *Acrocephalus*. These small birds look much alike, being uniformly colored gray or brown above and creamy white below, sometimes with darker stripes.

A member of the former genus is the bush warbler (*C. diphone*), so famed for its melodious and varied song that it occupies a prominent place in Japanese folklore. A fairly similar species, Cetti's warbler (*C. cetti*), is also found in Europe, but of even more interest to ornithologists than its song is the spectacular manner in which it has extended its breeding area; during the last few years, in fact, this bird has spread from the Mediterranean region to much of central Europe and has even reached the British Isles.

The reed warblers of the genus *Acrocephalus* are the most notable songbirds of swamps and marshes in the Old World. These birds are specialized inhabitants of aquatic vegetation consisting mainly of tall herbaceous plants with a continuous, dense spreading habit. Particularly widespread species are the great reed warbler (*A. arundinaceus*) and the reed warbler (*A. scirpaceus*), both birds of the marshes, building characteristic, well-fashioned nests hanging on the vertical reed stems a little above the water surface. This ensures that the clutch is protected from many predators, though not from the cuckoo, which frequently parasitizes these

Like the majority of other Sylviinae, the bush warbler of Japan almost always lives in the heart of low vegetation, sheltering there at the slightest alarm. Its presence, however, is revealed by its persistent, unmistakable call. Warblers feed mainly on insects and other small arthropods, but at the end of summer they may supplement this diet with berries and fruits.

Bush warbler
(*Cettia diphone*)

Some species of warblers.

Cetti's warbler
(*Cettia cetti*)

Grasshopper warbler
(*Locustella naevia*)

The characteristic cup-shaped nest of the great reed warbler, firmly anchored to the stems of reeds.

Fan-tailed warbler
(*Cisticola juncidis*)

When singing, the reed warbler perches in a prominent position.

Reed warbler
(*Acrocephalus scirpaceus*)

Great reed warbler
(*Acrocephalus arundinaceus*)

species, probably because the nest is so easy to locate. The birds of the genus *Locustella*, including the grasshopper warbler (*L. naevia*), constitute a very special group. They closely resemble the reed warblers in appearance and often share the same habitat.

Another very homogeneous group is that of the grass or fan-tailed warblers of the genus *Cisticola*, with some 70 species. This group has always presented taxonomists with problems, especially with regard to the differences and similarities among the various species. Although broadly distributed in tropical and subtropical regions, they almost certainly originated in Africa, where three quarters of the known present-day species reside. One of them, the common fan-tailed warbler (*C. juncidis*), has a very extensive distribution from North Africa to eastern Asia and Australia, and is also the only one found in Europe.

Woods, hedges, and scrub are the undisputed haunts of the members of the genus *Sylvia*, most typical of the entire subfamily. The type of vegetation preferred makes it possible to divide the group further into predominantly arboreal species, such as the blackcap (*S. atricapilla*) and the garden warbler (*S. borin*), and those which live in bushes, like the whitethroat (*S. communis*), making characteristic song flights. The plumage of these species is always plain brown or gray above, lighter below, with little sexual dimorphism, except in the case of the blackcap, the male's head being black and the female's reddish.

These timid little birds, too, are noted for their songs, often loud and melodious, and in some cases so complex and distinctive as to rank among the finest anywhere, particularly striking examples being those of the blackcap and the garden warbler. Much simpler, and perhaps for this reason even more individual and useful for identification, are the songs of the *Phylloscopus* species. They are very active birds, and for most of the time can be observed indefatigably exploring every inch of a bush or tree.

The most ingenious nest builders of all, however, are the tailorbirds of the genus *Orthotomus*. Of the ten known species, all from southern and southeastern Asia, a few are garden visitors, the most familiar being the common tailorbird (*O. sutorius*), which frequently lives and nests close to homes.

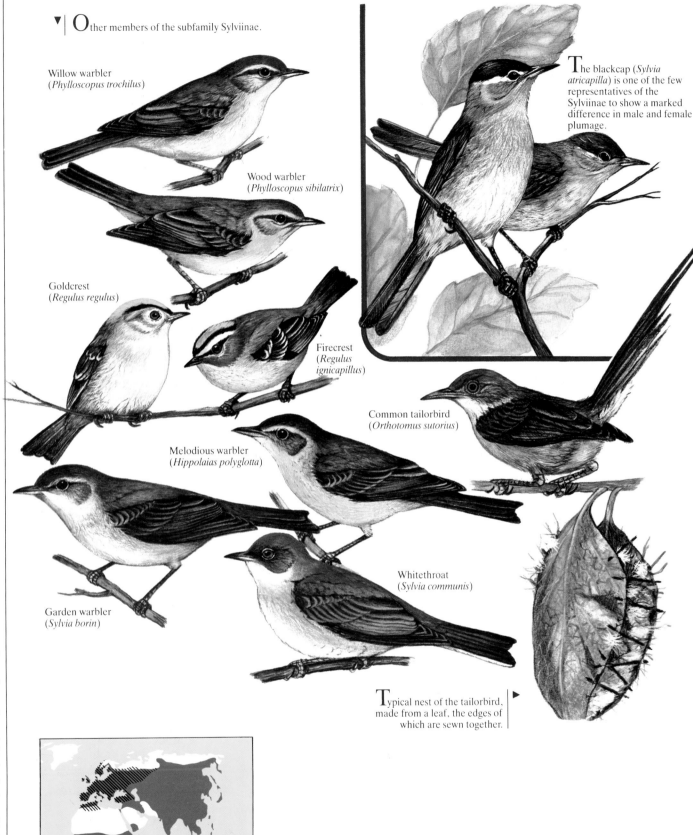

▼| Other members of the subfamily Sylviinae.

Willow warbler
(*Phylloscopus trochilus*)

Wood warbler
(*Phylloscopus sibilatrix*)

Goldcrest
(*Regulus regulus*)

Firecrest
(*Regulus ignicapillus*)

Melodious warbler
(*Hippolaias polyglotta*)

Garden warbler
(*Sylvia borin*)

The blackcap (*Sylvia atricapilla*) is one of the few representatives of the Sylviinae to show a marked difference in male and female plumage.

Common tailorbird
(*Orthotomus sutorius*)

Whitethroat
(*Sylvia communis*)

Typical nest of the tailorbird, made from a leaf, the edges of which are sewn together. ▶

◀ The Muscicapinae, commonly known as flycatchers, contain more than 300 species distributed over three continents of the Old World. Although these birds appear very different from the other subfamilies (Turdinae, Timaliinae, Sylviinae, and Pachycephalinae) of the large family Muscicapidae, the group as a whole shows various similarities in behavior and morphology to the Sylviinae, especially in the case of the 50 or so species inhabiting New Guinea. 1) Distribution of the subfamily Muscicapinae. 2) Distribution of the blackcap (*Sylvia atricapilla*), a member of the Sylviinae.

1   2

Paridae,
Sittidae,
Certhiidae,
Climacteridae

The family Paridae is comprised of 65 species commonly known as titmice or tits. The true titmice, belonging to the subfamily Parinae, are hole dwellers, for they not only nest but also spend the winter nights in cavities. The nest proper is a soft mass of hairs, feathers, and moss, on which the female lays her white, brown-spotted eggs, numbering up to 15 in temperate zones but rarely more than 4 in the tropics. Only the female attends to incubation whereas both parents care for the chicks.

Insects form the main source of food at all seasons, particularly when the numerous fledglings are being reared, for then the parents have to collect enormous quantities of grubs, spiders, and flies. During the winter much of the food consists of vegetation in the form of fruit, berries, and seeds. A few species, above all from northern climes, also have the habit of storing surplus food in bark or on the ground: this will be consumed when provisions are scarce but may equally be forgotten.

The typical members of the Sittidae family are commonly known as nuthatches, this name being derived from the fact that, in addition to insects, the birds collect acorns and nuts which, after being wedged into cracks in the bark, are hacked open with sharp raps of the bill. Some species are known as creepers, referring to their trunk-climbing abilities, and alternative names in other languages are associated with their typical use of mud to build a nest.

Nuthatches are small, stocky birds with a broad head and a short tail which, not being stiff, is useless for climbing; this is the job for the short, sturdy legs with their very long toes and claws. The bicolored plumage is also characteristic, the upperparts being gray and the underparts white; very often a black band extends from the sides of the head through the eyes. The beak is long and slender but quite

The golden whistler (*Pachycephala pectoralis*) is a representative of the small subfamily Pachycephalin (family Muscicapidae). It differs from the flycatchers having a broad head and a hooked beak.

The great tit (*Parus major*) is the best known and investigated member of the Paridae, being a very familiar garden bird that adapts itself easily to human presence. It often avails itself of artificial nests and in winter is a frequent visitor to bird tables. The tits, in general, consume large quantities of butterfly larvae as well as many other arthropods. In fall and winter they feed freely on berries and dried fruits.

Other representatives of the Paridae.

Blue tit
(*Parus caeruleus*)

Crested tit
(*Parus cristatus*)

Azure tit
(*Parus cyanus*)

Long-tailed tit
(*Aegithalos caudatus*)

Coal tit
(*Parus ater*)

Siberian tit
(*Parus cinctus*)

Sultan tit
(*Melanochlora sultanea*)

strong. The 20 or so species of the genus *Sitta* have a typically Holarctic distribution, namely Eurasia and North America, where they inhabit mixed woods and forests, only rarely leaving these haunts in winter to make short journeys; southern populations, on the other hand, are strictly sedentary. Other species live exclusively in rocky regions.

Nuthatches produce a variety of calls but the song proper normally consists of single, rapidly repeated notes which sometimes sound like a prolonged trill or even a whistle.

Particular mention must be made of one very highly specialized species which lives in mountainous regions, namely the wall-creeper (*Tichodroma muraria*). This is a splendidly colored bird with broad wings, a slender, curved beak and long, delicate legs which make it easy to clamber up vertical and projecting rock faces.

The tree-creepers belonging to the family Certhiidae bear a stronger resemblance to woodpeckers than do the nuthatches. Nowadays only five species are recognized, all very similar and all belonging to the genus *Certhia*. Their distribution is confined to wooded areas, both deciduous and coniferous, in the northern hemisphere. The common tree-creeper (*C. familiaris*) is found in the woods of North America and Eurasia, being the most widely diffused species. All the birds are sedentary, at most making brief moves to lower altitudes in winter; at that season they forgo their solitary habits, and in colder regions will collect together inside a single cavity to spend the night there, huddling close to one another.

The small family Climacteridae contains only six species, also known as tree-creepers, but only found in the eucalyptus and acacia woodlands of Australia. These birds illustrate once more the phenomenon of evolutionary convergence, for the same feeding habits have led to remarkable similarities, both in appearance and behavior, to the tree-creepers of the family Certhiidae.

In these species, too, the plumage is brownish above and white below, providing perfect camouflage as they clamber up and down the trunks like the true tree-creepers. The bill is likewise long and curving, ideal for digging out insects from bark, while legs, toes and, above all, claws are well developed.

Common tree-creeper
(*Certhia familiaris*)

Eurasian nuthatch
(*Sitta europaea*)

Red-browed tree-creeper
(*Climacteris erythrops*)

The wall-creeper (*Tichodroma muraria*) is a magnificent bird specialized in living in rocky, high mountain regions. It clambers over vertical rock faces with the aid of its long, slender legs, probing with its curved beak into cracks for the insects on which it feeds.

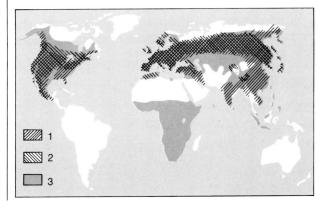

These birds, well suited to clambering up and down tree trunks and feeding on insects hidden beneath the bark, belong to three distinct families: the common tree-creeper to the Certhiidae, the nuthatch to the Sittidae and the red-browed tree-creeper to the Climacteridae.

1) Distribution of the members of the family Sittidae, commonly known as nuthatches. 2) Distribution of the tree-creepers, five species making up the family Certhiidae. 3)The family Paridae, containing the tits or titmice, is found all over the world, except for South America, Madagascar, Australia, and Polynesia.

DICAEIDAE, NECTARINIIDAE, ZOSTEROPIDAE, MELIPHAGIDAE

The flowerpeckers of the family Dicaeidae are small birds related to the sunbirds (Nectariniidae) and honeyeaters (Meliphagidae), with a distribution from southern China and India through the Philippines and Indonesia to Australia, Tasmania, and the Solomon Islands. The greatest diversity of forms is in New Guinea, where more than one quarter of the 56 known species live, and where it is thought this family originated. The most typical members of the family (the 35 species of the genus *Dicaeum* and the six of the genus *Prionochilus*) measure approximately 3½ in (9 cm). The short, slender, and slightly downward-curving bill has sharp edges, finely serrated at the tip. The tubular tongue, with its brush-like bristles, is made for sipping nectar. In most species the male's plumage is vivid, with black, white, and red being most evident, while almost all the females are a sober greenish yellow. These birds, inhabiting the middle and upper strata of the primary and secondary forests, are especially addicted to the berries of the tropical mistletoe (genus *Loranthus*).

The sunbirds of the family Nectariniidae are found almost exclusively in the warm zones of the Old World. Most of them live in Africa south of the Sahara (including Madagascar and other islands in the western Indian Ocean); indeed, over half the presently known species inhabit these regions. The range of the family also extends through Egypt, Arabia and the Middle East, India, Tibet and southern China, Ceylon, Indochina, the Philippines, New Guinea, and the Solomon Islands, to the northeastern tip of Australia. Food consists primarily of nectar, sugary pulps, and insects, caught both on the wing and from a still position. The spider-hunters, as their name would suggest, specialize in removing spiders from their webs. Many African species (*Cinnyris*, *Nectarinia*) have developed particularly

Mistletoe flowerpecker
(*Dicaeum hirundinaceum*)

Scarlet-backed flowerpecker
(*Dicaeum cruentatum*)

▲ The Dicaeidae or flowerpeckers feed especially on the berries of tropical mistletoe, the seeds of which, expelled with the feces, are scattered all over the place. Whereas substances of vegetable origin pass quickly through the digestive tract, small insects are diverted into the muscular stomach, shaped like a cecum. Here the proteins are decomposed and assimilated, the chitinous residues being regurgitated through the mouth in the form of small pellets.

Malachite sunbird
(*Nectarinia famosa*)

Olive sunbird
(*Nectarinia olivacea*)

▲
▼ With their lively colors and long, curved bills, the sunbirds of the family Nectariniidae look like hummingbirds. This superficial resemblance is misleading for they are only related to honeyeaters and flowerpeckers. They live in the warm parts of the Old World, frequenting almost all habitats from sea level up to more than 13,000 ft (4,000 m) on the southern slopes of the Himalayas.

Collared sunbird
(*Anthreptes collaris*)

Variable sunbird
(*Cinnyris venustus*)

Little spider hunter
(*Arachnothera longirostra*)

long, curving beaks for extracting nectar from deep flower corollas, either while perching or hovering briefly in midair. Short-billed species, like those of the genus *Anthreptes*, collect nectar more simply by perforating the outer base of the corollas. Sunbirds are not gregarious although fairly large flocks may sometimes be seen in areas with abundant flower growth.

Commonly known as white-eyes because of the spectacles of white feathers around the eyes, the Zosteropidae make up a homogeneus group related to the Meliphagidae and Nectarriidae, ranging over a vast area which comprises the Ethiopian, Oriental, Palearctic, southern Oriental, Australian, and Oceanic regions.

The white-eyes inhabit the upper layers of the primary forest but are more often seen in secondary woodland, on the edges of clearings, in plantations, in gardens and in mangrove swamps along the seashore. They have a habit of moving around in small, tight groups comprising males and females, so that if they are blown off-course by strong winds they can more easily settle in new zones. It is this capacity to adapt and expand that has enabled the birds to colonize some of the remotest islands in the Indian and Pacific Oceans, including the desolate Macquarie group at latitude 55°S.

The Meliphagidae family's center of diffusion is in Australia and New Guinea, but a few species range westwards as far as the Moluccas and Bali, to Hawaii and the Japanese island of Bonin in the north, to Samoa in the east, and southwards to New Zealand. The Meliphagidae occupy a large variety of habitats, including the different strata of the primary and secondary forest, open eucalyptus savanna, the enormous sandy wastes of the Australian interior, mangrove swamps and dense alpine scrubland up to a height of 12,000 ft (3,600 m).

Local forms along the mountain slopes of New Guinea regularly move up and down, while those living at or near sea level make seasonal migrations or simply wander here and there, feeding on the flowers of different eucalyptus species. Thrusting their beak or whole head deep into the large blossoms and deep corollas, the birds play an important role as carriers of pollen. In addition to nectar, they feed on ripe fruits, berries and sometimes small vertebrates.

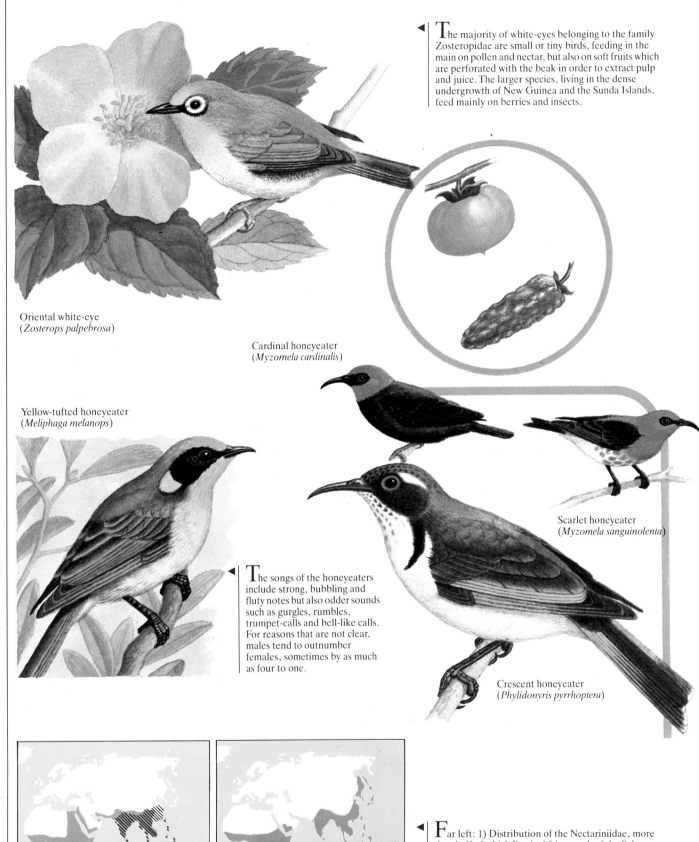

Oriental white-eye
(*Zosterops palpebrosa*)

Yellow-tufted honeyeater
(*Meliphaga melanops*)

Cardinal honeyeater
(*Myzomela cardinalis*)

Scarlet honeyeater
(*Myzomela sanguinolenta*)

Crescent honeyeater
(*Phylidonyris pyrrhoptera*)

The majority of white-eyes belonging to the family Zosteropidae are small or tiny birds, feeding in the main on pollen and nectar, but also on soft fruits which are perforated with the beak in order to extract pulp and juice. The larger species, living in the dense undergrowth of New Guinea and the Sunda Islands, feed mainly on berries and insects.

The songs of the honeyeaters include strong, bubbling and fluty notes but also odder sounds such as gurgles, rumbles, trumpet-calls and bell-like calls. For reasons that are not clear, males tend to outnumber females, sometimes by as much as four to one.

Far left: 1) Distribution of the Nectariniidae, more than half of which live in Africa south of the Sahara. 2) Distribution of the Dicaeidae, birds of southern Asia and neighboring islands. Left: 1) The Zosteropidae have a vast range. 2) The family Meliphagidae has its center of diffusion in Australia and New Guinea. The two large species from southern Africa have recently been included among the Nectariniidae, mainly for geographical reasons.

EMBERIZIDAE

According to the most recent, authoritative opinions, this family includes more than 500 species as different in outward appearance as buntings, tanagers and honeycreepers, previously allotted to separate families. On the other hand, there are so many similarities that it no longer seems reasonable to preserve the former distinctions so they are grouped together in this one vast family.

The buntings of the genus *Emberiza*, which have given their name to this subfamily and the whole family, are physically much alike. They are all small birds with fairly long legs and strong feet; and the short, conical bill, often swollen inside, indicates a diet based in principle on seeds, although other types of vegetable substances and insects are also consumed.

Buntings live for preference on level plains or in areas of scattered woodland and scrub; tropical species inhabit dense forests, especially around the fringes, but none of these birds can be truly described as having arboreal habits or tendencies. As a rule they nest in a low bush or tree, but never at a great height; the nest is often placed directly on the ground but alternatively in tree cavities or among rocks. It is built entirely by the female and consists of a fairly bulky bowl of grass, roots, and moss, lined inside with softer material such as hairs and feathers. The 2 – 6 eggs may be plain white or marked with dark wavy lines or spots. They are incubated by the female alone or by both parents, and the two adults normally rear the brood together.

The subfamily Cardinalinae is closely related to the Emberizinae, and comprises almost 40 species, commonly known as cardinals, grosbeaks and pyrrhuloxias.

The cardinals have a distinctly tropical distribution and are found only in the New World; the species which breed north of Mexico are often migratory and fly south to spend the winter in the northern parts of South America. The best known species is the cardinal (*Cardinalis cardinalis*), inhabiting the temperate regions of North America, ranging south to central America.

Another member of the subfamily is

Long-tailed bunting
(*Emberiza cioides*)

The buntings are birds of open spaces, notably grasslands and sparse woodlands, but they often frequent cultivated zones, nesting in hedges. Food consists mainly of seeds but the chicks are fed on insects and other arthropods. The long-tailed bunting is a very common bird of the Japanese countryside.

Yellowhammer
(*Emberiza citrinella*)

Reed bunting
(*Emberiza schoeniclus*)

Snow bunting
(*Plectrophenax nivalis*)

The most typical representative of the subfamily Cardinalinae is the cardinal (*Cardinalis cardinalis*), which lives on the borders of woods and feeds on seeds, insects, and berries. It is a familiar visitor to town gardens and bird tables.

Song sparrow
(*Melospiza melodia*)

Painted bunting
(*Passerina ciris*)

252

the dickcissel (*Spiza americana*), a typical bird of the western prairies of the United States, which exhibits polygamous behavior.

The subfamily Thraupinae is incomparably the most resplendent group of birds in South America, noted for the vivid coloring of their plumage. For sheer variety of brilliant hues and patterns, the small species of the genera *Tangara* and *Euphonia* are quite unrivaled. Both males and females possess the same multicolored plumage and the livery does not change from season to season. On the other hand, the species of the genus *Piranga*, from the United States and Canada, vary considerably according to sex and season.

Relatively few tanagers live in the darkness of the dense jungle, for most of them flutter continuously to and fro in the high forest canopy. Like other species who live in the treetops, they roam abroad to feed and nest among isolated groups of trees in glades and plantations. Some species live in the undergrowth but none is known to seek food directly on the ground. Fruit is the main ingredient of the diet, but this is almost always supplemented by insects.

One branch of this subfamily consists of a small and highly specialized group, namely the honeycreepers, sometimes regarded as a separate subfamily (Coerebinae) and sometimes treated as a proper family. They are small birds with a thin, curved beak, and the males, in particular, are splendidly colored in blue, turquoise, and green. Probably their most interesting feature is the tongue, which has been greatly modified in keeping with their very special diet: curved and fringed at the edges, subdivided at the tip, and in certain cases in the form of two tubes.

Two notably unusual species, also South American, are often allotted distinct subfamilies but have an uncertain place in classification. One is the plush-capped tanager or finch (*Catamblyrhynchus diadema*), a rare inhabitant of the high forests of the Andes, very little known, and the other the swallow tanager (*Tersina viridis*).

Finally, another group of very interesting birds assigned to the family Emberizidae is that consisting of the Darwin finches (subfamily Geospizinae). These 14 homogeneous species live exclusively on the Galapagos Islands, except for one of them which is found on the Cocos Islands, 600 miles to the northwest.

Plush-capped finch
(*Catamblyrhynchus diadema*)

Paradise tanager
(*Tangara chilensis*)

Swallow tanager
(*Tersina viridis*)

Western tanager
(*Piranga ludoviciana*)

▲ Tanagers and related species also belong to the family Emberizidae. Their name is a European version of the word *tangara* given to the birds by certain Amazon tribes. Tanagers are not greatly gifted singers and their vocal repertory is poor; this lack of aptitude is probably related to their territorial behavior, little evident and often completely absent.

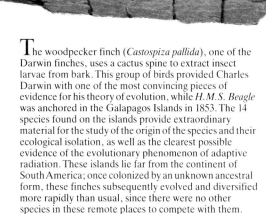

The woodpecker finch (*Castospiza pallida*), one of the Darwin finches, uses a cactus spine to extract insect larvae from bark. This group of birds provided Charles Darwin with one of the most convincing pieces of evidence for his theory of evolution, while *H.M.S. Beagle* was anchored in the Galapagos Islands in 1853. The 14 species found on the islands provide extraordinary material for the study of the origin of the species and their ecological isolation, as well as the clearest possible evidence of the evolutionary phenomenon of adaptive radiation. These islands lie far from the continent of South America; once colonized by an unknown ancestral form, these finches subsequently evolved and diversified more rapidly than usual, since there were no other species in these remote places to compete with them.

◀ The bill of honeycreepers is long and slender for extracting nectar from flowers.

Red-legged honeycreeper
(*Cyanerpes cyaneus*)

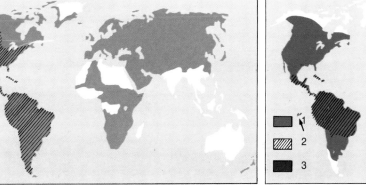

◀ Far left: 1) The cardinals (subfamily Cardinalinae) are tropical birds from the New World only. 2) The buntings (subfamily Emberizinae) have a wide distribution and have given their scientific name to the entire family; although the majority of species inhabit the Palearctic region, they make up a relatively recent group descended from American colonizing forms. Left: 1) The tanagers (subfamily Thraupinae) are almost exclusively South American. 2) Distribution of the honeycreepers, sometimes allotted a subfamily (Coerebinae) to themselves. 3) The Darwin finches (subfamily Geospizinae) are found only in the Galapagos Islands in the Pacific.

PARULIDAE, DREPANIDIDAE, ICTERIDAE

The family Parulidae is a relatively homogeneous group containing some 120 species found in the Nearctic and Neotropical regions, ranging from the southern limits of the Canadian tundra by way of Central America and the West Indies almost to Patagonia. It comprises two groups, the American warbler or wood-warblers, mainly insectivorous, and the bananaquits and conebills, feeding chiefly on nectar and fruit.

All Parulidae are small birds whose plumage consists of generally bright but not shining colors in which predominant hues are yellow, olive, chestnut, orange, red, gray, white, and black. The tropical representatives, mainly inhabiting mountain zones, have an almost identical livery in both sexes for the entire year. In the migratory species, however, which nest in temperate regions and winter in the tropics, the two sexes look very different.

Food consists principally of insects, caught in the middle and upper layers of the tropical and deciduous forests. The nest, almost always built by the female alone, is situated in a tree, often very high up, in a bush, on the ground, in a small cavity in a bank or in a rock cleft. The number of eggs in a clutch varies from a minimum of 2 to a maximum of 6. Incubation is carried out by the female alone; in migratory species this lasts from 13 – 17 days. The chicks, fed by both parents, stay for 8 to 15 days in the nest.

The Hawaiian honeycreepers of the family Drepanididae are birds measuring 4 – 8 in (10 – 20 cm), found exclusively in the Hawaiian archipelago. Some of the Hawaiian honeycreepers have an extremely long beak (in some cases up to one-third of the total body length), slender and curved downward so as to impale insects in cracks or probe deep inside flower corollas for nectar. One species, the rare akiapolaau (*Hemignathus wilsoni*), has a lower mandible half the length of the upper one, this structure making it easier for the bird to rip off bark, thus exposing insect larvae. Other species have a straight bill like that of woodpeckers,

The Parulidae are small birds with brightly colored plumage. Chicks of tropical species immediately take on the livery of the adults whereas the juvenile plumage of species breeding in temperate climes is more or less like that of the adult female. The livery is retained by males up to the spring following birth.

Ovenbird
(*Seiurus aurocapillus*)

Magnolia warbler
(*Dendroica magnolia*)

Painted redstart
(*Setophaga picta*)

Hooded warbler
(*Wilsonia citrina*)

Prothonotary warbler
(*Protonotaria citrea*)

Iiwi
(*Vestiaria coccinea*)

Kauai akialoa
(*Hemignathus procerus*)

Yellow Laysan finch
(*Psittirostra cantans*)

The present-day Drepanididae are descended from a single ancestor who reached Hawaii before any other tree-dwelling species, when the island was still covered by thick forest. To make best use of food opportunities and to avoid interspecific competition, the birds gradually evolved a whole range of different forms.

and still others, which feed mainly on seeds, possess bills that are shorter, heavier and curving.

The nest is a small, compact cup placed in a tree, a bush or tall grass, and it is built by both sexes. The clutch of 2 – 3 white eggs, spotted brown or russet, is incubated by the two birds in turn for a period of 13 – 14 days. The majority of these birds live in dense forest at heights of about 6,500 ft (2,000 m) where annual rainfall is in the region of 60 in (1,500 cm).

Of the 22 classified, 8 have vanished in quite recent times as a result of excessive hunting by natives, and the survivors are seriously threatened by changes to their primitive natural habitat.

The wholly American family Icteridae is made up of about 90 species distributed from the Arctic Circle to Tierra del Fuego, including the West Indies, the Falkland Islands, and the distant Easter Island. Their dimensions vary from 5 – 5½ in (13 – 14 cm) of the bobolink (*Dolichonyx oryzivorus*) to the 20 – 20½ in (50 – 52 cm) of the olive oropendola (*Gymnostinops yuracares*). The bill is conical, never longer than the head, straight or slightly downward curving, without notches. The plumage ranges from plain black (though often with strong blue, green or violet tints) to the most brilliant combinations of yellow, orange, red, chestnut, white, and black.

Males and females of the tropical species generally tend to look the same, while those breeding in temperate regions, are strongly differentiated. The former are usually sedentary while the latter set off on true migrations. The icterids are birds with many diverse habits and there is hardly any environment in which they are not at home, from tropical and deciduous forests to open, wet or semidesert regions, and from sea level up to altitudes of around 13,250 ft (4,000 m) in the Andes.

Food consists in the main of fruit, berries, nectar, seeds, insects, and small vertebrates often captured in unusual ways. Some ground-feeding species, such as those of the genera *Psomocolax*, *Cassidix* and *Dives*, turn over stones to disturb insects; and the giant cowbird (*Scaphidura oryzivora*), removes ticks and other parasites from the hides of grazing cattle.

Green oropendola
(*Psarocolius viridis*)

Great-tailed grackle
(*Cassidix mexicanus*)

Spotted-breasted oriole
(*Icterus pectoralis*)

The nests of the icterids, which seldom involves the participation of the males, vary greatly in shape, composition, and location; no other family of American birds, except the tyrant flycatchers and ovenbirds, display such varied architectonic skills. Almost all species are capable weavers, fashioning nests suspended from branches, but some build cup-shaped nests lined inside with mud and excrement.

Brown-headed cowbird
(*Molothrus ater*)

Giant cowbird
(*Scaphidura oryzivora*)

Eastern meadowlark
(*Sturnella magna*)

1) The family Parulidae inhabits the Nearctic and tropical regions of the American continent, from the southern boundary of the Canadian tundra through Central America and the West Indies, almost to Patagonia. 2) The family Icteridae is also wholly American and mostly tropical; it is found throughout the continent, including the West Indies, the Falklands, and Easter Island.

1
2

FINCHES
Fringillidae

Of the two subfamilies into which the whole group is divided, that of the Fringillinae comprises only three species, and only one of these, the brambling (*Fringilla montifringilla*), has a wide distribution; of the others, one is found exclusively in the Canary Islands, and the chaffinch (*F. coelebs*) does not range far beyond the western bounds of the Palearctic region. The brambling, however, inhabits a continuous belt over the Eurasian land mass, from Scandinavia to Kamchatka. They may be regarded as forms midway between the insect-eating Passeriformes and the more highly evolved seed-eaters. Their bill is relatively long, and this explains why they enjoy a much more varied diet than almost all other Fringillidae: in the summer they feed especially on insects. Because of the long beak and their method of feeding with rapid jabs, these birds seldom remove seeds from plants but almost always seek their vegetable food on the ground. The brambling has a slightly larger beak, indicative of its greater preference for beech seeds.

The second subfamily of Carduelinae displays much more variation in feeding habits and in the corresponding bill structure, which results from specialization. At one extreme are the representatives of the genus *Carduelis*, notably the goldfinch (*C. carduelis*) from Europe and the American goldfinch (*C. tristis*) from central–north America. These elegant, multicolored birds have a relatively slender and very pointed beak, which they use like pincers to extract seeds deeply buried inside certain types of flower parts, such as those of the composite plant family.

Species with a short, broad beak, like the linnet (*Acanthis cannabina*) and the redpoll (*A. flammea*), feed on plants whose seeds are directly attached to the stem, as in many grasses, or enclosed in pods and capsules, as in the crucifers. The redpoll, with its especially small beak, is closely dependent on the birch, feeding abundantly on its tiny seeds.

Among the most untypical members of the family is the bullfinch (*Pyrrhula pyrrhula*), sole European representative of a small genus from the Asiatic forests. This bird is therefore widely

Brambling
(*Fringilla montifringilla*)

▲ The Fringillidae are typical birds of wooded regions which eat large quantities of seeds from a variety of plants and trees. They are notable for their short, conical beak with sharp edges. Very often the distribution of individual species is associated with local tree growth, as is the case with the brambling, whose range coincides with that of the beech. The diet of these finches varies in accordance with the shape and size of their beak. The smaller species feed on the seeds of herbaceous plants, the larger ones on the fruits of trees (beech, alder, thorns, etc.). The fledglings are fed mainly on animal substances.

Linnet
(*Acanthis cannabina*)

Bullfinch
(*Pyrrhula pyrrhula*)

Hawfinch
(*Coccothraustes coccothraustes*)

Redpoll
(*Acanthis flammea*)

Goldfinch
(*Carduelis carduelis*)

Serin
(*Serinus serinus*)

Greenfinch
(*Carduelis chloris*)

▲ Other representatives of the family Fringillidae.

distributed in Asia, being a typical inhabitant of the taiga and coniferous mountain forests as far as the most easterly parts of the continent and Japan, where it appears as a distinct subspecies (*P. p. griseiventris*). The bill of this bird is short and very rounded, with sharp edges. Food consists of a large variety of seeds, but in comparison with other species the bullfinch has a special fondness for those of fleshy fruits such as sorb apples and blackberries.

Another extreme example of feeding adaptation is that of the hawfinch (*Coccothraustes coccothraustes*), ranging from the British Isles to Japan. This is a stocky bird with a short tail, strong neck and exceptionally large head and beak. The hawfinch is renowned for its remarkable ability to crush the stones of the toughest fruits, such as cherries and olives. For this purpose the internal structure of its beak is even more specialized than that of other finches. The normal diet of the hawfinch, therefore, consists of seeds of hawthorn, elm, hornbeam, maple, and beech; surprisingly, however, much of its food, at least around the beginning of summer, comprises butterfly larvae and cockchafers.

The strangest adaptation of all is displayed by the three species of crossbills (genus *Loxia*), found in northern Eurasia and America. These birds are wonderfully adapted to a diet consisting almost exclusively of conifer seeds: the particularly large, strong feet are used for grasping the cones and the crossed mandibles for opening them. In fact, the upper mandible curves downward and the lower one upward, so that they cross to the left and right of each other. The birds are also noted for their erratic behavior, causing them to appear in places at irregular intervals and, in the case of at least two of the species, to breed at virtually any time of the year.

As regards breeding behavior, there is a striking difference between the two subfamilies. The brambling and the chaffinch, for example, rear their chicks on insects and defend a fairly large area of territory, spending much of their time here looking for food and covering the terrain quite uniformly. The Carduelinae, on the other hand, feed their young mainly on seeds and nest in small groups that sometimes swell into colonies, defending only a small territory immediately adjacent to the nest.

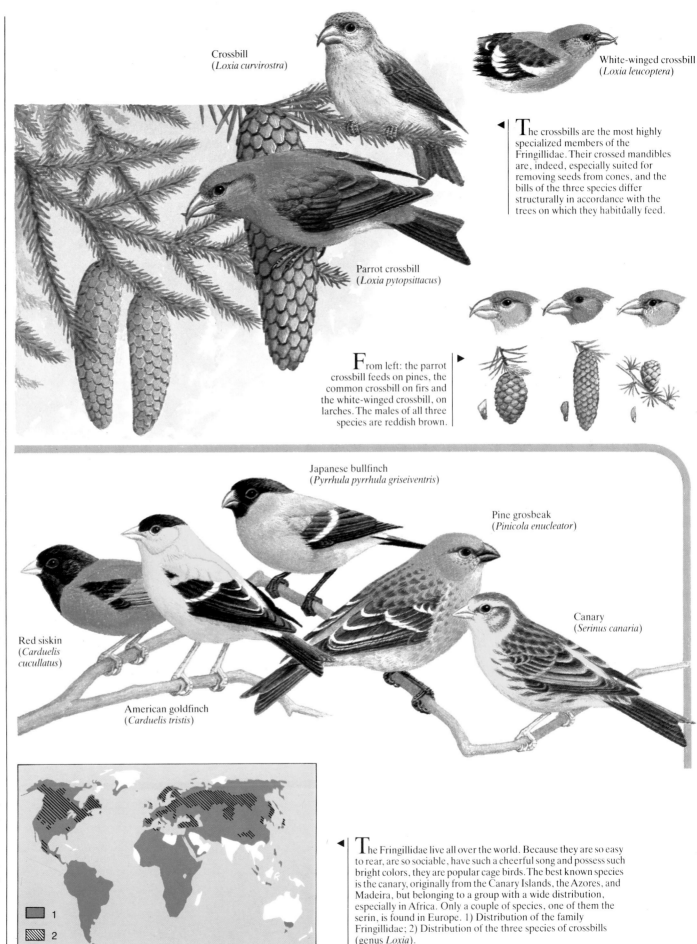

Crossbill
(*Loxia curvirostra*)

White-winged crossbill
(*Loxia leucoptera*)

Parrot crossbill
(*Loxia pytopsittacus*)

The crossbills are the most highly specialized members of the Fringillidae. Their crossed mandibles are, indeed, especially suited for removing seeds from cones, and the bills of the three species differ structurally in accordance with the trees on which they habitually feed.

From left: the parrot crossbill feeds on pines, the common crossbill on firs and the white-winged crossbill, on larches. The males of all three species are reddish brown.

Japanese bullfinch
(*Pyrrhula pyrrhula griseiventris*)

Pine grosbeak
(*Pinicola enucleator*)

Canary
(*Serinus canaria*)

Red siskin
(*Carduelis cucullatus*)

American goldfinch
(*Carduelis tristis*)

The Fringillidae live all over the world. Because they are so easy to rear, are so sociable, have such a cheerful song and possess such bright colors, they are popular cage birds. The best known species is the canary, originally from the Canary Islands, the Azores, and Madeira, but belonging to a group with a wide distribution, especially in Africa. Only a couple of species, one of them the serin, is found in Europe. 1) Distribution of the family Fringillidae; 2) Distribution of the three species of crossbills (genus *Loxia*).

1
2

ESTRILDIDAE, PLOCEIDAE

The seed-eating Estrildidae include in their ranks birds commonly known by such names as waxbills, cordon-bleus, avadavats, manakins, etc., and many of these exotic species are very popular cagebirds. All members of this family are very small, usually not more than about 4 in (10 cm) long, and almost always very vividly colored. Most of them have adapted to a granivorous diet.

All estrildids construct a fairly bulky nest in the form of a dome, a globe or a bottle; but the finished product is fragile and does not stand up well to bad weather. Incubation of the 4 – 6 pure white eggs lasts about 20 days. Courtship postures and attitudes are highly varied and very fascinating, but one thing common to all species is that they do not flick their wings, as do most other passerines; in these birds females inviting copulation vibrate their tail.

The family, with just over 100 species, has a limited distribution in the Old World, comprising the tropical regions of Africa, Asia, and Australia; favorite habitats are open, level grasslands, margins of forests, reed beds, and arable land, where birds of various species assemble in large groups.

The large Old World family of Ploceidae, with a particularly wide distribution in Africa, consists of birds collectively known as weavers, not easily described and individualized. Broadly speaking, they are sturdy in build, varying in size from that of a common sparrow to that of a thrush, with a short, stout beak. As regards behavior, none of them are notable for a complex, musical pattern of true song, their vocal expressions being limited to chirps, squeaks, and other sharp or humming sounds.

Most species are listed in two large subfamilies. The subfamily Ploceinae contains slightly under 100 species of true weavers, noted for their elaborate nests fashioned from interwoven plant fibers. Most of the birds live in Africa south of the Sahara, only a half dozen being found in southern and Southeast Asia. They often nest in large communities, assembling in isolated trees on the African savannas, where their

▲ The weavers are particularly well known for their skill in nest building. Species that inhabit the savannas, such as the Cape weaver (*Ploceus capensis*), usually nest in large groups.

One of the most colorful of the Estrildidae, and one of the most exotic of all cage birds, is the Gouldian finch (*Chloebia gouldiae*).

▼ The construction of the nest demands an elaborate series of complex and well-coordinated movements. The male begins the weaving process at the tip of the chosen branch. Knots are made in various ways, but all are perfectly adapted to the particular situation. Species which nest in the tropical forest, such as the crested malimbe, remain private, their nests having a typical tube-like entrance. The enormous constructions of the social weaver, with perhaps a hundred or so nests, are quite exceptional.

Social weaver
(*Philetairus socius*)

Crested malimbe
(*Malimbus malimbus*)

massive nests are sometimes among the most striking features of the landscape. Certainly this is true of the huge communal construction of the social weaver (*Philetarius socius*). This is probably the largest nest of any bird, with a diameter of up to 16½ ft (5 m). As many as 30 pairs of birds collaborate in building this structure, starting with the roof, using materials such as branches, twigs, and the stems of savanna grasses, continuously renewing it so as to obtain efficient shelter from wind and rain; in due course the birds build their individual nests, all close together and all with entrances low down.

The three genera making up the subfamily Passerinae are *Passer*, *Petronia* and *Montifringilla*. They are found all over the Ethiopian, Palearctic and Oriental regions, and with the recent introduction of two *Passer* species to the New World and Australia, are now virtually cosmopolitan in range. These sparrows are fairly small birds, from 4 to 8 in (10 to 20 cm) in length, with a stout, conical bill and inconspicuous plumage dominated by gray, brown, and black, but only rarely by brighter colors such as yellow or pure white. They are seed-eaters, finding such food mainly on the ground. They are not good fliers, traveling only short distances and at no great height.

There is marked sexual dimorphism in the 15 species of the genus *Passer*, the male having a typical black bib which comes down to about the breast and a jet-black line running from beak to eye; the exception is the tree sparrow (*P. montanus*), in which these features are present in both sexes, making them indistinguishable.

The sparrows of the genus *Montifringilla* live higher in the mountains, often at altitudes of up to 13,250 ft (4,000 m). They live almost wholly on the ground and only display gregarious habits in winter when groups of hundreds of birds abandon the now-inhospitable upper regions.

The five species of the genus *Petronia* can be distinguished by a conspicuous yellow mark on the throat, standing out against the remaining gray or brown of the plumage. The habitat varies according to the region, from sparse woodland to dry scrub, and sometimes higher up in rocky mountain zones. The species which nest in trees and bushes feed mainly on insects; those from the mountains nest and feed on the ground.

House sparrow
(*Passer domesticus*)

Snow finch
(*Montifringilla nivalis*)

Rock sparrow
(*Petronia petronia*)

Cape sparrow
(*Passer melanurus*)

Dead Sea sparrow
(*Passer moabiticus*)

The Ploceidae contain species which very often, as in the case of the sparrow, live quite happily alongside humans. They are sturdy birds with a powerful beak, feeding principally on seeds collected by hopping about on the ground.

Spanish sparrow
(*Passer hispaniolensis*)

Golden sparrow
(*Passer luteus*)

Tree sparrow
(*Passer montanus*)

The passerines are widely distributed over the Ethiopian, Palearctic and Oriental regions. Recently, with the introduction of two species to the New World and Australia, the subfamily has become virtually cosmopolitan. 1) Zones of recent introductions. 2) Original areas of the subfamily Passerinae.

Desert sparrow
(*Passer simplex*)

1
2

1
2

1) The Estrildidae inhabit the tropical regions of Africa, Asia, and Australia. 2) The Ploceidae are typical Old World inhabitants, particularly plentiful in Africa.

WAXBILLS, MANAKINS, CANARIES AND OTHER EXOTIC FINCHES

Lavender waxbill (*Estrilda caerulescens*). *Family*: Ploceidae. *Distribution, Habitat, Behavior, Food*: West Africa from Senegal to Central African Republic. Dry shrubland, forest fringes and gardens. Gregarious. Mainly granivorous. *Dimorphism, Size*: Sexes identical. Length 4¼ – 4¾ in (11 – 12 cm). *Breeding*: 4 – 6 white eggs are laid in a circular nest. Both sexes incubate in turn for 12 – 13 days.

Black-rumped waxbill (*Estrilda troglodytes*). *Family*: Ploceidae. *Distribution, Habitat, Behavior, Food*: Africa between the Sahara and the Equator, from western Ethiopia to the Atlantic. Open, arid, and semi-arid regions. Gregarious. Mainly granivorous. *Dimorphism, Size*: The female has less vivid pink areas on the belly and red patches around the eyes. Length 4 in (10 cm). *Breeding*: Pear-shaped nest with grass-lined floor, often divided into two, with one section for the brooding female and the other, more rudimentary, for the male. 4 – 8 white eggs.

Zebra finch (*Poephila guttata*). *Family*: Ploceidae. *Distribution, Habitat, Behavior, Food*: Australia and Lesser Sunda Islands. Found in all surroundings, except rain forest. Gregarious, with permanent pairs formed. Nomadic. Characteristic trumpet-like or mewing calls. Granivorous. *Size*: 4½ in (11 cm). *Breeding*: In colonies. The male courts the female by singing and dancing, elevating the feathers of cheeks, nape, and neck. The ball-shaped nest, with a hole at the side for entry, lined with tufts of grass, is placed in a tree hollow or a wall cavity. The 4 – 8 white eggs are incubated by both sexes for 13 – 15 days.

Gouldian finch (*Chloebia gouldiae*). *Family*: Ploceidae. *Distribution, Habitat, Behavior, Food*: Northern Australia. Open regions far from populated areas. Margins of mangrove swamps. Gregarious and partly nomadic. Fully active around midday. Feeds on seeds, vegetation, and insects. *Distinctive*

Waxbill
(*Estrilda astrild*)

Peter's twin-spot
(*Hypargos niveoguttatus*)

Tricolored manakin
(*Lonchura malacca malacca*)

Painted bunting
(*Passerina ciris*)

Black-headed manakin
(*Lonchura malacca atricapilla*)

Pin-tailed whydah
(*Vidua macroura*)

Java sparrow
(*Padda oryzivora*)

Red avadavat
(*Amandava amandava*)

Crimson finch
(*Neochmia phaeton*)

Features, Dimorphism, Size: Polymorphous species, with three different phases, black-, red-, and yellow-headed. The female's colors are more subdued, especially the violet of the breast. Length 5 – 5½ in (13 – 14 cm). *Breeding*: The highly ritualized courtship consists of rapid bows and swaying movements, the nape and breast feathers being ruffled and those of the graduated tail raised. The rudimentary nest is generally placed in the cavity of a tree or termite mound, very occasionally among bushes. There are 4 – 8 white eggs but more than one female may lay in the same nest. Both sexes incubate in turn for 13 – 16 days. During their first few days, the chicks display phosphorescent plates inside the mouth as an aid to feeding in semi-darkness.

Pale-headed manakin (*Lonchura maja*). *Family*: Ploceidae. *Distribution, Habitat, Behavior, Food*: Malaccan peninsula, Sumatra, Java, Bali, and other small islands. Open plains, rice fields, and gardens. Gregarious. A measure of nomadism is associated with availability of various foods. Mainly granivorous. *Dimorphism, Size*: Sexes identical, but the males often sing and dance before the females. Length 4¾ in (12 cm). *Breeding*: Round nest with side entrance, situated in low vegetation. 4 – 6 white eggs.

Waxbill (*Estrilda astrild*). *Family*: Ploceidae. *Distribution, Habitat, Behavior, Food*: Most of Africa below latitude 10°N. Open grassy regions, including those close to populated areas. Markedly gregarious. Granivorous. Partially insectivorous in breeding season. *Distinctive Features, Dimorphism, Size*: Very similar to black-rumped waxbill, but with a tail that is black below as well as above. Dimorphism as in black-rumped species. Length 4½ in (11 cm). *Breeding*: As for black-rumped waxbill.

Peter's twin-spot (*Hypargos niveoguttatus*). *Family*: Ploceidae. *Distribution, Habitat, Behavior, Food*: East Africa. Dense bush and margins of rain forest. In pairs or small groups. Mainly granivorous. *Dimorphism, Size*: The female has more subdued red zones, the sides of her head are brown and the center of the abdomen is grayish. Length 5 in (13 cm). *Breeding*: Round nest on ground or in a low bush. 3 – 6 white eggs which are incubated in turn by both partners for 12 – 13 days.

Pin-tailed whydah (*Vidua macroura*). *Family*: Ploceidae. *Distribution,*

Paradise whydah
(*Steganura paradisaea*)

Red bishop
(*Euplectes orix franciscana*)

Black-rumped waxbill
(*Estrilda troglodytes*)

White Zebra finch
(*Taenopygia castanotis* var. *alba*)

White-rumped manakin
(*Munia striata* var. *domestica*)

White Java sparrow
(*Padda oryzivora* var. *alba*)

Habitat, Behavior, Food: Africa south of the Sahara. Open regions, cultivated or uncultivated. Gregarious. Granivorous. *Distinctive Features, Dimorphism, Size*: The male in nuptial garb measures 14 in (35 cm) by virtue of his four central tail feathers. At the end of the breeding season these rectrices are replaced by feathers of normal length, and the entire plumage molts to leave a brown livery, more or less like that of the female (who is slightly smaller: 4½ – 4¾ in [11 – 12 cm] rather than 5¼ in [13 cm]). *Breeding*: Polygamous. Parasitic. Each male couples with 5 or 6 females. The white or creamy eggs are laid in the nest of another species, notably that of the waxbill, the yellow-billed waxbill (*Coccopygia melanotis*) or members of the genus *Cisticola* (fan-tailed warblers). One egg of the parasitized species is tossed out prior to laying its own. The baby is reared by its foster parents alongside their own chicks.

Black-headed manakin (*Lonchura, malacca atricapilla*). *Family*: Ploceidae. *Distribution, Habitat, Behavior, Food*: Southern India and Sri Lanka. Open plains and wet zones. Gregarious and partially migratory. Granivorous. *Dimorphism, Size*: Sexes identical. Length 4¾ in (12 cm). *Breeding*: Ball-shaped nest, low down among reeds and shrubs in swampy areas. 5 – 6 white eggs. Both sexes participate in breeding activities.

Red avadavat (*Amandava amandava*). *Family*: Ploceidae. *Distribution, Habitat, Behavior, Food:* From southern China and India across Indochina and Malaysia to eastern Indonesia (Lesser Sundas). Introduced to various countries, including Egypt, Philippines, and Hawaii. Open zones, preferably wet, up to 6,500 ft (2,000 m) above sea level. Gregarious. Mainly granivorous. *Distinctive Features, Size*: The male's red patches are marked according to whether it is of a western or eastern subspecies. In the winter his livery is similar to that of the female, but his throat and breast are grayer. Length 4 in (10 cm). *Breeding*: Ball-shaped or tubular nest among bushes, rushes or reeds, not far from water. 6 – 10 white eggs.

Java sparrow (*Padda oryzivora*). *Family*: Ploceidae. *Distribution, Habitat, Behavior, Food*: Java and Bali. Introduced to other Indonesian islands, eastern India, Malacca, Indochina, southern China, Philippines, East Africa, Seychelles, St Helena, and Hawaii. Rice fields, mangrove swamps, reed beds, scrubland, and city parks. Gregarious.

Long-tailed munia
(*Erithrura prasina*)

Yellow-headed Gouldian finch
(*Chloebia gouldiae*)

Pale-headed manakin
(*Lonchura maja*)

Zebra finch
(*Taenopygia castanotis*)

♀ ♂ Gouldian finch
(*Chloebia gouldiae*)

Lavender waxbill
(*Estrilda caerulescens*)

♂ ♀ Starfinch
(*Bathilda ruficauda*)

Granivorous. *Dimorphism, Size*: Sexes similar but the male has a slightly heavier beak. Length 5½ in (14 cm). *Breeding*: In colonies. Circular nest with side entrance, attached to a tree or beneath roof tiles. 4 – 8 white eggs.

Crimson finch (*Neochmia phaeton*). *Family*: Ploceidae. *Distribution, Habitat, Behavior, Food*: Northern Australia. Open regions far from water but also near populated areas. Moderately gregarious. Feeds on seeds, vegetation, and insects. *Dimorphism, Size*: The female's breast and abdomen are gray-brown. Length 4¾ – 5¼ in (12 – 13 cm). *Breeding*: After an elaborate courtship, executed by the male with a blade of grass in his beak, a bottle-shaped nest is built at the base of a palm leaf or under the tiles of a roof. 5 – 8 white eggs are incubated in turn by both birds.

White-rumped manakin (*Munia striata* var. *domestica*). *Family*: Ploceidae. *Distribution, Habitat, Behavior, Food*: The wild form, predominantly chestnut, is widespread through India, southern China, Taiwan, Indochina, Malacca, and Sumatra. Open regions, scrubland, and secondary forest up to 6,000 ft (1,800 m) above sea level. Gregarious and locally migratory. Granivorous. *Distinctive Features, Dimorphism, Size*: In Japan a variety of color forms have been selectively bred from wild stock. The most common are chocolate, fawn, isabel, spotted, and white, with or without a tuft. There is no difference between the sexes, but the male often sings to the female with a very faint voice and jerky movements of the body. Length 4¾ in (12 cm). *Breeding*: The wild form builds a ball-shaped nest with a tubular side entrance, not far from the ground. 3 – 8 white eggs. Both sexes share all reproductive activities and often two or three females use the same nest.

Canary (*Serinus canaria*). *Family*: Fringillidae. *Distribution, Habitat, Behavior, Food*: Western Canary Islands, Madeira, Azores. Woods and parks. Sedentary. In small groups only outside the breeding season. Mainly granivorous. *Dimorphism, Size*: The wild form is gray-green with dark stripes above, throat and breast being yellow and the abdomen white. The female has shades of brown above and less yellow underneath. Length 5 in (12.5 cm). *Breeding*: In spring the male marks out his territory with loud, melodious song. Cup-shaped nest, preferably on a conifer, at very variable heights. 3 – 5 eggs, pale blue or white with russet streaks.

Cut-throat
(*Amadina fasciata*)

Canary
(*Serinus canaria*)

Red-throated parrot finch
(*Erythrura psittacea*)

Orange Canary

Red Canary

Japanese Fancy Canary

Japanese Scotch Fancy Canary

The pictures on these pages and the preceding pages illustrate twenty or so of the best known exotic cage birds of the families Ploceidae and Fringillidae. Some live happily in the home, others not so happily. As far as the latter are concerned this does not mean that they cannot be kept at all in captivity, merely that they must be provided with roomy, well-planned cages instead of the traditional cramped cages generally available. The simplest and most practical cages are rectangular in shape, their length being greater than their height, enclosed on all sides except the front. Other fancy types of cage, in varying shapes, are inadvisable.

STURNIDAE, DICRURIDAE, ORIOLIDAE

The starling family (family Sturnidae) is made up of 111 species divided into 32 genera. It includes birds of small and medium size, sturdy in build, with a beak that is usually straight and fairly unspecialized. The plumage may be of various colors, black in the spotless starling (*Sturnus unicolor*), pink in the rosy pastor (*Pastor roseus*), blue, green, and purple with metallic tints in the glossy starlings.

Starlings are typical birds of Europe, Africa, and southern Asia. Generally sedentary, they may roam abroad in search of food, as in the case of the rosy pastor, a species which nests over a vast area extending from southeastern Europe to the Altai Mountains. They are, as a rule, highly sociable, living and breeding in groups of varying size according to surrounding conditions.

The birds generally nest in tree or rock cavities, but often make use of houses, particularly under the eaves. They frequent woodland as well as open zones and savannas. Their diet is extremely wide ranging, including both animals (arthropods and small vertebrates) and plant substances (shoots, seeds, etc.). Starlings also consume insects harmful to farmers, such as locusts, but at the same time take their toll of cultivated fruits (cherries, grapes, and olives).

Most species possess very remarkable abilities to mimic other songs and sounds. The common starling (*Sturnus vulgaris*) can imitate the calls of many species, but the most gifted in this field are undoubtedly the mynahs, a group of 12 species belonging to six different genera. Particularly well known is the hill mynah (*Gracula religiosa*), an inhabitant of the secondary forests of Asia, from India to the Sunda archipelago, which is regularly imported into Europe as an ornamental cage bird. Because of its astonishing capacity for mimicry, many people prefer it to parrots.

Oxpeckers are birds of average size, from 8 to 9 in (20 to 23 cm), found in Africa. Their rather large beak is admirably suited for the capture of

Common starling
(*Sturnus vulgaris*)

▲ Starlings display a high measure of sociability; indeed, they live and breed in groups that vary in numbers according to local conditions. Outside the breeding period they assemble in flocks that may contain thousands of individuals, both when feeding and roosting at night. The diet is varied, consisting both of animal prey (small vertebrates and insects) and vegetable matter such as shoots, seeds, and fruit.

Black-collared starling
(*Gracupica nigricollis*)

Rosy pastor
(*Pastor roseus*)

Bald starling
(*Sarcops calvus*)

Daurian starling
(*Sturnia sturnina*)

Gray starling
(*Spodiopsar cineraceus*)

Golden-breasted starling
(*Cosmopsarus regius*)

Hill mynah
(*Gracula relig*

ectoparasites (especially ticks) on the hide of large wild or domesticated herbivores. Sharp, curving claws enable them to move nimbly over the body of such animals, so that they can assume any position required wherever parasites are to be found. There are only two species, the yellow-billed oxpecker (*Buphagus africanus*) and the red-billed oxpecker (*B. erythrorhynchus*).

The family of drongos (family Dicruridae) is made up of one genus (*Dicrurus*) with 19 species living in the tropical regions of Africa south of the Sahara, Madagascar, southern Asia, the Sunda archipelago, and Australia. The family is particularly common in southern Asia, where ten species are found. These birds, measuring on average 8 – 15 in (20 – 38 cm), have black plumage and generally lack any pronounced sexual dimorphism. They live in forest and savanna, feeding on insects which they hunt with techniques similar to those seen among flycatchers and shrikes.

The Old World orioles (family Oriolidae) constitute a small family of 22 species found in Europe, western and southern Asia, Africa south of the Sahara, Indonesia, and Australia. Of average size, from 8 to 12 in (20 to 30 cm), they are powerfully built, with a strong, conical, hooked bill. There is usually a marked difference in the appearance of the two sexes. The wings are pointed and the tail is short, and the flight pattern is rapid and undulating. As a rule the orioles build a hanging, hammock-type nest, suspended from horizontal branches. The eggs are usually white or pink. The typical song is short and fluty. Their diet is quite varied and comprises arthropods as well as many types of fruit.

The family contains migratory species such as the golden oriole (*Oriolus oriolus*) and the African golden oriole (*O. auratus*). The former nests throughout Europe and parts of Asia, wintering in central Africa. The African species, by contrast, makes seasonal journeys but always remains in the tropics. There are two distinct races, one nesting to the north and the other south of the Equator. The southern subspecies (*O. a. notatus*) travels north, leaving Zambia and Zimbabwe and reaching Uganda and Zaïre, where it nests from April to August. The northern race (*O. a. auratus*), which lives in the savanna, moves southward to southwest Africa between November and April, then returns from June to February to Zaïre and Uganda.

Yellow-billed oxpecker (*Buphagus africanus*)

Like the red-billed species, the yellow-billed oxpecker spends its time perched on the back of large herbivores, feeding on the ectoparasites which burrow into their hide, and thus greatly improve the physical condition of the hosts.

The Dicruridae live in forests and savannas. They feed on insects using hunting techniques that are similar to those employed by flycatchers and shrikes.

Black drongo (*Dicrurus macrocercus*)

Black-naped oriole (*Oriolus chinensis*)

Golden oriole (*Oriolus oriolus*)

The golden oriole is a migratory species which winters in central and southern Africa, from Zaire to South Africa. In spring it flies back to Europe to breed.

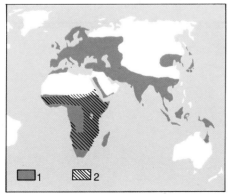

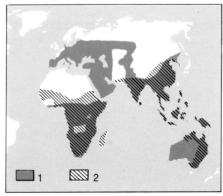

Far left: 1) The starlings (family Sturnidae) are typical birds of Europe, Africa, and southern Asia. 2) The oxpeckers (genus *Buphagus*) live only on the African savannas. Left: 1) The small family of orioles (Oriolidae) inhabits Europe, western and southern Asia, Africa south of the Sahara, Indonesia, and Australia. 2) The members of the family Dicruridae live mainly in southern Asia but are also to be found in Africa south of the Sahara and in Madagascar.

CALLAEIDAE, GRALLINIDAE, CRACTICIDAE, ARTAMIDAE

The wattlebirds of the family Callaeidae are inhabitants of the most inaccessible forests of the New Zealand hinterland, living in pairs within family groups. They frequently seek food on the ground, hopping and fluttering through the branches, but not really flying in the true sense of the word. The saddleback feeds principally on insects, as did the extinct huia, whereas the kokako mainly eats leaves and fruit. The open nest is a fairly shallow cup, made of rootlets, twigs, leaves, and ferns, often hidden behind a rock or in a tree cavity some way above ground. The 2 – 3 eggs in each clutch are gray or brown with darker stains and streaks. They are incubated by both sexes for about 20 days and both parents also rear and feed the young.

The so-called mudnest builders of the family Grallinidae are inhabitants of Australia and New Guinea. Although there are only four species, differences among them justify the classification of the two species of the genus *Grallina* in a separate subfamily (*Grallininae*) and the two monotypical genera *Struthidea* and *Corcorax* in another (*Corcoracinae*).

The magpie-lark (*Grallina cyanoleuca*), with its black-and-white coloration, is one of the best known Australian birds. The size of a blackbird, its head, back, wings, tail, throat, and breast are a brilliant black; the eyebrows, a patch below and behind the eyes, the base of the tail, the shoulders, the lower breast and the abdomen are pure white. The female's throat is also white and she has no eyebrow.

A bold nature and special breeding requirements have adapted the magpie-lark very well to urban environments, and it occupies the same ecological niche in Australia as the rook does in Europe. It feeds mainly on animals such as insects, earthworms, and freshwater snails.

Australia (including Tasmania), New Guinea and adjacent islands, and recently New Zealand (with two intro-

Kokako
(*Callaeas cinerea*)

The Callaeidae are passerines of average size. The most apparent external features are the wattles, originating from the fringes of naked skin which characterize the beak commissures of many passerines, but in this case become more conspicuous with age instead of disappearing. The kokako or wattled starling feeds on fruit and leaves; the huia, found only on the North Island of New Zealand, became extinct in 1808 as a consequence of intensive hunting by white colonists. The huia was an interesting bird because of the marked difference between the sexes in the shape of the bill, the male's being short and straight, the female's long and curved, enabling each to consume different types of food.

Grallinidae
Magpie-lark
(*Grallina cyanoleuca*)

Callaeidae
Huia
(*Heterolocha acutirostris*)

The magpie-lark remains near water not only for feeding purposes but also because it habitually builds a cup-shaped nest entirely of mud, this being anchored to a horizontal branch close to a river or stream. This dependence on mud obstructs breeding in years of drought but facilitates it, outside the normal season, during rainy periods.

duced species) are the homes of the Cracticidae family, uncertainly placed in systematics, which contains 11 species known by such names as butcherbirds, bell-magpies, currawongs, etc.

Dimensions vary from 10½ to 24 in (26 to 60 cm) and superficially they look like crows, rooks or even shrikes. The birds have a large, heavy head and a powerful, often strongly hooked, beak. In general the plumage is black, black-and-white or gray, but some species display brown color phases. The fairly long legs are very strong, resembling those of the Corvidae. The long, straight bill terminates in a hook.

The birds live in various forest environments, from the coast to the mountains, feeding on insects, fruits, birds' eggs, small reptiles, and mammals. In winter they come together in flocks, which break up at the start of spring as each pair departs to defend its own nesting site. The nest, placed in the fork of a tall tree, is a shallow cup of interlaced branches, lined inside with bark fiber. The 2 – 5 eggs are light brown or tawny with darker spots and streaks.

In addition to the aforementioned families, the Artamidae, known variously as wood-swallows and swallow-shrikes, also occupy an uncertain place in systematics, although they certainly originated in the Australian region. Despite these names, they are unrelated either to the swallows (Hirundinidae) or shrikes (Laniidae). They have a compact body and vary in length from 5½ to 8 in (14 to 20 cm). The plumage is black, gray or white in nine species and partially chestnut in the remaining one.

The center of the family's distribution is Australia and the islands of the southwestern Pacific. One species, the white-backed wood-swallow (*Artamus monachus*), ranges westward to Malaysia but does not actually touch the Asiatic continent; another, the ashy swallow-shrike (*A. fuscus*), is well distributed in Southeast Asia from India and Sri Lanka across Burma and Thailand to western China. In southern and western Australia some species migrate within the continent. All ten species are grouped in the genus *Artamus*. The nest is usually placed on a prominent branch, sometimes in a cavity or, as with the Indian species, at the base of a palm leaf, generally some 33 ft (10 m) from the ground.

White-browed wood-swallow
(*Artamus superciliosus*)

Fairly peaceful by nature, the wood-swallows usually perch conspicuously on a branch, waiting for insects to pass by and then launching themselves into the air to capture them on the wing. The birds form tight groups of several dozens at night, probably because their delicate plumage provides very poor insulation, so that only by assembling in such groups can they withstand excessively cold nocturnal conditions. On the left is the white-browed wood-swallow, one of the ten species of the genus Artamus.

The Cracticidae have a large, heavy head and a strong, often sharply hooked, beak. As a rule their plumage is black, black-and-white, or gray, but some species go through a brown color phase. The butcherbirds of the genus *Cracticus* are carnivores and particularly aggressive. They store up food, using the same technique as shrikes, impaling their prey (large insects, reptiles, amphibians, small mammals, and baby birds) on thorns or sharp-pointed branches.

Gray butcherbird
(*Cracticus torquatus*)

1) The distribution range of the Grallinidae comprises Australia and New Guinea. 2) The Artamidae inhabit the islands of the southwest Pacific as well as Australia. 3) The Callaeidae live exclusively in New Zealand. 4) Australia is the home of the Cracticidae, who also extend their range to Tasmania and New Guinea.

BOWERBIRDS

Ptilonorhynchidae

The size of the bowerbirds varies from that of a thrush to that of a rook, namely from about 7 to 12 in (18 to 30 cm). Males are, as a rule, brightly colored and ornamented in various ways. Among certain species the plumage takes on the most astonishing changes of tone depending on the angle of light incidence. Only rarely do the sexes look alike, the females being much more modest and subdued in color.

The bowerbirds are forest dwellers who spend the greater part of their time in the foliage, except when they come down to the ground to display. Although they eat fruit they may also consume insects and snails. The nest is a cup-shaped affair of roughly interlaced branches, situated up in a tree. The 1 – 3 eggs are white, with typical hieroglyphic markings. So far as is known, only the female incubates and rears the brood.

The bowerbirds are known only from New Guinea and Australia and have derived their vernacular name from the males' extraordinary habit of building special display grounds, known as bowers, avenues, and maypoles, designed simply to attract females for the complex phases of courtship ceremonies. Genuine bowers and avenues are constructed only by some species; they are always situated at ground level and often surrounded by exhibition arenas, and they have no connection with the nest which, as mentioned, is invariably placed in a tree. Some species assemble brightly colored objects inside their bower. The species of the genera *Ptilonorhynchus*, *Chlamydera* and *Sericulus* perform the almost incredible feat of "painting" the walls of their bower with the colored juices of certain berries, mingled with bits of charcoal and pulped grass held together with saliva, using as a tool a wad of leaves or bark.

The basic structure of a bower is a central post with a circular roof descending toward the base. Avenues have a basal platform, walls and an arch or roof of interlaced twigs and branches. Bowers, avenues and their immediate surroundings may be decorated at various points with fruit, flowers, beetles, and other colored objects.

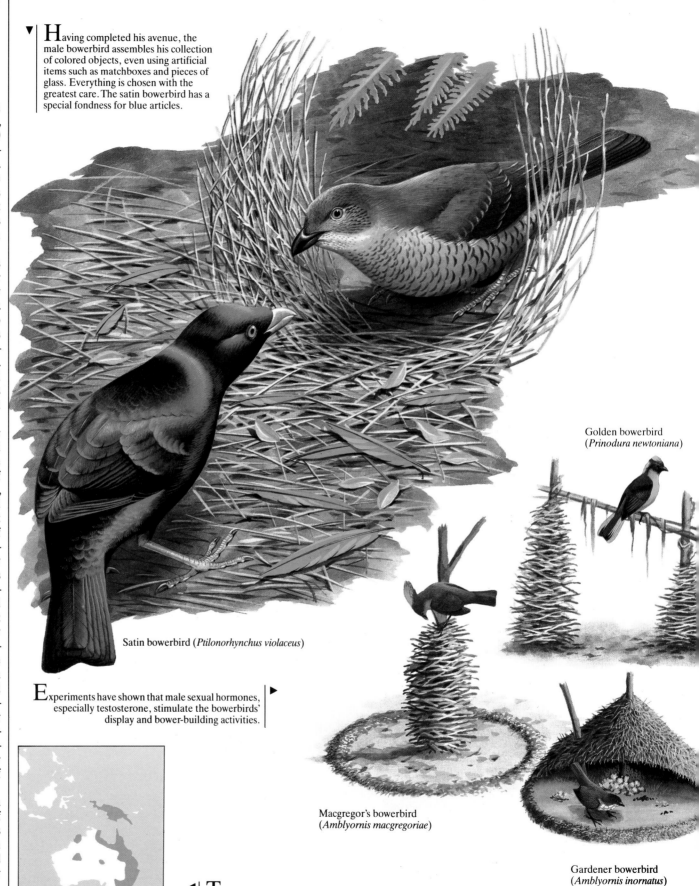

Having completed his avenue, the male bowerbird assembles his collection of colored objects, even using artificial items such as matchboxes and pieces of glass. Everything is chosen with the greatest care. The satin bowerbird has a special fondness for blue articles.

Satin bowerbird (*Ptilonorhynchus violaceus*)

Experiments have shown that male sexual hormones, especially testosterone, stimulate the bowerbirds' display and bower-building activities.

Golden bowerbird (*Prinodura newtoniana*)

Macgregor's bowerbird (*Amblyornis macgregoriae*)

Gardener bowerbird (*Amblyornis inornatus*)

The bowerbirds spend most of their time in the heart of the forest, feeding mainly on fruit. They appear to be related both to the crows and the birds of paradise, and they live only in Australia and New Guinea. 1) Distribution of family Ptilonorhynchidae.

BIRDS OF PARADISE

Paradisaeidae

The birds of paradise constituting the family Paradisaeidae are universally famous for the colorful, decorative splendor of their plumage and for their extraordinary private or collective ceremonial displays. It is not so well known, however, that these astonishing birds are very closely related to the Corvidae, which are notable, for the most part, for their lack of color. New Guinea and the adjacent islands form the evolutionary center of the Paradisaeidae, a few species of which are found in the northernmost parts of Australia and the Moluccas.

All species of birds of paradise are tree dwellers, inhabiting the most inaccessible mountain zones, often at very high altitudes. Food consists of insects, small vertebrates, and other animals, and some species also consume fruit. As a rule the birds are not gregarious by habit, being observed in small groups only where food is very plentiful or, in some cases, on display grounds. Certain species have black plumage, without special ornamentation save the metallic reflections of the feathers and the odd caruncle or wattle, the males differing hardly at all from the females. At the other extreme are species in which the females have fairly drab plumage while the males are either black with an adornment of strangely formed feathers or brightly colored in a blend of beautiful hues, further embellished by a variety of curious ornamental features.

The form of breed-behavior depends on the type and extent of sexual dimorphism. Species in which there is little or no distinction between sexes form monogamous pairs. But among species where sexual dimorphism is very marked, there is no pair formation. The males assemble in groups of varying numbers or exhibit themselves individually on display grounds. Some birds of paradise prepare an arena on the forest floor, clearing it of all large objects in order to perform their private displays. Others go through the ritual on a branch high above the ground; and the males of some species come together to perform collective dances.

For a long time Europeans believed birds of paradise to be divine because they were thought to lack legs and thus to have come from heaven. Actually they have very sturdy legs, but the skins which were dispatched to Europe had the limbs removed so as to avoid damaging the flimsy feathers.

Greater bird of paradise
(*Paradisaea apoda*)

Arfak
(*Astrapia nigra*)

King of Saxony bird of paradise
(*Pteridofora alberti*)

Magnificent bird of paradise
(*Diphyllodes magnificus*)

Emperor of Germany's bird of paradise
(*Paradisaea guilielmi*)

Magnificent riflebird
(*Ptiloris magnificus*)

The polygamous habits of many birds of paradise have led to the creation in the wild of many hybrid forms, these having often been described as separate species. The evolutionary center of the group is New Guinea and the adjoining islands, a few species being inhabitants of northern Australia and the Moluccas. 1) Distribution of the family Paradisaeidae.

1

CORVIDAE

The family Corvidae is part of the order Passeriformes, and, by reason of the complex structure of the syrinx or vocal organ, belongs to the suborder Oscines (songbirds). They are sturdy birds with a stout bill of varying length, though never short, either straight or slightly curved. The nostrils are covered by forward-directed bristly feathers. Lacking any particularly specialized features, the Corvidae are highly adaptable birds, endowed with considerable brain power. Many species display a high level of social organization.

The family is distributed virtually throughout the world, except in Antarctica, New Zealand, and parts of Polynesia. It is divided into two subfamilies, Corvinae, comprising crows, rooks, jackdaws, ravens, and nutcrackers, and Garrulinae, made up of jays, magpies and choughs.

Crows, rooks, jackdaws, and ravens. These birds are all grouped together in the single genus *Corvus*. Among them are the rook (*C. frugilegus*), the carrion crow (*C. corone*), the common crow (*C. brachyrhynchos*), the raven (*C. corax*), the fish crow (*C. ossifragus*), the jungle crow (*C. macrorhynchos*), and the jackdaw (*C. monedula*).

The raven is a large bird measuring 24½ in (62 cm) in total length, its plumage completely black with metallic tints. It has a very broad distribution, with various subspecies, throughout the northern hemisphere: in North America from Alaska and Greenland southward to Central America, and in the Old World from Iceland eastward to the shores of the Pacific and south to the Tropic of Cancer. It is an inhabitant of wild mountain regions and rocky zones, including sea cliffs. Sedentary by habit, its bulky nests are built on outcrops of rock, where 4 to 5 (sometimes 3 or 6) eggs are laid in February–March. The species feeds mainly on animal substances, flying in a straight line and often hovering at great heights. The birds usually live in pairs but will also gather into large flocks where abundant.

The carrion crow is a bird measuring about 18 in (46 cm), its legs and plumage completely black, with metallic reflections; but the hooded crow

Carrion crow
(*Corvus corone*)

► Carrion crows often gather on the seashore to feed on stranded fish and other marine animals. The fish crow of the North American Atlantic coasts is a specialist in this field.

◄ Crows, rooks, jackdaws, ravens, and choughs have an enormously varied diet which includes animal and plant food as well as carrion and human refuse.

▼ Rooks, like crows, feed mainly on the ground. The birds often take turns as sentinel, ready to sound the alarm for the flock in case of danger. Food items with very hard shells, such as snails and nuts, are shattered against stones.

(*C. corone cornix*), a subspecies, is gray with black head, throat, wings, and tail. The species ranges over much of Eurasia and Lower Egypt, the carrion crow inhabiting western and eastern regions and the hooded crow being found in central areas. These crows live alone or in pairs and may come together in flocks as they wander to and fro or make short migration journeys. They nest chiefly on tall trees but also on rocks, ruined walls, or old buildings, laying 4 to 5 (sometimes 2 – 3 or 6) eggs. They are omnivores, like most members of the genus *Corvus*.

In some regions certain types of crow frequent seashores, feeding freely on marine animals on the beaches. This is the specialty of the fish crow, which lives only along the Atlantic coasts of North America.

The jungle crow, with some dozen subspecies, ranges all over southern and eastern Asia.

The jackdaw is one of the smallest members of the family, measuring in all 12½ in (32 cm). It, too, is black with varying metallic reflections, but its nape is gray. It is distributed, with various subspecies, over Europe, western Asia and northwest Africa. Southern populations are sedentary, but northern populations migrate southward in winter. They nest in colonies in rock clefts and in trees, and sometimes in abandoned rabbit holes. Jackdaws are frequently to be seen in towns with a number of old buildings.

Nutcrackers. This group contains one genus *Nucifraga*, with two species, the nutcracker (*N. caryocatactes*) from Europe and Asia, and Clark's nutcracker (*N. columbiana*) from North America. They live mainly in coniferous mountain forests, building their nests in the trees and laying from 3 to 4 (sometimes 2 or 5) eggs. Food consists mainly of pine cones and hazel nuts, which are often stored in underground "larders," to be dug up in the heart of winter, even when below a thick layer of snow. Thus they play an important role in the propagation of pines and hazels.

Choughs. This group is also made up of two species belonging to one genus, *Pyrrhocorax*, both from the Old World. They are the alpine chough (*P. graculus*) and the red-billed chough (*P. pyrrhocorax*). Both species are completely black with metallic tints, and about the same size; the latter, however, has a red rather than a yellow beak, which is longer and more incurved.

Red-billed chough (*Pyrrhocorax pyrrhocorax*)

Jungle crow (*Corvus macrorhynchos*)

Nutcracker (*Nucifraga caryocatactes*)

Alpine chough

Jackdaw (*Corvus monedula*)

Rook

Hooded crow (*Corvus corone cornix*)

Raven (*Corvus corax*)

▲ To extract seeds, the nutcracker holds the pine cones firmly with the feet and lifts off the bracts with its beak. It opens walnuts and hazelnuts in the same manner.

▲ In the two illustrations at the top, we see members of the crow family collecting and storing shining objects, something for which they are famous. Actually this habit appears to be confined to birds that are either tame or in close human contact. Rooks have been known to swoop down and fly off with golf balls.

◄ 1) The family Corvidae is found almost all over the world. It has been introduced to New Zealand and is absent from Antarctica.

COMMON MAGPIE

Pica pica

Order Passeriformes
Family Corvidae
Length About 18 in (45 cm), of which
8 – 10 in (20 – 26 cm) is tail; wing of
male 7¼ – 8 in (18.6 – 20.4 cm); wing
of female 7 – 7½ in (17.5 – 19 cm)
Weight 5½ – 8½ oz (155 – 242 g)
Distribution Europe and temperate
parts of Asia, North America
Nesting On high trees, sometimes low
trees and bushes. One clutch per year.
Eggs From 5 to 8, sometimes 4 or 9,
exceptionally more, varying in color
from blue-green to yellowish with
brown or ash-gray spots
Size of eggs 1⅓ × 1 in (33.9 × 23.8
mm)
Incubation 17 – 18 days
Chicks Helpless (remain in nest for
22 – 27 days or more)

The magpie (*Pica pica*) is not a very
large bird and is notable mainly for its
contrasting black-and-white plumage
and its long tail. Most of the body
(head, throat, back, wings, and tail) is
iridescent, velvety black, while the
remainder (flanks, abdomen, outer
wing coverts) is white. The wings are
fairly short and rounded.

Typical habitats are open spaces
abounding in food and with sufficient
tree growth for nesting and roosting,
such as fringes of woods, thin undergrowth, bush, and scrub. As a rule the
magpie frequents plains and hills but it
may also range up in the mountains,
nesting in the Alps to a height of 5,600
ft (1,700 m), and along seacoasts.

Magpies live in pairs all year round,
but the young stay with their parents
for a long time after birth, often
throughout the winter. Breeding commences at the start of April when both
sexes construct a nest on a tall tree or
in a bush. This nest is a large, rough-
and-ready affair, although quite compact, made of sticks and dry branches,
strengthened inside with soil and mud;
normally it is surmounted by a dome
with two entry holes. The interior is
lined with rootlets, grass, hairs, and
feathers. Only the female incubates
and she is fed by the male.

The magpie's diet, like that of most
Corvidae, is characteristically omnivorous.

The magpie belongs to the same family as rooks, crows,
and ravens. It resembles them in general body structure
and bill shape, as well as in certain biological and
ecological features. Its colors and its long tail are,
nevertheless, unmistakable.

The bird is a typical omnivore and its food
sources vary considerably depending upon local
conditions.

In flight the magpie's
rounded wings and
graduated tail are
clearly visible.

Eurasian jay
(*Garrulus glandarius*)

Azure-winged magpie
(*Cyanopica cyanus*)

Blue jay
(*Cyanocitta cristata*)

The magpie is well distributed over much of the
Palearctic region, living in Europe, in central Asia to
the Pacific Ocean, in Indochina, in Arabia, and in
North Africa. It has also colonized parts of North
America. The azure-winged magpie, however, is
confined to two areas of the Old World, namely the
Iberian peninsula and central and eastern Asia, widely
separated from the geographical viewpoint. 1)
Distribution of the azure-winged magpie (*Cyanopica
cyanus*); 2) Distribution of the magpie (*Pica pica*).

PICTURE SOURCES

Oliviero Berni, Milan: 46, 96 – 97, 100 – 101, 136 – 137, 138 – 139, 146, 147, 196 – 197, 198 – 199, 234 – 235, 236 – 237.

Fausto Borrani, Brescia: 114 – 155, 122 – 123, 188 – 189, 190 – 191.

Trevor Boyer/Linden Artists Ltd., London: 38 – 39, 40 – 41, 42 – 43, 44 – 45, 48 – 49, 50 – 51, 52 – 53, 72 – 73, 74 – 75, 76, 77, 78 – 79, 80 – 81, 82, 83, 84 – 85, 86 – 87, 88 – 89, 90 – 91, 92 – 93, 126 – 127, 128 – 129, 214 – 215, 216 – 217, 220 – 221, 230 – 231, 258 – 259, 262 – 263, 264 – 265, 268, 269, 272.

Martin Camm/The Tudor Art Agency Ltd., London: 47, 60, 61, 62 – 63, 64, 65, 66 – 67, 68 – 69, 70 – 71.

Umberto Catalano, Bologna: 132 – 133, 134, 135, 204 – 205, 224 – 225, 226 – 227, 228 – 229, 232 – 233, 238 – 239, 240 – 241, 242 – 243, 244, 245, 246 – 247, 264 – 265, 270 – 271.

Piero Cozzaglio, Brescia: 26, 27.

Ezio Giglioli, Milan: 14, 156 – 157, 158 – 159, 160, 161, 176 – 177, 178 – 179, 192 – 193, 194 – 195.

Michel Guy, Noisy Le Grand: 144 – 145, 152 – 153, 154, 155, 212, 213.

Francesca Jacona, Rome: 180, 181, 200, 201.

Jan Maget/Art Centrum, Prague: 104 – 105, 148, 149.

Pavel Major/Art Centrum, Prague: 108 – 109.

Gabriele Pozzi, Milan: 110 – 111, 112, 113, 116, 117, 118, 119, 120 – 121, 124, 182 – 183, 184 – 185, 186, 187.

John Rignall/Linden Artists Ltd., London: 30 – 31, 32 – 33, 34, 35, 36, 37, 54 – 55, 56 – 57, 218, 219, 248 – 249, 250 – 251, 252 – 253, 254 – 255, 256 – 257.

Aldo Ripamonti, Milan: 29, 125, 150 – 151, 162 – 163, 164 – 165, 166, 167, 168 – 169, 170 – 171, 172 – 173, 174 – 175, 266 – 267.

Sergio, Milan: 10, 15, 58 – 59, 94 – 95, 98 – 99, 102 – 103, 106 – 107, 130 – 131, 140 – 141, 142 – 143, 202 – 203, 206 – 207, 208, 209, 210 – 211.

David Wright/The Tudor Art Agency Ltd., London: 136 – 137.